THE EMBLEM

THE EMBLEM

John Manning

REAKTION BOOKS

For my Father and Mother

Published by Reaktion Books, Ltd
79 Farringdon Road, London EC1M 3JU, UK

First published 2002

Typography by Ron Costley

Printed and bound in Great Britain by
St Edmundsbury Press, Bury St Edmunds, Suffolk

British Library Cataloguing in Publication Data

Manning, John, 1948–
The emblem
1.Emblems in art 2.Emblems in literature
I.Title
704.9'46

ISBN 1 86189 110 5

What thou seest, write in a book . . .
Revelation 1. 11

NIL SIT IN ORE, QVOD NON
PRIUS IN SENSU
Nothing can [be spoken] by the mouth,
which was not previously [experienced]
by the senses.

CALICES VOLO, VERBAQUE LIBERA,
LUDOS ATQUE IOCOS . . .
I want cups [of wine], and free words,
games and jokes, too
Sambucus, *Emblemata*, page 80

EGO VERA LOQUOR
I speak true things.
Le Centre de l'Amour, page 5

If [this book] shal seeme to light to be read of the wise, or to foolish
to be regarded of the learned, they ought not to impute it to the
iniquitie of the author, but to the necessitie of the history.
Lyly, *Euphues*

An *Emblem* without a *Key* to't, is no more than a *Tale of a Tub*
Sir Roger L'Estrange, 'Preface', *Fables of Æsop*
and other Eminent Mythologists

Contents

Preface

Peter M. Daly, the most tireless modern apologist for the emblem, has conservatively estimated that there are 'perhaps as many as two thousand' emblematic titles in all European languages. Collectively these can be seen to impinge on every aspect of Renaissance and Baroque culture.[1] The inference from this has frequently been that emblems might be used as a peep-hole into the cultural assumptions of the period. This surely places too great a burden on the narrow shoulders of a form that began life as no more than a series of terse epigrams. The pervasiveness of the emblem surely leads us in a different direction: that the emblem itself can only be understood in terms of the broad cultural assumptions that produced it. This present book attempts to do so by setting the emblem against the backdrop of a shared European neo-Latin culture of festive celebration.

My original aim was to offer an alternative to studies of emblems, which were either synchronically or unhistorically conceived, or which were essentially motif studies, which unrealistically pretended to unlock the coded conceptual allegories of Renaissance and Baroque art or to deliver the 'meaning' of literary texts. My method was to have provided a historical overview of the form. Beginning with the sixteenth century, each chapter would unfold successive 'centuries' of emblems. The Ariadne's thread through this labyrinth was bibliographical: dates of first editions would determine where a work was discussed. Orderly and rational though this might appear, it did not take long to realize that it was based on the naïve assumption that the calender was a real guide to generic developments.

'Origins', for instance, had the disconcerting habit of receding, or paradoxically appearing much later than one had at first believed. 'Beginnings' could coincide with a first edition, but equally emerge in a later editorial innovation. Nor were later editions or texts an infallible 'advance' over their predecessors. Woodblocks and copperplates archived in the printing-houses could be taken up and reused. And symbolic forms persistently replicated themselves through ingrained rhetorical habits of imitation, so that a 'new' emblem book could accommodate persistent survivals of traditional habits of thinking, writing and reading. The regulation, ordering and systematizing of symbolic forms might induce innovation, but equally could act as a conservative brake on novelty. It was clear that notions of chronology had to be reconfigured and rethought.

As with origins, the 'end' of the emblem tends to be grossly exaggerated. Rosemary Freeman in her history of the English emblem book was confident enough to date the demise of the emblem. This was, apparently, in 1686, when John Bunyan dedicated his emblems to boys and girls. Yet, inconveniently, emblems continued to be published and sold. Since the myth of their 'decline' has been so persistent, some consideration of the influence of a new, juvenile readership on the development of the genre was needed, and the adoption of the form by writers and artists in the twentieth century needed to be examined.

New readers produce new emblems. With the advent of amatory and devotional emblematic sub-genres at the beginning of the seventeenth century, a traditional image stock was recirculated within a different context. Miniature forms were elaborated according to evolved rules, where, in a species of semiological overcoding, a more restricted application procured innovation.

Ends are often dictated by distinct purposes and designs. All writers and artists were under obligation to an epideictic rhetoric of praise and blame. This social function dictated that many emblem books subserved occasional and local circumstances, particular historical events and perceptions of a national history. Grounded in a historical moment, emblems can be misunderstood, or be totally incomprehensible, unless there is an awareness of the immediate temporal context. Chronology, the moment of utterance, is a clue to meaning.

Nor did the early modern period compute and record time in the same way we do. The culture of holiday mirth that surrounds calendar festivals shapes the form and content of many emblem books. And, while annual festive celebrations inform some emblem books, so others are modelled according to a more sombre teleology of world history: the prophetic, apocalyptic endgames of the four last things.

Many of the strategies and conclusions of this study may be genre specific, but they may have implications for the way we read other early modern literary forms.

Acknowledgements

There will inevitably be objections to what I have done in the following pages, and for that I am pleased. What I have attempted is to place emblems into a context of ways of thinking and ways of feeling, ways of conceptualizing what we are and what we might be. But in a single volume, no one can do everything (*non omnia possumus omnes*).

The materials I discuss are a matter of choice, and inevitably some will complain that my system of choice is erected on a narrow base. My motto in all of this might be 'Obscura promens' (Horace, *Odes*, I, xxxiv, 14): I have brought the obscure into undue prominence, and exalted the unworthy. Some readers will find far too much Palmer, Whitney, Quarles, Wither and Stevenson, but most of my readers will be Anglophone and will probably assimilate these examples quite readily. I make no apology for the number of examples drawn from Alciato. He was the gold standard of emblematic writing, and his influence runs through the whole tradition. His book remained in print for 350 years. Unfortunately no English translation does justice to his robust Latinity. I have no ambition to write a book on the 'English Emblem'. The English examples I discuss are there not because they are English, but because they are good examples of a Europe-wide phenomenon. I attempt to provide a polyglot cultural context against which these can be seen. Any notion of a narrow national ownership of this tradition is ludicrous. Unless it can be seen against the background of a neo-Latin, pan-European tradition, it becomes virtually invisible. And the same might be said of various vernacular European linguistic appropriations. Except, of course, that some vernacular cultures in particular locations planted the form in vernacular soil and made it thrive. I resist any temptation to extend the polyglotism of this theory to encompass oriental ideograms, much less to authentic Egyptian hieroglyphs. When anti-matter confronts matter, when authentic philology confronts linguistic speculation of the highest possible imaginative order, all inevitably must fly *in fumo*.

Claude Mignault, attempting in his oft-reprinted preface to Alciato's *Emblemata omnia* to win assent for his argument, disarmingly concludes his *Syntagma de symbolis* with a quotation from Horace (*Epistles*, I, vi, 67–8): 'si quid novisti rectius istis / candidus imparti; si non his utere mecum (If you know something better than these precepts, share it, my brilliant fellow; if not, join me in following these). I can do no better than commend the sentiment to my readers.

That I have done what I have done has only been made possible by my conversation and friendship with many scholars in this field. They will know my extreme debts. I mention with particular warmth Bob Cummings, Marc van Vaeck, Karel Porteman, Peter M. Daly, Michael Bath, Alan Young, Daniel S. Russell, Pedro Campa, Jean-Michel Massing, Dietmar Peil, Wolfgang Harms, Karl-Josef Höltgen. All have generously shared their compendious erudition in matters emblematic, *die et noctu*. To my mentor, Alastair Fowler, I owe a particular debt: neither knew quite where the clue would lead, when he introduced me to this emblematic labyrinth. Among others, I would particularly wish to mention Lyndy Abraham and Sabine Mödersheim.

Various libraries and librarians have also been of enormous assistance: Edinburgh University Library; the Herzog August Bibliothek, Wolffenbüttel; Glasgow University Library; the Bibliothèque Nationale, Paris; the British Library; the Bodleian Library; Cambridge University Library; the National Library of Wales; Queen's University, Belfast; the Founder's Library of the University of Wales, Lampeter.

In all of this my wife, Shawn, has exhibited the thoroughly emblematic virtue of *patientia*. She read the complete text and made innumerable suggestions for its improvement. To her I owe more lessons in the Counter-Reformation principles of *lætitia* and *fristitia* than anyone could deserve.

Introduction

Had I a hundred tongues, a hundred mouths, and a voice of iron,
I could not sum up all the forms of *emblems*, or rehearse all the
names of devices.[1]

No one is compelled to perform the impossible.[2]

'To think is to speculate with images', pronounced Aristotle.[3]
Centuries later, Coleridge would buttress the principle with a
specious etymology: 'To think is to thingify'.[4] The Renaissance and
Baroque periods would have little reason to disagree with either
view. But their images were not – or at least not exclusively – those
pale shadows of sense impressions the Greek philosopher meant.
The image stock that sustained these Early Modern thought
processes derived from a complex visual and verbal culture. Actual
buildings, books and objects – galleries, libraries, and collections
of ancient artefacts, inscriptions and archaeological finds –
provided part of the mental furniture. And since there were no
restraints imposed by any viable formal theory of image production, the generation of new imaginative forms and structures was
technically limitless. The sources that fed the image-making
faculty were wonderfully varied and philosophically irreconcilable, though some hardy spirits would attempt the feat: Graeco-
Roman, Judaeo-Christian, archaeological, theological, literary,
historical, artistic, heraldic, mythological (see illus. 1), scientific,
astrological. This fantastic repertory of images and mythologies, a
heady cocktail of fact and fiction, firm articles of faith and will-o'-
the-wisp nonsense, lent form and substance to unspoken assumptions, inarticulate unconscious hopes and fears that went to make
up a culture in the process of being formed. The fabric of medieval
faith and thought was eroding under a steady tide of religious,
political and intellectual upheaval and change. Yet, the anxieties
created by enormous innovations – the Reformation, the discovery
of the New World, new astronomical theories – exerted a pressure
on the cultures of Europe to look afresh at the things that sustained

1

their imaginative life. But the image stock of the past was to assert a continuing pressure. The scholarly reader was probably more likely to glean his knowledge of astronomy from a better edited text of Hyginus than from Copernicus (illus. 2). The culture of the Renaissance and the Baroque oscillated between past and present. The classical world of Greece and Rome was dead, but still exerted a powerful influence. The present was in the process of being born. More accurately and insistently, it required articulation. The past was drawn into that present. But wherever the images came from, thought of whatever kind would be absolutely dependent upon them. In some cases, the images were fragments stored against impending ruin, in others, they nourished the hope of a new imaginative synthesis, a new beginning.

Any approach to the terms 'symbol' and 'symbolism' of the Early Modern period has to begin by admitting that both terms had already become blurred in antiquity, and the situation did not get any better as time went on. Antiquity bequeathed a linguistically contaminated term that led to the point where at least seven different meanings could be assigned to the word.[5] When the emblem emerged as a distinct literary form in the first half of the sixteenth century, its species of symbolic representation was also called a *symbolum*. Being a new invention, however, the emblem was free to define itself. Thus, it could be 'a species of epigram',[6] or 'a symbolic, identifying attribute held by an allegorical personification'. The *Oxford English Dictionary* can define the term as a verbal construct, 'fable or allegory that might be expressed pictorially', or as an image, 'a drawing or picture expressing a moral fable or allegory'.[7] Flags, identifying marks, familial or national coats of arms,

2

mottoes, even war-cries, might all spring to mind as possibly relevant. The taxonomical question becomes further muddied when we look at closely related linguistic forms in various vernacular traditions: *impresa* in Italian and *empresa* in Spanish in many cases also refer to what we would commonly accept as emblems. *Symbola*, like their vernacular equivalents *devises*, or devices, could also refer to emblems or to *imprese* or to both. 'Poosees' (posies) became an English appropriation of the term *emblema*. The hieroglyph inspired and formed the basis of emblematic constructs. Collections of learned imagery, iconologies, images of gods and goddesses were also sources for, or drew on, emblems and emblem books. I say nothing at this time of the parable, the illustrated beast fable, the illustrated proverb, the reverses of medals, the rebus or the enigma. A cautionary case, which illustrates the depth of the problem, is the term *theologia symbolica*. To a seventeenth-century German Protestant theologian, it would have referred, not to a book of Christian symbols, but to theological arguments concerning the Creed.

What one can say with certainty, however, is that around the beginning of the sixteenth century, a number of essentially new symbolic forms were invented or rediscovered. Variously described as *imprese*, emblems, iconologies, symbologies, *Imagini de i Dei*, *Mythologia*, hieroglyphs, *symbola* or *icones*, these works collectively bear witness to a systematic programme of composing, compiling, transposing and recording allegorical imagery. The task was taken up by humanists, theologians, courtiers, heralds, academics, antiquarians, philologists, rhetoricians, esoteric philosophers, alchemists, hermeticists, Jesuit educators, poets, artists, *literati*, mystics, architects and polemicists of every colour of sectarian persuasion. Together they presided over a major shift in sensibility that fundamentally altered the perceptions of the Middle Ages and lasted until the dawn of Romanticism and beyond.

One cannot understate the variety as well as the pervasiveness of emblematic modes of thought and expression during this period. Without exaggeration, from Catholic Spain to the Protestant Netherlands and from England to Russia the emblem impinged on every aspect of European Renaissance and Baroque life – and death. Over 2,000 titles of printed books in who knows how many editions, manuscripts and various printed ephemera are only part of the surviving legacy of a phenomenon that decorated every aspect of domestic and civil life, however noble, however menial. Yet this terrain still remains largely uncharted. There are bibliographical maps, but they are incomplete or unreliable.[8] The essential tasks of analytical and descriptive bibliography, textual history, the construction of stemmata on which textual authority might have been firmly established, have not, in the majority of cases, even begun. Modern editions tend to be in the form of facsimile reprints, expensively preserving the errors and typographical idiosyncrasies of individual copies, even down to the accidents at the press, the ink blots and scribbles left by early readers, which render, on occasions, the printed text illegible.[9] These reproductions further distort, blur and degrade to varying degrees the quality of the original. When the book is particularly fat, reproduction of some openings render the text illegible in the inner margin of the recto and the outer margin of the verso. Biblio-biographical information on authors, artists, engravers and publishers exists, but the record is patchy and has never been collated. Historical and theoretical certainties hardly exist; philosophical and epistemological orientations are unreliable. Academic ground-work that took place for 'respectable' literary and art-historical national traditions at the end of the nineteenth century and at the beginning of the twentieth failed the emblem and its related kinds, partly because of its bastard and uncanonical status. It was neither Literature nor Art, although it was spawned and secretly nourished by both.

There exists an eloquently specific, but, I would claim, a representative example of just this kind of collusion and obfuscation from a period at the end of the nineteenth century, when much of the scholarly work that went to the establishing of national literary disciplines was being done. In Britain, for example, the *New English Dictionary* and the *Dictionary of National Biography* were being compiled. At this time Edmund Gosse wrote of Robert Louis Stevenson's *Moral Emblems*, that 'these volumes were decidedly occult. . . . [T]hey leave something to be desired. *Non ragionam di lor, ma guarda*, if you be lucky enough to possess them, *e passa*.'[10] By implication, the dark quotation from Dante's *Inferno*, iii, 51 ('I will not speak of them, but look and pass on') consigns the poems to a place somewhere on Lethe's far bank. But no reader who had actually seen these little booklets could easily recognize them from Gosse's description: they are anything but occult. Of course, Gosse knew that his statements were almost certain to go unchallenged, partly because of his secure position within the literary establishment of the day, but also because few readers would have actually laid eyes on the texts in question. At this date, they were extremely scarce, and had only appeared in their first, limited, ephemeral editions. Even the British Museum did not hold a full set. But Stevenson had sent Gosse copies of all the productions of Lloyd Osbourne's press. Gosse knew that what he wrote of them was sheer hokum. His specious misrepresentation was deliberately designed to exclude them from consideration as part of Stevenson's legitimate output. Gosse recommends the booklets only to the bibliophile and the collector, not to read them, but to 'possess' them.

It is time to explore the emblem phenomenon more fully. Barriers between Literature and other kinds of writings and inscriptions, we are led to believe, have been eroded. Let us, therefore, explore this illegitimate phenomenon, even though the way may sometimes be dim. Theorists are at best blind guides. Answers to questions may not always be satisfactorily forthcoming. Fortitude and patience are required.

What is an emblem? What is a symbol? Nothing, one might think, could be more natural than to ask this at the outset. Let us rehearse, by way of dialogue, some assumptions, and confront them with the facts as they are found in real examples of the form.

The emblem consists of three parts – a 'lemma' or motto, a picture, and a following explanatory text.

But this three-part structure is not the exclusive property of the emblem. It occurs in texts that are certainly not emblems. Illustrated Ovids, Aesops, Virgils, and fable books (see, for example, illus. 3) have a page layout that consists of a title or caption, the picture, and a following text, which teases out the implied narrative of the picture. The format existed before emblem books as such were invented, and derived from a healthy manuscript tradition. Of course, it is not unlikely that this format might well have influenced the decision of the printer of the first published emblem book to commission pictures to add to the motto and text that the author provided. But a three-part structure is not all that makes an emblem. Nor did emblem authors feel constrained by the mystic number Three: there are various layouts: two, four, six, eight, or more parts have seemed variously viable. It was not for nothing that Jacob Cats christened one of his books of emblems *Proteus*!

However many parts it has, one, at least, must be a picture?

Yes ... except sometimes the picture is lacking. The emblem is then said to be 'naked'.

Surely this is a printer's oversight, or an attempt by the press to save money?

Sometimes it might be doubted if an illustration ever formed part

88 *VENEFICA, ET QVIDAM.*

Π.

Γ῾υνὴ μάγος, καὶ τις ἄνθρωπος.
Ο᾽ργὰς θεῶν τις μάγος ἐπηγγέλετο γυνὴ
Α᾽ποτρέπειν, ἐνθένδε πολλὰ φερομένη,
ἔαλω, ἰδὼν δέτις εἰς θάνατον ἀπαγομένην.
Α᾽ δωάτος ἔφη ἀνδρῶν, ἐπαγγείλου θεῶν.
Ε᾽πιμύθιον.
Πολλοὶ τελοῦσ᾽ οὐδὲν μεγάλ᾽ ὑπισχνέμενοι.
LXXX.

Venefica, & quidam.

Mulier venefica iram Deûm se auertere
Iactabat, inde plurimum faciens lucri,
Fit rea, trahi quam homo ad crucē videns, ait
Hominem haud fuit mutare pollicitam Deum?
Sensus fab.
Plerique magna promittunt, praestant nihil.

EVTA-

3

of the author's intention. Even within the same book, some emblems may have pictures, others not.

How long should an emblem be? Doesn't it have a short accompanying verse epigram?

Yes, except when the verse is prose, and the text – whether verse or prose – can stretch from a pithy distich to several pages. But does the verse epigram 'accompany' the emblem, or is the epigram the emblem?

These are works of mysterious, esoteric symbolism.

The 'darkness' of these books is often greatly exaggerated. But the emblem was never meant to be obvious. There may, indeed, be some deliberate obfuscation, for it had to have something *plus in recessu quam in fronte* More that is hidden than is openly displayed. Authors with an interest in the occult did appropriate emblematic formats for obscure purposes. But it is more usual to find that the imagery is very plain and taken from ordinary, everyday objects: a mop or a comb might serve as the basis of an emblem. In these designs, of course, it has to be realized that cleanliness is often next to godliness.

I have seen some emblems that contain music.

Yes . . . and the format of many printed emblems resembles that of the seventeenth-century song books. But music is not always or necessarily part of an emblem. But there are, indeed, musical emblems.

Well, I know this much: these are usually works of morality or devotion.

In many cases, yes. But they could also be works of social satire, esoteric science, philology, or libidinous speculation. Content is no certain guide. *Emblemata* or 'emblem books' formed no discrete category in Early Modern libraries. Some books of emblems were shelved in the poetry section, others catalogued as legal or medical, still others as ethics, or politics, or divinity, or natural history. Occasionally in early libraries multiple copies of the same book were each classified in different sections. Emblems could also be found within larger works of reference: rhetorical manuals, educational treatises, encyclopaedias, dictionaries, and scientific reference works on botany, ornithology, herpetology, etc. Nor was the emblem – whether 'naked' or otherwise – always to be found between the sheets of a printed volume. Sometimes it was part of some public celebration, festive, gratulatory or funerary; sometimes it formed the basis of a sermon; sometimes it decorated the interior or exterior of religious or civic buildings.

It is apparent, even at this stage, that we have taken the wrong track. *What is an emblem?* is not even a good question. It implies that the answer lies in the same eternal present as the question, and that there is *an* emblem, a normative type, that the emblem is one thing at all times in all places. But before a barrage of *excepts* and *buts* begins, polite enquiry ought to cease. This game of verbal tennis might continue endlessly, each observation countered by negative qualifications or ever-more subtle refinements. One quickly realizes that a few superficially innocent enquiries have yielded so many answers, many of which are stale, flat and unprofitable. This question can prompt those who know into a Prufrockian evasiveness ('Oh do not ask what is it . . .'), or a Faustian horror ('*Homo, fuge!* Oh turn from these labyrinthine, dusty, theoretical arguments!) The question *Quid emblema sit?* is the very riddle of the Sphinx, that dies when answered.

One might wander endlessly within the Early Modern academies of critical interrogation of the form. The answer one gets from earlier records is not consistent. Authorities repeat the solemn pronouncements of their predecessors – even those of the medieval schoolmen – without any noticeable advance or improvement. What is most disturbing is the constantly defeated expectation that these pronouncements should bear at least passing resemblance to what we find when we actually see the thing itself. Even in this present century, normative, formalist approaches to the problem – the Germans' hunt for the fabulous *Idealtypus*,[11] which never did nor ever could exist in nature, only in a speculative museum to be looked at by academic specialists – have suffered, when applied to the actualities of the case. It does not survive the kind of rhetorical enquiry that even schoolboy rhetoricians of the Renaissance would have subjected it to: the time when; the manner how; the place where. Not even the fertile hunting grounds of the Renaissance emblematists – the deep forests of Germany, or the wildernesses of North Africa and Ethiopia – have yielded a satisfactory specimen! It exists only as a convenient subterfuge, the product of hypothetical reasonings, that can be arrived at only by setting aside all the historical facts. We must be wary, too, of applying a post-Romantic or Postmodern critical theory to a period that constructed visual, lexical, and typographical space in radically different ways to our own. Yet the Victorians had their emblem books (see illus. 4), which repeated or redesigned those of earlier centuries. There are, too, Postmodern emblems: notably those of Ian Hamilton Finlay.[12] Some Surrealist experiments, in which objects were signed and given a new name, have much in common with many emblematic procedures.[13] Although proceeding in an independent direction without reference to the emblem, when a poet such as Bernadette Mayer can write of the 'obfuscated poem' that it 'bewilders old meanings while reflecting or imitating . . . a beauty that we know', she asserts, knowingly or unknowingly, a fundamental continuum between a Postmodern poetic and the best traditions of the art of the emblem. Then, as now, it is just as true to say that

> to be alive as a poet is to be
> *in conversation with one's eyes*[14]

These broad kinships show the futility of attempting to establish synchronically viable generic markers that would reconcile different productions at different times under the same broad label. 'Exceptions' co-existed at the same date, even within the same volume. Nor can we take refuge in the feeble construction of emblematic subspecies – the love emblem, the Jesuit emblem, the humanist emblem, the alchemical emblem, the heart emblem, the *impresa* – where different but consistent rules and conventions might apply. Each sub-genre, it will be found, replicates in miniature the contradictions that run through the entire corpus.

Literary practitioners did not think of generic 'rules' as tyrannical edicts. Ben Jonson robustly rejected the notion that 'authenticity' can only be achieved by adherence to certain 'laws'. 'I can conceive of no such necessity', proclaims Cordatus, Jonson's *alter ego*, a character 'of a discreet and understanding judgment'. Speaking of comedy, a not irrelevant consideration, since it has been argued by more than one person that the emblem to be considered a *genus jocosum*, he states:

> If those lawes . . . had beene deliuered vs, *ab initio*, . . . there had beene some reason of obeying their powers: . . . yet how is the face of it chang'd since! . . . [it is] augmented . . . with all liberty, according to the elegancie and disposition of those times, wherein [various authors] wrote? I see not then, but we should enioy the same license, or free power, to illustrate and heighten our inuention as they did; and not bee tyed to those strict and regular formes, which the nicenesse of a few (who are nothing but form) would thrust upon vs.[15]

EDITED BY

MARTIN GERLACH.

ORIGINAL DESIGNS

BY THE MOST DISTINGUISHED MODERN
ARTISTS: ALSO REPRODUCTIONS OF OLD TRADE
ARMS AND DESIGNS FOR MODERN ONES IN THE
RENAISSANCE STYLE.

EXPLANATORY TEXT BY

DR. ALBERT ILG

CUSTODIAN AND PROV. DIRECTOR OF THE ART-HISTORICAL COLLEC-
TIONS OF THE IMPERIAL FAMILY AT VIENNA.

VIENNA 1882.

PUBLISHED BY GERLACH & SCHENK.

4

As with comedy, there were no 'lawes' laid down to govern emblematic composition *ab initio*. Indeed, 'liberty', 'license', 'free power . . . to illustrate and heighten' were also the hallmarks of the emblematist's art. Part of the emblem's distinction – as was recognized early on – was its diversity. To slightly paraphrase Gabriel Rollenhagen's prefatory epistle to his first readers, changing his words, but not his sense, to apply his statement specifically to emblems: 'But just as there is great diversity in virtually every other thing in spite of their being put together under the same genus, such is also the case with *emblems*'.[16]

In answer to the question with which we began – *What is an emblem?* – it may be safest to assume a somewhat radical, nominalist position: everything that was called an emblem *was* indeed an emblem. Even here we are insufficiently liberal, for we really ought to embrace its various synonyms: *emblema, emblemata, emblème, Sinnbild, Sinnebeeld, Sinnepoppen, Zinneminnebeeld* . . . . At this stage the faint-spirited might wish to give up, and simply concede that different linguistic and national traditions had their own way of dealing with this particular word-image collocation and abandon them to their own devices! But even were one to respect discrete linguistic boundaries, one would find that these terms within the same linguistic borders would have to be stretched to encompass some local variation: – the *emblèmes* of Lyon are not necessarily those of Paris; the Florentines and the Romans dealt with these matters in different ways; Nuremberg is not Frankfurt; the academic *emblemata* of Leuven are not those of the more commercially orientated Antwerp printers. Yet the portability of the printed book, and the various swift communication networks across Europe, could ensure that a book printed in Lyon could normally be available in Geneva, Antwerp or Madrid in a short space of time and could there make its contents known.

We probably need to go even further and accept for the sake of argument whatever definition, and whatever fabulous and unlikely explanation that early writers gave for the beginnings, origins developments of the form, as well as relations to their various cognate manifestations, even though with the benefit of hindsight we now know these to be philologically and linguistically mistaken, if not totally fanciful. The polymath Athanasius Kircher, for example, pursued his deluded symbological and philological investigations back beyond the Tower of Babel to the *lingua adamica*![17] Luca Contile, more modestly, traced the history of symbols to the time of Noah – the divine *impresa*, a rainbow with the motto NEQVAQVAM VLTRA INTERFICIETVR OMNIS CARO AQVIS (From henceforth all flesh shall not be rooted out by the waters of the Flood).[18] Others cite the secret writings of the Egyptians via the esoteric tradition of Moses, Zoroaster, Orpheus, Pythagoras, Plato and Proclus. Others claim to be heirs to a line of occult wisdom enshrined in the oral tradition of the Cabala, which began with a theosophical school established by God himself with the help of the archangel Raziel. He instructed selected angels in the art, who in turn instructed Adam. These imaginative constructions of the form, however dubious or ludicrous, formed part of their real thinking about the genre, influencing the way it was uttered and its uses. Whatever was thought to be the case actually changed the form itself.

All this, of course, is simply part of the stubbornly healthy refusal of genres to conform to static theoretical constructs. All literary forms change, mutate, evolve and eventually die, sometimes to be resurrected in more glorious embodiments. And the emblem has, as we have indicated above, proved to be particularly vigorous in adapting itself to different uses: academic, pedagogical, satiric, decorative. It became the plaything of such various and mutually irreconcilably different groups as Jesuits, Lutherans, Behmenists, Paracelsians, Aristotelians, Neoplatonists and alchemists. It flourished in the courts of absolute monarchs, as much as under republican rule. Its pervasiveness and its progress went unchecked by local outbreaks of iconoclasm and iconophobia. The rage for book-burning and the hysterical violence against objects of wood and stone seem to have been directed more against the medieval legacy of images of saints than against contemporary images of vices and virtues. Nor should we be surprised that emblems should be any less flexible than most other forms. They were spawned under the aegis of the Sphinx, whose stony features twist into a smile at our attempt to bind this Proteus. The following chapters will seek to illustrate by particular examples some of the ways in which this form spectacularly adapted itself to diverse uses over the centuries. The mistake that so many theoreticians make is that they look for a normative embodiment of the form, which denies the very flexibility that gave the genre life. One hesitates, for various reasons, to invoke the magisterial put-down of Dr Johnson against those who sought to apply Neo-Classical 'rules' to Shakespeare – 'the petty cavils of petty minds' – but it is all but irresistible when applied to the field of emblematics.

If the emblem was not generated from a theoretical matrix, where did it come from? The best approach that I can suggest to this question of image generation is to look at the customs and practices that went into making the emblem. And both were as various as they were pervasive and obtrusive.

No domestic or public space was left unfilled by some appropriate emblematic decoration. Each part of the day from dawn until the evening announced *finis coronat diem* (The end crowns the day) and afforded opportunities for reflection. As one progressed from the bedroom, to the hall, to the library, to the garden, ceilings

could catch in mid-career a falling Phaeton, or a fireplace suspend
a Quintus Curtius at the apex of his heroic leap; overmantels
might display a merchant's profession; on walls, tapestry hangings
showed the cardinal and the theological virtues; curtains, cabinets,
and bed-hangings might depict the exploits of Cupid or the loves
of the gods; windows instructed the eye as much for what was
written on them as for what could be seen through them; pictures
of famous worthies of the past inspired the viewer to present
emulation; vases, statues, pillars, rings, clothing might represent
private resolutions; table ornaments, trenchers and glassware
would remind the diner of the tortures of Tantalus or the advisa-
bility of Temperance – at such feasts, the motto surely was *Gustate
et videte* (Oh taste and see); inlaid cabinets might celebrate the
Labours of Hercules or of Cupid; furniture, mosaic floors, swords,
armour, flags, standards, might form spurs to valour and noble
enterprise. Even the smallest room in the house – the newly-meta-
morphosed Ajax – and the humble chamberpot did not lack
appropriate emblematic adornment. Certainly, in the first half of
the sixteenth century it was fashionable to wear emblematic
badges or to have some mute sign embroidered on cloaks, caps or
sleeves. Some of these images and words were from the pages of
printed emblem books. Others became part of printed books,
many of which have not survived. Nor are we necessarily dealing
with actual houses and buildings. Some of these things existed
only within the mental architecture of a memory theatre.

No opportunity was lost to surprise the eye and the mind into
moral reflection. Wise words, witty sentences, allegorical images
and visual puzzles – a Saturn's head, Hercules' Hydra, Oedipus'
Sphinx, Cupid's bow – waited in ambush to remind one of moral
duties or religious truths. This scope and perspective on the individual marked this symbolism off from medieval patristic readings
of the creation as universal sign. A striking phrase from some
better author – Virgil, Ovid or Horace – a proverb, a biblical verse
could be joined to an eyecatching image to constitute a miniature
religious sermon or moral essay wrought into the material fabric
of an individual's daily life. This was attention-seeking poetry
addressed *to* someone, and demanded or challenged interpretation. Discrete traditions normally kept apart – the Classical and
the Christian, fabulous myth and the scientific observation of the
natural world – were collapsed together in a mutually illuminating
flash of understanding. If what was discovered was not always new,
it was at least reinforced by copious and various repetition. Knowl-

edge was, after all, a process of remembering, recollecting, recuperating and reminding. Nature was observed through the 'spectacles of books', for reading could only be useful if it moderated and shaped perception and understanding.

The duties, offices, and potential pitfalls of every station in the social, secular hierarchy from prince to servant, and of every stage in the human progress from the cradle to the grave, from infant to corpse, were prescribed in symbolic form and outlined according to a moral heraldry. Princes and courtiers more than most other stations in life were subjected to emblematic targeting. They were surrounded by the symbolic attributes and appendages of power – the orb, the sceptre, the rods of office, flags, standards – and instructed in the mysteries of state from the entries that greeted their arrival to the masques that entertained them after dinner. Political resolutions and treaties were preserved in visual form on standards and medals. The royal personage would display his personal ambitions and desires in coded form in the decoration of his palace (see illus. 5). François I's famous, amorous salamander adorned each nook and cranny of his palace at Fontainebleau. It was a mark of ownership that he stamped upon his dwelling. But, as it also declared his noble, but secret passion, it also managed disconcertingly to obtrude his private desires on public, 'official' space. The effect is thoroughly Manneristic. In detaching an image from one sphere of existence (here, the private, the amorous, the personal) and attaching it to another (the political, the official, the public), it is quintessentially emblematic. It tests, and perhaps serves to define, boundaries and limits by embarrassingly, if artfully, overreaching them.

But also, more generally, in respect of the less privileged, the new-born babe was surrounded by emblematic gratulation, even if it took no more grand form than a 'Latin' christening-spoon; schoolchildren cut their wits on emblematic exercises; the dragon-guarded maid, the torch-bearing lover, the yoked newly-weds commended with pomegranates (see illus. 6), the wife with her tortoise, the lion-hearted soldier, the blindfolded or clean-handed judge, the scholar, whose learned tomes rivalled the elephant in the term of their gestation, and the dove-like widow did not lack for emblematic advice. Last, of course, the corpse was attended with customary suits of woe to its final resting place in a well-wrought urn or a half-acre tomb adorned with emblematic trappings. In cypress-planted churchyards, hieroglyphic serpents twisted themselves into stony hoops, biting their tails in defiance of depleted

SYMBOLA
Nutrisco & extingo.

Fuit hoc nobilissimi ac magnificentissimi
Galliarū Regis Francisci insigne symbolum: Sa=
lamandra flammis incubans. Salamandram au=
Plin.   tem tanto frigore præditam scribit Plinius, vt i_
gnem, velut glacies, petenter extinguat. Alij in
flamma vitam agere: quin & ali vulgò creditum
est. Atque memini me vidisse effigiem Regis
huius

hourglasses and eyeless skulls – an ancient intimation, or pious hope, that the triumph of eternity would succeed the triumph of time. There could be few surprises in a world in which each stage of life had its expectations penned and delimited by churchmen, jurists, moralists and teachers. It must have all been very comforting – and severely controlling.

6

Life was essentially emblematic because, to some degree, many aspects of daily experience were self-consciously presented as part of an emblematic theatre, in which no event could be presented without an accompanying gloss. For this reason human history, legend and myth needed to be taught and remembered, because these fictions and constructions of the past repeated themselves in essence, and could, in turn, throw light on present events and happenings. Time had penned its lessons; men and women repeated them.

Yet even the most mundane or trivial aspect of everyday life could afford a useful moral to the curious and inquisitive eye. There was literally nothing under the sun that was not emblematic – at least potentially. The four elements, the heavens, four-footed beasts, birds, fishes, plants, stones and insects could all instruct the 'eye of understanding'. What made this symbolic universe different from the medieval 'Book of Nature' was the active participation of the individual within the construction of significance. Abraham Fraunce, following Luca Contile, noted that 'The one and the same image of any animal or plant can be used to unfold various ideas conceived within the mind'.[19] This symbolic process originated within, and was generated by, the human mind. It was not a gift from God. Instead of a world divided Thomistically into the celestial and the mundane, one is presented with a curious knot that ties together the creation, so that spiritual realities can be seen within the created world as impinging on the individual, in so far as that individual participated within larger social and religious networks and within his or her own cultural history. The very terrain of the individual soul could be mapped. Not only physicians, but preachers and moralists became cosmographers: the physical world rendered tangible by a process of forged analogies that linked the invisible world of moral, spiritual, political and psychological entities. It was not so much a matter of a leap of faith, but a metaphorical leap that could be triggered by any number of rhetorical ploys, or by a Neoplatonic awareness of parallel emanations that descended from the world of the divine to the physical universe as perceived by the senses.

This moralists' map bore some relation to what has familiarly been called the 'Book of Nature' or the 'Great Chain of Being', which stretched in an ordered hierarchy from the Throne of God through the Choirs of the Blessed Angels and the celestial spheres, down to the smallest, though far from insignificant, pebble on the face of the earth. Even Hell itself might inversely replicate such an order. This world picture was a conservative, medieval survival, and the notion of a simple, ordered scale of creatures corresponding to established moral, political and spiritual meanings bore only a superficial relation to the complex harmonies that the Renaissance and Baroque mind could form from occult correspondences between the visible and the invisible. For this later age the 'Book' was more like a folio volume, its indices compendious and various, and its author, God, more a Baroque concettist than a simple preacher. Nor was there only a single book in this library exclusively concerned with Christian devotion. One image (illus. 7) from Otto Vænius's *Emblemata horatiana* shows that the humanist revival of Classical learning provided a repertory of Classical moral virtues that could exist alongside the Christian message. Hardly a polished mirror, which reflected exclusively Christian, spiritual truths, it was a dark glass, a cipher, a labyrinth of significance. It was, moreover, alive. At this time the earth began to move. The planets danced, the stars sang. Nature was also wittily pregnant. 'All things are big with jest', exclaimed the poet George Herbert. Later, it would 'breathe', 'whisper', 'intimate'. Emblem books were not reprints of the old 'Book of Nature' of fixed allegorical types, but made from moveable type and formed of metals – those infernal practices of the printing house, the casting of molten lead, the scraping and cutting of woodblocks, or the corrosive, sulphurous and nitrous burnings on copper plate – to reveal, in William Blake's phrase, the 'Seven deadly Sins of the soul'. This art was no easy transcription from the world of nature, but the result of

> The secret of dark contemplation
> By fighting and conflicts dire
> With terrible monsters Sin-bred
> Which the bosoms of all inhabit.[20]

One thinks of the earlier Anton Wierix plates in which Christ 'searcheth out the monsters lurking in the darke corners of the hart' and sweeps away the 'viper, serpent, [and] toad'.[21]

Symbolic equivalences were an art of the fugue, where a simple theme could be twisted and restated in different keys and registers: the sunflower (illus. 8), which followed the sun in its daily journey across the sky, might show the influence of the heavenly on the mortal and transitory world, or the secret harmonies that connected our rooted but transitory earthly existence to the immortal. In terms of human spirituality, this motif might show how the soul, trapped in its mortal body, attuned itself to divine influence; or, in the world of the Court, it could intimate the courtier's attendance on the monarch, or, in erotic allegory, a lover's reverential devotion to the distant object of desire. In one emblem (illus. 8), Camerarius combines half a line from Virgil with a Christian message. Nor does this list exhaust the potential

B

XLIX.

NON INFERIO-
RA SECVTVS.

Solis vt hunc florem radiantia lumina versant,
Dirige sic mentem Christe benigne meam.

Q 3   Est egre-

applications of a single symbolic motif across discrete bands in the spectrum of existence, ranging from the privately intimate to the overtly public. Replicated over the range and variety of potential motifs, the number of variations that might be played on such an instrument is exponentially increased. Understood in this way, one might endorse Christopher Smart's rapturous observation, 'flowers are musical in ocular harmony'. The emblematic conceit, derived in some cases from the harmonies of a traditional keyboard of correspondences, was based on a conservative world view; in other cases writers wandered within the zodiac of their own wit, seeking analogies and individually dissonant metaphors in other worlds and other seas. It is important to remember that the universe during this period was constantly expanding, and changing. Our epistemological map has certainly changed since the Renaissance. Not only do the mental sets of the twentieth century differ from those of the artists, writers and scholars who produced the first emblem books, but the mental map was being revised and redrawn even during the period in which emblem art was being produced. It ought to be obvious that the symbols and the symbolic philosophy of the early sixteenth-century humanist were not those of the seventeenth-century Jesuit, the Enlightenment *philosophe* or the Victorian sage. But even within a shorter historical span there were radical disparities and shifts in emblematic meanings and usage. Tension between the innate conservatism of conventional arts of visual representation and swift changes brought about by the sudden expansion of knowledge in the Renaissance meant that within the sixteenth century we see a number of different uses of the same emblematic design, and a process of adaptation and change, of competing modes and fashions of symbolism. Differences of ideology, geography and vernacular traditions could at times override the false impression of unity within an international Neo-Latin culture. This richness and diversity of the emblematic tradition makes normative definitions suspect, while providing a rich and polysemous visual repertory of signs and meanings. When Martin Gerlach produced his *Allegories and Emblems* in 1882, he could not merely repeat the iconographic codes of the past centuries. He had to find ways of presenting entirely new concepts, as in 'Electricity' (illus. 9). Although this was a new concept, he could also use this as something of an excuse to display the female form, by appealing to the conventions of seventeenth-century allegory. The emblem was actively engaged in negotiations with all aspects of the culture of its time – literary,

theological, political, popular and artistic – and these various demands required it to be various, aware of its different potential exploitations.

Our safest procedure is to allow the emblem practitioners to answer for us. They invite us to step through their ornate frontispieces and command our attention: *Aspice* (Look!), *Vide* (See!) and, ultimately, *Elige* (Choose!).

ONE

Talking with the Dead: The Beginning and Before the Beginning

This chapter deals with the beginnings of certain symbolic forms: the emblem, the hieroglyph, the *impresa*. Or rather, it might better be said to deal with certain myths of their creation. As Daniel Russell has persuasively shown, there was a vigorous visual and verbal culture that was emblematic in all but name before the 'emblem' was officially invented.[1] We should be careful not to overestimate the importance of accredited 'beginnings'. Yet, for all the Renaissance preoccupation with origins and with pedigree, the earliest form in which a book was uttered, the manuscript or the first edition, did not necessarily prescribe its public future appearances, much less the ways an author would be later read and used. Nor, given the large license accorded the printing trade in the early modern period, could there be any guarantee that a book's first public utterance would correspond with the author's intentions. Nor would later readers in succeeding decades have been aware of the publishing history of the book they had recently bought. There may have even been an expectation that the book in their hands would have materially departed from the author's copy. Although the printing trade was by inclination conservative in its practices, the publisher would naturally have been conscious of current tastes and fashions in the art of the book and would be inclined to issue a book in a form that would appeal to the contemporary reading public. Who would actively prefer the crudely executed woodcuts of an earlier generation, when finely executed copperplate engravings were in fashion? There is no doubt that pedigree conferred authority, but this was more likely to spring from the printer's *imprimatur*, or from the materiality of the book itself, than from a mere author. When dealing with these early symbologies, modern readers should be careful not to be narrowly bound to definitions, which place an excessive reliance on printed 'origins'.

It is a needless truism to state that the early modern period was in a state of change and flux. But some literary historians, when dealing with the emblem, *impresa* and hieroglyph, tend to forget this.[2] Whatever such theorists state or piously wish, symbolic forms did not remain as they were first pronounced. Nor did the different genres stay chastely separate. There was inevitably inter-penetration and cross-pollination. Beginnings, of course, were important; how otherwise could these things *be*? But it was soon realized that no one was bound by the 'earliest' conception of a genre, or the 'earliest' construction of a particular meaning attached to a particular symbol. These 'earliest' meanings could be discovered by a process of scholarly interrogation and contested inference. But there was no lexicon that systematically gave the dates, places and authors that identified a particular symbolic equivalence at any particular time. The situation was altogether too fluid to allow such a thing. The grammar of symbolic forms was in the process of being intuited. And what should prevent anyone, at any date, attaching a different symbolic equivalence to any object? After all, in emblematic composition part of the chal-lenge was to see how far one could go in extending the applica-tion of a given symbol, or in developing a copious thesaurus of images to express the same idea. Given this possibility of the construction of new meanings, there seems no reason why the earliest significance should weigh more heavily than a later. Authority, in this as in so many other areas, was severely contested. But we have to begin somewhere, and the beginning, wherever that is and however we might construct such a notion, seems the most logical place.

Andrea Alciato: Emblematum pater et princeps

Rarely can the birthdate of a genre be established so precisely, and its 'father' so clearly identified, than in the case of the emblem. Notwithstanding all its lookalike proto-manifestations, on 9 December 1522 the academic lawyer Andrea Alciato wrote to Francesco Calvo, a printer, announcing the invention of a new species of literary composition: 'During this Saturnalia, I have composed a little book of epigrams, to which I have given the title *Emblemata*'.[3] Alciato saw these 'emblems' as recreative and enter-taining: a relief and respite from serious academic work during the holiday period. He also hoped that these elegant trifles might entertain his intimate circle of erudite, humanist friends. The festive, saturnalian provenance of these compositions is not to be underestimated and was to exert an enormous influence on the tone and substance of the emblem tradition as a whole. I propose to deal with this in detail later, in chapters Six and (in particular) Seven. Alciato certainly seems to have had no intention to publish these works. In all probability, this may well have more than a little to do with their festive provenance, their Rabelaisian, even Fescennine, mirth. Private jests uttered in a Bacchanalian setting rarely translate well when reproduced in the sober light of print. Such intimate 'mysteries' are not intended for publication. Nor, during a period in which a manuscript culture was still vigorous, is there any reason to expect that the printed format was the most acceptable or usual means of publication. The holograph – now presumed lost – was for a small, intimate, intellectually elite group of erudite, humanistically trained readers, who would appreciate the poems for the festive utterances they were.

Modern scholars would dearly love to know what this manuscript looked like. In their later published and printed form, the emblems were usually set out as in 'Maturandum' (We must make haste; illus. 10): a short motto or lemma above a woodcut; the *pictura* (here, the slug-like remora wound around an arrow). Beneath would be a short epigram, describing the significant parts of the image, here unpacking the comical paradox that a creature proverbially a symbol of sluggish inertia can possibly recommend haste.[4] This tripartite layout became the most usual format for the emblem. Yet, it is highly unlikely that Alciato's first holograph presented it in this way. It is probably wise not to be over-confident about the lost manuscript's exact form and content. But we can make some likely inferences on the basis of the bibliographical evidence of subsequently published editions and the likely processes of textual transmission that lay behind it. In the absence of truth, the best we can hope for is a likelihood of truth.

Alciato published some epigrams in 1529 in a collection of Latin translations made from the *Greek Anthology*.[5] These texts are identical to some of the subscripted epigrams in the *Emblemata*, except that the texts do not have mottoes. The Latin anthology was, admittedly, a different publishing venture with different aims, but it is a legitimate inference that these texts may be those referred to in the earlier letter to Calvo, or that the *emblemata* described therein may have closely resembled them. On this basis, we might assume that, in at least some earlier states of Alciato's emblems, there was no *lemma* or motto. Such a structure is generically feasible. Some of the first published emblem books, for example, La Perrière's, also lack any sort of motto.[6]

ī2ō   AND. ALC. EMBLEM. LIB.

Maturandum.   LII.

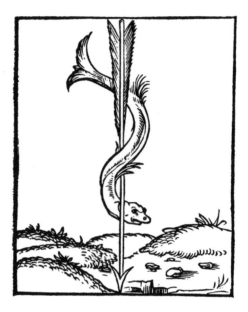

Maturare iubent properè & cunctarier omnes,
Ne nimium præceps,neu mora longa nimis.
Hoc tibi declaret connexum Echeneide telum,
Hæc tarda est,uolitant spicula missa manu.

10

If there was no motto to the first holograph emblems, it is even
less likely that there was an image.[7] To judge from the evidence of
authorially approved printed editions of the *Emblemata,* Alciato's
original manuscript epigrams were 'naked' – i.e., devoid of
pictures. When Alciato published his complete works at the end of
his life, they appeared simply as lemmatized epigrams.[8] This
format, therefore, had the author's sanction. During his lifetime
and in the early posthumous editions many of his emblems
appeared in exactly this way,[9] though he seems also to have been
prepared to acquiesce to the provision of woodcuts. It was far
from unusual for later editions of the *emblemata* or for Alciato's
imitators to adopt an unillustrated format that simply consisted
of a lemmatized epigram. It should therefore come as no surprise
if the author's original holograph lacked visual material. After all,
the image implied or described by the epigram was plain enough

SIGNA FORTIVM.

Quæ te caufa mouct uolucris faturnia magni,
    Vt tumulo infideas ardua Ariftomenis?
Hoc moneo quantum inter aues ego robore præfto,
    Tantum femi deos inter Ariftomenes.
Infideant timidæ timidorum bufta columbæ,
    Nos aquilæ intrepidis figna benigna damus.

11

to anyone who could read the Latin. Or, if it was not plain, that was the author's intention. There is a calculated ambiguity in some of the emblems that meant they could not be visually construed with absolute confidence. In one example (illus. 11), we see the tomb of the mighty Aristomenes. However, the eagle in different editions is found either chiselled into, or sits on top of, the monument. The precise visual specifics are not clear, for the Latin, '*insideas*' can bear both possibilities with equal justice. Woodcut artists could not indulge in the Latin text's imprecision. They had to choose what to depict. Alciato seems to have had no particular preference, for finally it is immaterial whether the eagle is a sculpted effigy or incised onto the lid of a sarcophagus. Here the erudite and the learned had the advantage over the illiterate artisans who designed and cut the woodblocks for the printed texts. Few artists at this date could read any learned tongue. For

Alciato's first intended readership, the image was easily visualized through the words of his poem, and any provision of a graphic image would have been an otiose tautology.

Alciato's *Emblemata* appeared for the first time as a distinct work in printed form in 1531, almost a decade after the letter to Calvo. How the manuscript came into the hands of the Augsburg printer Heinrich Steyner is not known. When they were thrust into an unprepared world in print form, their appearance came as a complete shock to the author. He even tried to have the volume suppressed. It may have been that he was embarrassed by the public appearance of things he had intended strictly for private circulation. These were the licensed jests of the Saturnalia, uttered *festivis horis* (at a time of convivial merriment).[10] The term *festivus* also implies that the poems were witty, even salacious. They were not meant to be repeated or released to the larger world. For works that were meant for the private amusement of some friends to be put abroad in print was a betrayal, a breach of decorum. Some of their humour, we will see in a later chapter, could be so very broad that it caused some of his later commentators to blush. But we are in no position to judge the strength of the author's annoyance, for the book appears to our casual observation to be exactly what an emblem book should look like: a collection of poems with mottoes and accompanying woodcuts. Such was the success of Steyner's inspirational publishing *coup* that the design he hit on became the most usual form in which a publication of this kind would be issued for the entire history of the genre. But this was probably not the book our author invented. It appears, from Steyner's prefatory address to the reader, that it was the printer's own idea to commission the illustrations. A valid implication from this is that there were no illustrations before, and that Alciato's text consisted only of mottoes and epigrams. Six emblems remained inexplicably unillustrated in Steyner's edition, those printed on the openings on sigs E_4^v / E_5^r and F_2^v / F_3^r, and these might be regarded as more accurate reflections of the copy text, which Steyner had acquired. For the rest, he had simply taken over the author's manuscript, however he may have come by it, and fitted it to the existing popular publishing formats of the illustrated fable, the illustrated bestiary, the *Bilder-bibel* and collections of illustrated proverbs, which were designed for a more general readership.[11] This was the emblem's first gigantic stride towards a distinctly popular culture. And the emblem never fully recovered.

Whatever other reason Alciato may have had for suppressing

the volume, there can be no doubt that Steyner's edition was a travesty of Alciato's erudite, humanist emblems. Their utterance in this form must surely have embarrassed the learned jurist. They looked distinctly popularist and down-market. Also, given the iconological inexactitude of Steyner's commissioned woodcuts, it is inconceivable that they could have derived from an author's sketch or verbal directions to an artist. Even the specifications of the images described in the words of the epigrams are ignored or misunderstood. The artist–designer seems to have regularly misconstrued the iconography and meaning of the Latin, often in such a way as to fly directly in the face of the text's precise details. There was also an unacceptable number of embarrassing typos, which the printer hastened to put right by issuing a new edition within weeks of the first. Inevitably, while correcting some compositorial blunders, he added new ones. Yet, for all its faults, from this modest beginning sprang the most frequently reprinted emblem book in history. It appeared in over 200 editions in the sixteenth and seventeenth centuries alone, and almost immediately was translated into the vernacular. It spawned Latin imitators, and its repertory of images was appropriated by the material culture and reproduced in tapestry hangings, plasterwork and domestic ornament. Others, prompted by Alciato's example, repeated or extended this image stock.

Even in 1531 it was too late for Alciato to put the genie back in the bottle. The emblems were in the public domain and they could not be recalled. The distinguished, academically respectable, Parisian printer, Christian Wechel, persuaded the injured author to entrust him with the printing of a new, corrected edition with cuts by Jollat, which he would commission at his own expense. From 1534 until 1542 a series of editions of the *Emblemata* flowed from the Wechel press, along with a French translation by Le Fèvre and a German one by Wolfgang Hunger. During this time Jollat's woodblocks, which had initially largely followed the designs of Steyner's artist, Jörg Breu, with all their faults, were progressively modified and corrected. New cuts with a different iconography were substituted for the old (see illus. 14, 15, 16). All these changes brought the blocks more strictly in line with the images described in Alciato's epigrams. It is tempting to think that Alciato himself had a hand in the process. That Alciato approved of Wechel's enterprise is indicated by the fact that he continued to communicate newly composed emblems to the press: in 1534 nine emblems that had not appeared in Steyner's edition were incorporated into the

Wechel text, and two new emblems were added at the end of the 1542 edition.

Alciato went on composing emblems for the rest of his life, and collaborated with a number of publishers, sometimes happily and sometimes not. In June 1546 some 86 hitherto unpublished emblems, complete with illustrations, were issued from the Venetian press of the heirs of the distinguished Aldus (illus. 12). How the texts came into their hands, and the dates of their composition, are far from certain. It may be, but this is the purest conjecture, that

Alciato, or those who placed these emblems with this publishing house, wanted to associate the *emblemata* with the Aldine press. In the first years of the century, the great Aldus Manutius was in the forefront of the current interest in Egyptian hieroglyphics and was the first to put Horapollo into print. As it was thought by many to provide the key to Egyptian hieroglyphic wisdom encoded in an ideogrammatic picture script, the text exerted enormous influence on the development of the emblem tradition as a whole.[12] But the 1546 edition of the *Emblemata* is fraught with unanswered questions. Again, it is not known whether the author's holograph, if that was the copy text, contained illustrations, but on previous evidence, this is unlikely.

At about the same time Alciato was negotiating with the Lyon printer Sebastian Gryphius over an edition of his *Reliqua opera*. These included all the *emblemata* from both the Wechel series and the new Aldine texts. In Gryphius's edition they all appeared without illustrations as 'naked' emblems. Gryphius passed the text of the complete series of emblems to his former apprentice, Jean de Tournes, who went on to publish the *emblemata* in a single volume composed of two books, the first comprising the Wechel suite, the second the Aldine emblems. Jean de Tournes commissioned new woodcuts for 'Liber I' from the renowned Bernard Salomon. 'Liber II' was not furnished with cuts. The implication is that custom and practice had associated the earlier suite of emblems with the tripartite illustrated form, but the author's copy of the new emblems, as communicated to him by his fellow Lyon printer, had no such visual embellishment. Jean de Tournes was probably unaware of the illustrated Venice edition, which seems to have exerted little influence on the subsequent iconography of Alciato's emblems. Thuilius, Alciato's most diligent editor, appears to have been unaware of it. For 'Liber I' Salomon adopted some of the iconographic detail from Jollat's illustrations to the Wechel editions, but did not hesitate to change or reinterpret Alciato's epigrammatically defined images. Jollat's brilliantly spirited designs became the models that many subsequent artists would follow. Towards the end of Alciato's life, the bookseller Guillaume Rouillé, in collaboration with the printer Macé Bonhomme and the artist Pierre Vase, brought out an edition of the *Emblemata omnia*, which provided illustrations for 211 of the 212 hitherto published emblems.[13] Alciato's *Emblemata* proved to be a title that both de Tournes' and Rouillé's publishing houses would keep in print well into the next century.

What emerges from this compressed publishing history of the

Emblemata during Alciato's lifetime is that it would be a mistake to assume printed versions were faithful or even consistent reproductions of the author's first poetic thoughts as embodied in his original manuscript(s). The printed book had a life of its own, and its shape and destiny was controlled by various hands – booksellers, printers, artists, compositors and editors. Each would assume an almost total authority over one part of the production process. Consultation seems to have been a difficult concept. If it occurred, it was probably after, rather than before, the event. The author's role, once he had wittingly or unwittingly supplied the initial text, seems to have been at best marginal, one more concerned with damage limitation than anything else. The process of innovation and change to the published format was not arrested with the author's death. New cuts with different iconographic motivations were commissioned, and the book acquired a body of annotation and commentary. I will deal with some of these changes in chapters Two and Three. Suffice it to say, if Alciato were to have returned to the world and sought to buy a copy of his emblems some 80 years after his death, he would scarcely have recognized the book as his own. We might also go further and make the not unfair assumption that, even in his own lifetime, he regarded the subsequent public appearances of his poetic offspring with some bemusement. At various times he seems to have allowed, if not actively approved, different visual interpretations of his epigrams. It was probably a matter of indifference to him, as long as the artists' interpretations did not render his text totally ridiculous. After all, the humorous, the preposterous, the exotic and the strange were not altogether removed from his original sense of festive emblematics. It is also worth mentioning that he had no financial interest in the publication of his emblems.

But, even if the publishers, printers and artists do not seem to have cared very much, it seems legitimate to ask what Alciato's original intentions might have been. Although he left no formal theoretical utterance that sets this out with any clarity, we can infer certain things from the different states of the printed emblems, which represent initial misunderstanding and subsequent correction to and accommodation of the author's ideal intentions.

In Alciato's letter to Calvo we witness a lawyer's fussiness over what amounts to the announcement of a new genre – this *libellus* is, after all, Alciato's poetic child. There is even something affectionate in his choice of the diminutive. Though internal evidence suggests he must have begun composing these epigrams around

1517, at that time the book cannot have been large. If not a *libellulus* (a very little book), it was indeed small. It probably contained fewer than the 104 emblems that were published by Steyner in 1531. It had a long way to go before it would assume, under Thuilius's editorship, the mammoth proportions of Tozzi's 1,000-page Padua edition of 1621. Alciato's choice of the name *emblemata* for his contribution is revealing. At that time absolute novelty was neither desirable nor a recommendation, so Alciato decided to dignify his new creation with a classical pedigree, and thereby sought to confer on it some species of cultural legitimacy. He hit on a Greek word with a sound Ciceronian provenance: *emblema*, from a Greek verb meaning to set in, or on, to put on, to graft on.[14] But the new name was always going to cause problems. Classically, it referred to mosaic tiles, or the grafting of a shoot onto a stock, or detachable decorative ornaments. Never had it been thought of as a kind of literary composition or epigram, though it had been applied to a mannered, precious style of speaking or writing.[15] In this latter sense there may even be a sense of knowing self-mockery in Alciato's choice of the name.

When Cicero had used the term,[16] he was referring to encrusted ornaments stuck onto plate or vases for decoration. In classical times, it seems, these could be removed from the object (the Ciceronian context implies that they were indeed purloined by violence – 'ripped off'). They could be transferred to another object. Instead of incurring the expense of having many elaborately decorated objects, in the interests of domestic economy one could have *emblemata*, which could dress up everyday household objects for special occasions. The implications for Alciato's 'emblems' are many. This imagery is decorative and designed to impress. It is not for the everyday. There may be, further, a hint of deception, dishonesty, even pretentiousness. In the re-application of these *emblemata*, something plain and ordinary could speciously acquire an appearance of greater worth than it normally had. The decoration disguises the object. It is deliberately made to seem other than it is. Metaphorically, then, *emblemata* are veiled utterances. The rich design appropriated from somewhere else might merely clothe a simple idea with a portentousness it does not deserve. Or, the applied ornament might reveal a hitherto unsuspected significance. Meaning is generated by dislocation: the familiar, everyday or commonplace is changed by virtue of being placed in another context: it has become the bearer of unsuspected meaning, a metonym for a previously hidden reality.

We cannot be sure what Alciato's intentions were for the new genre, though we can make some guesses. From his dedicatory epigram to Peutinger, the preface to almost all the editions of the *Emblemata*, it seems he considered his emblems as poems – epigrams that cleverly describe images, statues, pictures and similar kinds of visual shows. He was happy enough for the images so described to be taken up and used as patterns for badges and decorations. But this task he relegated to artisans. As a scholar and a poet, Alciato styled himself, with whatever degree of self-mockery, as '*vates*' (a bard): [17] he was more interested in the fact that images could acquire or be endowed with meaning, could be used to communicate ideas. His intention was 'to describe in each epigram some object from history or the natural world in such a way that it might be endowed with some chosen significance'.[18] The nub of the emblem, however, lay in its gnomic allegory – not so much its image, but the compressed verbal utterance of a Pythagorean *symbolum*.[19] Alciato tells us that sometimes the emblem is based on puzzling occurrences in nature, hidden arcane secrets, the sacred wisdom of the ancient sages, the true doctrines concealed beneath the fictitious cortex of a fable, or the learned sayings of philosophers or historians.[20] The epigram would be occupied in setting out and explicating the meaning of such recondite facts and problems not so much because they were difficult and strange and required explanation, but because they implied some useful advice that might be applicable to one's everyday life. This advice was rendered memorable, because it could be summed up in a corresponding image. These images were 'invented' in the sense that contemporary rhetoricians used the term. They were not so much 'made up' as found (from the Latin verb *invenio*, find). As a true scholarly humanist, in his poetic work, as in his legal scholarship, Alciato was keen to return *ad fontes* (to primary sources): historical facts, archaeological records, the literary evidence, etymological inferences or grammatical analysis. He did not disdain the traditional poetic euhemeristic allegories of the gods, demi-gods or heroes or physical allegories of the forces of Nature that 'Poetry' from earliest times was held to wrap in 'Fables and darke stories'.[21]

Alciato's emblems sprang from an essentially verbal culture. His 'In Occasionem'[22] (see illus. 13) does not confront a statue, as much as a verbal description of an artefact elicited by a process of question and answer. It is the verbal artificers, the ancient poets, who exert a shaping force on his imagination when he confronts the creatures that lurk in the recesses of rumour and imagination:

Scylla, whose white waist is girt with barking monsters, exultant
Discord, impious Rage, the snake-eating hag, Envy.[23] These are no
new inventions, but memories of, and appropriations from, a classically biased education. They provide archaeological literary sites
that the emblematist could visit and pillage with profit. The
process is one of inexact repetition, for the original is wrenched
from its narrative context, fragmented and put together to form a
newly constituted verbal artefact. Instead of an image or a memorable phrase being tied inextricably to a given meaning, the essence

13

of this species of symbolism is its *extricability*. The processes of
detaching words or images from one context and transferring
them, with whatever violence, to another are the means by which a
chosen significance can be achieved or enhanced. There is a subtle,
sardonic distance between the initial recognition of what is already
known, and known to have once belonged to someone else, and
the coming to terms with the novelty of its relocation. Alciato
deliberately emphasized the shock value of this tactic by his wilful
roughness of metre, a deliberately licentious poetic style that won
admiration and provoked imitation.[24]

    Elsewhere an emblem might be based on a material object – a
statue, a monument, a painting, an inscription. The tomb of Aristomenes (illus. 11) is a case in point. The epigram expresses curiosity as to why an eagle should adorn this sarcophagus. The
questioner is soon told that the eagle is on this tomb because it is
an appropriate sign of the fearless qualities of the dead hero that

lies beneath: just as the eagle is pre-eminent among birds, Aristomenes is among men. The enigma, if there really ever was one, is soon solved. Yet what is important here is not only the simile that links the bird and the man, but the ontological status of the image itself. It has value because of its physical actuality in validating some moral or spiritual reality. Elsewhere, in similar vein, we have among the emblems little images (*sigilla certa*) on the tomb of Archilochus (Emblem 51), marble embodiments of the waspish tongue that characterized him in life. Niobe, too, presents a witty case of *habeas corpus* for the jurist: her tomb does not contain a body, for her body is its own sarcophagus (Emblem 67).[25] These symbolic images are material entities – it matters little whether they are described in words or physically present to the eye. The emblem reminds us both of the materiality of the sign, and of the materiality of meaning itself.

In still other architectural encounters, question and answer dialogues structure the iconographic interrogation of pieces of ancient statuary. Indeed, we might say that in the *corpus emblematum* the whole known universe is placed under interrogation. It is not surprising that Alciato should have been a lawyer. But Alciato is particularly drawn to the monumental. Through tactile admiration of the workmanship of the past a hidden allegory is literally anatomized, tied to particular attributes and body parts. This technique is familiar in the epigrams of *The Greek Anthology*, which Alciato used as the basis of 'In Occasionem' (illus. 13) and elsewhere. The famous classical statue stands on tiptoe, wears winged sandals, holds a razor in her hand, the back of her head is bald, a long forelock famously hangs before her face. Each of these details is interpreted in relation to the central concept she embodies: Opportunity. The iconographic syntax is based on a visually structured model. It is the opposite of what we would usually term 'abstract', for there is no abstraction here that does not correspond to some obtrusive visual fact. The description is pointed in such a way that the details require, even demand, elucidation and explanation. In Alciato's epigram and in the *Anthology* the statue stands in a civilized portico ('pergula aperta'). But it could not be long before such powerful images would break free from such containment. In the 1583 *pictura* here reproduced, Occasio towers over sea and land, dwarfing the tiny ships that sail past her ankles. The artist has added his own iconography, for the craft that sustains her in her ocean voyage is none other than Fortune's wheel. Her habitation amid the waves also associates her iconographically with

Fortune. Further, her image accommodates an even more popular iconography. As she outbraves the elements of wind and tide, she embodies the vernacular form of *una fortuna*: a storm, a tempest. It is entirely unlikely that such a figure would patiently endure a passing scholar's polite enquiries in the civilized retirement of a Renaissance garden.

Part of what we see in the gap between Alciato's 'In Occasionem' epigram and the woodblock cutter's interpretation is a manifestation of the cultural difference that divides one half of the sixteenth century from the other, and a widening separation between a learned, erudite, literary iconography and the more popular forms of contemporary visual culture. This mismatch between the author's ideal classical image and those provided by the artists did

14

not arise simply because the author, after his death, could no longer control what went on. Nor can we attribute this to the production of new editions that were less in touch with the author's original intentions. That Alciato's iconography was genuinely neoteric – or, at least, unknown or unusual, in that it recovers and reintroduces elements from classical antiquity hitherto not generally current – had caused problems from the beginning. The first state of Jollat's woodcut for Alciato's emblem 'Anteros, id est amor virtutis' (illus. 14) was modelled on Jörg Breu's woodcut for Steyner's edition, and, while it corrects some of Breu's blunders, it perpetuates his principle error. *Ubi sunt pennae?* (Where are your wings?) asks the epigram. But the question is rendered faintly ridiculous by the *pictura*, for Jollat's Anteros is fledged in truly magnificent fashion. The point of Alciato's epigram is that this virtuous Love is far different from the conventionally flighty and fickle Cupid. The blunder shows not only the artist's misunderstanding of Alciato's text, it also indicates that in

no way could the artist have been following an author's manuscript containing an image to accompany the epigram. Any accompanying image, however roughly drawn, would have made clear
the author's meaning.

Jollat's error was quickly corrected. A second Wechel edition
appeared in the same year, 1534, and in it Anteros' splendid wings
were clipped by the simple expedient of chiselling away the offend-
ing parts of the woodblock. In the process the overhanging limb of
the tree, in whose shade the god sat, was also lopped. It may be that
the author himself drew attention to the error, or the mistake was
caught in-house. But, whatever happened, for the first time in its
printed form the epigram's question, 'ubi pennae?', makes sense,
when referred to the *pictura*. The corrected state of the block was
used for all subsequent Wechel editions, and served as a model for
the later designs from other presses. So conservative were these
that even Jollat's totally redundant background tree was retained.

The significant thing here is that correction is made retrospectively. This is not a case where there is a decline in iconological
exactitude, as each subsequent edition departs one step further
from the author's holograph. The later editions are more accurate
than the first edition, as each subsequent variant is gradually
brought into line with the author's intention. The second Wechel
edition did not complete these processes of emendation, correction and revision. Alciato's 'In adulatores' (On sycophants) is a case
in point (illus. 15). This was one of the non-illustrated lemmatized
epigrams in Steyner's edition. Jollat did not have Jörg Breu's design
to follow, and was free to interpret the image as he wished.
Steyner's text, however, offered a hanging side note, which refers
the reader to Pliny's *Historia naturalis*,[26] which describes the exotic
beast thus: 'It has a tail that tapers towards the end and curls in
coils like a viper, and crooked talons.'[27] It may well be that this
marginal note derived from Alciato's holograph, and that this was
as far as he was prepared to go in giving actual visual cues to his
readers: he expected them to bring to mind the visual specifics laid
down by classical precedent. Jollat did his best to render such specifications to our view, and in its first state his woodcut for this
emblem is thoroughly uninhibited. He depicts a fierce monster,
with eagle-like claws, a scaly body, prominent snout and sharp
teeth. Further, the 1534 text is further muddled by a significant
typo, which renders the motto as 'In adultores' (On adulterers): the
protruding snout, stiff tail, and fishy scales may well have been
thought congruent to such a predatory beast. However

compelling, this imaginative creation totally ignores the point of Alciato's epigram, which is based more on Plutarch and Erasmus than Pliny,[28] and is concerned with court flatterers, not marital infidelity. In a new edition in 1536 the misprint in the motto was corrected, and the earlier woodcut was scrapped. A more plausible, egregiously smiling chameleon was substituted, and the connection between the animal's hypocritically adaptable behaviour and the *mores* of the court was established in visual terms by the provi-

15

sion of a fortified tower in the background (illus. 16). The implication is that the chameleon is to be found not only in its wild natural habitat, but its human equivalent is equally at home in the prince's court. The revised design, whether it originated from the author's advice to the printer or from Le Fèvre's attentions as a translator or *correcteur* to the press, is probably immaterial. The effect was to bring the *pictura* in line with the author's ideal intention. Had there been authorial directives from the beginning, these expensive corrections would not have been needed (the revised design was retained in all later Wechel editions). However, a castle background was not considered *de rigueur* for subsequent woodcut designers at other presses.

What we may conclude from the above is that the printers and publishers packaged the author in a different format than he envis-

aged. When the illustrators took his matter in hand they seem to
have seen this as an invitation to create the author's imagery in
terms of their own visual conventions: they came at it from a
different iconographic tradition, that of the popular fable books,
illustrated proverbs and a popular tradition of mythography,
which provided renditions of the images of classical gods and
goddesses in the image and likeness given to them by the sixteenth
century. And, although the trade was fundamentally conservative

16

in these matters, one artist did not necessarily feel absolutely
bound by the example of his predecessors. The emblem was
quickly accommodated to other aspects of this popular contemporary visual culture: that of the heraldic device, the fable, the parable, adages, proverbs, the enigma and the rebus. Alciato's text, on
the other hand, was classically learned and with an antiquarian
bent. The first emblems, in more than one way, belonged to a
different, earlier age. He recovered a number of ancient images
from the past, which were strange to the workers at the press, who
simply drew what they knew and thought they saw. But in other
ways, too, it had more in common with the literary culture that
prevailed at the turn of the century than that of the 1530s.[29] To
some extent, Alciato's first emblems had more in common with
Pierio Valeriano's *Hieroglyphica* and the excitement engendered by
the mystery of the Egyptian sacred script, not to mention
Francesco Colonna's erotic novella, the *Hypnerotomachia* – his

encounters with ancient ruined architecture, his tactile admiration of cunning workmanship, its visual and verbal puzzles, his adventures with typography, and the delight in the broken and the fragmentary. The rest of this chapter will look at this cultural context. But it is important not to over-generalize. Alciato's complete emblems were composed over a long period, and they reflect and preserve different literary enthusiasms that he indulged at different periods of his life: hieroglyphs; the artful epigrams of *The Greek Anthology*; fantasy archaeology; historical narratives; fables and jests. These represent not so much a palimpsest, but the growth rings of a poet's mind, which reflect the shaping influences on the emblem genre.

The reading public at large – as opposed to the intellectual elite for which the manuscript was first designed – was left to puzzle out meanings in the new emblematic construct, which brought them in touch with a territory that was at one and the same time familiar and unfamiliar. But Alciato's success was that he looked forward as well as back to the erudite labours of the beginning of the century. He did not leave his readers with dry-as-dust conundrums. He discovered a syntax and a grammar of symbolic forms, which encouraged others to imitate him. Or, to use another metaphor, Alciato was the Euclid that provided exemplary symbolic axioms on which a geometry of meaning could be postulated. The underpinning principle of these would be *homo omnium mensura*: in all his emblematic equations the key point of reference is the human. The punishment of Prometheus, after all, taught him that 'What is above us has nothing to do with us'.[30] This definition of the scope and focus of the emblem was formulated in a theoretical preface to a later emblem book as 'ut in mundo, sic et in homine' (As it is in the world at large, so also with humankind).[31] The emblem is frequently built on an actual or an implied simile, which relates even the most surprising objects back to the private, the public, the moral, the social, the ethical, the physical, the spiritual, or the financial. In this the emblem has much in common with the *Parabolae* of Erasmus. As such, they are based on a wide reading of classical and contemporary authors. Animals, trees, flowers and almost everything else assume symbolic roles expressing human values, emotions and ideas. The whole world becomes a literary device, a rhetorical strategy, for exploring these. They are bookish, but always the emblems are concerned with the business of living. Alciato commends the sound and healthy, he reproves the sick and the vicious. The phrase from the Roman comic poet Terence could well be used to sum up Alciato's attitude: 'Homo sum; humani nihil a me alienum puto' (I am a man; therefore I think nothing human is foreign to me).[32] In the course of this book, we will see how true that can be.

Egyptian Mysteries

It was thought that the Egyptians had contrived a means of evading the curse that followed the fall of the Tower of Babel, by preserving their esoteric wisdom in picture script. The carved stone monuments presented a lasting record, and the symbolism was thought to erect a hedge around their learning, rendering their meaning comprehensible to the learned, while baffling the vulgar and the profane. These hieroglyphic obelisks and pillars were veritable mountains covered with strange characters formed of birds, beasts, discrete human body parts, agricultural implements and kitchen utensils. The ancient provenance of these objects gave them enormous authority. They could not help attracting attention, if only by their sheer bulk, and they continued to exert a mysterious fascination on the Renaissance and Baroque mind. An enduring paper monument to this is the massive three-volume folio of Athanasias Kircher, *Oedipus Aegyptiacus* (illus. 17). This 'Egyptian Oedipus' was none other than Kircher himself, master, according to the fulsome dedicatory verses that prefix the volume ,of 'chain'd mysterious emblemes, holy rites, / Close riddles, obscure symbols'. The English poem is found on signature '+++++$_2$^v' of volume i.

Attempts were made early to crack the symbolic code. Greek and Roman authors left a number of tantalizing, scattered references to this ancient script that suggested that it was nothing less than a cryptic record of arcane, sacred knowledge, a whole system of law, theology, philosophy and esoteric wisdom in carved, visible shapes.[33] The Roman general Ammianus Marcellinus assumed that 'individual characters stood for individual nouns and verbs; and sometimes they meant whole phrases'.[34] Diodorus Siculus had earlier tried to read this picture script, and was regarded as something of an authority. He saw it as a series of transferred metaphors. Thus, the falcon, the swiftest of birds, became a sign for swiftness, or something done quickly; the crocodile, an evil creature, became a metonym for evil. Ammianus Marcellinus added that 'scientifically' recognized and agreed properties of living things and objects ('rationes physicae') stood for concepts

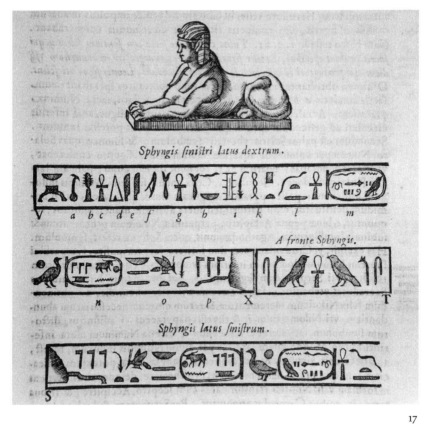

Sphyngis finistri latus dextrum.

A fronte Sphyngis.

Sphyngis latus finistrum.

17

by a similar process of metaphorical transference:

> [B]y a vulture they represent the word 'nature', because, as natural history records, no males can be found among these birds; and under the figure of a bee making honey they designate 'a king', showing by this imagery that in a ruler sweetness should be combined with a sting as well.[35]

'Et similia plurima' (And many similar things more) the Roman general added, possibly becoming a little impatient with all of this. These were inferences drawn from a number of scattered interpretations. One can imagine the excitement when, in 1419, a manuscript attributed to 'Horapollo' did surface (illus. 18). It purported to be the key to deciphering the Egyptian mysteries and it represented a huge increase in the repertory of interpreted images. We now know it to be a late antique forgery, and the meanings it assigns are ingenious fantasies. But the Renaissance regarded it with unquestioning belief as a sacred text, on the basis of which a lexicon of visual signs could be generated. Ammianus Marcellinus

could not have even suspected the huge collection of *plurima* that
Pierio Valeriano Bolzani and his imitators would provide, based on
these few classical clues. Writers of emblems could not but be
drawn to this cognate body of symbolism.

Alciato's first description of his collection of emblems in the
letter to Calvo as a *libellus* nudges us towards the possible 'Egyptian' provenance of his book: for the Latin, *libellus*, could refer to a
papyrus scroll. We know Alciato had studied hieroglyphics at
Bologna with Filipo Fasanini, the Latin translator of Horapollo,
and Karl Giehlow has persuasively demonstrated that Alciato used

18

Fasanini's translation when composing his emblems.[36] The fashionable enthusiasm for things Egyptian at this time can only be
compared to the rage for such things a   millenium-and-a-half
earlier, when Sylla introduced the cult of Isis to the ancient Roman
matrons. Apuleius' description of her rites (illus. 19) in Book II of
the *Metamorphoses*, includes a fancy-dress parade of mythological
figures – Ganymede, Bellerephon, Pegasus, satyrs – as well as a
monkey with a Phrygian cap and a bear dressed as a fine lady.
Dionysus of Halicarnassus adds a host of other sacred and profane
figures in his description of the Roman festivals: the Sileni, the
images of the gods and goddesses with their symbolic trappings,
the Graces, the demi-gods, Hercules, Aesculapius, Pan. These
remind us of emblems as much for their cast list as for the shared
sense of the ridiculous and spirit of festive jollity. Apuleius' image

19

of an ass with wings glued to its back forms the source of one of Vænius's love emblems.[37]

The 'Bible' of hieroglyphic symbolism must surely be the *Hieroglyphica* of Valeriano. Although not an emblem book itself, it was the source of many emblems. The emblem and the hieroglyph were believed by some to be cognate forms.[38] And there are many interconnections. Valeriano and the emblematist Achille Bocchi were friends, and Book VII of the *Hieroglyphica* is dedicated to him. Thomas Palmer, the first English emblematist, did little more than turn selected passages of Valeriano's Latin prose into English eights and sixes.[39] As if to emphasize their connection, or their confusion in many minds, the fact that although the first published texts of Horapollo and their Latin translations appeared in non-illustrated form, from the 1550s editions of the *Hieroglyphica* employed the common tripartite structure of many published emblems (illus. 20).

Valeriano's attitude to this inherited body of symbolic lore is found in Book VI under the chapter heading 'arcana tegenda' (The sacred mysteries must be concealed): 'the Egyptians had sculptures of Sphinxes in all their temples, to indicate that divine knowledge must be protected from the vulgar by enigmatic symbolism'.[40] He believed that God himself was held to communicate with us in just such a sacred script. In the Old Testament the Mysteries of the

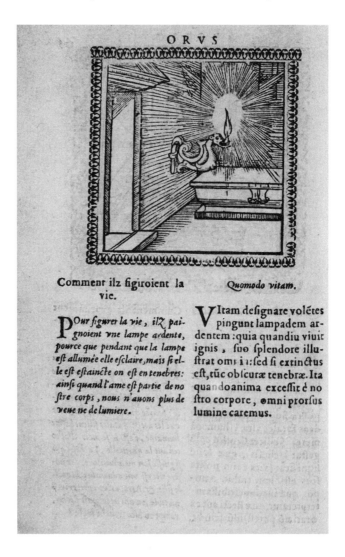

ORVS

Comment ilz figuroient la vie.

Quomodo vitam.

POur *figurer la vie*, *ilz pai-gnoient vne lampe ardente, pource que pendant que la lampe est allumée elle esclaire, mais si elle est estaincte on est en tenebres: ainsi quand l'ame est partie de nostre corps, nous n'auons plus de veue ne de lumiere.*

VItam designare volétes pingunt lampadem ardentem :quia quandiu viuit ignis , suo splendore illustrat omi i ı :sed si extinctus est,tūc obscuræ tenebræ.Ita quandoanima excessit é nostro corpore, omni prorsus lumine caremus.

Gospel were thought to have been delivered to the Children of Israel under the veil of allegorical types and figures, so God's great book of Nature was believed to contain mysterious impressions of the Creator, natural hieroglyphs, significant images that declare His glorious Being. These witty contrivances of the Egyptian priests were designed to bring the human race to a greater knowledge of the meaning of God's works and of the Creator himself.

For those approaching the *Hieroglyphica* with such lofty expectations, what is revealed when the mysteries are unveiled must come as something of a disappointment. Indeed, at first glance, it is hard to know what the excitement was all about. Valeriano certainly expanded on what he found in Horapollo. He works his way systematically through the whole animal world, starting with the King of Beasts and so on down through the created universe. Browsing through his pages, we find that an angry man was depicted by a lion eating his prey, ... a religious person by a lion running away from a cock, ... a whore by a lion with a woman's head: her face is fair, her speech pleasant, her charms powerful, but she preys mercilessly on a man's body and fortune. The merciful were shown as a lion with a lamb lying at its feet, ... an impatient lover as a lion devouring a heart. The elephant signified a king, because it never bows its knee. It is an enemy to serpents, as rulers are to the serpents of the state. It hates swine and filthy creatures, therefore the Egyptians saw it as the promoter of Justice, Peace, and moral Virtue; it was resolute in overcoming difficulties, merciful to the humble, and punished those that resisted royal authority. The elephant, because it was believed to do obeisance to every new moon, was made a hieroglyph of Piety. A priest was depicted by a *cynocephalus*, a kind of dog-headed ape, riding on a fish in a river: the river is the inconstant world, the fish, the passions, which must be subdued by those who aspire to be worthy of divine office. The learned were signified by a stag, lying on its side. A resourceful timeserver was imaged as a hedgehog: it changes its dwelling with the weather. A babbler, ignorant of good manners, was represented by a grunting pig, as was the voluptuous man, wallowing in ease and pleasure. Someone with a facility for acquiring knowledge was signified by a she-goat, because of her acute hearing. A whore was depicted as a wolf: a visual translation of a pun, for in Latin, *lupa* signifies a prostitute, *lupanar* a brothel. Someone in doubt how to get out of present difficulties was shown as a man holding a wolf by the ears, ... a hypocrite, or a dissembler, by a leopard, which was believed to hide its fearsome head, so that it might the more readily catch its beguiled prey. And thus it continues.

It probably comes as no surprise that a stupid and ignorant person was signified by an ass!

The illustrated editions of Horapollo attest to a visual culture that represented the perceived universe in quite different ways. Amputated body parts – hands, heads, eyes, feet, ears – are wrested from their normal context, and hang in the sky above a miniaturized landscape that stretches beneath (illus. 21). They inhabit a conceptual rather than a naturalistic space. This dislocating strategy was a challenge to the observer to interpret the world from a non-mimetic perspective.

One such observer is Valeriano. What is genuinely impressive about his work is the range of erudition he brings to bear in reading this world. Like Alciato, the scholar wishes to return *ad fontes*. He utilizes all available codes and systems that collectively make up his culture. These are widely scattered and dispersed – literary allusions, metaphors, analogies, proverbs, etymologies, verbal echoes, visual commonplaces, scientific and pseudo-scientific discourses. His list of works consulted stretches to over 200 authors. In one short paragraph on the herb hyssop, for example, Valeriano cites the Old Testament psalmist, the cleansing rituals of the Israelites, the allegories of St Eucherius and two passages from Cicero. A marginal note refers us to Pietro Andrea Mattioli's botanically authoritative commentary on Dioscorides. It should be remembered that this was an age in the habit of making 'consents' of Scripture and of keeping commonplace books, even though we should acknowledge Valeriano's erudition as impressively broad and eclectic. His work is not, however, a rag-bag of citations. It is built on a disciplined scholarly approach: he collates relevant biblical and classical texts, he is aware that these traditions have been moderated by recent developments in learning, and he applies the tools of etymology and philology in an attempt to crack the code of concealed meaning. Elsewhere he unpacks unsuspected metaphors in a disciplined, analogical process, likening physical to moral, divine to human, or the world of creatures to that of man, adeptly playing up and down the Neoplatonic scale according to the esoteric principle *Quod superius, sicut quod inferius* (That which is in the higher world is like that which is in the lower world). Frequently, the different points of reference, classical and Christian, antique and modern, do not triangulate on a single significance, but offer various possibilities of meaning. At other times he sought to establish the common agreement of several authorities to buttress an interpretation.

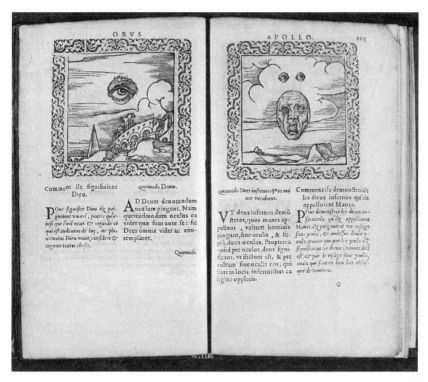

21

The iconographic codes so derived, we realize, were designedly anti-mimetic, or, to put it another way, we can say that poetic, moralistic or doctrinal motives radically moderated any literal mimesis. Images subserved a theological, moral or political purpose, as here in the image of the elephant as a hieroglyph of piety (illus. 22), and therefore did not need to be grounded in 'fact'. Highly dubious constructions of the natural world promulgated by classical or Christian authors were miraculously preserved in a literary and symbolic posterity long after their 'scientific' life ought to have been rendered extinct. So absolute were the conservative powers of theology, politics and education, that symbolic representation of the natural world based on impeccably edited classical texts survived any interrogation grounded in empirical principles. There were many things, in Sir Thomas Browne's memorable phrase, 'neither consonant unto reason, nor correspondent unto experiment', on which symbolic meanings were based, and which were supported only by various authorities cited in the marginalia. The allegorical habit was deeply ingrained from earliest youth through a religiously based education system. Observation of the natural world was occluded by literary, theological and classical

22

reading. Patristic and classical texts provided a stock of presuppo-
sitions about the meanings that may be found in Nature. The
world, to adapt Dryden's phrase, was perceived 'through the spectacles of books'. Or the world may be populated by monstrous
forms that step forth from the pages of printed volumes (illus. 23).
The dog-headed Egyptian god Anubis is an image of shameless
Impudence.

The primacy of the bookish and the verbal in the formulation of
allegorical images was pervasive. When Valeriano read the hieroglyphs and parables placed for our edification in the natural world,
he did so with the aid of textual guides. There was for him more
than one clue by which to thread the labyrinth of the created
universe. He systematically collates references to biblical, classical
and 'Egyptian' symbolic equations. Programmatically it can be
compared to Guillaume Budé's remarkable piece of scholarship in
which he established the weights and measures of the ancient
world by systematic comparison of ancient texts. In such a way
Valeriano hoped to establish the moral and theological equivalences of ancient symbolism.

Although not published until 1556, Valeriano's *Hieroglyphica*,
like Alciato's manuscript emblems, belongs to the first decades of
the century. At this time the enthusiasm for hieroglyphs was great.

23

Celio Calcagnini was translating Plutarch's *De Iside et Osiride*, one of the most difficult Greek texts, and attracted the praise of Erasmus for doing so. Petrus Crinitus, in his *De honesta disciplina*, began to collect some notes on the meaning of particular Egyptian symbols. The origins of Valeriano's treatise lie even further back in the previous century. Some of his images derive from newly devised hieroglyphs from that time: a 'novum commentum' or a 'iuniorum commentum'. One such is a goose attached to anchor for *firma custodia*,[41] which derives from the *Hypnerotomachia*. In a more blatant fashion, Valeriano's friend, Achille Bocchi, borrowed *verbatim et literatim* (or, in this context, we might add, if we can be permitted the term, *picturatim*) some of Colonna's hieroglyphic imagery (see illus. 29). The symbolism of the late Quattrocento is thus preserved, or still current, in the mid-sixteenth century, when there seems to have been a revival of interest in such things. Not only was Valeriano's book printed, but Jacques Kerver in Paris brought out a new edition of Horapollo, but this time with illustrations, making it look like an emblem book. Kerver also at around this date brought out a new edition of Colonna's erotic romance, while in Rome appeared the first edition of Paolo Giovio's treatise on *imprese*.[42]

The dedicatory epistle to Book xxxiii of Valeriano's *Hieroglyphica* tells of the origin of the work. This account takes us back to the first years of the century, when the author and some of his young friends visited his uncle, Fra Urbano da Bolzani. They found the old man teaching Greek. He broke off his lesson and they spent the rest of the day in erudite and pleasant conversation. It was, Valeriano recalls, one of the happiest days of his life. The topic discussed was the hieroglyphic meaning of the eye, which Fra Urbano expounded with uncommon erudition, derived from his wide-ranging reading. In the course of the symposium the general enthusiasm for matters hieroglyphical was raised, and Fra Urbano refers to Aldus Manutius' edition of Horapollo and the Table of Cardinal Bembo.[43]

When, years later, Valeriano's treatise appeared in print, the symposium format had been abandoned. The book was a vast encyclopaedia of symbolism. It was no longer the nostalgically remembered, erudite table-talk of a sophisticated coterie from a previous generation. It was a reference work, one that was to spawn a flood of new symbolic utterances. At the top of the engraved title-page to one collection of Egyptian wisdom (illus. 24), for example, is what looks like a Parnassus or the cloud-covered Mt Sinai,[44] around which are seen the flying angelic ministers; the Lamb of God presides at the fountainhead of symbolic wisdom, the 'FONS SAPIENTIÆ', which flows through secret conduits, and threatens to overflow out of the bottom of the engraving. On either side, the Lamb is flanked by two tables of stone, hieroglyphic obelisks: the one on the left is dedicated to the sun (Osiris), the other, to the moon (Isis). At the base of the first, the *fauna*, at the base of the second, the *flora*. The allusion of the frontispiece would seem to be to God's speaking to Moses on the sacred mountain. His cloudy utterance as revealed in Exodus was given material shape in the Tables of the Law. Here, the modern Moses is none other than a member of the Jesuit order, Nicolas Caussin, whose stony tablets are not so much those of the Law, but contain the sacred lore of the

De symbolica
AEGYPTIORVM
Sapientia, in qua
SYMBOLA, PARABOLÆ,
HISTORIÆ SELECTÆ,
quæ ad omnem
EMBLEMATV, ÆNIGMATV,
Hieroglyphicorum
Cognitione via præstat
Autore Nicolao Caussino
Trecensi è Soc.
IESV

COLONIÆ AGRIPPINÆ
Apud IOANNEM KINCKIVM sub Monocerote
ANNO M. DC. XXIII.

24

Egyptians, the myths of the poets and the figures of the created universe. From these secret conduits flows the fountain of wisdom. To emphasize the Egyptian source of this wisdom, the river deity who pours from his abundant urn the waters of knowledge rests his elbow on a gaping crocodile. What Shelley said in quite another context may with some justice be applied to this image and to the hieroglyphic floods of symbolism:

> [A] great poem is a fountain forever overflowing with the waters of wisdom and delight – and after one person or one age has exhausted all its divine influences which its peculiar relations enable them to share, another and yet another succeeds, and new relations are developed, the sources of an unforeseen and unconceived delight.[45]

The floodgates of Valeriano's hieroglyphic 'Bible' of esoteric wisdom, based on its heterogeneous collection of 'peculiar relations', provided the means by which a torrent of 'new relations' could be developed by others. He did indeed prove the source 'of an unforeseen and unconceived delight'.

Franceso Colonna: The 'Hypnerotomachia'

The *Hypnerotomachia* has been mentioned several times in this chapter, and it is necessary to give some account of it, at least as to how it relates to the emblematic tradition. It is not an emblem book, and this is not the place to give a full reading of the work. It was written before 1467, but not published until 1499. It has the distinction of being one of the finest books Aldus Manutius's press produced.

Thomas Nashe scoffingly described Colonna as 'one of those Hieroglificall writers, that, by the figures of beasts, plants, and of stones, expresse the mind, as we doe in A. B. C.'[46] To be fair, the meaning of the whole allegory is a little more opaque than A. B. C. What we see in process in the book is the evolution of various semantic structures in a hermeneutic synaesthesia. But Nashe was correct in observing that one of Colonna's strategies was to work into the fabric of his dream romance certain hieroglyphic designs, in which he translates words into images. In one image (illus 25), the phrase 'semper festina tarde' (always hasten slowly) is rendered by a circle ('semper'), a dolphin, the swiftest of fishes ('festina') and the anchor ('tarde'). This was not, of course, the true grammar and syntax of the Egyptian hieroglyph, even as it was imperfectly understood by the Renaissance. But it is a good indication of the larger communication strategies developed elsewhere in the book, which invoke a syntax based on visually structured models. This is what Colonna refers to as 'emblematura' (mosaic work).[47] The Egyptian script is only one of the many polyglot forms used in the text as a whole. He brings languages together, combining them into a style all his own. In this dream romance a word is sometimes rendered visible in new ways and is taken as an image to be displayed on a plinth, a pediment or an architrave of a building. Colonna becomes a semantic architect using the spaces created by his visually sensitized pages. Typography structures meaning, as the very textures of words are looked at for their physiognomies in a book that plays with various fonts. These are typefaces after all. Even broken letters are part of its design. It, too, is the opposite of the abstract, demonstrating the same dependence on the materiality of meaning that we have seen in Alciato's emblems. The world of the dreamer is a literary creation made up of linguistic signs.

25

The woodcuts of the *Hypnerotomachia* show a good deal of wit and humour. They also present something of a thesaurus of visual motifs that homonymically illustrate the same thing. There are more than 80 variations of the hieroglyph in one cut (illus. 25). These symbolic variations on the theme of 'mature haste' are

26

APOLLO.　1044

Quomodo laborem.

LAborem adumbrare cu-
pientes Bouis caput de-
lineabant , carne nudatum:
Bouis, inquam ,caput: quia
bobus terra aratur, qui præ-
cipuus labor est & magis.
necessarius, carne aut nuda
tum:quoniam laboriosi ho
mines plerumque macilenti
& pallidi.

Comment ilz demonstroiét
labeur.

POur entendre labeur ilz pai-
gnoient vne teste de beuf,de-
nuée de chair : la teste debeuf,
pource qne auec les beufz on faict
tout labourage:et denuée de chair
pource que gens de labeur & qui
souuent trauaillent sont commune
ment maigres.

27

deliberately comical, as elephants turn into ants, and ants into
elephants (illus. 26). There is a delight in oxymoronic absurdity as
we see a precariously balanced, half-seated girl, who in the act of
raising her left leg, has a tortoise weigh down one hand, while the
other is furnished with wings that lift it on high.[48] The bucranium
as a symbol of patience is as we find it in the illustrated editions of
Horapollo of the next century (illus. 27). The book presents a
continual process of instruction and initiation through ciphers,
visual puzzles, moral marvels and myths.

Colonna's dreamer, like the interrogator in Alciato's *Emblemata*,

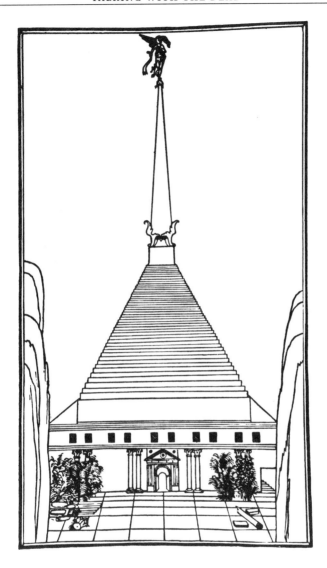

28

is faced with ruins, heaps of stones. In confronting a literary and artistic past, which exists in his present as ruins, reliefs and carved lettering, the dreamer discovers his oppressive individuality: often he is confronted by himself. The buildings echo and resonate with the dreamer's sighs, his longings, his desires. Dead things participate in his life. By classical precedent the fearsome Medusa that greets his gaze at the outset ought to have turned him to stone, and made him of like substance to that which he beholds. Instead, he is awakened to his emotions – fear, wonder, puzzlement – and to a vivifying awareness of the meaning of what he sees. His exploration

CCCXLIIII   **LIB. V.**

PYRRHO BOCCHIO FILIO.
Ex MYSTICIS ÆGYPTIORVM LITERIS.

Symb.   CXLVII.

of the past becomes a kind of burial in it. He is the living anatomy memorialized in the discretely labelled body parts with which he is confronted. The text lovingly recreates the textures, the feel, the colour of what is seen. He explores a statue by climbing inside it, in a sequence that anticipates later heart emblems, where the heart is entered, explored, cleaned and swept.

Elsewehere in the romance, an implied or cited text will frequently form the key to unlock the mystery of some strange, unnatural visual construct: an obelisk with Fortune at the top, turning with a grinding, strident noise (illus. 28) is an observation from Horace translated into the architecturally visible: 'From one man Fortune with shrill whirring of her wings swiftly snatches away the crown; on another she delights to place it.'[49] The sequence of architectural rooms visited by the dreamer and the sights seen can be related to divisions of a significant topos.

In Colonna, too, we have early evidence of the Renaissance habit of transferring a pagan myth to a Christian subject, and vice versa, which will become a stock-in-trade for the emblem writer. But, if we were in any doubt as to the influence of this work on later emblematic developments, it is sufficient for us only to cite Bocchi's wholesale pillaging of one of Colonna's hieroglyphic fragments in his *Symbolicarum Quaestionum* (illus. 29). Bocchi also took up the challenge of finding variants on Colonna's favourite theme of 'mature haste' when designing a medal for the Governor of Bologna with the motto *Matura Celeritas*. Nor was Bocchi alone in finding Colonna's inventions congenial. Valeriano, as we have seen, cites his work with approval. He anticipated many developments in emblems before the emblem was truly born.

The 'imprese' of Giovio

Paolo Giovio (1483–1552), Bishop of Nocera, historian, antiquarian and friend of Alciato, is frequently credited with writing the first treatise on *imprese*, the *Dialogo dell'Imprese Militari et Amorose*.[50] Even though it was not the first (Claude Paradin's *Devises heroiques* predates it by four years), this enormously influential treatise went through a number of editions before the end of the sixteenth century. Neither can it be said to be a particularly theoretical work. But Giovio was acknowledged by many as the inventor of the 'new science' of the *impresa*. Even if he did not actually invent it, he established rules for the form, which would be discussed for the next 150 years. The impression that this was a 'new' science, though invented earlier than 1555, was reinforced by Giovio's own device (illus. 30), which he had placed prominently at the entrance of his villa in Como: *Recedant vetera* (Let ancient things depart). Historically, this device commemorated the amnesty of 1495 that ended the French invasion of Italy. As we can see, it shows a burning book. This, in fact, is an account book, and its burning signified that with the truce, old scores had now been settled. But when applied to Giovio's *Dialogo*, it also suggested that the art of the *impresa*, which he described, was a new art

30

form, which put antiquity ('veteres') to shame, or, at least, politely rendered the ancients obsolete. If the *impresa* as an art form was not absolutely new, it represented such a degree of improvement over what had gone before that it might as well be said to be new. That which had its beginnings in the rude and uncouth Egyptian carvings was now brought to its subtle perfection by the addition of material from the Greeks and Romans, gnomic proverbial utterances, dark enigmatic sentences and emblems. The evidence for the newness of the *impresa* lay in the fact that there was at first no Latin word for it, and, rather unfortunately, and in a way that further complicated a complicated case, contemporary theorists, forced to find a Latin equivalent for the new creation, fell back on the over-loaded term *symbolum*. Although some would argue that the Renaissance *imprese* descended from the standards of the ancient military divisions,[51] Giovio, and others, would have none of it. Modern devices were aimed not at establishing the collective identity of a Roman Legion nor at repeating the historical precedents set by antiquity, but recorded a specifically modern, individualistic sense of the self: they were designed to declare individual passions and states of mind.[52]

Giovio's *Dialogo dell'Imprese* was first published in 1555, but it reflects not the world of the mid-sixteenth century, but an earlier period, the close of the Quattrocento. His long life also gave him the advantage of having known a lot of people, and in the book he casts his mind back to the glittering society of the rich and famous that he had known in his early life. He thinks of the military pageantry, the tournaments and gallantry he observed when the French invaded northern Italy in the last years of the previous century. He thinks of the ways in which rich, famous and notable people of the time intimated their hopes, fears and desires by means of coded, visual allegorical shows. His book is an anthology of such practices, and it is laced with adjectives that bespeak his high admiration for the people and the times. They are invariably either 'bellissima' or 'nobilissima'. The noble, seductively beautiful Hippolyta, for example, who spread out a garment dyed dark blue and adorned with an inlay of golden gnats so that her lovers would realize they ought not to come any closer to her fire lest they suffer the fate gnats do when they fly about a flame for too long, paying the penalty for their light-mindedness and foolhardiness.[53] He thinks fondly, too, of the punning laurel tree *impresa* of Lorenzo de Medici;[54] the columns of Charles v with the motto 'Plus ultra' (Further onward), commemorating the daring of the man, who strained at the limits of the known world; Erasmus's device, 'Cedo nulli' (I yield to none), thought by some to betray his intellectual pride; and Stefano Colonna (illus. 31), who took his device from his family's coat of arms, a siren, and displayed his own noble temperament by declaring that he would calmly endure all the storms of fortune.[55]

For what they are worth, Giovio's five rules for the perfect *impresa* are these:

> There should be a just proportion and agreement between its 'soul' and its 'body', i.e., the motto and the image.

> It should not be so shrouded in darkness and obscurity that it needs some Sibylline prophetess to interpret it; nor should it be so obvious and plain that even an ignorant, low-class individual could read and understand it.

31

Its exterior form should appear so beautiful and charming that the minds of those that see it are overcome with the greatest and most delightful pleasure.

No human figure should be used.

A motto should be added to the image, as the soul is married to the body. This motto should be in a different language than that which the inventor of the *impresa* 'sucked out' when he imbibed his wetnurse's milk. In this way the meaning is more concealed.[56]

In all of these there was an element of sophisticated game-playing, self advertisement and self display. Where the emblem and the hieroglyph were intended initially for a learned audience, *imprese* were designed for a different social milieu, people in the very public sphere of court life. Under the veil of an *impresa* they could insinuate private ambitions and desires – in this culture rebuses, monograms, ciphers and symbolic colours had earlier served much the same purpose. And to add to the pleasure of the game, Giovio's five rules could be used to judge the success of such witty contrivances. To the delight granted the eye and the mind in beholding such things could be added the pleasure of arguing and debating the respective merits of these visual shows. The social ambiance is aristocratic, the emphasis is on wit and verbal subtlety. There is an additional pleasure in intrigue, secrecy and conceal-ment, though, of course, it would defeat the purpose if the cloud of

secrecy were so impenetrable that no one could see the point. The whole requires just enough 'concealment' to make the game teasingly interesting. And Giovio's rules inserted a certain challenge and difficulty: this was not an exercise that allowed the imagination total freedom to do as it wished.

The rights and wrongs of these rules were debated at length in the Italian academies, where the pleasure in argument was taken to refined levels. Notable contributions were made by Girolamo Ruscelli, Alessandro Farra, Luca Contile and Scipione Bargagli.[57] Lodovico Domenichi's and Gabriele Simeoni's treatises were frequently printed along with Giovio's.[58] There was a particular delight derived from pointing out the fact that many of the examples cited by, and praised by, Giovio did not conform to his own rules. But for all the objections that were made to them, the discussion always came back to Giovio's rules. This they did with a vengeance in Boschius' *Symbolographia*, where they are versified in seven books on the pattern of Horace's *Ars Poetica*. There follows a collection of over 2,000 *imprese* that the author has collected.[59]

While some drew a sharp distinction between the emblem and the *impresa*, the one being general, the other particular to an individual, there can be no doubt that the symbols migrated backwards and forwards from one genre to the other, and both contributed to the image stock, whether these were to be uttered in emblem books or in collections of *imprese*. Indeed, allusions to the one could inform the other. In Simeoni's *Le Imprese heroiche et morali* (1574) we see how Colonna's earlier hieroglyph of the

Anchor and Dolphin is newly pressed into service as an *impresa* (illus. 32). Alciato would appropriate it as an emblem.[60] Aldus Manutius already owned it as the device of his publishing house, and it appears as the printer's mark on title-page of the works issued from his press (see illus. 12).

What may be said is that Giovio's example informed not only subsequent *imprese* treatises, but also books of 'Heroic' emblems. The form was persistent, and surprisingly long-lived. One of the more recent, and most successful, exercises in the genre is that by Ian Hamilton Finlay. His and Ron Costley's *Heroic Emblems* (1977) include a commemoration of the Battle of Midway in *impresa*-like emblems. This, like Giovio's treatise, celebrates warfare in what we might say is a fascination with the aphrodisiac of power. In choosing weapons of mass-destruction he follows the Renaissance interest in the machinery of war as a potential symbol – how many traditional emblems are devoted to bombs, catapults, siege-engines, battering-rams, swords, spears and the like? Finlay brings together quotations from classical sources with a conscious allusion to Renaissance symbolism. Some of this has a *trompe-l'oeil* effect, as helicopters are turned into bees, the aircraft-carrier into their hive, its fuel the honey in an oxymoronic allegory of military might: 'Out of the strong came forth sweetness'. The modern radar screen can offer an insight into the power of such gnomic utterances to offer revelations of what might have been otherwise hidden and obscure: 'Hinc Clarior' (By this means it becomes clearer), or, as Finlay has it, 'Hence Brighter'. Finlay, as so many emblematists before him, is guided from the visible to the invisible.

In all of these symbolic forms, emblem, hieroglyph, *impresa*, it would be wrong to assume that the printed image, wherever it came from, simply restates the text as a kind of visual tautology. The strategy here is, at bottom, crudely rhetorical. The image is designed to catch attention, and having caught it, to move and persuade. It is also designed in such a way that it demands interpretation. The challenge it provides to the ingenuity reinforces the coded message once the puzzle is solved. The image is striking in its strangeness, even though, to some extent, we find we are confronted by things we already know. Therefore the rhetorical catachresis of rendering the highly abstract in highly literalistic terms has the purpose of refreshing a familiar text. The author of the preface to the *Hieroglyphica* was aware that 'things which are too well known lose their reverence and authority and fall into contempt and low esteem'. The strategy, therefore, was to present them in a way that removed them from the common and the usual by formulating the message in veiled, allegorical terms. It may have been the stated desire of some to address the learned, while concealing esoteric wisdom from the vulgar, or to claim that the recourse to poetic veils was the only way mortal eye could behold the dazzling ray of divine truth. But the real motive behind much symbological activity was *periphrasis*: at all costs, to avoid the bald statement of what was, at bottom, trite and obvious.

TWO

Towards an Emblematic Rhetoric

Here may'st thou scant or widen by the measure
Of thine own will; make short or long at pleasure;
Here may'st thou tire thy fancy, and advise
With shows more apt to please more curious eyes.[1]

cramben bis coctam apponere (The same again and again in other words).[2]

Imago fallit (The image deceives).[3]

Writing Emblematically

The publication of Alciato's *Emblemata* aroused immediate interest, and immediate imitation. Part of their early assimilation by French authors, such as La Perrière and Corrozet, is due to the fact that the format of the early editions of Alciato looked like illustrated fable books and collections of illustrated proverbs, with which they were already familiar.[4] '[V]aleat tacitis scribere quisque notis' (Let everyone have the ability to write in secret ciphers), Alciato decreed in his dedicatory epigram to Peutinger that was to preface all editions of his emblems.[5] And by the beginning of the next century, it seems that everyone was doing precisely that: even 'common' people had taken up the habit of writing *emblematicè*.[6] Though far from 'common', Gabriel Rollenhagen's *Nucleus emblematum selectissimorum* (1611) shows that Alciato's successors had learned from his example of using the hieroglyphic codes described in the previous chapter.

In one example (illus. 33), Rollenhagen passes on exactly the same prudent advice as Alciato does in his 'Maturandum' emblem (illus. 10), but applies a new device: not the remora and the arrow, but the spider and the butterfly. This elegantly varies the symbolic utterance, the outward show, while retaining the inner meaning and substance. The debt to the earlier emblematist is declared, while it is simultaneously concealed. The ethical content is conservative, the visual homonym inventive. In his prefatory letter Rollenhagen is quick to draw attention to the improvements he has

18

A M O R A L

NATVRA mora longa nocet spes omnis in alis
Instat qui te vult prendere Papilio.

33

made over his predecessors, and to the fact that he has taken some control over the provision of the illustrative materials:

> For I am presenting images cut not in wood, as they did, but in bronze, and they are not naked, but embellished with adorn-ments not lacking in charm. The [subscripted] lines are few but suitable, clear and polished.[7]

Here he insinuates that he has abandoned Alciato's roughness of diction and metre in favour of a clearer, more rotund poetic utter-ance. He sees the function of the poetic part of the emblem as explicating the meaning: these lines are 'perspicui' (clear, and, by implication, clarifying).

Otto Vænius, too, as an artist, exercised control over both the images and text. His aim, like Rollenhagen's, was to produce a work 'not lacking in charm'. He also shows that he, too, had learnt to string together hieroglyphic symbols in the new syntax laid down by the hieroglyphical writers of the last century. 'Amor aeternus' (illus. 34), can be read in the light of, and may owe something to, Colonna's 'Egyptian' translation of the maxim *Semper festina tarde* (illus. 25). In Vænius we have the familiar figure of Cupid, who may legitimately be understood as the 'Amor' of the motto, sitting within a circle formed by a snake in the act of biting its own tail, a Horapollonian hieroglyph for Eternity, and therefore a visual metonym of the motto's adjective 'aeternus'. Colonna had earlier used a circle as an exact equivalent to the Latin 'Semper' (always).

34

What Vænius does is to develop and embroider the hieroglyphic art initiated by his predecessor.

Many examples of these kinds of derivative symbols, and variations on them, could be cited. But the development of an emblematic syntax and rhetoric did not stem solely from the processes of imitation or quotation of earlier examples. The generation of new emblems came from a combination of sources that arose from the necessity of collaboration at various levels between author, printer, artist, editor and publisher. Sometimes the printer, at other times an author or the artist or the editor, might be the driving force behind a new emblematic book. At other times, the publishing venture might be driven by political or religious patronage. In this chapter I will attempt to provide some examples of how these various forces interacted at different times and places in the history of the genre. While such bibliographical and contextual evidence does not offer the solution to the whole mystery of emblematic art, it can throw some light in that direction.

The Primacy of the Word: Imitation

Rollenhagen could look back over almost a century of emblem writing and give a succinct overview of the literary history of the form. For all his pride in his innovations, and the obvious superiority of the quality of the De Passe copperplate designs, he acknowledges the achievement of earlier writers:

> Andreas Alciato . . . by publishing the small but learned *Emblematum libellus*, achieved great fame. Sambucus, Hadrianus Junius and others followed him, albeit at a different pace.[8]

Rollenhagen identifies the fact that others had followed Alciato's example in emblematic composition, notably the humanist Hadrianus Junius and the Hungarian court poet Joannes Sambucus. Their *emblemata* were first published by the Plantin press in the 1560s and went through various editions until the end of the century. Although this does scant justice to the number of 'others' caught up in the enthusiasm for the new form, he identifies the 'best' writers in the tradition and he signals the importance of Alciato's original example. He is seen not only as the first, but the best. The compliment is made by means of an elegant allusion to Virgil (*Aeneid*, II, 724). Describing Aeneas's son, Virgil says, 'sequiturque patrem non passibus aequis' (He follows his father with steps that match not his). Rollenhagen thereby implicitly recognizes Sambucus and Junius as the 'sons' of Alciato, but also proclaims Alciato's superiority in this species of composition: he was its 'father'.

Such recognition is conferred on the author not with the first, or even subsequent, early editions, but retrospectively. It is unlikely that Rollenhagen knew the slim volume that had appeared in 1531, although he refers to the 'libellus' (possibly one of Wechel's editions), and talks of the collection as 'small'. But by the time Rollenhagen wrote the words quoted above, the *Emblemata* had long outgrown these humble beginnings, and had assumed a more bulky format thanks to the attentions of editors, commentators and publishers. The posthumous *Emblemata* became a work with an imposing textual presence and a life of its own. The text spawned explications; a theoretical preface was deemed *de rigueur* for what was assuming the status of a modern classic; the dedicatory matter grew; a list of works consulted emerged; additional annotation supplemented the already lengthy commentaries; the whole agglomeration generated a substantial index. All these editorial and typographical changes affected the way the book was viewed, and they all contributed to the authoritative status that the text had acquired.

That there was a growing prestige attached to the emblematic format may be seen in the example of Geffrey Whitney, who followed Alciato, Sambucus *and* Junius, in Rollenhagen's phrase, 'quamquam dispari passu' (At a different pace). Literary imitation there certainly was, and Whitney had the further advantage of being able to use many of the very same woodblocks cut for the editions of these three authors' emblems. Whitney's *A Choice of Emblemes* (Leiden, 1586) gained some authority and legitimacy in that it emerged from the Plantin press, which had established a substantial corner in emblematic publishing, and from a generic context, which was bound to appeal to the intellectual, humanist elite of the University at Leyden, where the author was enrolled as a student. But the publication and format of his volume were motivated less by humanistic ideals of literary imitation than by his patron's current political imperatives. The adopted emblematic mode might be seen in itself as something of an implied compliment to his Dutch hosts at a time when the English forces under Robert Dudley, Earl of Leicester, were present in the Low Countries opposing Spanish oppression.

As with Whitney's *Choice*, many emblem books can only be fully understood against the backdrop of the complex network of inter-relationships between authors, publishers and patrons, and the political agenda that underlies a book's composition and publication. Place of publication and date are often keys to understanding these things. Additional pointers can be picked up by looking at contemporary items in the publisher's list. Julius Wilhelm Zinc-gref's *Emblematum Ethico-politicorum Centuria* (Oppenheim, 1619) is a case in point. The book was published by Johann Theodore de Bry, who had moved his business from Frankfurt to set up near the Palatinate Court at Heidelberg. His motives would seem to have been equally political, religious and financial. Hopes of anti-Habsburg political and religious reforms centred on Frederick v and his English bride, Elizabeth Stuart. Oppenheim was not only near the royal castle, it was on a European axis that stretched from London to Prague. From Oppenheim at this period emerged an outpouring of works concerned with magic and hermetic philosophy – by, among others, the emblematist Michael Maier and the English philosopher Robert Fludd. These were intended to indicate support for the Protestant dissidents in Bohemia and were designed to influence public opinion in favour of the political ambitions of Frederick to become King of Bohemia. There seems to have been no shortage of money to subsidize the publication of such books. Zincgref's emblems were part of this campaign. They were dedicated to the Elector Palatine. That the publisher was in sympathy with the project is indicated by the fact that the engravings were by Johann Theodore de Bry's son-in-law, Matthäus Merian. The sense of a divinely-guided Protestant cause is reflected throughout the book: one emblem, for example, shows the Israelites ('God's chosen people') being led toward the promised land by the pillar of cloud. The Palatinate lion is seen in a number of emblems, and the fantasy architecture of Heidelberg castle appears in the background of others. The politics of the volume were recognized even by Frederick's opponents. When his ambitions were suddenly checked, many of the motifs in these emblems were used in visual satires against him.[9] De Bry moved his operations back to Frankfurt in 1620.

The Primacy of the Word; The Fallacy of the Image

After Alciato's death in 1550, publishers commissioned artists to supply new suites of cuts for the *Emblemata*. This independence in the generation of the visual material continued the process that had begun with the very first edition, and it carried on whether the author was alive or dead. Thrift may have dictated to the Frankfurt publisher Sigmund Feyerabend the expedient of using some of his woodblock designs three times over: in 1567 for a new edition of Alciato, in 1581 for Reusner's *Emblemata*, and in an edition of Aesop.[10] The emblem cut is variously detachable, and the same cut might at one time be emblematical and at another no more than an illustration of a fable's narrative. The implication of this is that the woodblock image was not emblematic in itself, but only when attached to emblematic verses. Further, the same cut can be read differently, according to its context. There can be little in the way of surprise in the provision of an illustration to a short narrative. But when the cut becomes the bearer of a hitherto unsuspected significance made explicit in the emblematic verses, we have the very essence of emblematic wit – the evocation of a new significance hitherto unsuspected in the previous life of the image. This is a species of metamorphosis. Similarly, in taking up the cuts used for an edition of Alciato and applying them differently to other interpretations, Reusner showed his capacity for emblematic invention. A parallel process can be observed within the pages of the polyglot emblem book, where the same cut is anchored by various visual cues to different vernacular texts, each of which might take a slightly different interpretative stance. These visual–verbal analogies, depending as they often do on jokes, allusions and puns that are linguistically and culturally specific, do not necessarily readily translate from one language to another. Jacob Cats assembled Latin, Dutch, French, Spanish and English texts, which mirror a different species of emblematic polyglotism wherein the writer moves between the languages of love, morality and the sacred, variously transposing the same image into an amatory, ethical or spiritual key. Cats alludes to this protean nature of the emblem in the very title of his *Silenus Alcibiadis, sive Proteus*. Originally composed love emblems are revisited and given moral applications.[11] And then, later in the same book, he could turn the same emblems into *Sacræ Meditationes*. Vænius also moves from *Emblemata amatoria* 'ad sensum spiritualem ac divinum' (To a spiritual and divine meaning). This shows that an emblematic cut is not in itself tied to a single meaning, but is at the disposal of the verbal text. The text is what does the work in making the cut convey the meaning.

That the expository strategies of the emblem book are carried on in the epigram, rather than in the cut, might appear to be self evident. But it is one of the things that seems to be advertised by the decision to use the term *choice*, or in Latin *selecta*, to describe many collections of emblems. Obviously, this term implies a process of culling. Many more emblems were written than were actually published or survive. Rollenhagen's *Selecta emblemata* are, he tells us in his preface, 200 of the 500 he has written. But on another level it is a piece of self-congratulation, a piece of magnificent self-advertisement: *choice* also means fine, and *selecta* excellent. These are *Imagini illustri* – not just the devices of famous people, but illustrious images, which, decorum demands, are fit for famous people.

This notion of 'choice' also directs us towards a particular emblematic expository strategy: the process of choosing a specific meaning from the many possible meanings that could attach themselves to an image. As Alciato said, 'aliquid elegans significet', an object, by means of the way it is described, might be endowed with some chosen significance.[12] This negotiation with the lexical potential of an image is carried on in the epigram. The verses, it will be noticed, contain few daring metaphors, no 'metaphysical' conceits. Rollenhagen describes his epigrams as brief but 'perspicui', that is, plain: they are designed to make known or to declare the meaning of the image. Francis Quarles, the most reprinted English emblematist, we should remember, expressed a distaste for 'strong lines'. These, after all, would confuse and distract from the relationship between text and printed image, running the risk of imposing another layer of metaphor and simile on what is already an implied metaphor or simile. The emblematic epigram exerts an insistent, if gentle, pressure on the reader towards an authorial choice of meaning from a whole lexicon of possible applications, some of which were in the process of being generated. Frequently this choice is sustained by a number of potential parallels between image and text, and the decision between them is recorded in the subscripted epigram. These can be pursued relentlessly, and can lead to some unintentional humour. Quarles invokes the commonplace simile of death being like sleep, which he attempts to enliven by a further parallel: in this sleep of death, the 'bed' is the 'grave'. The sobering effect of this is then somewhat lost, when he pushes the point somewhat further than it could be seriously sustained by adding the further analogy, that the fleas in this cold bed are 'worms'.

In considering the priority of text over image, one ought to take account of the notorious iconographic instability throughout the publishing history of those emblem books that went through a number of editions. The text will usually remain fairly constant, though subject to changes in house style from printer to printer, and prey to manifold compositorial errors. But different editions of reprinted emblem books bear witness to large-scale shifts in iconographic fashion, or to later artists' differing interpretations of what constitutes the significant features of a particular symbolic representation. A printer's financial commitment of resources to commission a new set of plates probably indicates, among other things, that the perceptions of the earlier illustrations were beginning to be considered no longer fashionable, interesting, useful or viable. There was an active pursuit of a novel freshness of design. Even when the replacement of a set of blocks or copperplates was forced on the printer simply because they had been damaged or become worn and illegible (a more serious problem in the case of metalcuts, which were more prone to wear), it is rare to find that the new cuts are exact copies of the old. We may therefore conclude that, in some cases, when a sequence of illustrations needed to be re-done, the opportunity was taken to up-date the designs, and that the earlier cuts had ceased to communicate their meanings effectively. A later generation of readers may have been unfamiliar with the visual conventions that had guided the earlier artists. Significant features of the abandoned designs had become obfuscated with the decay of earlier iconographic codes.

An example of this may be found in the history of the emblematic designs for the *picturae* for Alciato's Emblem 27, 'Nec verbo, nec facto quenquam laedendum' (We must not offend, neither in word, nor in deed). Alciato's epigram described an image of Nemesis as a female figure pursuing the footsteps of the wicked and holding in her hand a bridle and a cubit rule.[13] However, the various cuts that accompanied Alciato's verse in editions of the *Emblemata* from 1531 to 1621 frequently depicted quite different images from the one described in the text. Two examples will suffice. Jörg Breu, the designer of the woodcuts for the first edition of the *Emblemata*, did not illustrate the image Alciato described, but a Nemesis conceived according to a somewhat different iconographical tradition. She has wings on her shoulders, stands on a wheel, and looks towards Heaven. But this is the iconography of Dürer's Nemesis, not Alciato's. The only points in common between the figure described by the emblematist and that drawn by the artist is that both are women and both hold a bridle.

Subsequent illustrators did not take Breu's design as a model, but adopted different iconographical conventions, which were still inaccurate representations of the image Alciato described. Later in the century, for example, when Plantin commissioned a new set of cuts for his editions of Alciato, his woodcut artist imaged Nemesis as a female figure carrying a bridle. He discarded the wings and wheel – if, indeed, he ever knew of them – but still failed to provide her with the iconographic attribute specified in the author's epigram. She is closer to Alciato's description, but it would appear that the woodcut designer, the monogrammist 'A', was influenced not by a new fidelity to the emblematist's text, but simply by a different, currently fashionable, iconographical tradition, which stemmed from Macrobius. These details had recently been codified and recorded in the work of the mythographers Giraldus and Cartari. The sun, a significant symbolic attribute of the goddess according to Macrobius, is prominently displayed behind Nemesis's left shoulder.[14]

Eventually, some decades after the author's death, in Richer's editions of the *Emblemata* (see illus. 56), which began appearing in the 1580s, the goddess is depicted for the first time with the attributes that Alciato described in his epigram, and which his first illustrators ignored. This should alert us to the fact of the often genuinely neoteric quality of the imagery introduced by Alciato, which appears not to have been immediately understood by his illustrators, and only gradually won acceptance and authority.

In other cases, we find a publisher deciding to 'emblematize' a previously published work. A book that had hitherto happily appeared without cuts is later provided with them, in some cases long after the author's death. Alexander Pope comments acidly on the practice, when he refers to certain books adorned with engravings ('sculptures') in the Dunce's library, 'where, by sculpture made forever known, / The page admires new beauties not its own'.[15] But Pope's Parnassian disdain simply affirms that these books sold, however much he might disapprove. If it were not for profit, it is unlikely that a printer would go to the trouble and expense of commissioning an artist to do them. And, if authors were safely dead, there was no need to consult with them over the matter.

Bunyan's *A Book for Boys and Girls* (1686), not mentioned by Pope, though it may well have come under his scornful gaze, is a case in point. The plates were added only after the author's death, to the ninth edition of 1724, when the book was retitled *Divine Emblems: or, Temporal Things Spiritualized, Fitted for the Use of Boys and Girls*. The title-page advertizes 'large additions', and these probably refer to the cuts rather than the text. The tenth (corrected) edition includes a new set of copperplate engravings. In this form it went on being reproduced with various numbers of illustrations (18, 46, 47, 48 or 50) for another 150 years.

Yet an emblem book cannot simply be defined as a book with symbolical illustrations. Its 'emblematic' qualities do not reside simply in the presence or absence of cuts. There must be, in Quintilian's phrase, when he was talking about the mysteries hidden beneath the surface of a poem, 'plus in recessu, quam in fronte' (More lying behind, than shows on the surface).[16]

The correlative verses that appear in the early non-illustrated editions of Bunyan's book advertize yet another of the many verbal strategies that might be identified as a symptom of an explicitly emblematic rhetoric. Bunyan, for example, anatomizes the 'comely sight' of a blossoming apple tree. With a final 'Behold then', he sums up the sobering reflections he has already verbally illustrated:

> Behold then how abortive some Fruits are,
> Which at the first most promising appear.

The Frost, the Wind, the Worm with time doth shew,
There flows from much Appearance, works but few.

The effect is identical to that of many emblem books that do have
cuts. Bunyan's verbal strategy is indistinguishable from them.

Spenser's *Faerie Queene*, though not an emblem book, can be
described as an emblematic text, which displays 'admirable wit' in
its emblematic rhetoric. Although it contains but one heraldic cut,
the Garter George and Dragon, its verse is full of emblematic
devices: masques, shows, processions, spectacles, portrait galleries,
tournaments, *impresa* shields, curious painted imagery, symbolic
tapestries, embroidery and antique statuary. Spenser refers to these
'outward shows' as designing or 'shadow[ing]' 'inward sence';
'signs' are the means by which we 'understand', if only we can 'read'
or 'know' them aright.[17] His visual symbolism is interpretative
rather than mimetic. What he has in his sights, are 'ensamples':
'Behold th'ensamples in our sights'; 'Behold . . . and by ensample
see'. The instruction to 'Look', 'Behold' and 'See', together with the
frequent use of the deictic 'Lo!', is exactly what we find in all
emblematic epigrams.[18]

Any imbalance between words and illustrations, where the verbal
far outweighs the visual, should come as no surprise. The economics of the printing process can account for this: one copperplate cost
more in terms of initial production, and was more labour intensive
to reproduce by mechanical means, than many typeset pages. Yet,
the cost to the printer does not completely explain why many
canonical seventeenth-century emblem books have comparatively
few plates, and a large number of closely printed pages. The
primacy of the word over the image is a habit of mind that was
merely reinforced by the economics of the printing house.
Mechov's *Philosophia paraenetica* (Frankfurt am Main and
Hannover, 1671) is a good example. It has but seven engravings,
each prefacing a long essay on a different moral virtue. The plate
catches the attention and arouses the curiosity, but the verbal argument is what bulks large. But, apart from symbolizing a particular
virtue, the cuts have another function. They direct the text towards
its noble recipient, and are motivated by the politics of patronage.
Each plate depicts a horse, which is the ensign of Lower Saxony. The
philosophical text is designed for an ideal reader, who is to be
educated to be the head of an ideal Platonic state, where rulers are
philosophers, and philosophers rule. The book thus becomes a
collection of seven rather long-winded *imprese*, in which the author

has no intention of becoming obscure through being over-brief. In Jean Baudoin's two-volume *Receuil d'Emblemes* (Paris, 1638–9), we have not an epigram following the cuts but separate longish essays. These, in the manner of Francis Bacon, address a number of subjects, moral and ethical. The expansion of the notes to Alciato's emblems also provided the opportunity for the commentator to insert large-scale thoughts and opinions on sundry topics. These began to assume the shape and scale of mini-essays. The process was one of gradual accretion, as each subsequent edition of the notes 'improved' on the former. After 30 years, the original author, Claude Mignault, looked at the result with some incredulity. He expressed surprise at the sheer bulk of the commentary. They had started out in 1571 as rather brief expository notes. He even claimed that much of the commentary in these later editions was not his. Generously, however, he claimed that he would adopt all these 'illegitimate children' that had been foisted on him.

Other books, unsuspected of initial emblematic provenance, were later issued with cuts. Their text was subjected to what we might term a 'retrospective emblematization'. The first edition of Drechsel's *De Aeternitate considerationes* in 1620 had but one emblem 'Consideratio vii: Quomodo Christiani pingant Aeternitatem' (Contemplation No. 7: How Christians should depict Eternity). The Cologne 1631 edition, however, adorns the text with nine. *Nicetas*, a dialogue on sexual continence, was first published in 1624 without cuts, but was furnished with them seven years later. The *Heliotropium* was innocent of emblematic adornment on its first publication in 1627. By 1630 it had acquired five emblematic plates.

But, if we are thinking of retrospective emblematization, these examples are as nothing to the posthumous emblematic treatment given to Johann Gerhard's *Meditationes*. Almost 70 years after its first publication, 50 heart emblems were added in 1707 to bring it belatedly into the emblematic fold.[19] Who could have suspected at its first appearance, or in its numerous seventeenth-century reprintings and translations, that this book of Protestant meditations was susceptible to generic transformation to the emblem mode?

King James's *Basilikon Doron*, which had an international reputation as a work of statecraft, was reconstituted in emblematic form several times by Henry Peacham, once in print, and also in the form of manuscripts dedicated to the royal author himself.[20] It was a transparent method of seeking patronage to offer an emblematic glass on which the recipient's image was already engraved.

Aristotle could not remotely have expected the later attentions of Bartholomeo del Bene, whose *Civitas veri sive morvm* compendiously reduces the *Nichomachean Ethics* to emblematic form in folio format.[21] The prefatory material is dated 1585, long before the book was first published, and it was signed not by Del Bene himself, but his editor. The manuscript must have been completed before that date. Hieronymus Drouart, whose lavish format and large-scale illustrations did the enterprise proud, constructed huge imaginary utopias and dystopias out of a reading of the philosopher, which was designed to generate moral allegories. The ruinous 'Palace of Intemperance' (illus. 35) was designed on the same plan as the earlier Palace of Temperance, but this one has fallen into disrepair. Intemperance sits in a myrtle grove – the plant of Venus – where she is regaled by Cupid and Bacchus. She spurns Right Reason under her naked foot. Before her are prepared three tables: one consecrated to Gluttony, the next to cures for her inevitable hangover, the last is furnished with incitements to Lust – make-up, cosmetics and perfumes. An opengrave lies at the foot of the plate. Even the annotations to the text are supplemented by similar engraved plates. Its author's thoroughly emblematic motivation was the praise of virtue and the reprehension of vice. It is not known whether the plates were copies of Del Bene's original manuscript, or independently conceived by the publisher.

More selectively, Otto Vænius would emblematize the text of Horace in his *Q. Horatii Flacci Emblemata*. In one plate (illus. 36) he translates the Horatian phrase 'Raro antecedentem scelestum deseruit pede poena claudo' (Rarely does punishment, albeit of halting gait, fail to catch the guilty though he has a headstart).[22] Part of the plate is concerned with a bloody narrative, which has no counterpart in the textual part of the emblem. A man, presumably the guilty individual in Horace's text, with a drawn sword in one hand, and a woman's head in the other, flees a scene of carnage. He can be recognized from Cesare Ripa's handbook of personified abstractions, where 'Homicidio' holds 'una testa humana tronca dal busto'. There is no narrative to explain what has happened, or who these characters are or what they have done. But the figure that dominates the plate is a woman, who vigorously pursues the fleeing malefactor, in spite of the fact that she has a wooden leg. This, we find, is a grotesquely literal translation of Punishment's metaphorical crippled foot ('pede claudo') in

A. Intemperantiæ palatium, ſtructura eiuſdem modi qua illud Temperantiæ,
    ſed caducum & ruinis deforme.
B. Effigies Intemperantiæ quam Cupido ſuauiatur F.
C. Bacchus pocillans quaſi heræ ſuæ Intemperantiæ.
D. Recta Ratio quàm Intemperantia pedibus ſubiectam habet, & quaſi con-
    temtim conterit.
E. Platanus ingens huic choro vmbram faciens.
F. Myrtus arbor ſacra Veneri.
G. Adparatus Gulæ.
H. Adparatus & inſtrumenta curandis morbis, gula crapuláq. contractis.
I. Fuci, pigmenta, odores, aliáque inuitamenta Veneris.
K. Mors voluptatibus accelerata.

36

Horace's poem. Had it not been for the prior text, the plate would not have looked like this. But the visual translation is thoroughly un-Horatian. Vænius hardly feels himself absolutely tied to a plodding literalism, for he indulges in melodramatic visual excesses: the disabled woman vigorously wields a scourge of snakes over her head, in spite of the fact that she is further encumbered by the basket she carries, containing various emblematic accoutrements, including a bridle. Further textual support for the visual construct is cited, not least Valerius Maximus's sentiment that 'Divine wrath proceeds to vengeance with a slow step: but it makes up for its slowness with its severity'.

If Aristotle and Horace are the textual antecedents of much emblematic activity, they are as nothing compared to the influence of the Bible as a prioritized text. Many examples could, of course, be cited. But one will have to suffice in this place, from Quarles's emblems, which renders into emblematic terms the text of Philippians 1. 23: 'I am in a straight between two, having a desire to be dissolved and to be with Christ' (illus. 37). The emblem is based on Herman Hugo's *Pia Desideria*. Yet there is no attempt to translate the text into an image word by word: William Marshall simply copied the emblematic iconography of Boëtius à Bolswert's corresponding plate – the Soul leaps up, and seeks to fly to Heaven, only to be pulled back by the huge ball and chain that shackles her to the things of this world. This is not a translation into visual terms of the biblical text in Vænius's manner discussed above. It is, however, eye-catching and memorable. The Poet Laureate, Southey, in the nineteenth century could still be struck by it. He speaks of 'the picture in Quarles' *Emblems* of a soul with wings trying to fly and chained by the leg'.[23] Ultimately, the image is shaped by the hieroglyphic tradition: Colonna's comical half-sitting, half-rising girl, whose empty, winged hand is counterpoised against the weight of the tortoise she holds in the other. Alciato's emblem of the poor scholar held back in his intellectual progress, with one winged hand held aloft, the other weighted down by a stone, may also inform the image. Both iconographical types are appropriated to encompass an entirely different spiritual anguish, hitherto unsuspected by either visual antecedent. There is a radical, though literal, recon*text*ualization of these visual motifs that is conditioned by its application to this particular biblical text.

The primacy of the verbal is frequently evident in the construction of *imprese*. In fact, the images are frequently incomprehensible without it. The device of the doctor Gabriello Frascato turns on the verbal hinges of the motto *Temperat arva*, which may with equal justice be translated as either 'he' or 'it' waters the fields (illus. 38). It is this grammatical facility, invisible in the Latin, that enables the device to negotiate between the image of the rain dropping gently from the heavens and the qualities of the man known as 'Il Rapito' (the enraptured one) to his fellow academicians. A poetic allusion to Virgil, *Georgics*, 1, 110: 'scatebrisque arentia temperat arva' (And with its gushing streams slakes the thirsty fields), takes us a step further to appreciating the witty justice of the composition. But, where, on a physical level, the rain soaks the fields, when applied to this physician it refers to the refreshing waters of truth, which cure the sick and morally infirm. As doctor, philosopher and theologian he dispenses these healing waters. This is a man who liberally pours out his knowledge for the benefit of others.

I am in a straight between two, having a desire to be dissolved and to be with Christ.

Philip. 1. 23.

P. 224.

37

38

Cesare Ripa's *Iconologia* is an encyclopaedia of symbolically conceived personified abstractions. This science of 'iconology' could be defined through its Greek derivation as 'speaking pictures', or a 'discourse in images'. Violent passions, heroic virtues and vices of various complexions could be presented to the view by means of the conventional attributes that have been associated with them by poets and orators. But what is important to realize at this stage is that, although the book spawned many fine illustrated editions, the generation of these images springs from a pre-eminently verbal culture. Significantly, the first edition was non-illustrated, and simply (if that is the word) describes the various personifications. The suites of woodcuts or engravings in later publications do not illustrate all the images, nor do they present any consistent iconographic translations of the text. These were commissioned, of course, not by the author but by various publishers. In text, and later in picture, the human form is made to bear meanings through the activity of supporting masses of emblematic clutter. The hands hold sundry and various objects; the body is either naked, or clothed in garments of different colours and textures; strange headgear is sported for defence or significant adornment. Underfoot, despised objects or vile creatures are spurned; or the feet are painfully pricked or chained. 'Inganno' (illus. 39) has no feet at all, but rather the body tails off into snaky coils. This is Deceit, a creature whose monstrous form never did, or could, exist in nature. The compendious 1645 edition of the *Iconologia* presents no less than four verbal description of this vice. The cut below illustrates one of these; but in 1945 all of the attributes and symbols from the various literary descriptions were amalgamated into one composite figure. The goat-hair shirt, for example, comes from an Alciato emblem, whose text appears in Italian translation; the serpentine tail from the deceptive Sphinx; the panther, hiding its head, is unacknowledged, but possibly from Valeriano, or taken directly from Valeriano's sources; the hooks can be traced to a line of Horace's (*Epistles*, I, 7, 74). The net comes

from yet another source. The illustration, while ignoring some attributes mentioned in Ripa's text, overgoes any one single description of various ways that the idea might be embodied. The goat-hair shirt is appropriate to one kind of Deceit – specifically the deceptions involved in sexual entrapment – but is inconsistent with the hypocritical golden garment that clothes more than one of the personifications Ripa's text describes and that we see in the image oppostie (illus. 39).

It must be admitted that, when presented to the view, some of the figures are more than faintly absurd. The personification ought not really be visualized on the page, but in the mind. Ripa's descriptions are a means of fixing a text in the memory, as its significant features are distributed to the different body parts. And Ripa himself asserted the primacy of the verbal and the bookish in forming images of this kind: 'Images made to mean more than meets the eye have no other nor more universal foundation than the imitation of the memorable images found in books'.[24]

The Primacy of the Image

In some emblematic texts the visual dominates, and the words become redundant or at least are marginalized. Johannes Sadeler's brilliant large-format engravings of Alciato's emblems shrink the words and the emblematic event by placing them within a large and detailed landscape.[25]

While we have noted some instances where later editions expand the verbal matter and commentary, in other cases quite the opposite process can be discerned. Later editions cut and prune the text severely. Augustin Lubin's translation of Augustin Chesneau's *Orpheus Eucharisticus*, for example, abbreviates the original by about one third. The translator, obviously tiring of its long-winded piety, suspected that his readers would too, and made no apology for his abbreviation: 'the fire of devotion is lost and extinguished by a rambling sermon',[26] he opined with more than a little justice.

Other emblem texts are greatly helped by the quality of the engravings: an example from Achille Bocchi's *Symbolicarum Quaestionum* (Bologna, 1574), is attractive in a way that Bocchi's text is not (illus. 40). But it draws us into the rich variety of the universe, where myth and natural objects – the raw materials of occulted significance – are combined. The first causes of wisdom are, in Platonic terms, the Ideas. But what draws us back to them is

40

the visual. The title-page of Gabriele Simeoni's *Le imprese heroiche e morali* plays with much the same idea through a comical wood-cut of the author literally with his head in the clouds (illus. 41). His eyes are on higher things, presumably. But the reader is faced not with these higher invisible matters, but with the rest of his visible body: his lower limbs. Though the scope and end of these compositions points to the *invisibilia*, the base, common currency of this species of composition is more basic: it deals, at very least, with the *visibilia*, and, as we shall see in more detail in a later chapter, concentrates its vulgar attentions on the more grossly lower rather than the higher.

On occasions the genesis of an emblem book lies in its illustrative matter. Barthélemy Aneau's *Picta poesis* (Lyon, 1552) is a case in point. When the author saw in Macé Bonhomme's printing house some woodblocks being prepared for an illustrated edition of Ovid, he decided to write emblematic verses to accompany them. These were not to be explications along the lines of a medieval moralized *Metamorphoses*, but new poems that would take these illustrations of Ovid's narrative and metamorphose them into whatever theme the emblematist wished.

41

Robert Whitehall's *Hexastichon hieron* (Oxford, 1677) began with certain 'imported foreign pictures' ('Iconum Quarundam extranearum'). These originally were innocent of emblematic intentions, being Merian's illustrations of the Bible narrative from Genesis to Revelation. Whitehall would turn them into emblems by adding a motto furnished from a Classical author or a biblical text, and by appending his six-line English epigram – the hexastich. These would not tell the story of the plate, but would tease out a witty moral in what the title-page advertises as an 'Explicatio Breviuscula & Clara'.

Apart from the engraved frontispiece by William Marshall (illus. 42), all the cuts in Wither's *Emblems* came from Gabriel Rollenhagen's emblem book published more than 20 years earlier. Wither had acquired the copper plates, and found them shorn of their

'mean' (by which he implies 'brief' or 'concise') verses. He cheerfully admits that he has no intention whatever of explicating, or providing a commentary on, the original plates

> little care I take
> Precisely to unfold our Authors minde;
> Or, on his meaning, Comments here to make[27]

He is fully aware that Rollenhagen's images are modern inventions and have nothing to do with 'Ancient *Hieroglyphick*'. What Wither is concerned with, he tells us in his epistle 'To the Reader', is a way of teaching and reinforcing a 'usefull *Morall*'. He has in view the 'common *Readers*', to whom rhetorical elegance would serve only to obscure meaning. His plainness derives as much from a lack of genuine poetic talent, as from a suspicion of '*Wordy Flourishes*' and '*Verball Conceites*'. These devices are nothing more than opportunities for '*Wittie men* to shew *Tricks* to one another'. He scornfully adds: 'the *Wise* need them not'.[28]

The change from Rollenhagen's original octavo format is what chiefly undoes Wither. His folio, apart from distorting the neat proportion between image and text that characterizes De Passe's well-designed book, requires him to fill a lot of white paper with his original compositions. Rollenhagen's succinct verses can supply at best only two to four lines as a basis for the new text. Wither mostly disregards them altogether and is thus thrown back entirely on his own verbal resources. This necessity to procure a 'comely Vniformitie in the Pages', even Wither admits, 'much injured the libertie of my *Muse*'.[29] What he complains of here is not that he had to write so much, but that he wanted to write more, and was constrained by having only the rest of the folio page to fill!

To call them verses is kind, because they read in many places like rhyming prose. He deprives himself of the opportunity for compressed wit, which would leave the reader to absorb the point. Instead, Wither has to tell us at length what that point should be. Exhausting the imagery of the plate, he often then needs – an invitation to further disaster – to find material of his own to fill the page: additional images, anecdotes, allusions. By the end of the emblem we have meandered far from our starting-point. If we have not exactly fallen off William Marshall's frontispiece allegorical mountain by this stage, we may well have fallen asleep.

The primacy of the image can be seen, too, in some of Alciato's emblems, where the starting-point is not an engraving, but an ekphrastic description of a piece of ancient art work, for example

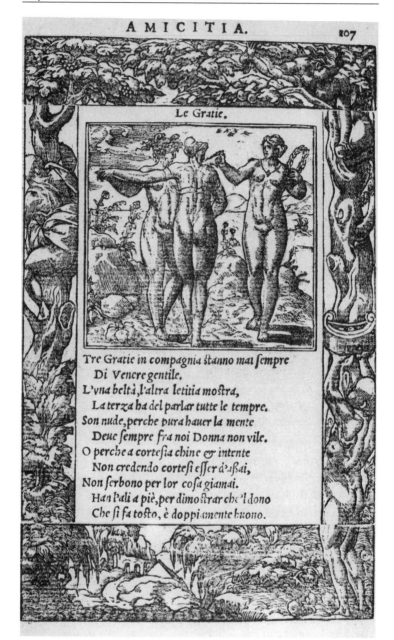

AMICITIA.

107

Le Gratie.

Tre Gratie in compagnia stanno mai sempre
    Di Venere gentile.
L'vna beltà, l'altra letitia mostra,
    La terza ha del parlar tutte le tempre.
Son nude, perche pura hauer la mente
    Deue sempre fra noi Donna non vile.
O perche a cortesia chine & intente
    Non credendo cortesi esser d'assai,
Non serbono per lor cosa giamai.
    Han l'ali a piè, per dimostrar che'l dono
    Che si fa tosto, è doppiamente buono.

the Three Graces (illus. 43). This Classical marble statue, preserved in the texts of Pausanias and Seneca,[30] aids him in his attempt to act as a Renaissance poet whose aim is to find and invent notable images of virtues and vices. He ransacks not only books, but Classical works of art as well. Like some village assembled from the stones of a disused and ruined monastery, or better, like the Renaissance city of Rome, assembled out of the stones from the ruins of classical buildings, the Renaissance emblematist would take a tag from Horace, an hieroglyph from Horapollo, an elegant gem from the *Anthology*, and assemble it into a new, meaningful structure.

Iconographic Redundancy: The Decay of Images

A small, instructive example of this can be found in Geffrey Whitney's use of a woodcut originally designed for Sambucus's *Emblemata* some twenty years earlier (illus. 44). Sambucus's 1564 motto, CONSCIENTIA INTEGRA, LAURUS (The laurel, an unsullied conscience), Whitney changed to MURUS ÆNEUS, SANA CONSCIENTIA, which he borrowed from Horace:

> hic murus æneus esto,
> nil conscire sibi, nulla pallescere culpa

> Be this our wall of brass to have no guilt
> at heart, no wrongdoing to turn us pale.[31]

Horace's lines had acquired almost proverbial status. Whitney is hardly displaying any uncommon erudition, but rehearses a commonplace, which he might have found in any of the florilegia, encyclopaedias or dictionaries of the period under the alphabeticized heading CONSCIENTIA. The appropriation of the classical text may also, of course, be part of Whitney's larger programme (discussed more fully in a later chapter) of translating the moral virtues of Augustan Rome to a new English environment. The central business of the woodblock, however, the unharmed laurel tree and Jupiter armed with his thunderbolts, a visual metonym in contemporary iconologies for storm and tempest, as well as God's wrath towards man's wickedness, passes unimpaired from the Hungarian physician and court poet to the English student without any risk of misunderstanding. However, Sambucus's epigram and the crispness of the woodcut impression in the first edition make clear there is also a bird in the background – a swan crowned with laurel. Sambucus devoted several lines of verse to an explication of this laurel-crowned swan, which forms a significant restatement of his moral. The man sheltering beneath the flourishing bay and the laurel-crowned swan both indicate the security of a sound conscience. Whitney's verse, on the other hand, omits any

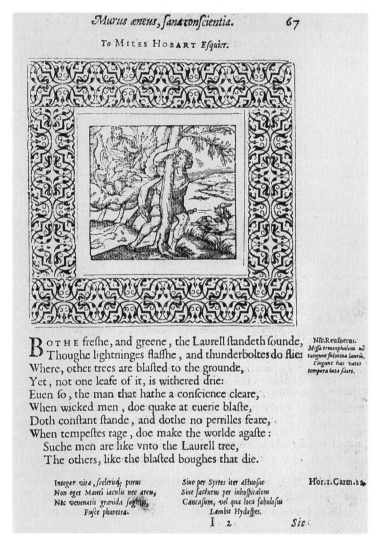

Murus æneus, fana conscientia.   67

To MILES HOBART *Esquier.*

BOTHE freshe, and greene, the Laurell standeth sounde,   Nic.Reusnerus.
Thoughe lightninges flasshe, and thunderboltes do flie: *Missa triumphalem no*
Where, other trees are blasted to the grounde,   *tangunt fulmina lauru,*
Yet, not one leafe of it, is withered drie: *Cingunt hac vates*
Euen so, the man that hathe a conscience cleare,   *tempora læta sacri.*
When wicked men, doe quake at euerie blaste,
Doth constant stande, and dothe no perrilles feare,
When tempestes rage, doe make the worlde agaste :
     Suche men are like vnto the Laurell tree,
     The others, like the blasted boughes that die.

Integer vitæ, scelerisq; purus   *Siue per Syrtes iter æstuosas*   Hor.1.Carm.22.
Non eget Mauri iaculis nec arcu,   *Siue facturus per inhospitalem*
Nec venenatis grauida sagittis,   *Caucasum, vel qua loca fabulosus*
     Fusce pharetra.   *Lambit Hydaspes.*
         I 2   *Sic*

44

mention of a bird, and after two decades and several reprintings, this portion of the woodcut design has become worn and its impression blurred. But more, it has become unnecessary to his allegorization. A whole area of the woodcut has become not only hard to read, but dead – literally desensitized. It has ceased to communicate. Sambucus's swan had its symbolic origins in Horapollo. Valeriano's *Collectanea* of 1613 still includes the swan as a hieroglyph of CONSCIENTIA PIA. Its meaning must have been still current for Whitney in 1586, even though he chose to disregard it. We may possibly infer from that fact that this symbol's emblematic potency and viability was beginning to wane, or perhaps that such symbolism was considered too recondite, and therefore less appropriate in a published vernacular emblem book. It is crucial that readers of emblematic texts should be aware that all meanings that were ever attached to a symbol were not all equally available. The system was under constant interrogation.

Emblematic Negotiations: Past and Present

In the foregoing discussion we have seen that the generation of emblem texts depends on images and texts being brought together in hitherto unsuspected ways. It also points to a knowing self-consciousness and allusiveness. The game ought to have been well and truly up for the emblem, spawned as it was on a wrong-headed enthusiasm for hieroglyphic mysteries, when one of Napoleon's soldiers turned up the Rosetta Stone during the Egyptian campaign that centred on the Battle of the Nile. At a single stroke this discovery exposed as vain, centuries of erudite labour devoted to deciphering the mysteries of the Egyptian script. By rights, the books that derived from so much misguided effort ought to have been swept away as mere cobwebs of learning, useless, erudite fantasies. This has not been the case. In fact, the realization of their fictive nature, their playfulness, has given a greater sense of freedom. We have seen some of this in Ian Hamilton Finlay's works.

Although other recent examples could be cited, Robert Southey's experiments in emblem composition are an interesting case in point. Southey discovered that he was actually related by marriage to the seventeenth-century poet George Wither. He obviously knew the emblems well. He specifically uses the term 'emblem' in his poem 'To a Spider' (first published in *The Morning Post*, 23 March 1799), though oddly, as an active verb: 'thou emblemest the ways / Of Satan'. More traditionally, he sees the emblem as built on 'likeness true'. The spider's web is seen

> To emblem laws in which the weak are caught,
> But which the strong break through

just as Petrus Costalius, La Perrière, Claude Paradin and Thomas

Palmer had done before him. The proverb, 'Laws catch little flies, but let great flies go free', was still current, and can be traced back to Erasmus's *Adagia*, 'Aranearum telas texere' (To spin spiders' webs), to Diogenes Laertius and St Basil's Homilies on the *Hexameron*. But Southey's immediate source is probably none other than Wither (*Emblems*, p. 18):

> The nimble Spider from his Entrailes drawes
> A little Thread, and curious art doth show
> In weaving Nets, not much unlike those Lawes
> Which catch Small-Thieves, and let the Great-ones goe.

Wither goes on to compare the spider to those 'curious . . . in Trifling things', and, further, to those whom 'silly Men unwarily abuse', and to the greedy, who bring 'the *Poore* to utter Desolation'. But Southey is not bound by Wither's precedent. He at once alternatively and variously moralizes the web in resemblance after resemblance: it is 'young hopes and Love's delightful dreams', the Statesman's schemes, and, finally, the Poet's brain. The 'nice geometry' that the author spins between the natural world and the world of religious, political and moral truths is wittily acknowledged as just as flimsy, and as easily swept away. Less obviously, Southey's 'Holly Tree' owes some debt to Wither's description of Virtue (p. 23):

> her Sweetnesse [must] fast be closed in
> With many Thornes, and such a Prickling-Guard.

Southey's emblematic vision of the world is explicitly stated in the third stanza of his poem:

> I love to view these things with curious eyes,
> And moralize:
> And in this wisdom of the Holly Tree
> Can emblems see . . .

These emblems provide the substance for his rhyme, and yield some profitable moral.

Other more recent writers will seek to align themselves not so much to a particular writer, but to an emblematic mode of writing. This may be simply be an allusion in the title, or may be more deeply informed by the conventions of the genre. Hugh Buchanan and Peter Davidson style their *Eloquence of Shadows* (Fife, 1994) as 'emblemata nova'. These conform to our expectations of the genre in their artful intimations of mortality, as ruins, architectural fragments and Arcadian landscapes are tied to lines from classical poets. Daniel E. Kelm reworks Michael Maier's *Atalanta fugiens* in a sequence entitled *Neo-emblemata nova* (Easthampton, Mass., 1990). This signals his modernizing intent, which is part and parcel of the emblem's traditional format. Others will invoke the name of 'emblem' without the substance. Glynne Ivor Hughes in his *Spice of Life* (Leicester, 1970) promised some 'Immoral emblems'. But these are pointed epigrams, that can support a consistent ethical approach to modern living. But Hughes would seem to miss just how 'immoral' many traditional emblems are (on which, see my chapter Seven). Alan Halsey promises *An Alphabet of Emblems* (Market Drayton, 1987), a title that takes us back to a long line of popular works that began in the 1850s as 'The Language of Flowers'. The modern designs and the playful verses offer no traditional moralizing of the natural world. But they retain in their playfulness part of the essence of emblematic wit. In all of these modern appropriations, some cultural legitimacy is offered by reference to the form, which, if anything, allows for imaginative play.

THREE

The *Imaginotheca*: Curators and Janitors

He rambles over all the faculties
Ransacks the secret treasuries
Of Art and Nature, spells the Universe
Letter by letter, can reherse
All the Records of time . . .[1]

Holy and cold, I clipped the wings
Of all sublunary things . . .[2]

The Reading Room

Although the ambitious promises of analytical bibliographers and textual critics have never been even half-way fulfilled, in the case of the emblem the history of textual transmission can offer some guidance. The development of the genre can be seen in many cases to be reliably, if partially, reflected in the history of the publication of Alciato's *Emblemata*. The rearrangement of the order of Alciato's book under *loci communes* in the editions published by Rouillé at Lyon from 1548 onwards marks a radical departure in the way the book was used and perceived. It may be tempting to see it as marking a fundamental change in the reading habits of the early modern period. The book in this new format was widely disseminated, whether because of the appeal of the new arrangement or because of this publisher's strategic geographic location at the crossroads between Protestant Geneva and Catholic Spain, and on the road north from Spain and thence to Paris and on to Antwerp, which was the trajectory that followed one of the more successful Habsburg expansionist ambitions. Between 1548 and 1616 the book appeared in at least 35 editions published by Rouillé, Bonhomme, and their associates. It should also be noted that in the sixteenth and the seventeenth centuries Lyon was the most productive source of illustrated books in France.

Rouillé's edition recognized a different kind of reader, one who would come to the book seeking some lively illustration of a particular theme or topic: God, Religion, the Virtues (Faith,

Prudence, Justice, Fortitude, Hope), Concord, Vices (not the traditional Seven Deadly ones, but Treachery, Foolishness, Pride, Envy,
Lust, Sloth, Avarice, Gluttony), Nature, Astrology, Love, Fortune,
Honour, the Prince, the State, Life, Death, Friendship, Enmity,
Revenge, Peace, Knowledge, Ignorance, Marriage. The volume
concluded with an emblematic arboretum – a collection of moralized trees, which would form the model of so many subsequent
emblematic groves and pleasure gardens.[3] The rearranged contents
proceed in an organized fashion, from the greatest to the least, to
produce a book that was now a work of reference. Rouillé, in his
prefatory epistle to the reader, with some witty justice, styles it a
'promptuary', a well-stocked notebook,[4] but one designed to
appeal as much to the eye as to the mind: the Latin *promptus*
implied 'rendered visible', 'exposed to view'. From this point on, in
probably more cases than not, Alciato's *Emblemata* came to be
issued as a collection of visible commonplaces. Starting at the top
of the chain of being, with God, readers could pleasantly survey
the realms of knowledge with a compendious gaze that swept from
superior theological matters through the moral universe to the
very bottom of sentient life: the vegetable kingdom. At every stage
there were observations and lessons. There was no obligation to
peruse the volume from beginning to end. A reader could enter or
exit at any point. Those interested in one particular topic could
find several variations on a single theme, or, if they wished, be led
helpfully to closely related notions – one virtue leading to another,
one vice to the next. Or they would be confronted by binary opposites: life/death, knowledge/ignorance. Flagging invention could
thus be stimulated or sustained in copious exploration through
variations on a theme. These very topics were ones that would
provide Jesuit schoolmasters with lesson plans for their classes in
emblematic composition for the next century and more.

But most users of reference works want answers rather than
stimulus to further inquiry. An even more decisive step along the
road towards the classification and commodification of Alciato's
emblems was taken when emblematic epigrams were assigned to
alphabetically arranged topical headings in Langius's encyclopaedic
edition of the Mirabellius *Dictionarium*, the *Polyanthea*.[5] By this
time, Alciato's emblems, through no fault or ambition of their own,
had attained authoritative status on matters moral, ethical and
theological. The sheer bulk of Langius's volume would discourage
any scholarly bee, however industrious, who might be tempted to
slip from one philosophical bloom to another. The alphabet does

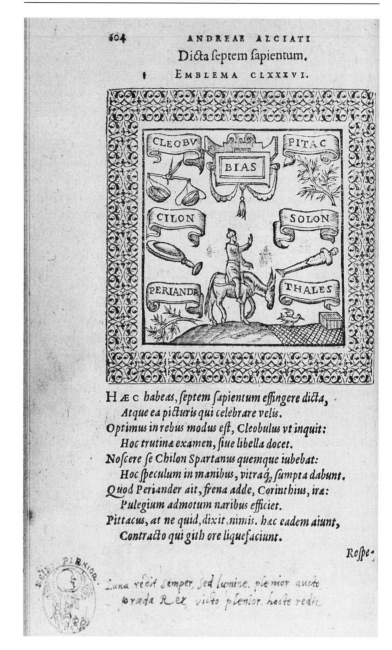

504   ANDREAE ALCIATI
Dicta septem sapientum,
EMBLEMA CLXXXVI.

H æ c *habeas, septem sapientum effingere dicta,*
Atque ea picturis qui celebrare velis.
Optimus in rebus modus est, Cleobulus vt inquit:
Hoc trutinæ examen, siue libella docet.
Noscere se Chilon Spartanus quemque iubebat:
Hoc speculum in manibus, vitraq̄ sumpta dabunt.
Quod Periander ait, frena adde, Corinthius, iræ:
Pulegium admotum naribus efficiet.
Pittacus, at ne quid, dixit, nimis. hæc eadem aiunt,
Contracto qui gith ore liquefaciunt.

Respe-

Luna redit semper, sed lumine. plenior aucto
orada Rex victo plenior. hoste redi

45

not normally provide nearly such a useful bridge from one concept
to the next. Only the most muscular of enquirers would not be
deterred from straying far from the narrow focus that had brought
them to the weighty tome in the first place.

Alciato apparently saw the emblem's potential for classifying

118   I. SAMBVCI
Partes hominis.

PRÆCIPVAS *noſtri partes tribuere vetuſti*
Diis, quorum ambigua vertitur ordo via.
Linguam Mercurio, cuius facundia pacem
Nunciat, & Diuûm bella minatur ope.
Splenem Saturno, tetra non bile feneſcit,
Triſtibus & vitam fuſtinet ille modis.
Iupiter aſt hepar proprium depoſcit, amoris
Namque putabatur fons, & origo noui.
Sanguinis eſt cupidus Mauors in prœlia ducens,
Cor, cerebrum Phœbi, quippe calore vigent.
Sed ſtomachus Lunæ, quia debilis, humidiorque
Renes & generis membra cupido fouet.

Ambi-

46

knowledge, reducing it within the span of a particular, individual emblem, to a neat and easily memorizable formula: Emblem 186 in the Tozzi edition deals with the ethical wisdom of the seven sages (illus. 45); Emblem 138 neatly allegorizes the twelve moralized Labours of Hercules; Emblem 118 exposes the significance of colours. When his editors turned the volume into a commonplace book, they did no more than expand a strategy that pertains in particular emblems, and apply it to the book as a whole. Sambucus learnt the lesson of his master. Some of his individual emblems systematize bodies of knowledge. One shows this in quite literal fashion, where 'Partes hominis' depicts a melathesia, showing each vital organ under the astrological governance of one of the seven planets (illus. 46). Nor is it uncommon for other early emblem books to take on the task of subjecting whole bodies of knowledge to emblematic treatment. Achille Bocchi's *Symbolicarum Quaestionum de universo genere*, divided into five books, takes as its subject the whole of universal knowledge: physics, metaphysics, theology, dialectic, Love, Life, and Death, packaging them under the veil of fables and myths.[6] Valeriano, as we have noted, also seems to have changed his original conception of the format of his *Hieroglyphica* from a symposium-style dialogue to that of an encyclopaedia cum dictionary. In 1613 the addition of a *Collectanea* enabled the reader to look up the abstract concept and to find the symbols associated with it. The effect of this was, as it were, to turn the original concept of the book upside down or inside out. From that edition onwards one could access the moral meaning directly without penetrating the poetic veils of symbolic flora and fauna.

Antiquities and Relics: Coins, Rings, Medals, Seals, Inscriptions

Rouillé visually enhanced his edition by using elaborately ornamented typographical borders around each page. These borders were originally commissioned for a book of Offices of the Virgin.[7] The style of these borders is traditional in missals, as Byron would later note:

> ornamented in a sort of way
> Which ancient mass-books often are, and this all
> Kinds of grotesques illumined; and how they,
> Who saw those figures on the margin kiss all,
> Could turn their optics to the text and pray
> Is more than I know —[8]

Although they perhaps might be seen as more appropriate to the emblems than the Hours of the Virgin, in no way might they be seen as an iconographic commentary on the emblems they frame. They do, however, alter the way we look at Rouillé's volume. It becomes a kind of humanist reliquary, a secular counterpart of a religious Book of Hours. Rouillé probably had not even an inkling that, later in his century and in the next, emblem books would become manuals of devotion in their own right, and that both sides of the sectarian divide would take up the form and use it for their particular purposes.[9] For Rouillé, Alciato and their contemporaries, these books were reliquaries of a different kind, cabinets of precious rarities, paper museums of architectural antiquities, lapidary inscriptions, gems, coins and medals. There were also more exotic creatures and delicate monsters than could ever fill any princely *Wunderkammer*. Claude Paradin and Gabriele Simeoni would include descriptions of antique coins (illus. 47) in their collections of 'Heroical' devices. Sambucus devoted several pages of his *Emblemata* to numismatics, suggesting thereby that ancient medals were an important source for emblems, and that there was a generic relationship between them. In explicating the *imprese* of the Accademia d'Urbino, Giovanni Andrea Palazzi would need to draw on the ancient and modern medallic devices of Hadrian, Antonino Pio, Julius Caesar, Claudius, Darius, Faustina, Germanicus, Caesar Augustus, Titus and Vespasian.[10] Hubert Goltz's authoritative work on numismatics was a prime source for many subsequent emblem writers and editors.[11] All emblematists, to greater or lesser extent, had to be expert iconographers, interpreting the symbolic paraphernalia that adorned ancient statues. Little wonder, then, that emblematic volumes would advertise themselves on their title-page as a 'Repositorium' or 'Cabinet' or 'Schatz-Kammer', containing works of art by painters, sculptors, glassmakers and engravers, designed to delight the eye and the soul. Claudius Clemens was to style his work *Musei, sive Bibliothecae*, while Johann Georg Schiebel would see his book as an emblematic exhibition hall.[12] Claude-François Menestrier would assemble a contemporary iconographic history of the reign of Louis XIV based on a gallery of medals, *jetons* and devices.[13] He was, in effect, the curator of the royal image, and the iconographer to the court of Louis XIV. John Evelyn thought that reverses of medals inclosed 'Morals, recondite Mysteries and Actions; recommending and representing the most conspicuous Virtues'.[14] In this their subjects were identical to those emblems, hieroglyphs and devises that treat of piety, honour, virtue, equality, religion, concord, peace, hope, justice, clemency, providence and fortune.

Rouillé's publishing house, in collaboration with a number of local printers, had a broad interest in device books, antiquarian symbolism, and iconographic curiosities. He produced another 'promptuary', his *Prontuario de le Medaglie de piu illustri, e fulgenti huomini e donne* was frequently reprinted, and appeared in Latin,

French, Italian and Spanish editions.[15] The Italian version was dedicated to 'la sereniss. et christianiss. Caterina, Regina di Francia', the highest placed representative of Italianate culture in the land. But the success of the volume obviously depended upon a contemporary curiosity for antiquities. Rouillé's editions of Guillaume du Choul's *Discours sur la castrametation et discipline militaire des Romains* and his *Discours de la religion des anciens*

47

Romains (1556), which treated the symbolic meaning of ancient medals, statues, inscriptions, intaglios and bas-reliefs, also fed the reading public's huge and curious appetite for such matters.

Yet, as far as the iconography of the Alciato emblems was concerned, Rouillé's antiquarian labours came in for a good deal of criticism, as did the whole tribe of artists who slavishly copied the images laid down in earlier editions, without regard to their accuracy. Lorenzo Pignoria, himself the owner of a library and museum of antiquities, advised the Paduan printer Tozzi on the production of new set of cuts for a new edition of Alciato's *Emblemata*.[16] These cuts would be used again in the magisterial 1621 edition of Alciato edited by Thuilius. Pignoria's scorn for the unscholarly habits of his predecessors is withering. 'The power of habit is very authoritative', he lamented.[17] How unfortunate that these irresponsible artists, so in love with their own misconceptions and ignorant of classical antiquity, have chosen to meddle in what they do not understand! Proper representation should be in agreement with the subscripted verses, and in accordance with classical precedent. What we find, however, in many cases, is that the images stand in flat contradiction to the under-printed epigrams. How ridiculous, he claimed, is their representation of Mercury at the crossroads! The verses below say that the god's statue is 'mutilated', 'lacking in some of its parts' (*trunca*). Many of the earlier plates show a fully formed young man, wearing a winged hat and carrying a caduceus. The artists obviously did not read, or could not understand the Latin. Pignoria respected Alciato as an antiquarian scholar, and felt that the ignorant woodblock artists disgraced his memory. Alciato, in his eyes, was not so much a learned jurist, but an art historian and iconographer, a reader of the statues of Phidias, Chrysippus and Praxiteles. Pignoria also realized that Alciato's admiration of these works of art was moderated by a highly literate and literary culture. In all probability, if it were not for the epigrams of the Planudean *Anthology*, these statues would not have been considered as fit subjects for emblems. But that is to speculate beyond what one can legitimately affirm. One can, however, with some certainty say that Alciato's and Pignoria's reading of classical texts severely moderated and controlled the way ancient statuary was seen. The Three Graces are seen, but they are only emblematically noticed because of the text of Seneca's *De beneficiis*. Their nakedness is seen not with the eye of the connoisseur, but through the lenses of textual glosses.

Pignoria, who produced an authoritative commentary on Egyptian hieroglyphs, continued to engage in learned correspondence on the meaning of ancient gems. He brought a curator's eye for detail and accuracy. Eschewing allegorical inferences and intuitions, he offered no meaning for which he could not cite evidence in classical texts. Since poetry and painting were held to be sister arts, men of letters could be trusted to give symbolic readings. He castigated the iconography of the earlier editions, claiming that the artists who produced them were either ignorant, drunk or mad. It was one of Pignoria's articles of faith that 'There is nothing trite, common or empty of mystery among our ancestors'.[18] It was therefore absolutely imperative that the artist should get the images right according to the archaeological evidence and textual authorities. Some of his favoured classical sources were the sections on art in Pliny's *Natural History* and Philostratus' *Imagines*. Far from advocating slavish transcription, he recognized that the artist rearranges what he sees, selecting in order to create perfect creatures. The sheer variety of things in the created universe allows the artist to work with a great alphabet. The antiquarian scholar, on the other hand, can read this alphabet and syntax by means of hieroglyphs and emblems. Thus, for example, Fortunio Liceti in his *Hieroglyphica sive antiqua schemata gemmarum anularium quaesita moralia, politica, historica, medica, philosophica et sublimiora explicata* (Padua, 1653) uses various symbolic forms, analogies and allegories to decipher the images on ancient gems. These, he believed, were images of occult power, talismans and amulets that could harness astrological and magical influences. Such potent forces demanded scholarly rigour, respect and, above all, precision.

The Catalogue

Increasingly, authors, their editors, or publishers began to think of the emblem book in terms of an overarching design. It is hard to underestimate the Renaissance passion for order and their encyclopaedic curiosity, the fetishistic need to catalogue, compile and classify. Even if efforts in this direction amounted to no more than a Rabelaisian list, it was a permanent feature of humanist culture. It is therefore no surprise that publishers should seek to appeal to these mental habits of their reading public. The title-page (illus. 48) of Jeremias Drechsel's emblematic *Opera*, produced by Melchior Segen and Nicolaes Henricus in 1628, advertised each of the works in the volume under its own neat *impresa*. The design of the page offers more than a mere table of contents, for it emblematically advertises the complex symbolic inter-relationships between the works. At the top of the page sits *Aeternitas*, its tail-biting serpent superior to the world of time. The temporal world occupies the next rung down in this hierarchical ladder: on the left of the page is the *Zodiacus*, and on the right, the *Horologium*. Descending lower we come to the moral, human world: on the right, *Nicetas*, which deals with Continence's triumph over immoderate desires through anorexic fasting and moral diligence; on the left, *Trismegistus Christianus*, the three-headed prophet of conscience. On the lowest rung stand representatives of man-made objects, and the botanical kingdom: *Amussis* (the rule or level), a treatise on right judgement, and lastly, the *Heliotropium*, the

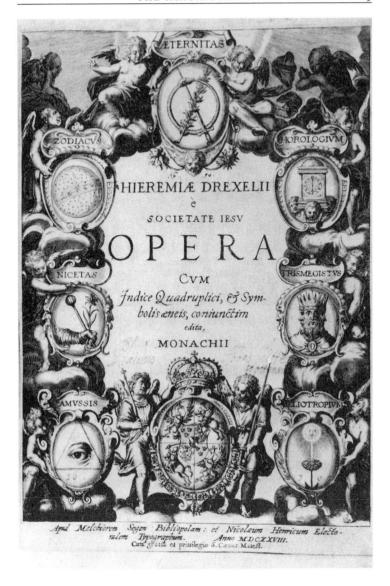

sunflower, dealing with the right orientation of the will. Each work takes its place in an overall hierarchical order of things. Pious thoughts and meditations can ascend and descend up and down this scale of creation.

While some emblem books attempt to replicate the structure of the whole created universe, others confine themselves to a single subject or object, using this self-imposed limitation to give some focus and design to the volume, and, in so doing, to expose the cunning variety that might be found in such supposed unity. The

49

Jesuit Alard le Roy would see the religious life in herbs and flowers.[19] Later, the birds of the air would provide him with emblematic sermons on Virtue.[20] Franciscus Reinzer's *Metereologia Philosophico-Politica* (Augsburg, 1698) is divided into twelve dissertations on different aspects of the geo-physical environment: volcanoes, hot springs, frozen landscapes, mining. These, in turn, are linked to axioms of political philosophy and statecraft. Camerarius devoted each of his four centuries of emblems to a different corner of the created world (illus. 49): herbs and trees; quadrupeds; birds and flying insects; sea creatures.[21] The completed design surveys the four orders of created things, each book confining itself to a single province. Thomas Palmer's emblematic manuscript, 'The Sprite of Herbes and Trees', draws all its images from the botanical kingdom.

Often we see writers imposing such restraints on themselves, working within narrow definitions and specifications. This particularly pertains in the field of religious or 'sacred' emblematics. Although at first glance this might strike one as surprising, it must be recognized that the topics of devotion are relatively few. Augustin Chesneau's *Orpheus eucharisticus* takes as its subject the Holy Eucharist. But, having begun with this apparently narrowly restricted topic, he elaborates on his subject, drawing on the profuseness of creation, showing all creatures, whether they fly, crawl, walk, swim or hop, participating in joyous communion with their Creator.[22] Antonius Ginther devotes his *Currus Israel, et Auriga ejus* to the Crucifixion.[23] His chariot of biblical history is driven to a single destination, and each emblem records a typological prefiguration of the same turning-point of religious history. His book records the iconography of a particular ecclesiastical building at Biberbach, on the pilgrim route from Catholic Germany to Rome. The early emblems deal with typological foreshadowings of the Crucifixion. Ginther, Leenheer, Henry Hawkins and Van der Sandt (Sandaeus) focus intently on the Madonna and arrive at a thesaurus of symbols that might apply to her: flowers (the rose, lily, pansy, sunflower, hyacinth), precious stones, the sun and the moon, mountains and stars.[24] Georg Stengel's *Ova Paschalia* provides 100 egg-shaped emblems.[25]

Many emblem books work with traditional schematic and topical arrangements. Guilelmus Hesius based his book on the three theological virtues, Faith, Hope and Charity.[26] Others took the four classical virtues, while others provided a suite of the full seven and for good measure add the corresponding Vices.[27] Emblematic triadic structures involved the three parts of the human soul, the Holy Trinity, or the trinitarian structure of Ignatian meditation.[28] The four cardinal virtues, the four ages of the world, the four seasons, or the four elements provided another strategy.[29] Sevens recommend themselves not only because this is the number of the Virtues and the seven Liberal Arts, but also the number of the days of the week, the planets, and the ages of man.[30] Arrangements by twelves are also common: the twelve months, or the twelve zodiacal signs form the ground plan of several books.[31] Jacob Harrewyn brought together four's, seven's, and twelves, collecting together all the rags of time in his emblematic survey of months, days and seasons.[32] The letters of the alphabet, usually numbered in this period as 25, form the basis of other emblem books.[33] Fifty is the number of celebration and jubilee, and festive emblem books frequently find themselves planned on the basis of this number or its multiples.[34] 'Centuries' of emblems are, after all, nothing more than double jubilees.[35]

But the chief works of this schematized kind are those by Filippo Picinelli and C.-F. Menestrier, two Jesuits who attempted to bring the whole sphere of emblematics into order and design.[36] Their anthologies – and it would be wrong to call them anything but that – are conceived on a grand scale. Since it was recognized that anything under the sun could be an emblem of something, then order and rationale were clearly necessary. The basic tenet that informs their work is that the world is an emblem of God, and that the emblem is the means by which the divine Creator can be seen. They therefore imposed a map of the cosmos on the field of emblems and brought the diverse productions of different authors under this universal cataloguing device. The sheer variety of creation allowed them to work with a great alphabet, but their activities may be referred to what Coleridge would later describe as 'Fancy': the rearrangement of ready-made and pre-assigned images into new patterns. Any poetic or 'imaginative' intent before this must be considered secondary, for other considerations entered therein: political, theological, sectarian. This was no pure, disinterested activity. The Jesuits in particular obviously revelled in a delighted taxonomy of the *theatrum mundi*, and their aim was to establish normative hierarchies, vital distinctions between virtue and vice, good and evil. Control over these aspects of intellectual life was clearly something to be fought for, even if the territory gained could be measured only on paper.

Among these schematizers, none was more ambitious than Picinelli, whose intellectual curiosity may indeed be said, in the words that form one of the epigraphs to this chapter, to ransack 'the secret treasuries / Of art and nature'. When he began sorting his primary materials for his emblematic encyclopaedia, he found them at first a bundle (a 'manipulus'), which grew into a heap ('acervus'), which in turn became a huge, shapeless mass ('molem vastam').[37] He felt compelled to dispose this chaos into some ordered design. Taking his cue from the Creator at the beginning of the Book of Genesis, he brought order and design into the 25 books of his *Mundus symbolicus*. He first separated things occurring in nature, those created by God, from those that were formed by art, those created by human ingenuity: Part One is therefore devoted to *Corpora Naturalia*, Part Two to *Corpora Artificialia*. Part One contains thirteen books, beginning with the highest orders of creation and descending to the most lowly. Book One of the first part, therefore, deals with the celestial bodies – the planets, the stars, zodiacal signs, and the constellations; Book Two descends to the building blocks of sublunary nature according to the physics of the age, the four elements: Fire, Air, Water, Earth. Next he surveys the animate creation. Book Three deals with humans: the classical gods and goddesses, created in our image and likeness, and famous figures of world history. Succeeding books deal in turn with birds, four-footed beasts, fish, serpents, insects. He then moves on in turn to trees, plants, flowers, precious stones, rocks, and metals. The man-made objects in the books of the second part of the volume are, in turn, ecclesiastical objects, domestic utensils, buildings, machines, toys and games, the alphabet and all things to do with writing, nautical craft, scientific instruments, military equipment, musical instruments, agricultural tools. His final book brings together anything that could not be found a place in the preceding books! Chaotic variety is brought into order. His symbolic imagination was of the truly epic proportions described by Tasso:

> in this admirable realm of God called the world, the sky is seen to be scattered over and beautified with a great variety of stars, and descending lower from region to region, the air and the sea are full of birds and fishes, and the earth harbours many animals both fierce and gentle, and in it we can see many streams, fountains, lakes, fields, plains, forests and mountains, here fruits and flowers, there ice and snow, here dwellings and cultivation, there solitude and wild places. Yet for all that, the world, which includes in its bosom so many and so diverse things, is one, one in form and essence, one the knot with which its parts are joined and bound together in discordant concord; and while there is nothing lacking in it, yet there is nothing there that does not serve either for necessity or ornament.[38]

It is this 'knot' of discordant concord that Picinelli both ties and unravels. His work is mimetic in that it mirrors the design of the created universe, but it is not content to merely conform to the precepts of an Aristotelian poetic. He imitates, but he also interprets. His imitation of 'the admirable realm of God' is filtered through textual lenses, as neat and succinct citations from good authors are applied as interpretative labels to the 'stars . . . the air and the sea . . . birds and fishes, and the . . . many animals both fierce and gentle, . . . streams, fountains, lakes, fields, plains, forests and mountains'. It is as an interpreter that he is most engaged, and most interesting, inasmuch as it is here that he reveals his curious cast of mind. But it would be wrong to think of him as eccentric or out of step with his age. He was at one with many of his contemporaries. Nor did he superimpose moral meanings on a universe that his contemporaries observed as totally innocent of any such textual gloss or moral purport. Many works of 'legitimate' science at this time by no means ignored the symbolic equivalences of created things.

Picinelli's gaze is most impressively focused when he descends to minute particulars. Most of his books treat their subdivided contents in alphabetical order, but this is not inevitable. Book Three, for example, first deals with figures from classical mythology (chapters 1–59), and then with characters from biblical history. The latter are then further subdivided. Those from the Old Testament are treated first, then those from the New. While New Testament figures are dealt with in alphabetical order, the earlier are treated chronologically, so that Picinelli provides in miniature nothing less than a history of the world from the Creation to the birth of Christ. These organizational devices are on rather a grand scale, but Picinelli exercises a curious control over the details of his design. Thus, when he comes to consider timekeeping devices in Book 21, he distinguishes hourglasses from clocks and sundials. Clocks in turn are considered according to their various motions: whether driven by weights, or by a pendulum, or by clockwork cogs and wheels.[39] Each yields a congruent moral meaning. Picinelli in this way may indeed be said to 'spell the universe / Letter by letter' and 'rehearse / All the records of time'.

He was certainly not the first to attempt a symbolic overview of the known universe. He depended on his predecessors. Valeriano was, inevitably, one of his sources. As was the French Jesuit Nicolas Caussin, who was equally dependent on Valeriano and Horapollo. Caussin's modestly titled, twelve-book digest of the symbolic universe, the *Polyhistor symbolicus*,[40] must have provided Picinelli with a model on which to work. Caussin also began with the universe and then considered human history, dealing with the exemplars of the good and the bad. His fifth book was given over to the form and manner of religious worship. He then proceeded from the human to the animal kingdoms, dealing in turn with birds, four-footed beasts, fish, serpents and insects. Book 10 considered plants, Book 11 stones. The final book was devoted to manufactured objects. Each symbol is commented on in protases and apodoses from an erudite stock of Greek and Latin texts, which 'substantiate' any particular moral he wishes to promote. Broadly speaking, Picinelli was to cover the same topics in much the same descending, hierarchical order from the greatest to the least, from animate to inanimate. Where Picinelli overwent his predecessor was in the minuteness of his attention to detail, and awareness of the subtle interconnectedness of things. It was as though, in constructing his symbolic *Mundus*, his eye had traced the complex interconnectedness of creation as if it were a huge spider's web. That object, of course, he saw as a fit emblem for (inevitably, among other things) the *vanitas* of *Mundanus labor* (the workmanship of this world).[41] It was subtle, it was intricate, it was painstakingly curious, but it was also useless.

Picinelli's emblematic vision was based on the authority of St Paul. 'For the invisible things of God from the creation of the world are clearly seen, being understood by the things that are made' (Romans 1. 20).[42] The Latin motto is clearly placed on the title-page of Augustin Erath's translation of the book. This Pauline symbolic strategy underpins not only Picinelli's, but other emblem books as well. Thomas Jenner, without acknowledging the biblical source, states on his title-page: 'by the outward and visible we may the easier see that which is inward and invisible'.[43] The geography of the created world may be imposed like a net over the invisible intellectual, moral and affective universe of thoughts, feelings and emotions, enabling these insubstantial things to be seen and handled with more assurance. But for all the detailed intricacy of the design of Picinelli's globe, surveyed through the his microscope or telescope, his work is not theoretical or analytical. It also, if anything, underrates the complexity of the associative iconographic interrelations that formed the early modern mind. These could derive from the wastepaper basket of outmoded and discredited pieces of scientific knowledge, 'Hieroglyphical fansie[s]', in Thomas Browne's phrase, 'neither consonant unto reason, nor correspondent unto experiment',[44] images from paintings and statues, ancient or modern, as well as from dreams and fantasies. Picinelli's book functions most seductively and successfully as a massive database, which is variously accessible, and the information retrieved from it can surprise and delight through the unforeseen variety of the many conjunctions between familiar objects, classical tags and moral meanings. This book, and those like it, could arguably be seen as successors to the medieval *speculum*, encyclopaedic 'mirrors' of human knowledge. Yet these

Baroque emblematic 'mirrors' were something of the 'through-the-looking-glass' variety: one enters via a visible physical universe, which has been severely moderated by odd, bookish accretions, and then one is confronted by moral and metaphysical abstractions. Little wonder, then, that the human mind itself was configured as a species of mirror.[45] Every *thing* meant something other than itself. This philosophically unsatisfactory state of affairs can be summed up pithily in the timeserving insubstantiality of the mirror emblem (illus. 50) from the *Imago primi sæculi*: 'Omnibus omnia' ([It is] all things to everyone). The verbal trick of

Omnibus omnia.   { *Ghelÿck*
                    Aen ieghelÿck.

50

the motto indicates that the emblematic mirror gallery gives back slightly altered, even inexact, reflections: *omnia* is reflected in *omnibus*. The motto also shows that these mirrored analogies have a spectator as their focus, and are meaningless without that point of reference.

The mirror also recommends itself as a self-reflexive emblematic model in that it alludes to the production process of the printing of its illustrative matter. The right of the engraved plate or woodblock appears as the left on the printed page, and vice versa. The further implications of this reversed, inside-out process will be discussed in chapter Seven, but at the moment it is enough to record many emblematists' awareness of the unreliability of their medium, the essential falsity of their methods.[46]

But it was the comprehensiveness of Picinelli's volume that made it so seductively attractive to those who came after. It was the model for Claude-François Menestrier's monumental *Philosophia imaginum*,[47] which, for all the promise of its title, does not offer a theory or 'philosophy' of images, but an elaborate catalogue, which shows how the created world can provide the ground plan of numerous emblematic inventions. This hugely erudite librarian was more interested in cataloguing than theorizing. This was as true of the images he collected, as of the part of the volume that was turned over to theoretical concerns, where he simply summarized the different, opposing opinions of 49 authorities.[48] Since the subject was so contentious, and there was no agreement about the 'laws' of emblematic composition, he was not prepared to offer any rules of his own. Johannes Michael von der Ketten would even later produce his irregularly paginated two-volume *Apelles symbolicus* on the same model: the first volume of 894 pages, the second weighing in at a mere 552.[49] The most recent in this line of Picinelli imitators are the twentieth-century German scholars Arthur Henkel and Albrecht Schöne,[50] whose anthology of sixteenth- and seventeenth-century emblems was loosely based on Picinelli's hierarchies, but without Picinelli's exact and discerning discrimination. What all these volumes crave is a huge, coherent, ordered and capacious design in order to harness good, emblematic practice. But the problem is that most individual emblem books are not like this at all. Nor is Picinelli's the only, or the most reliable, guide.

Galleries

Works on *imprese* are a case in point. Apparently designed as discussions of the theory of the form, they quite often merely repeat or refine the same five rules laid down by Giovio, and they quickly become anthologies of good, or bad, practice, not so much in the construction of such devices, but of ideals that have guided men and women to the good life. What one has is a portrait gallery, not of the faces of the individuals mentioned, but a gallery that exposes the very souls of the noble and famous, revealing their aims, thoughts, ambitions and desires under penetrable poetic veils. What in Italy flourished as books of *imprese*,[51] north of the Alps became volumes of *Icones illustrium*, the images of famous people.[52]

A detail from the engraved title-page of Drechsel's *Opera omnia* (Antwerp, 1643) depicts a further alternative method of emblematic organization and a strategy of emblematic reading (illus. 51). It is, as can be seen, based on a series of triads. The central figure sustains the threefold emblematic triad which is, as might be expected from the work of a Jesuit, the Holy Trinity. She supports in her right hand the emblems of the Son, the Lamb standing on a Book (presumably the Gospels); her left hand sustains the dove of

51

the Holy Spirit. On her head, at the apex of the triangle formed by these symbolic motifs, sits a rooster, the herald of the morn, and here a sign of the Father/Creator, whose voice called light out of darkness. Still another triad is formed by the outer female figures who iconologically represent different aspects of the religious life. On the left is Christian Piety, who sits above an elephant, Valeriano's hieroglyph of *Pietas*. She holds a Crucifix. On the right sits Eloquent Virtue, a helmeted Minerva, the goddess of Chastity and Wisdom, who holds Mercury's caduceus on her arm, the sign of eloquence and peace. The central figure, sustaining the emblems of the Trinity, is Divinity. The three female figures might also shadow an analogous microcosmic trinity, the three parts of the human soul: memory, will and understanding. The whole engraving is involved in a negotiation between overtly Christian and pagan symbols: the crucifix; the hieroglyphical elephant; the caduceus; the classical, helmeted Minerva; the Lamb that taketh away the sins of the world; the dove-like Holy Spirit. The crowning rooster at the top of the engraving is a particular case in point, for not only is it the bird that heralds the new dawn and a new spiritual light, but from classical times was dedicated to the pagan god of healing, Aesculapius. Socrates, on his death, left in his last testament 'a cock to Aesculapius'.[53] The title-page expands itself into a larger schematic trinitarian structure as it negotiates between the interests of divine spirituality, of necessity at the apex in this wider intellectual scheme of things, and the interests of eloquence and morality, already foreshadowed in the figure of Minerva with the caduceus. These concerns are now iconographically elaborated and, to some extent at least, unpacked in 'Copiosè' (illus. 52) and 'Moraliter' (illus. 53), to be discussed in further detail below. These stand necessarily on the lower plane in this iconographical species of solid, theological geometry.

52, 53

These negotiations between eloquence, morality and religion are part and parcel of a Jesuit post-Tridentine rhetoric, which pressed the fables and symbols of the ancients into the service of Christian truth. The accommodation of the two traditions, however, was made more intellectually plausible by the theory that held that the hieroglyphs of the Egyptians were, in fact, vestiges of the first truths imparted to Adam and Eve in the Garden of Eden. These, in turn, were preserved by the Egyptians. Further, since the Greeks and the Hebrews learnt from the Egyptians, it was also apparent that all religions are nothing less than corrupt degradations of this Adamic wisdom, and they could be thought to preserve some shadow or kernel of this truth. Antonio Ricciardi in his *Commentaria Symbolica* discussed this theory of the transmission of the arcana, as it progressed from Adam to the ancient Egyp-

Kircheriana Domus naturæ artisq theatrum
Par cui vix alibi cernere posse datur.
AMSTELODAMI.
Ex officina Joannis-à-Waesbergiana Anno MDCLXXVIII.

tians, and to other races via Orphic Philosophy.[54] The theologians and philosophers of the ancient world could be seen to treat the arcana under allegorical shadows (mythic, iconographic) or through similitude and metaphor, for the face of Truth had to be veiled, and could not be revealed to the vulgar populace.[55] Athanasias Kircher developed this approach. He was so convinced of this method of reading that it sustained him through volume after volume in his pursuit of ancient symbolism.[56] In a view of the interior of the Jesuit College at Rome (illus. 54), we see him leading a small tour party through the antiquarian holdings there: obelisks, ancient monuments, books, paintings, vases. . . . A stuffed crocodile is even suspended from the ceiling. The long gallery might almost be an externalized depiction of the contents an erudite Baroque mind. If the ancient Egyptians preserved their wisdom in veritable mountains of stone, this seventeenth-century polymath erected his monuments out of paper. He indefatigably tracked various analogously related triads through the whole world of myth and religious history: Father, Power, Mind; Faith, Truth, Love . . . . His belief that different cultures all restate the same hidden mysteries can only be described as a scholarly delusion of mammoth proportions. Never once did it occur to him that some of these Egyptian monumental inscriptions were, in some cases, totally devoid of mystery, recording only very ordinary, wholly unremarkable statements. Never once did he doubt that he was dealing with the earliest surviving human records, closest in time to the date of the Fall itself, and which appeared to endorse a Christian interpretation of these ancient records. In fact, in many cases, his readings were more frequently based on late antique sources, post-dating the birth of Christ, which freely and exotically mixed pagan and Christian references.

The Subject Catalogue

There were other ways of classifying and cataloguing. Menestrier classified emblems according to 'subject', which we might see as some sort of anticipation of the Dewey system. The director of the Jesuit library at Lyon from 1667 assigned emblems to categories: 'Moral, Political, Doctrinal, Chemical, Heroic, Satiric, and Emotional'.[57] Any one of these could become the dedicated focus of a single volume. Huddlestone Wynne and Francis Tolson produced volumes of *Moral Emblems*; John Thurston a book of

Religious Emblems; Jacobus à Bruck and Marcus Boxhorn called their volumes *Emblemata politica*. Ludolph Smids stood in a whole line of *Emblemata heroica*, famously initiated by Claude Paradin. Daniel Stolcius's *Viridarium Chymicum* could be seen as one in Menestrier's classification of *Emblêmes Chymiques*, which must include the works of Michael Maier and Johan Daniel Mylius's *Opus Medico-Chymicum*. These generic classifications attest to continuities that might be seen to be the basis of an emblem tradition, as well as to a sharpening of focus and definition, that would, in turn, lead to the evolution of emblematic sub-genres.

But these different emblematic kinds did not always remain chastely separate. They could be found mixed together under one cover. Jakob Bornitz occupies a certain moral high ground already claimed by Julius Wilhelm Zincgreff when he called his collection *Emblematum ethico-politicorum*. These high moral positions were possibly trumped, when Ægidius Albertinus titled his book *Emblemata hieropolitica*. Here we see an erosion of the hard and fast distinction suggested by Menestrier's catalogue. The ethical encroaches on the political; the sacred on the moral and the political. Schoonhoven's title-page acknowledges the fact that his book crosses certain generic boundaries: it is partly 'moral' but also partly 'political'.[58] Reusner's *Emblemata* are, according to the book's frontmatter, 'partly ethical', 'partly to do with natural history', 'Historical', and 'Hieroglyphical'. For good measure, it also contains some *imprese* of famous people and some descriptions of statues.[59] Reinzer's *Meteorologia* (Augsburg, 1697) is described as 'Philosophico-Politica'. But when Martin Meyer's *Homo, Mikrokosmos* (Frankfurt, 1676) is advertised as *Ethico-Politico-Theologicis Moralibus*, generic refinements reach Polonius-like proportions. Ottavio Scarlattini overgoes even this when he provides moral, mystical, proverbial, hieroglyphical, physiognomic, iconographic, religious and calligraphic emblems drawn from prodigies, histories, statues, coins, fables, marvels and dreams.[60]

The Verbal Laboratory

In the light of all of this, it is instructive to refer back to Whitney, to see how far the emblem had come by the end of the seventeenth century. Whitney attests to the earliest forms of emblematic production. Although Rosemary Freeman styled Whitney's

A Choice of Emblemes (1586) as an anthology of commonplaces, we can readily see that the author does not seem to have designed it for use in this way. He eschewed the current format of Alciato's *Emblemata omnia* as digested into the *loci communes*. Editions of Alciato in the form they were first published still continued to appear, and these were more in line with Whitney's presentation of his material. These books were not so much organized collections, but aggregations of compositions assembled throughout a lifetime of emblematic extemporization. Whitney's *Choice of Emblemes* or Henry Peacham's *Minerva Britanna* (1612), for example, appeared in this 'old fashioned' form. Peacham (or his publisher) advertised the 'sundry nature' of his emblems on his very title-page, while Whitney's term 'choice', of course, suggests 'miscellany', a variety of different emblematic kinds. The very term *emblema*, after all, implied a mosaic that brought together many single, individual pieces assembled from a number of smaller constituent parts. Accordingly, Whitney's and Peacham's collections drew on a host of different literary kinds that had no absolute connection to one another except that they lay within the frame of a single volume: jokes (Whitney's of a man who searched for his drowned wife upstream rather than downstream: since she never did what was expected during her life, why should she change at this stage?); hieroglyphs; fables (the clay and the iron pots, the ass bearing the mysteries); witty sayings of famous philosophers; historical anecdotes concerning the famous and powerful; beast fables; moralized natural histories; parables; images of the classical gods and goddesses. Peacham, in deference to his royal dedicatee, Henry, Prince of Wales, includes a number of noble devices and *imprese*. These emblem books continued to present all the organization of a heap, apparently flung together adventitiously, without apparent regard to any neat, coherent design. One might invoke the inset design of Drechsel's 1643 *Opera omnia* (illus. 52), where winged *putti* pour out emblematic riches, 'Copiosè' (abundantly, fully, at great length). Narrowly configured, this is representation of the abundance of divine Grace and eleemosynary relief. Yet these playful, naked, winged children steadying their curiously shaped vessel, the one from above, the other from below, can also be seen to represent emblematic negotiations between higher and lower things, between the sacred and the profane, the Christian and the pagan, divine love and human. This vessel is a cornucopia, a horn of plenty, which dispenses the inventive *copia* of emblematic devices. Yet these outpourings do not, as they hit the ground, present any neat, ordered form.

Perhaps what Freeman was responding to when she recommended the *Choice* as an 'anthology' of commonplaces was Whitney's only partially acknowledged use of such compendia, dictionaries and anthologies in the composition of the volume. In common with other Renaissance authors, Whitney made use of classical compilations of miscellaneous information, such as Aulus Gellius's *Noctes atticae*[61] and 'Suidas'.[62] By far his greatest debt, however, was to a contemporary compilation of quotable quotes – Nicolaus Reusner's *Polyanthea, siue Paradisus poeticus* (Basle, 1578), which he cites as 'Nic. Reusnerus',[63] or under its alternative title, 'Paradisus poeticus'.[64] He acknowledges his dependence on the commentary by Claude Mignault on Alciato's *Emblemata* – the Plantin editions of 1573, 1574, 1577 and 1581 were available to Whitney : the hanging side-notes cite him as 'Minos' or 'Claudius Minois' or 'Claud. Min.'.[65] There is also some unacknowledged borrowing. It is probably more than coincidence that the marginal note on p. 174, 'Locus e nuce Ouidiana', also appears in Mignault's commentary on Alciato, emblem 192. An unacknowledged source may well be a school textbook, J. Sturmius, *Poeticum volumen (primum – sextum)* (Strassburg, 1565), which assembles suitable quotations from classical authors under relevant mottoes. The quotation from Horace under the motto *Vlyssis abstinentia*[66] also appears in *Choice*, p. 82; the side-note to Whitney's 'Biuium virtutis et vitii' (*Choice*, p. 40) can also be found in Sturmius, III, 6: no. 2. Elsewhere, Sturmius lists convenient schemes, such as the Four Ages of gold, silver, brass and iron, with relevant classical quotations that may have been useful to Whitney. The scaffolding of Whitney's secondhand erudition, his reliance on commentaries and works of reference rather than on primary sources, lies so close to the surface of many emblems, and so often seems to support his writing, that it must necessarily obtrude itself on our attention.

The moral world of emblems can be seen as constructed in rather different ways than that ordered by Caussin, Picinelli and Menestrier. This is indicated by Drechsel's countervailing winged putto in the 1643 title-page (illus. 53). Where one frame shows the pouring out of oratorical *copia*, the other, 'Moraliter', indicates a stricter code of imagery. Within its narrow frame, this *putto* is surrounded by the conventional hieroglyphs of the Virtues: the sleeping lion (Magnanimity), the pillar (Fortitude or Constancy), the set-square (Temperance or Prudence). Yet the inset image also suggests how carefully (*moraliter* in another sense) the emblematic moral universe ought to be carved out on the workbench, using a set-square to trace almost mathematical correspondences between the physical and the ethical. These are derived from the four-square rhetorical bases of different kinds of similitude:

Sameness
Difference or opposition
Metonymy (the transference of properties from one object to
    another)
Allusive reference to some other literary text.[67]

What the disproportionate symbolic universes of Picinelli and Menestrier sometimes appear to ignore is that the Creator was held to have designed the world by number, weight and measure. Although many emblems are based on medical, botanical or zoological 'facts', the stress on allusion, the last of the four bases of rhetorical similitude, indicates that emblematic culture participates in a verbal, bookish universe rather than the 'real' world. It is important to remember that the Renaissance and the Baroque set a high value on verbal skill and ingenuity, the culture participated in a common literary tradition, whether Judaeo-Christian or classical, which was appreciated both for its own sake and for the use that could be made of it in appropriating it to any new topical context.

Yet other emblem writers sought to win assent to their imaginative constructions of the universe by an appeal to scientific authority. Many emblems are based on mathematical and scientific instruments – the plumb-line, the astrolabe, sets of scales, clocks or dials, the set-square, the telescope, reading glasses, the file, the scissors and the saw. Gabriel Rollenhagen's 'Suum cuique tribue' (Give to each what is due) shows the scales of Justice supporting the author's citation of Cicero's standard definition of Justice (illus. 55); the emblematist characteristically measures, weighs, and inspects, perhaps in an attempt to underpin and buttress the moral truths that are being propounded. In Van Haeften's and Harvey's *Schola cordis*, the human heart itself is variously weighed, measured, refined, irrigated, printed, pressed, plumbed, and refined. Alciato alternatively takes as his measure of Justice the cubit rule (illus. 56). Both Alciato and Rollenhagen base their symbolism on a faith that such invisible and abstract notions can be exactly determined, measured and proportioned.

In Drechsel's 'Moraliter' figure, the title-page putto and the emblematist draw a precise metaphorical line. The physical and the

55

56

moral do not coincide in every way, but the wit and the cogency of the emblem depends on the exact precision of a particular relationship. Sometimes the angle of correspondence will be 'right', at others obtuse, and at still others, but perhaps more rarely, acute. These variable relationships underlying the emblematist's art are perhaps more shrewdly imaged in Costalius's 'In normam Lesbiam' (On the Lesbian rule), which depicts a cunning device (illus. 57) invented by the builders of Lesbos, who found they needed a flexible measure, one that could bend with the object. Such an approach underlies Emanuele Tesauro's survey of the witty justice of this symbolic architecture, for he grasped the fact that the mirror of the human mind that feigns these contrivances is not always constant, but in a state of flux, always changing, colouring what is observed by the tinctures of emotions and associations. Through his Aristotelian glasses, he examines these shifting images. These images are metaphors. For example, a diamond struck by a hammer should not be seen as an illustration of some industrial process, but as a symbol of dauntless resolution in the face of adversity.[68]

In discussions of encyclopaedic iconographic compilations, one cannot omit the work of Cesare Ripa, whose *Iconologia* first appeared in unillustrated form in the last decade of the sixteenth century. It was translated into various European languages, and appears never to have been out of print in one edition or another through the next 250 years. An English imitation by the architect George Richardson, containing 'upwards of four hundred and twenty remarkable subjects' appeared in 1778. 'We are', remarked the dramatist John Webster, 'phantastical puff paste'. And, Ripa, as a cook, in charge of preparing actual feasts for the eye and the palate, would know exactly what was allegorically required on such occasions to simultaneously edify the mind. He took as his foundation the human figure – Giovio, as we have noticed above, excluded it from *imprese* altogether – and in the concoction of his brain baked it into fantastical shapes. In various physical contortions and distortions he rendered visible the hidden thoughts, fancies, emotions, ideals of the mind and heart. The symbolic appurtenances that accreted around these depictions most frequently derived from books and other works of reference.[69] The body now became the means to access a library of information. It became an actor in a memory theatre.

Later editions of Ripa themselves became valuable works of reference. From the beginning the work was arranged in alphabet-

In normam Lesbiam.

Bonus iudex.
21

A ſpice vt in partes ſemper tornatilis omnes,
Se ſubieƈtam operi Lesbia norma facit.
Intus ſæpe latet ſcriptæ ſententia legis,
Quæ ſolet in tota iudicis eſſe manu.
Hanc ille in varijs rerum variare figuris
Debet,non vnum ſemper,idémque ſequi.

E iiij

57

ical order, but what made it more accessible to readers was the editorial apparatus, which kept on growing: its indices and lists which enable the reader to access the contents of the volume from various points of entry. The Venice 1645 edition, for example, is prefaced by 56 pages, which list iconographical attributes and their literary sources. We are presented with tables of gestures and postures, lists of manufactured objects, plants, animals, fish, inscriptions and ancient medals, which are tied to some symbolic equivalent in the following text. The image stock, however, was not

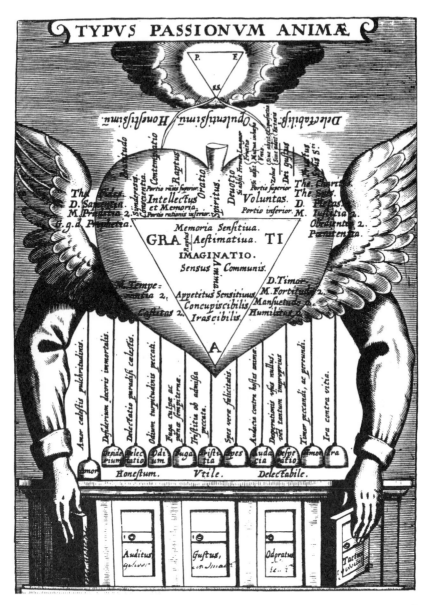

58

stable and constant. Matteo Florini's edition of 1613, for example, was six years in preparation and substantially altered the iconographical register of earlier editions: many symbolic attributes of the personifications, as well as background details, were omitted or changed.

Ripa should not be considered eccentric in his habits of thought. The very popularity of the book from its first publication shows it to be no odd sport of an idiosyncratic imagination. Or, if it was so at first, it was remarkably quickly absorbed into the contemporary culture. Others easily appropriated the iconographical technique to their own purposes: a number of the entries in later editions were not by Ripa at all, but by various others, who added their conceitful addition to the book. When the book was translated into Dutch (Amsterdam, 1644), Jegher dressed Ripa's allegorical types in contemporary costume, transposing the figures to bourgeois Holland. There seems to have been a deliberate attempt to de-emphasize the grotesquely over-subtle, fantastical quality of earlier editions, in an effort to naturalize these personifications. They were not 'other', but recognizable contemporaries, living and moving in the artist's own time. It was as much as if to say that he saw Anger, Greed Gluttony and their like walking around him in daily life. This must have had the effect of endowing Ripa's compilation with a satiric intent.

The schematic illustration 'Typus passionum animae' (illus. 58), shows again that Ripa's approach to the symbolic universe was far from unique. The human body could become nothing less than an elaborately organized set of pigeonholes for thought. This relates to a meditative technique that traces a sure path from the earthly to the heavenly. As the devotional manuals have it:

> as the Bodye hath his fiue exteriour Senses . . . : so the Spirit . . . hath fiue interiour Actes proportioned to these Sences, . . . with the which hee perceiueth the inuisible, and delectable things of God. . . .[70]

FOUR

Children and Childish Gazers

'vain amusement to wch I Boldly gave the Name of Wisdom.'[1]

Who would have thought that Jove was touched by love of children?[2]

If authors, artists, publishers and editors had a shaping effect on the emblem, so too had the presumed or ideal reader. The fact that many emblem books were directed to or at children exerted an enormous influence not only on the content and subject-matter of the book, but also on its format and strategic formulations.

One of the simplest and most affecting examples of this is Charles Jourdain's *Le Blason des fleurs* (Paris, 1555).[3] The book's unusually diminutive format may at first strike one as odd, until one realizes that its intended reader was but eleven years old, and it was designed to fit the small, sixteenth-century female hand that was to hold it. This particular book was probably a one-off, and it exists possibly in a unique copy in the Pierpont Morgan Library. Yet it is symptomatic of an early appreciation of the suitability of the emblem for an under-age readership. Alciato's German translator, Wolfgang Hunger, knew that playful emblematic images would instantly appeal to children,[4] and, from at least that time onward, children and childish readers were to dictate at least one direction the emblem was to take. But the involvement of children with emblem books is a subject that has been so consistently misunderstood that it warrants some detailed discussion.

Emblem books literally teem with children, engaged in every imaginable childish activity. Their presence is notable from the very beginning. Thomas Palmer's 'table of ... pictures' reflects his various sources when it lists 'A boye with winges on th'one arme and a great stone on the other'; 'Boyes clyminge the palme tree'; 'A Boy holden vp by the chin whyle he swymmes'; 'A boye hangyinge by a boughe of the palme tree'; 'A boye with a naked sworde'.[5] Ganymede (illus. 59), the lovely boy, is borne aloft on Jove's eagle with the full sanction of Christ's words in the Gospels: 'Suffer the little children to come unto me' (Mark 10. 14);[6] the laudable or reckless deeds of mythological sons – Icarus, Aeneas, Phaeton and, pre-eminently, Cupid – are held up for scrutiny. Children literally spring out of the ground in Taurellus's *Emblemata Physico-Ethica*,[7] and again in the *Thronus Cupidinis*, where they symbolize love's fruitfulness.[8] Thousands of naked babes, we are told, crowd around the aged Genius waiting to be let into the Garden of this world in the proto-emblematic *Tabula Cebetis*.[9] Nor should we be altogether surprised at this preoccupation: one of the guiding paradoxes of emblematic composition was *multum in parvo* (much [matter compressed] in a little [space or person]).

59

Other writers took childish toys, games and pastimes as their principal images. From the very beginning Alciato identified the composition of emblems with child's play. His dedicatory emblem to Conrad Peutinger parallels the making of emblems to children playing with nuts and other toys.[10] First place is given to children, and the line opens up a lifetime of holiday sport in its allusion to the proverb *Ad nuces redire* (to return to one's childish games), which can be applied to any age, any time.[11] Recreation and play are recognized as important not just to children, but for each stage of development from the cradle to the grave –'perdere nolo nuces' (I don't want to lose my nuts), cried Martial.[12] The bawdy innuendo, of course, may be taken as read, but the poet plainly endorses the enduring importance of child's play for adults as well as for children. Alciato's Emblem 100, 'In iuventam', erects a temple to eternal Youth, whose patron saints are the youthfully beardless gods Apollo and Bacchus. His Emblem 130, 'Semper praesto esse infortunia' (Misfortune is always close to us), shows three young women playing dice. Palmer, via Petrus Costalius, in his Emblem 86 commends 'the top and scourge' to boys. La Perrière's fifth emblem presents the image of a tennis-player, while Henry Peacham later introduces a game of football to show how 'worldly wealth is tossed to and fro'. Wither expresses a 'childish delight in trifling objects' – 'Rattles, and Hobby-horses'. He includes a 'Game at Lots', and he describes the book as 'a Puppet-play in Pictures' and the emblems as 'Play-games'.[13]

But this is as nothing compared to the huge catalogue of games and toys covered by Jacob Cats's 'Kinderspel' from his *Emblemata moralia et economica*.[14] It was not for nothing that he was styled 'Father' Cats, when we consider his amused overview of children's play. Against the staid backdrop of a city hall, tops spin, hoops bowl, stilts totter, bubbles blow, acrobats roll, somersaults turn. Boys and girls grope their way through blind-man's buff, they skip, leapfrog, turn handstands. Hobbyhorses are ridden, marbles shot, whirligigs turned, dice thrown, knucklebones tossed, dolls nursed and kites flown for a brief triumphant moment before their inevitable catastrophic fall back to earth. The Erasmian motto that stands over this whirling, energetic activity is plain: *ex nugis seria* (from trifles, serious matters). Indeed, Erasmus's statement could be set at the head of this whole emblematic tradition, in which Wither, for one, unashamedly stands: 'I ... have alwaies intermingled *Sports* with *Seriousnesse* in my *Inventions*'.[15]

Like Alciato before him, Cats, in his preface to *Silenus Alcibiadis*, embraces the parallel between emblematic composition and children's games: 'You may laugh and think this is but childish work ... well laugh away'. Cats invites his readers to participate in play, and involves them in the recognition that they, too, have a childish streak. Readers are invited to lay aside their sober facade, and to enjoy. Indeed, as Cats says in his verses to 'Kinderspel', his readers, if they care to look, can see themselves mirrored in these children's games.[16] Adults have not entirely left behind the child they were and are. Play becomes a mirror of instruction not just for the children who do it, but for those that watch. One might say, *particularly* for those that watch. Each activity carries its consequential emblematic moral baggage. It is not all, as the Erasmian motto warns us, simply fun and games. There is a moral translation at hand for most activities: stilts (pretention); the kite (soaring ambition, which has its fall); the whirligig (restive discontent); balloons and bubbles (*vanitas* and transitoriness). Such translation exercises are a fairly simple matter once one has cracked the basic code. As Cats states in his Preface to *Silenus Alcibiadis*: 'The world ... is but a children's game'. This can be taken in two ways. First, and most obviously, as a comment on the vanity of many of the world's 'serious' concerns. But also it recognizes the humanistic principle that childhood is a preparation for the whole of life.

Nor was Cats presenting a blindingly new insight in seeing the business of the world as mirrored in play. In Mignault's commentary on Alciato, Emblem 130, 'Semper praesto esse infortunia', we are told that Socrates compared human life to a game of dice. Whatever happens, we cannot roll the dice again. Terence agrees in *Adelphis*: 'It is just the same in life, as when you play with dice.'[17] So in Hugo's *Pia Desideria* (I, xiv), the dice-game of life has serious consequences viewed in the light of the soul's eternal destination: 'nos dubio manet alea iactu', or, as Edmund Arwaker expanded it into couplet form:

> For *that* or *this* must be doubtful *cast*,
> Nor may we *throw* agen when once 'tis past.

Horace, too, agreed in a line quoted more than once in connection with emblematic games, even if the games Horace refers to were played by political and military heavyweights: 'The game of dice is full of danger'.[18] The commentaries on games and pastimes in and annexed to emblematic descriptions of them recalls the education of the young Gargantua:

> they ... brought into use the antique play at tables .... In playing they examined the passages of ancient authors wherein the said play is mentioned or any metaphor drawn from it.[19]

The quantum physicist thinks that God, too, plays dice, but Plato was there first: 'May we not regard every living thing as a puppet of the gods, which may be their plaything only ... ?'[20]

Cats was not alone in pointing out that moral wisdom lay just beneath the surface of children's play: Visscher sees the boy bowling a hoop as a type of futility (see illus. 67). His Emblem 40, 'Leert het u kinderen niet', depicts games of chance, dice and cards presided over by a hovering crab. The moral is that one should not commit oneself to Fortune: the Christian path is straight and plain, the way of the Devil is crooked. Cramer (illus. 60) applies stilt-walking to 1 Corinthians 10. 12: *Qui se existimat stare, videat ne cadat* (Wherefore let him that thinketh he standeth take heed lest he fall). His sensible motto is MELLIVS IN IMO (It is better on the ground).[21] He also likens a child on a swing to the child in faith (illus. 61), swayed by every wind of doctrine: 'now he swings this way, now that'.[22] Alonso de Ledesma, the Spanish translator of Vænius, saw the spiritual sense in a whole range of children's

MORALE VII.   25

Qui fe exiftimat ftare, videat ne cadat.

MELIVS IN·IMO.

Ne labare cave, dum ftare videris: ab alto
Lapfus ad ima gradu præcipitante datur.

B   5   Wachet

games. A bouncing ball shows the conversion of St Paul: thrown to the ground, he bounces right up to the third heaven. Counting to ten on the fingers of one's hands teaches the Ten Commandments, if we count using 'the fingers of the soul'.[23] Melchior Glarus proposed in his *Confusio Disposita* (Augsburg, 1725) four 'Lusus Satyrico-Morales' (Satiric Moral Plays), digested into scenes and adorned with emblematic plates – the first a highly instructive play depicting girls ('Lusus filium bene imbutus'), the second, about naughty boys ('Lusus puerum male educatum').

MORALE XIV. 53

Vt iam non fimus paruuli fluctantes, & circumfe-ramur omni vento doctrinæ in nequitiâ homi-num.

RECTUM NON VENTI-LAT AVRA.

Error doctrinæ nunc hàc nunc fluctuat illàc :
Pendula mens vento ducitur, ergo volat.

D 2   Die

William Blake dedicated his *Songs of Innocence* and *The Gates of Paradise* to children, and he pictures numerous sports and games within the borders and headings of his poems. Children not only read, as in the *Songs of Innocence* frontispiece, but they dance, embrace, march, sing and play games. They pet a whole menagerie of animals – lions, lambs, serpents. 'The Echoing Green' depicts children flying kites and playing with bats and balls. A boy with a cricket bat, and another bowling a hoop along the ground, flank the margins of the first stanza. 'The Nurse's Song' shows the little ones laughing, leaping and dancing for joy, while the echoing hills resoundingly endorse the cry 'let us play, for yet it is day'. 'The Laughing Song' gives triumphant approval to childish mirth and merriment with its chorus, 'Ha, ha, he'. Unlike Cats, or those at the Jesuit College at Brussels, Blake did not attach a specific moral to these activities, for play and laughter and the very children themselves were, for Blake, implicitly and powerfully emblematic. They *are* the State of Innocence, and close to the Eternity from which they came. Pointing to a group of children playing, Blake is reported to have said to Samuel Palmer, 'That is Heaven'.[24] Nor does Blake always see them as little angels. They have tantrums. They can be loud and unruly. In the 'Songs of Experience' they can be like fiends. But their very energy is what commended them to him, for it is an energy that pulsates with new life.

A Postmodern appropriation of these ludic motifs should not surprise us. Until recently certain images were concealed from us, not so much by poetic veils, but by the Iron Curtain. Among the holdings of paintings in Russian galleries that have come to light since the end of the Cold War is a Picasso in St Petersburg's Pushkin Gallery: *Devochka na sharye* (Young Girl on a Ball). It is unmistakably indebted to the iconography of Alciato's emblem *Ars naturam adiuvans* (Art assisting nature): 'Just as Fortune stands on a sphere, Mercury is seated on a cube'.[25] But Alciato's Mercury has become, for Picasso, a circus strongman, while Fortuna is now a young acrobat balancing *en pointe* on a ball. The circus was not a remarkable subject for Picasso to undertake. But what we find here is Picasso's deliberate appropriation, quotation and recontextualizing of Alciato's iconographic motifs. Both, however, teach the same lesson out of Ovid: 'Disce bonos artes' (Learn good arts). For Alciato, the choice was between the cultivation of intellectual skills and base, mechanical arts; in Picasso's modern topsy-turvy world, the tricks (Alciato's 'mechanema') of the circus are more appropriate contrivances against the harsh effects of fortune than academic disciplines.

The Child as Reader

Many emblem books were directed to or at children, taking the opportunity to overcome any resistance to moral advice by using the pleasing amalgam of words and pictures to catch a reader's attention. 'Even children can readily understand pictures', Abraham Fraunce and the composers of *imprese* knew.[26] There was a specialized trade in such illustrative materials, which were known at that time as 'gays'.[27] Wither describes his plates, shorn of their verses, as 'delightfull . . . to *Children*, and *Childish-gazers*'.[28] Further, early copies of emblem books bear marks to prove that children visited them with active, even assiduous attention – not always necessarily to the benefit of the child or the book. In a letter to Southey (10 October 1798), Charles Lamb describes a 'detestable' copy of Wither: 'Some child . . . hath been dabbling . . . with its paint and dirty fingers'. Lamb's disappointment is far from unique.

A specific child-centred emblematic strategy devolved responsibilities on authors, which essentially changed the way in which attitudes to virtue and vice were portrayed. This can be seen in Jacob Cats's tenth emblem of his *Spieghel van den Ouden Ende Nieuwen Tijdt*.[29] It depicts a toy-shop, at which a little girl gazes with rapt enchantment before a wonderful array of toys and playthings – dolls, whirligigs, hobby-horses, drums, rattles. In the background, a well-dressed young woman displays her wares to a youth who eyes her with evident interest. The motto that covers background and foreground activities is 'Schoon voor-doen is half verkocht' (Well displayed is half sold). It is a commercial advertising strategy that applies equally to toy shops, to love and to the purveyors of moral advice. Virtue must at least look attractive and pleasing, if we want anyone to 'buy' it. How much more potentially effective than the earlier tactic of telling people how 'vneasye, paynful, ieapardouse, [and] harde' the path of virtue is?[30] The young pupils at the Altdorf Academy of an earlier generation were treated rather more sternly: 'The path of virtue is difficult' was one of the emblematic themes they were set.[31] The Jesuit scholars at the Brussels College were likewise encouraged to consider that 'The thorny path is the way to the stars, the easy path is the way to Hell.'[32] Gabriel Rollenhagen similarly pointed to the 'right path' taken by the Muses' winged mount, Pegasus: but this route leads over the rocks and thorns of Pindus:

> To attain the summit of the Æonian mountains [i.e., Mt Helicon] by the right path, the mind traverses the rocks and thorns of Pindus.[33]

It is a route map based on a harsh moral geography. Immortality has to be gained through rough and unpleasant toil. In case we missed the point, Rollenhagen restates the message elsewhere in the combined hieroglyph of his Emblem 5: a spade (toil) encircled by a serpent (eternity/wisdom). The meaning, 'wisdom is gained through toil', hardly takes an Oedipus to decipher.

Two paths were presented to young people, one broad and pleasant, the other, thorny, narrow and difficult, where bears and lions lurk, where there are ditches into which the unwary foot will almost certainly slide. Which, one might ask, would you recommend? While earlier moralists had no hesitation in pointing to the rough and thorny path, the immediate rewards of Virtue were recommended by later authors. Even John Milton conceded that the road of Virtue should at least present the *appearance* of being 'easy and pleasant', even though it was 'rugged and difficult indeed'. Thus 'the book of sanctity and virtue' should be moderated to those 'of soft and delicious temper, who will not so much as look upon Truth herself, unless they see her elegantly dressed' – like the young woman in the background of Cats's emblem.[34] Of course, Milton's iconographic joke depends on the fact that Truth is traditionally naked.

Children and Literary History

Rosemary Freeman simply misread the involvement of children in emblem books. She identified John Bunyan's *A Book for Boys and Girls* (1686) as marking the end of the useful life of the emblem tradition in England: 'the first [English] emblem book intended specifically for children [was published] in 1686, a date which can be taken as marking the end of the life of the convention'.[35] Despite the seductive neatness of her literary history ('The first English emblem book', according to her, appeared in 1586), the 'end' came in 1686. Yet she was as wrong about the end as she was about the beginning. Bunyan's book became *Divine Emblems: or, Temporal Things Spiritualised* in 1724, after the author's death. The woodcuts, presumably the 'Emblems' referred to in the new title, were added to this edition. An estimated further twenty editions were published between 1701 and 1867. If the emblem's life was over in 1686, it took a remarkably long time to die. And during this period the emblem book was not the only thing to change. The status, position and perception of the child and the reading habits of the young were also being looked at and revised. In William Holmes's *Religious Emblems and Allegories* (1854), Envy is still chewing on her snakes and painfully supporting her steps with a 'thorny cane', just as she had done in Alciato (illus. 62). She is still going strong well into the nineteenth century. Here she is offered by Holmes as a piece of morally improving bedtime reading for the young. Of course, this 'threefold demon' is the stuff of juvenile nightmare.

62

But behind Freeman's suspect literary history, there lurks an unstated value judgment. To commend a work to boys and girls is usually to imply that it is not worth reading at all. It is an insult Martial precisely and ironically levelled at the bland epigrams of his rival, Cosconius, when he said of them that 'they deserve to be read by boys and girls'.[36] But Bunyan does not really interest Freeman. He is merely a convenient peg on which to hang her evaluation of the direction in which the whole emblem tradition was headed in 1686 or thereabouts. Somehow, she implies, the governing human-ist principle that had sustained emblematic production to this date, *ex nugis seria* (from trifles, serious things), had suddenly been turned upside down. What we have in its place is *ex seribus nugae* (from serious things, trifles) – a process of intellectual degradation that renders the form unworthy of serious attention.

What we do have to face is the fact that the emblem as a form was seldom classed among the *seria* (serious things), and that it shared with its purely verbal sister art, the epigram, a dedicated commitment to the trivial and the nugatory. If it was serious, then it must be said that it was serious in its pursuit of the trivial. The trivial and the nugatory absolutely defined the form: 'they are trash and trifles', Martial cheerfully acknowledged of his epigrams.[37] Giovio's treatise on *imprese* is full of silly foolery ('ineptiae') in Abraham Fraunce's opinion.[38] The fourth part of Harsdörffer's *Frauenzimmer Gesprechspiele* (1644) contains an emblematic addition, which he revealingly entitles *Mantissa* – i.e., a worthless make-weight.

Freeman's analysis misses the fundamental biblical grounding that informs the emblematic child-like vision – whether Bunyan's, Wither's, Cats's or anyone else's. The use of the trifling and silly to impart spiritual truths is a method that derives from God himself: 'God hath chosen the foolish things of the world to confound the wise; . . . And base things of the world, and things that are despised, hath God chosen . . .' (1 Corinthians 1. 27–8). Christian emblematists – of whatever sectarian persuasion – tended to identify themselves with God's perspective in these matters. Besides, His preference for *discordia concors* must have appealed to any Baroque concettist.

While recognizing that there is little point in flogging a dead literary historian, one cannot help but niggle just a little further at Freeman's view of the history of the genre. Her argument rests on extremely narrow ground – it is a suspect interpretation of one feature of a specifically English literary history. Johann Michael Dilherr's *Christliche Gedächtnis-Münze* (Nuremberg, 1655) was proposed as a 'Kinderlehre' (a lesson for children). Jan Luyken's *Des Menschen Begin, Midden en Einde* (Amsterdam, 1712) was dedicated specifically to children, and Cats's advice-book, *Maechden-plicht ofte ampt der ionck-vrouwen* (Middelburg, 1618), obviously targets its audience in its title – girls and young women. No one would say that Dilherr, Cats or Luyken marked 'the end of the life of the convention'. Indeed, if we simply look at the continued reception of this one book of Cats's, we would see that such a view is palpably unsustainable. Apart from its numerous reprints, it was translated into major European languages for at least another 250 years: it became 'An Emblematicall Dialogue' in Thomas Heywood's *Pleasant Dialogues* (1637), and an emblematic 'school' for young ladies in eighteenth-century Germany: the *Neueröffnete Schule vor das noch ledige Frauenzimmer* (Frankfurt and Leipzig [1720]). As late as 1886 a French translation appeared: *L'Amour virginal ou le devoir des jeunes filles dans leurs chastes amours.*

Nor should we single out Bunyan or Cats. There are other emblematic works, even within English literature, that were directed to or at children at or around the date Freeman has in mind. The intended recipients of Robert Whitehall's *Hexastichon Hieron* were apparently the youthful scions ('Epheborum Praenobilium') of a few select, noble houses, the book being primarily devised, according to the statement on the title-page, as a means of encouraging these young Protestants to read their Bibles.[39] It is not uncommon for emblem books to be dedicated to the children of the rich or powerful. At the beginning of the century, Henry Peacham dedicated his *Minerva Britanna* to Henry, Prince of Wales, the son of James I and heir apparent, although at this date he could hardly be considered a child. But this, as with Whitehall, may not necessarily lead us automatically to conclude that the authors thought that emblems were more appropriate to children than to adults. It was determined by a more obvious, mercenary plea for patronage – a strategy, not unknown in theological circles, whereby an approach is made to the father through the son.

Freeman makes a false inference in attributing a change in literary history to an author's decision to dedicate his work to children. The whole genre did not at a single stroke become any more or less 'childish' simply because one volume was directed to under-age readers. And, as we have seen, the presence of children in emblem books was not suddenly introduced at this time, but was there from the very start. Freeman was clearly responding to a number of changes. One is signalled in the revised title of Bunyan's work, *Temporal Things Spiritualised*. This points to a shift in the iconographic repertory. Familiar, everyday images increasingly take precedence over those drawn from a more classically orientated, mythographic tradition. The symbolic lexicon had expanded to include this more accessible material for the purposes of providing instructive analogies between the exterior world and the spiritual life. Yet the classically inspired, literary iconography did not disappear on the crowing of this particular cock. Its continuance indeed became ghostly – the manifestation of an older tradition that continued to be evoked, enforced and summoned.

What we do have, though, is probably an even broader change in the cultural history of laughter, play and festivity, which emblem books may symptomatically exemplify. Keith Thomas cites a contemporary comment from 1649 that identifies those 'most apt to laughter' as 'children, women and the common people'.[40] Even by 1635 George Wither had frankly acknowledged the appeal of emblems to 'common Readers', the 'vulgar Capacities', and to '*Children*, and *Childish-gazers*'. In this he anticipated Spinoza, who regarded mythologies and emblems as 'extremely necessary ... for the masses, whose wits are not potent enough to perceive things clearly and distinctly'.[41] Yet, unlike Spinoza, Wither regarded this vulgar appeal, rightly or wrongly, as a positive recommendation, as did Jacques de Zetter, the French translator of Andreas Friderich's *Emblemata nova*.[42] Nor are we dealing simply with a debased vernacular tradition: Charles Musart's *Adolescens academicus* (Douai, 1633) is firmly directed to schoolboys. All this is some 200 years before 'Aunt Judy', 'Miss Thoughtful' and Mrs Gatty appropriated the emblem for their young readers. What we are forced to conclude is that this is a continuation of a tradition, not a decline or attenuation. Gatty's material, as Wendy Katz has shown, came from the standard emblematic sources.[43]

Around the middle of the seventeenth century, however, emblems in certain quarters began to be judgmentally dismissed, sneered at, as 'childish'. In the 1740s William Ayre refers to 'the Children's Poet, Mr Withers'.[44] Of Quarles and Wither, he states: 'Their writings were always recommended to those under twelve Years of Age, especially Female, by the three beforementioned great Wits' (i.e., Atterbury, Swift and Pope). Pope, of course, set his face firmly against popular culture, but he explicitly condemned the taste for emblems as 'Gothick' – not only old-fashioned, but crude and barbarous. Accordingly, in Pope's revised *Dunciad*, I, 294–6, Wither is found 'among the dull of *ancient* days' (my emphasis). Similarly, a contributor to the *Gentleman's Magazine* in 1738 called Wither 'the worst of all bards' – where 'bard' carries the pejorative connotations of venerably obscure portentousness. Pope scored many other palpable hits when he set up Quarles and Wither among his satiric butts in his *Dunciad*. The books in the Dunce's library inevitably include 'Withers, Quarles and Blome' (*Dunciad*, I, 126). 'Quarles is sav'd by Beauties not his own' (*Dunciad*, I, 139–40) – the saving atonement stemming from the 'quaint' engraved plates by William Marshall, which, in Pope's view, reprieve the book from the sentence the verse deserves: to be consigned to the pie-shop or the privy. In the third book of the revised *Dunciad*, during the visit to the poet's underworld, Benlowes, Quarles's patron, appears, as in life, 'propitious still to blockheads' (line 21).[45]

But such superior scorn the wits poured on the judgement of those they considered no better than children or imbeciles should not be taken as typical or representative of the reading public as a whole. These were 'advanced' views. Sir Roger L'Estrange could condemn them roundly as a fashionable pose of a set of 'unsociably sour, ill-natur'd and troublesom' men, who affected to scorn what others liked:

> There are ... a certain Set of morose and untractable Spirits in the World, that look upon precepts in Emblem, as they do upon Gays and Pictures that are only fit for Women and Children, and look upon them to be no better than the Fooleries of so many Old Wives Tales.[46]

If we were to follow the 'morose and untractable' down this path, we would be in danger of losing sight of an essential emblematic strategy and lively developments in popular culture. What has been constructed as a symptom of its decline is, in fact, a consistent, coherent development of a fundamental, underpinning motif that existed from the beginning: serious play, or, as Achille Bocchi advertises it on his title-page, 'serio ludere' (to play in earnest).[47] This doubly commits emblematic authors both to a serious endorsement of play and to a requirement to deal with serious things in a playful manner. In similar vein the alchemist Michael Maier produced a *Lusus serius* and a *Iocus severus* with a view to uncover the serious lessons beneath the ludicrous surface of the created universe.[48]

The Foundations of Knowledge

L'Estrange repeats a humanistic, educational truism: 'The *Foundations* of *Knowledge* and *Virtue* are laid in our *Childhood*'; 'The *Principles* that we imbibe in our *Youth*, we carry commonly to our *Graves*'.[49] The reason why emblems were addressed to children is not so much that they were only fit for fools and simpletons, but it was a basic humanist principle to instruct children in morality from their earliest youth. Horace influentially stated, 'The jar will long keep the fragrance of what it was once steeped in when new'.[50] Erasmus saw no difficulty in including this maxim in his *Adagia* (II, iv, 20). Quintilian (I, i, 5) likewise recommended that the best things should be learned even from our youth. At a young age, the earlier the better, lessons are more likely to be remembered, and, for the early modern pupil, the emblematic method of instruction was considered both congenial and suitable. It was implicitly and exactly recommended by the educational metaphor of cultivation in which the young shoot is grafted onto an old

63

stock: this is itself literally an emblematic process.[51] *Fit surculus arbor* (The young shoot will become a tree) and *Ex ramo nascitur arbor* (The tree is born from the twig) were the two maxims that became emblematic mottoes.[52] Emblem books self-referentially justify their existence by showing bears licking their formless cubs into shape (see illus. 83),[53] Cupid bending the supple cane,[54] or showing the folly of trying to uproot a tree once it is fully grown (illus. 63).[55]

Jean-Jacques Boissard's first emblem, *Educatio prima, bona sit* (One's first education is good),[56] is a veritable miniature anthology of such motifs (illus. 64). The mature branch breaks, but the young, tender shoot easily bends; a woman pours some presumably desirably fragrant liquid into a presumably new jar. In the foreground, a book is pressed into the hands of a young child. From the nexus of visually realized metaphors we might conclude that the child itself is the unopened book. In the facing prose commentary Boissard stresses that education should begin as early as possible, even from the cradle ('à primis cunabilis'). Its function, he goes on to say, is to repair the ruins of the knowledge of our first parents, lost through their primal transgression. The casting of the educational imperative in such terms puts the whole human race in the position of sons and daughters. Thus Harvey's

64

CONTAGIO CORDIS

Cr de bibis stigiun morbi mortisque venenum.
Hic te dum blandis decipit illecebris.

The INFECTION of the HEART.

While Satan thus deceives with flattring Breath,
Thy Heart drinks Poison in Disease and Death.

65

66

School of the Heart opens its curriculum with Eve's first sin of disobedience (illus. 65); this is followed by the sequence of instructive lessons learned by the childlike heart.

'*Children* are but *Blank Paper*, ready indifferently for any Impression', stated L'Estrange.[57] The scholars of the Altdorf Academy implied the same thing by a mirror, which indifferently reflects whatever is shown to it: a military hero, a satyr or a devil. 'Objecta refert' (It gives back what is shown to it).[58]

Reading is a childish pastime, which is encouraged in life and reflected in emblems. L'Estrange talks of the educational benefit of '*Sights*, and *Stories*' and children's pleasure in 'applying a profitable *Moral* to the *Figure*'.[59] Stevenson in the first of his *Moral Emblems* shows children running to a book 'to see what's in 't'. They are enjoined to 'Seize and *apply*' the volume (illus. 66). Stevenson, to some extent, might be seen to appropriate the substance of Blake's frontispiece to *The Songs of Innocence*, where two children stand at their mother's knee. They look eagerly at a book, which she holds open on her lap. But in Blake's frontispiece, we might make the additional inference that the children are themselves the 'Blank Paper' of as yet unwritten emblematic volumes.

Old Infants

When, however, L'Estrange stated 'The *Principles* that we imbibe in our *Youth*, we carry commonly to our *Graves*', he did more than merely repeat a humanist commonplace. There are important implications for our reading of the early modern child, and its involvement in emblematic structures. L'Estrange saw a continuous line that runs from infancy to adulthood and on to old age, and which circles back on itself to connect the extremes of youth and age. Biblical constructions of human life underpin such a view of a complete continuous circle of existence: 'Naked came I out of my mother's womb, and naked shall I return thither' (Job 1. 21). The notion is wittily, if grotesquely, illustrated by Cramer as an infant crawls through two holes in a giant globe: from the left-hand opening emerges the child's head and naked torso, the right-hand opening exposes the bare bottom, legs and feet. Head and feet are separated by the great globe itself, visually distorting the child's body to suggest a stretched, elongated, worm-like creature.[60]

Part of the iconographic effectiveness of Roemer Visscher's emblem of futility, which depicts a boy bowling a hoop (illus. 67), is that it reflects the cycle of existence, which is imaged variously elsewhere. Beginnings confront endings in the final epigram of Quarles's *Hieroglyphikes of the Life of Man*, which is addressed 'To the Infant'. It directs the child's gaze to the final scene of life, played out with 'eyes ... dimme, ears deaf, visage pale, teeth decayed, skin withered, breath tainted, pipes furred, knees trembling, hands fumbling, feet failing'. 'Old' and 'young', 'Infant' and 'old Man', become matters of little or no distinction:

> He's helpless, so art thou; what difference then?
> He's an old *Infant*; thou, a young *old Man*.

Eschewing the fashionable vein of *memento mori*, L'Estrange connects the child to the man: '*Boys* and *Men* [are] indifferently of the same Make'.[61] It is a tantalizingly short verbal distance to Wordsworth's 'The child is *father* to the man' – but the paradox is as much beyond L'Estrange as is the sensibility that informs Wordsworth's line. L'Estrange's distinction between child and adult becomes simply one of size. It is worth noting that the point is conceitedly made in a new preface added along with a new set of cuts to the 'tenth edition' of Bunyan's *Divine Emblems* (1757), which addresses 'the Great Boys in Folio, and The Little Ones in

67

Coats'. The child is the 'epitome' of the adult 'folio'. Or, to refer to
another, more organic metaphor from John Huddleston Wynne,
'the Rose, in its infant state, while in its bud, contains in epitome all
the sweetness, bloom, and beauty of maturity' (sig. A4v). If the
difference is only one of size, it follows, according to L'Estrange,
that both children and adults are 'accountable to the same Faculties and Duties' (sig. A3v). The child is nothing more than a miniature adult, a full member of society no less governed by its rules
and principles.

The World in Miniature

If play allows children an environment in which they can safely
learn and prepare themselves against the pitfalls of adult life, the
activities of what is sometimes absurdly referred to as 'the real
world' can be viewed satirically through the opposite end of the

telescope. We enter a Lilliputian state where ambitious worldly plans and schemes can be reduced to nothing more than a child's game. This is not so much the morally proportioned world where the microcosm, the *parvus mundus*, reflects the greater world of the macrocosm, but a satiric distorting mirror, a *mundus parvulorum*, a world that shrinks the adult. Cats's disingenuous prefatory words to his *Silenus*, that 'The world . . . is but a children's game', can be taken in a bitingly satiric sense. The world of children's play becomes a satiric mirror of adult folly: the *stultus puer* (foolish child) reflects in miniature an even more *stultus homo* (foolish adult). According to Taverner's evaluation, 'a foolyshe and ignoraunt person . . . in dede differeth no thynge from a chylde'.[62] Cramer addresses the '*Stulte puer*', whose wish exceeds his grasp. But anyone who does this, at whatever age, must be seen as involved in 'Kinderwerck'.[63] Hugo and Arwaker, building on an emblematic idea treated first by Theodore de Bèze,[64] develop this perspective in *Pia Desideria*, Book I, Emblem 2:

> How does our toil resemble Childrens play,
> When they erect an Edifice of Clay?
> How *idly* busie and imploy'd they are?
> Here, *some* bring Straw; there, *others* Sticks prepare;
> *This* loads his Cart with Dirt; that in a Shell
> Brings Water, that it may be temper'd well;
> And in their work themselves they fondly pride,
> While Age the *childish Fabrick* does deride:
> So on *our Work* Heav'n with contempt looks down:

'Ridemus' (We laugh) at such a sight, de Bèze agrees. Arwaker's God looks on this spectacle 'with contempt', but Hugo's sees it as a joke: 'Superis dant nostra negotia risum' (Our affairs are an object of mirth to the gods). Unlike Arwaker, Hugo's Baroque, post-Tridentine Latinity allows him to make an easy identification between the Olympians and the Christian God, yet his view is thoroughly supported by biblical authority: 'Hath not God made foolish the wisdom of the world?' (1 Corinthians 1. 20).

Here the rage for building, 'improving' as it was called, is derided, but the emblem proceeds to anatomize the whole of the adult world throughout its history as just so many more examples of different species of childish folly. How otherwise could these things be viewed, since we follow in the footsteps of our first foolish parents, who so frivolously traded their primal innocence for an apple? The contrast between Youth's silly, pointless games and

Age's superior derision ('Age the *childish Fabrick* does deride') works to the greater disparagement of Age, for it turns out that children know more than the adults. Age, it seems, cannot even grasp the rudiments of what every schoolchild knows:

> For [*Boys*] from Counters currant Money know,
> Almost as soon as they have learnt to go :
> But *Men* (oh shame!) prize counterfeit delights
> Before the Joys to which kind Heav'n invites.

Yet Hugo and Arwaker reserve a saving grace in this satiric condemnation. If we accept this evaluation, that all we hold dear in this material world is puerile and silly, we might just perhaps be able to pass off what are actually 'sins' as mere 'folly'. If the subterfuge works, we might escape the punishment those sins deserve by appealing to God's amused, parental indulgence.

The Child as Emblematic Author

It ought not come as a surprise that various games should figure among the subject of a number of emblems composed by the pupils of the Jesuit College in Brussels. For them, emblematic composition, working through coded moral signs and spiritual allegories, was a species of academic play, heavily seasoned with the spice of strong competition. Furthermore, the games imaged pointed to intensely serious issues. There were, inevitably, the usual conventional, satiric *vanitas* motifs. But we also have pointers to the fate of one's eternal soul, heroic martyrdom, the promises of the faith. ÆTERNITAS-TEMPUS depicts a circus acrobat in the midst of a possibly death-defying metaphysical leap through the hoop of eternity: 'Eternity is the gateway to either life or death'.[65]

MORS-VITA depicts the conventional *vanitas* motif: a child blowing bubbles.[66] While it might be tempting to sentimentalize the image and to interpret it as a symbol of an all-too-brief childhood – a reminder not simply of the distressingly high incidence of infant mortality at that period, or every infant's inevitable 'death' into adulthood – the realization it imparts is more brutal than that. As the beautiful bubble shines all too briefly, so childhood, youth and the rest of life vanishes far too quickly and is gone, as if it never was. The bubble may be compared, according to Junius in his notes to his Emblem 16, to 'an image of our fallen human condition' – 'there is nothing more deceptive or empty'.[67] The fleetingness of time renders the evanescent distinction between youth and age hardly worth making. 'The Bubble's Man', Quarles firmly tells us.[68] In Adrianus Poirters' *Het Masker van de Welt afgetrocken*, the child's fascinating, heavenly bubbles are symbols of the transitoriness of a woman's beauty.[69]

The same MORS-VITA manuscript shows boys whipping a top. The motto, taken from Virgil's epic simile of boys playing the same game (*Aeneid*, VII, 383, 'Dant animos plagae', The blows give it life), is now applied to heroic martyrdom: 'It stands firm amid the blows'.[70] This constancy even unto death is mirrored in the paradox of stillness achieved through motion. The joys of eternal life are shown in the image of boys and girls dancing in a ring.[71] 'For of such is the Kingdom of Heaven . . .' (Matthew 19. 14) gives the appropriate biblical sanction to a vision of eternity mirrored in childish play. In a stone fired from a sling we see how the heaviest heart positively flies when directed towards the prospect of eternity: 'it may be heavy, but it will fly to the stars'.[72] Archers shooting at a target (fol. 54) show how we all aim at the same mark – eternity. Skaters on a lake teach that in the slippery course of life we must be careful not to fall: 'he who stands, let him see that he does not fall' – an idea that had already been used by Roemer Visscher in his *Sinnepoppen*.[73] While the treacherous appearances of life are shown by a skater falling through the ice on a sunny day: 'there is no trust to be had in fine weather'.[74] Further examples from the manuscripts could be cited, which would add to this list of moralized games.

John Huddlestone Wynne's *Choice Emblems* (1772) were written 'for the amusement of a young nobleman not more than nine years old', but, in publishing them, he had in view an audience that included adults.[75] A century later, Stevenson produced his two volumes of *Moral Emblems* in active collaboration with a child. These rose out of what might be considered child's play. Indeed, it is hard to know whether the boy or the man was the more committed to the project. During his treatment for tuberculosis at the Swiss clinic at Davos-Platz, Stevenson wrote the verses and cut the woodblocks, and his newly acquired stepson, Lloyd Osbourne, printed them off on a toy printing press brought from California. But, although produced in collaboration with a child, the works themselves were intended for an adult audience. They were to be sold to the residents of the hotel. The sheer fun of the enterprise was what Stevenson repeatedly emphasized. One does not progress far into the *Moral Emblems* before one realizes that these are written in a high vein of serious silliness.[76] Whatever Stevenson's reading in canonical emblem literature (his letters attest to his reading of Quarles), he drew on a stock of recognizably emblematic images, themes and rhetorical strategies. The figures of paradox, prosopopoeia, periphrasis and even the playful choice of rhetorically licentious rhymes are markers of an emblematic verbal style. 'The pauper by the highwayside', as elsewhere, is an encouragement to charitable almsgiving.[77] Exemplary heroes, here 'adventurous Cortez' (illus. 68), are praised.[78] Stevenson, drawing on the emblematic book of creatures, writes of pines, eagles, the elephant and the 'sacred Ibis', the last-named probably because of its explic-

68

itly Egyptian, hieroglyphic associations (illus. 69).[79] We may recognize the 'careful angler' and the endangered, storm-tossed ship from earlier emblem books.[80] These emblems' moral preoccupations, like so many others, are to recommend industry,[81] or to warn against the 'unfortunate effects of rage'.[82] But Stevenson's recommendations to virtue often take a decidedly odd turn. The 'unfortunate effects of rage' are no more than indigestion, while his exemplar of virtuous industry, who secures for himself a comfortable and respectable retirement, is none other than an 'industrious pirate'.[83] Moral instruction is often pointedly absent or withheld. The dispute between the pines closes with no firm conclusion. One recognizes here the continuation of the humanistic *serio ludere* tradition of jocose seriousness and earnest comicality. Yet by means of such a boyish sense of humour, rage is condemned, industry commended.

Writing to Edmund Gosse, Stevenson, with his tongue firmly in his cheek, bestowed on himself the portentous Blakean title of 'Bard' ('Who Present, Past, and Future sees / . . . Calling the lapsed soul . . .').[84] But the pride in his achievement is undisguised, even if Gosse may have expected rather more from him than these humorous trifles. The woodcuts are meant to show tropical scenes, yet the stark black forms caught against the white page bring to mind a landscape nearer to hand: dark, desperate, flailing figures

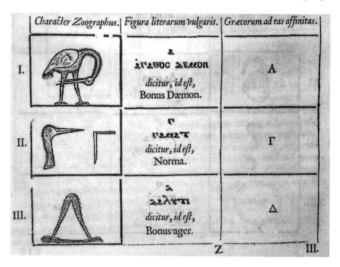

Charaĉter Zoographus.	*Figura literarum vulgaris.*	*Græcorum ad eas affinitas.*
I.	₂ ⲓⲅ₂ⲃⲟⲥ ₂ⲉⲙⲉⲟⲛ *dicitur, id eſt,* Bonus Dæmon.	A
II.	ⲅ ⲅ₂ⲙⲙ₂ⲧ *dicitur, id eſt,* Norma.	Γ
III.	₂ ₂₂λⲥⲧₓ *dicitur, id eſt,* Bonus ager.	Δ
	Z	III.

silhouetted against the blank whiteness of an Alpine winter (illus. 68). On April Fools' Day – the date is significant – Stevenson sent a copy of *Moral Emblems* to Dr Alexander Japp.[85] He described them as 'replete with the highest qualities of art'. The letter also reveals that Fanny Stevenson had by this stage also entered into the inspired silliness of the whole endeavour. Lloyd had recruited the whole family to his back room printing house. It was a way for Stevenson to occupy his mind, and to keep morbid thoughts at bay that might otherwise turn to his disease and the alien environment. So great was his application that *Moral Emblems: A Second Collection of Cuts and Verses* quickly emerged from the press of 'S. L. Osbourne & Company'. Ninety copies were printed, and the price was ten pence for the 'Edition de Luxe'. Eight pence for the 'Popular Edition' was obviously, therefore, the 'great bargain' it was advertised as.

The second volume proves that they thought the joke needed

further development. Stevenson went about designing a 'device' for the young printer: a heavily self-conscious, symbol-laden woodblock with an accompanying Latin motto, 'LABOR, CRUX, CORONA' (Work, Cross, Crown). Karl-Josef Höltgen has suggested that the symbolism was probably modelled on the title-page of W. Harry Rogers's *Spiritual Conceits* (1862), with its motto 'No cross, no crown'. Stevenson's design included more text in a cryptic acrostic, fusing the words 'typo' and the first four letters of the boy's name, 'Osbo'.

The period of these productions was one of particular closeness between the author and his stepson. But after the move from Davos, and a period of estrangement, when Lloyd was sent to boarding school, the fun seemed to go out of the enterprise, and an awkward distance, exacerbated by encroaching adolescence, meant that the collaboration came to an end. Symbolically, the printing press broke. Another planned emblematic production, *Moral Tales*, was never completed. Like Alciato, Stevenson maintained a huge affection for his emblems to the end of his days. When plans for his Collected Works under the editorship of Sidney Colvin were under way, he dismissed any pressure to suppress the emblems, and declared them, with whatever degree of self-mockery, 'far the greatest of my works'.[86]

Conclusion

The use of children in emblem books was part of a palpable design on the reader, and it mattered little during the seventeenth century and early eighteenth whether this reader was an adult or a child. The division did not matter, because it dissolved under a construction of human history that made one and all the erring offspring of the first parents, Adam and Eve, and which saw each and everyone as potential children of God. It was believed that our genealogy condemned us all to a lifetime of vain silliness, destined only to repeat the errors of the past. The possibility of divine adoption referred to in the biblical account contained a message of hope that spoke of spiritual rejuvenation and spiritual renewal, that promised a new beginning and a new life, if anyone was prepared to undertake a second, spiritual infancy. Calendar age ceased to matter under Christ's Gospel imperative to become as little children.

FIVE

Carnal Devotions

'Fancy's images'
(*A Midsummer Night's Dream*, v, i, 25)

The last chapter dealt with the influence of readers on the emblem. This chapter turns to another class of readers, who exerted just as strong an influence over the genre's shape, format and development: lovers, newly-weds, and those whose desires passionately turned from the carnal to the spiritual. This readership was, at least at first, conceived as predominantly female.

If the emblem book is a purveyor of the mysteries, there is no greater mystery than that of *eros* and *agape*, of human love and the divine. The imagery deployed for these subjects is not confined to books, but adorns all kinds of lovers' gifts – cameos, cabinets, hangings and plasterwork. The appeal was to be long-lived, and extended into the twentieth century. The designs were easily and endlessly adaptable. They appear in Neoclassical guise in a collection of engravings in the shape of cameos and brooches at the end of the eighteenth century.[1]

As in the last chapter, we enter a miniaturized world. Here the passions are enacted by appealing *putti*. Cupid is the archetypal actor in this emblematic drama. His exploits came to form a sub-genre of emblems, the love emblem. This forerunner of the modern Valentine card manages to mix advice with teasing eroticism, ribaldry, jocosity, and the softest of soft porn. Later, but not very much later, the winged *putto* was pressed into the services of religion, to become *amor divinus*, a provocative object of spiritual longings, desires and fears.

At first glance it looks as if these emblems are played out by children. The initial effect seems to infantalize the emotions invoked. But the passions involved are anything but childish. There is something distinctly odd about seeing these passionate scenes enacted by childlike figures. Alexander Grosart, when planning a nineteenth-century edition of Quarles's emblems, registered what he described as the 'grotesque' effect of all this: 'the chief figures are . . . childish even when adults are necessary to the "moral" of the verse'.[2] This comes from a man who was not entirely out of sympathy with earlier sensibilities. The relegation of adult emotions to the playground might be thought of as a conceited *discordia concors*: childlike figures enact scenes that can only be rightly understood by reference to adult experience. The books require a readership able to recognize these feelings for what they are. Cupid, after all, was not a child, but one of the oldest and most powerful of the gods.

In 1640 Fortunio Liceti produced an encyclopaedic commentary, *Ad Alas Amoris Divini a Simmia Rhodio compactus*, which must be seen as an erudite attempt to legitimize a shift in the emblematic repertoire, that had taken place earlier in the century, in which Christianity thoroughly appropriated erotic images and allegories. But the 'new' sacred Cupid did not entirely usurp the dominion of the profane. In spite of calls from various quarters to 'thrust forth th[e] wicked brat of that *Cyprian* strumpet out of doores. Break his quiuer, snap his shafts' and to exalt Christ, the 'Chaster *Cupid*',[3] both the sacred and the profane Cupids continued to overfly emblematic territory. Indeed the profane supported the sacred. In this theatrical *erotomachia*, this contest between two loves of comfort and despair, *amor divinus* and *amor humanus*, *eros* and *anteros*, it is sometimes hard to know which represents 'comfort' and which 'despair'.

Profane Love

Daniel Heinsius, the Leiden professor and editor of classical texts, was the first, albeit anonymous, author to open the sluices to what was to become an overwhelming flood of works in this amorous vein with *Quaeris quid sit Amor, quid amare*. The dedication is to the young women of Holland: 'Aen de Ioncvrouwen van Hollands'.

But from the beginning Love had played a part in emblems. Colonna's *novella* offers initiation into sacred erotic mysteries; Giovio saw the *impresa* as part of an amatory social game, in which the lover would find ways of insinuating his suit by secret signs and covert messages. The eye-catching device was designed for one particular female eye. The 'heroic' devices of Gabriele Simeoni and Claude Paradin pre-eminently included those of lovers, while Giordano Bruno devoted a whole volume to explicating the dark riddles and conceited conundrums of such 'heroic enthusiasms'. La Perrière, in his Emblem 62, shows Cupid teaching an ass to dance.

Alciato translated some of the anacreontic exploits of Cupid from the Planudean Anthology: *Potentissimus affectus amor* (Love is the most powerful emotion), features Cupid's abilities as a lion-tamer: the most savage of beasts are brought under his yoke, and they now draw his chariot; *Potentia amoris* (The power of love), celebrates Cupid's rule over land and sea: he holds a fish in one hand, a flower in the other; *Vis amoris* (The strength of love) shows that Cupid's fire is more powerful even than lightning: love yields to none; *In studiosum captum Amore* (On the scholar who has fallen in love) is not about Cupid at all, but a satire on the 'wise' scholar who becomes a fool, when, against the settled habits of a lifetime, he is entrapped by love. In *Anteros, id est amor virtutis* (Anteros, i.e., the love of virtue), Alciato literally clips the lascivious Cupid's wings in order to define a different, virtuous kind of Love, identifying it by the absence of Cupid's traditional iconographical attributes: this Love does not have wings, and does not carry a bow, arrows or fire-brands. *Anteros, Amor virtutis, alium Cupidinem superans* (Anteros, the love of virtue, overcoming the other Cupid) continues this theme. Alciato argues for the, albeit painful, necessity for the mutuality of love. The pair of emblems, *Dulcia quandoque amara fieri* (Pleasures sometimes cause pain) and *Ferè simile ex Theocrito* (Much the same from Theocritus), treat the Greek poet's charming narrative of Cupid the honey-thief stung by bees, running to his mother, Venus, for comfort, after his disappointing discovery that bees, as well as Love, bear sharp stings. Here Cupid appears as a weeping child, but the emblem switches sympathy from the injured boy to the lovers that Cupid daily wounds. The pains of Love are sharper than those caused by any bee! *In statuam Amoris* (On the statue of Love), provides a satiric interrogation of Cupid's traditional iconography: if he cannot see, why does he need a blindfold? Why is he depicted as a child, when he is as old as Nestor? How can he survive the cold, if he is naked? Why does he need wings, when he does his daily business on the ground, creeping into people's hearts? How can he possibly fly? Everyone knows he is as hard as stone. The epigram ends with a spoof heraldic blazon, which I will discuss in a later chapter.

What is interesting about this group of emblems is that they are either short narratives or discussions of iconographic conventions, which may be traditionally applied, sceptically interrogated or withheld altogether. There is a notable absence or restraint in the invocation of the currently fashionable Petrarchist conceit, which was the basis of the literary vogue for the sonnet.

In the editions of Alciato's *Emblemata omnia*, which dispose the different emblems according to their common subject-matter, these emblems appear unsurprisingly under the heading *Amor*. In Tozzi's 1621 edition, for example, they lie between Emblems 105 and 114, and, of course, they exist alongside a whole variety of other topics. Subsequent writers took this section out from that broader context and developed the theme in isolation, devoting whole books exclusively to the exploits of Cupid. This became a separate emblematic genre. The potential for this development was most fully realized in the Low Countries. Strangely, the genre does not appear to have been much practised in Italy, apart from the highly derivative *Emblemata amatoria* (Venice, 1627) of George Chambers, an expatriate recusant Scot.

But one of the most successful of these enterprises was Otto Vænius's *Amorum Emblematum* (Antwerp, 1608). In it Alciato himself is cited as an authority, along with classical love poets and moralists. What Vænius has collected here is an anthology of classic statements on love, or opinions that can be taken from their original context and applied specifically to human sexuality. Plutarch, Aristotle, Ovid, Seneca, Propertius, Cicero, Philostratus, Leone Ebreo, Porphyry, Lucretius, Plato, Tibullus, Publilius Syrus, Virgil and Horace are all cited. Yet there are numerous unacknowledged borrowings from a host of earlier emblematists: Simeoni, Paradin, Scève and others. The book is an anthology of such scattered material, and the fact that it is also very attractively presented contributed to its enormous popularity. The general sentiments or aphorisms of love would, of course, be personalized and particularized when the book was a gift from one lover to another. Yet the erotic polyglottism of this and other works of the kind suggest a whole linguistic universe ruled by Love, which is investigated by the poet in an effort to map its hidden interconnectedness by means of visual and verbal puns, textures and physiognomies.

Love is seen in many guises. He is instantly recognizable from neat visual citations of antique gems and pictures: as when *Eros* and *Anteros* wrestle for the palm, just as they had done in Philostratus' *Icones*. Elsewhere, he playfully usurps the mythographic attributes of most of the classical pantheon. He is the god of emblematic silence, Harpocrates, and holds his finger on his lips. Later, we find that he has filched Mercury's caduceus, because he has become eloquent. He carries the weight of the world on his shoulders, like Atlas or Hercules, but he is stronger than both. Like Jove or Erasmus, he confronts the god Terminus, the god of limits and boundaries. He is greater than Jove, when he violently ejects the leader of the gods from his bedroom. He gets the better of Phoebus in an archery contest. He spurs Hercules on to his virtuous labours. The implication of this playful process of redistributing and reappropriating these iconological attributes and symbols of the ancient gods is to suggest that there is now one true God, who rules the universe. This God is the God of Love: Cupid.

In the book, Cupid also engages in recognizably human activities: he is a soldier, a huntsman (who may try to chase two hares at once), a farmer yoking an ox, and, on several occasions, he appears as a mariner, whose compass points to the pole-star of his mistress's eye, who brings his ship safely to port, and who is the steersman on the lovers' prosperous voyage: 'Qvam bene navigant, qvos amor dirigit' (How well they sail, whose course love directs). He is a gardener, too, grafting a new shoot onto an old stock, so that two might become one: the motto is grafted onto the emblem from classical stock: Virgil's *Eclogues*, 10, 54: 'crescent illae, crescetis, amores' (They will grow, thou, too, my love, will grow) similarly links agriculture and love. He waters his tender plants, he marries the vine to the aged elm and cites Alciato's emblem of love enduring even beyond death (*Etiam post mortem*).

On a baser level, he is a thief, or a cook, boiling his pot over his own flames, or a woodsman, felling a tree by repeated blows: *Patience vaincqt tout*. He is a distiller, extorting tears by means of his secret fires. He is a bad innkeeper, serving poison instead of wine.[4] Who would take up lodgings with him! Some emblems function on an almost purely narrative level, for he does some of the things one expects ordinary lovers to do: he is garrulous, he is silent, he gives gifts, he gets letters, he dreams, he looks wistfully at the dawn.

The diversity of sources and the anthologizer's editorial genius in bringing them together play their part. But the charm of Cornelis Boel's engravings is what makes Vænius's book. There is a versatility here, ranging from 'learned' mythographic allusions to playful scenes of everyday activity. What unity the book has, is achieved by dint of the fact that one character appears in each emblem: the winged boy. But however ordinary the scene, however much the activities of the god might be drawn from 'normal' life, the emblems never thoroughly participate in that realistic, domestic environment that is altogether familiarized by Cats and Visscher. The presence of the winged *putto* transposes the familiar to a thoroughly new poeticized environment. On the other hand, it seems that this child has ransacked learned libraries for the citations from classical poets, moralists and philosophers. When introduced alongside the everyday activities of cooking and gardening, this erudition is thoroughly familiarized. The effect is to surprise, even disarm, the reader, who finds august phrases and sentiments recontextualized, reassigned, redefined.

Given that he is blind, lame and deaf (or at least ought to be),[5] it may seem odd that Cupid has an aversion to the medical profession.[6] He knows his Ovid well enough to realize 'Nullis medicabilis herbis' (There is no medicinal herb) to cure his affliction.[7] Love is his own doctor. He advances on his patient brandishing a specimen bottle, announcing 'To identify your disease, is the beginning of the cure'.[8] Subtle diagnostic skill may not be necessary, however, for the cause of the patient's discomfort is plain for everyone to see: he has been shot in the heart by an arrow! Cupid also engages in strange, comical biological experiments: he transplants Pegasus's wings onto an ass.[9] In pursuit of the same point he flogs a tortoise with his bow.

Vænius reads lectures in number theory according to love's higher mathematical paradoxes: Love is not perfect unless it [is directed] towards one; [Love] makes one harmonious concord from two lovers; the end of love, is that two might become one. Elsewhere he rehearses a Socratic theorem on friendship: one soul in two bodies. He encourages the lover to speculate on infinity and beyond: there are as many shells on the sea shore, leaves in the forest and stars in the sky as there are pains in love.[10]

One of the appeals of the volume is as a pattern book, and Vænius conveniently collects together various symbolic attributes of Love: mirrors;[11] the bee; the salamander; the crocodile; the chameleon (more changeable than Proteus); the compass; the touchstone; the sunflower; the rabbit; the bridle; the moth drawn to the candle flame; various fires that bring light (torches, lanterns and firebrands) or heat (for the use of the distiller or the cook); the churn; the cooking pot; tears; a wreath; a storm-beaten rock caressed and uncaressed by wind and waves. In his immoderate desire he spurns underfoot the yoke, the grain-measure, the mask and the peacock's tail.

The effect is very appealing, which depends in part on Cupid, at least some of the time, being seen as a child. He clings, in one emblem, to his nurse, who happens to be Hope. He cries, when Time attempts to clip his wings. He engages in winsome play: Love applies his shackles amid his pleasant games.[12] More, or perhaps just as, cruelly, he uses a lover for target practice.

Vænius presents no coherent 'philosophy of love'. Many of the emblems are mutually contradictory. Love chastises the tortoise for its tardiness, but the same animal is praised for its perseverance in the story of the tortoise's famous victory over the hare, where it illustrates the paradox *Festina lente* (Hasten slowly). Love is silent, but elsewhere garrulous; he is brave, but can also be fearfully timid. The advice is sensible. The underlying refrain is a warning against love, but it is recognized that it is unlikely anyone will be able to resist the power of the god. The love recommended is, for the most

70

part, honourable, prudent, honest: this Cupid scorns to hide himself under a deceitful mask of subterfuge.

There is also considerable good-natured visual and verbal wit and humour in all of this. This winged infant is able to speak, and though his words give rise to no absolute *nefanda* (impieties), he is certainly guilty of some *nequitiae* (naughtiness). The myth of Daedalus and Icarus is amorously allegorized (illus. 70): one's choice in love should not aim too high, nor too low: marriage should be between those of an equal social station.[13] Erasmus's *Adagia* had given the same forward-looking, sensible advice in a period when, we must remember, many marriages were arranged. However, there is a knowing lasciviousness that peeps around the edges of such decorous commonsense. The usual motto from *Metamorphoses*, II, 137 is extracted from Daedalus's advice to his son in Ovid's story: 'Medio tutissimus ibis' (In the middle you will travel most safely). Other emblematists had earlier used the subject and the motto to recommend, more often than not, the classical

Golden Mean, Horace's 'aurea mediocritas'.[14] However, Vænius was not entirely disingenuous when he knowingly relocated Ovid's 'MEDIO' to a new erotic context: the 'middle', in the fashionable anatomical geometry of the day, centred on the genitals. This centric part is invoked in several engravings. Love, like some seventeenth-century boy scout, kindles his fire by rubbing two sticks together (illus. 71). He holds them, St Andrew's Cross fashion, at the centre of the engraving, decorously concealing his complete nakedness. Of course, the position of the flaming fire that results

71

from this friction indicates only too plainly from whence his flames arise.

Elsewhere Vænius revels in some emblematic *double entendres*, as when he recommends the builder's plumb-line as an invaluable tool in constructing a relationship: 'Verus amans recto nunquam de tramite flectet' (The true lover never bends from the right [or the upright] path). The sentiment so rendered is unobjectionable. The Paris publisher Félix de Magnier had earlier used the motto 'Tramite recto' (By a straight flight) with the image of a hawk soaring upwards from the pages of an open book towards the sun. It symbolized the mind's flight to higher, celestial things.[15] But Cupid's flight does not aim so high, and the thing he aims at is of a more carnal kind. In the engraving Cupid stands meaningfully astride the plumb, revealing a blatantly physical measure, which should, for best results, stand *recto tramite*, upright, or straight up. In these engravings there is an obvious self-conscious and self-reflexive emblematic playfulness: apparent concealment transparently reveals the *res significans*, the significant thing, in its fully engrossed anatomical sense.

Vænius set a fashion for this sort of thing, and his *Amorum Emblemata* appears to have sold well. It gave rise to a whole host of *Zinneminnebeelden* and *Philothecae*. Cupid sported in his pleasure garden: Willem van der Borcht placing him in a *Blom-hof* (Brussels, 1641), W. I. Stam in a *Lusthof* (Amsterdam, 1613). He sits regally enthroned in De Passe's *Thronus Cupidinis* (illus. 72), which

72

continues the Vænius tradition of elegant figures tied to an artful lasciviousness. Cupid's acolytes lie prostrate before him. But how could they otherwise? Each and every one of them has been well and truly shafted by the contents of the fatal quiver. The captioned heading 'Lascivus puer' plays on a double meaning of *lascivus*: sportive, playful, wanton, on the one hand, licentious, lewd, on the other. Lovers die like flies around this wanton 'boy'.

The rest of the book rehearses some naughty Ovidian narratives and depicts appealing *putti* at suggestive erotic play. Cupid disports himself at blind-man's buff, a game to which he is well suited in iconographical terms (illus. 73). *Quid Amor quam vera Palaestra?* (What is love other than a real wrestling school?) makes its own point through the children at play (illus. 74). It conceals at least two further jokes: *palaestra*, a wrestling school, was also a term applied humorously to a brothel. In Greek, various lovemaking postures were called after wrestling holds. The *palaestra*

73

74

was also a school of rhetoric, and we can see that love becomes a subject on which one can cut one's wits.

Vænius's and de Passe's knowing allusiveness and sly lasciviousness are very proper and polite compared to some erotic manuals. The *galans et facetieux* emblems of *Le Centre de l'Amour* (published, we are told, by Cupid himself, but in fact a reissue of the plates of Peter Rollos's *Vita Corneliana*) unashamedly steers its course directly to the middle region.[16] The 'truths' the book pronounces avoid any intellectual complications, addressing themselves to the eyes rather than to the mind: 'Les titres n'en sont embarassez ni enveloppez de mysteres, pour ne pas fatiguer l'esprit pendant que les yeux sont occupez à contempler le Tableau.'[17] The book insistently parodies the emblematic form, while it invokes it. The figures in the emblems are dressed in antique garb not as a recommendation of the sages' classical virtues, but to remind us that Love has been known in every age since the days of Adam: 'What we do to-day, the ancients knew how to do'.[18] The implication is that we should do as they did, not as they say: past precedent condones, or even positively recommends, the indiscretions of the present. Here, as elsewhere, the book adopts a consciously libertine ('libre') approach to its subject, versification and meaning in the interests solely of giving pleasure to its readers – moral distractions are assiduously avoided. The author's guiding principle is the Latin tag *Natura diverso gaudet* (Nature delights in diversity), at once an advertisement for the book's various delights, and a frank recommendation to promiscuous enjoyment. This 'natural' sexuality is, of course, unfettered by conventional morality.

The activities and games the book deals with are more fashionably adolescent – one hesitates to use the word 'adult' – than those Jacob Cats dealt with in his *Kinderspel*. The young people play skittles, tennis and bowls. Each activity carries its own *double entendre* involving balls, shuttlecocks, the middle-region, cones[19] or feathers. These objects are rather monotonously stroked, pushed, knocked, hit, struck, rubbed or touched. As one might assume, the standard of wit is not high. Some of these collections of emblematic *erotica* were designed for, and even by, students. The very title of the *Pugillus Facetiarum* (A Fistful of Witticisms), for example, advertises its undergraduate humour and its dedicatedly relentless, self-pleasing intention: the *res*, significant or otherwise, is firmly taken in hand with pleasure aforethought.

Sacred Love

The sacred appropriation of carnal appetites and desire was long established in Biblical precedent in the Song of Solomon. Here a love poem had been incorporated into the Scriptures as a type of the love between Christ and the Soul, or Christ and the Church. Herman Hugo in the last book of his *Pia Desideria*, and, following him, Francis Quarles and Edmund Arwaker, take up certain scenes from this Biblical narrative. These serve as emblematic idylls –

'framed pictures' describing moments of heightened, passionate longing, in which the human spirit enjoys an intense and exhilarated state of mind. The Beloved and the Spouse leave the city behind and disport themselves in a pastoral setting, an enclosed garden of earthly delights, which shadows heavenly contentment.

Earlier I dealt in some detail with Vænius's erotic emblem book, because in some ways it set a trend in both sacred and profane emblematics for the rest of the useful life of the genre, which did not end in 1686. Indeed, the engraver of the collection, C. Boel, negotiated a successful route from the sacred to the profane and back again: he was responsible not only for Vænius's Cupids, but also for the title-page of the King James Bible.

The vogue for *erotica* was accompanied by an opposite tendency, which directed the reader away from the profane towards the sacred. Or, rather, the fashion was ripe for exploitation as a means of using human lusts to lead one to God. The Jesuits were keen to use popular emblematic forms for the cause of religion – here the love emblem, but elsewhere they exploit the popular appeal of the horoscope, the almanac, the prophecy, and 'Egyptian' wisdom.[20] Vænius, we are told, at the invitation of Queen Isabella of Spain, turned his erotic conceits into spiritual allegories, tracking the profane Cupid step by step with answering spiritual longings and desires. Love is similarly a mariner; the sunflower looks towards heavenly things. Again, Love's mathematics dictate (illus. 75) that 'Love is not perfect unless it is directed to one [person]', 'in unity there is perfection', and that 'the end of love, is that two might become one'.[21] The iconography of the last-named cut shows some iconographic wit: the figure of Terminus, the severe Roman god of boundaries and death, is here reconceived as a hermaphroditic figure on a plinth to intimate the seraphic union of the soul with its divine lover. Each of Vænius's emblems is based on the central symbols of his earlier erotic emblem book, but now conceitedly yoked to a particular spiritual state or doctrinal point: Love is eternal; love instructs; love is pure; perfection is unity, etc., etc. Sometimes the dislocation of a motif from its original erotic context may surprise, even shock, by its reappearance as a religious emblem. But that, as we have seen, is the essential nature of emblem: a detachable and re-attachable ornament. All this is consistent when perceived by the eye of faith: God is everywhere and in all things.

Throughout the collection of religious emblems, Vænius's Amor does not disport himself as the anacreontic, naked, winged

In unitate perfectio .

75

boy. He is decorously clothed, and his companion, Anima, wears a
chaste gown that reaches below the knee. But Vænius does not
simply re-run his erotic emblems in decent costume. There is a
new emotional charge in seeing these slightly chubby children play
out the mysteries of the faith, the spiritual longings, fears, doubts
and despair: the soul is in danger, peril, suffers pain, anguish, longs
for martyrdom. She flounders amid the waves, and cries out, in
fear of drowning. She is hunted by hell-hounds. She weeps under
the lash of her Divine Tormentor.

The eyes of the soul are fixed on heavenly things, yet even in this life, the collection intimates, there are celestial satisfactions to be had. The miniaturized figures give a sense of comfort and reassurance, even joyous celebration. The sanction for this is biblically sound: Christ's words in the Gospels, 'Whosoever shall not receive the kingdom of God as a little child, he shall not enter therein'.[22] Yet, while the figures are childlike, the emotions in many cases are not.

The Amor–Anima formula worked, and became extraordinarily popular. This was a kind of puppet-theatre – or 'poppet-theatre' – that could play out the spiritual fears and longings of the age. Herman Hugo, or rather, we should say Hugo's illustrator, adopted the childlike figures for the *Pia Desideria*. This seems to have been determined by the local visual convention initiated by Vænius, rather than by most of the substance of Hugo's text. Yet Hugo's Anima has a childlike fear of the dark, is lost, engages in silly games when her eternal fate is at stake. In an image of infant helplessness, Anima's first steps in the Faith are supported by the mechanical contrivance of a child's walker (illus. 76).[23] In their verses Arwaker and Quarles do not describe the image in the plate, but render its meaning: 'I am thy child. Teach thy child to go'.[24] Yet the affecting image had an enduring appeal. For Jan Luyken, as for Hugo, Quarles and Arwaker, it was the way God's child was sustained on the road to Heaven: 'den gang ten Hemel'.

But mostly, the emotions invoked by Hugo (and his illustrator) or by his imitators cannot be said to be childish. In the emblem cited immediately above, Arwaker knows that he is not referring to a child, but is caught in 'ambiguous terms'. His real subject is the weakness of the adult *mind*. Nor can the text, as opposed to the images, be said to be designed to make any appeal to childish readers. Hugo's subscripted verses are long, full of a highly wrought Baroque oratory: he heaps up adjectives to create emphasis, there are allusive, periphrastic exercises in metonymy, the conceits are elaborate similes based on Classical mythology or otherwise learned references. The emblem verses are followed by pages of citations from the Church Fathers that refer to the doctrinal issue dealt with earlier in the emblem. Furthermore, Hugo's third book introduced the explicit eroticism of the Song of Solomon into his text.

Quarles had William Marshall copy the plates, but did not feel himself bound to follow Hugo's text slavishly. Although he took much from his original, he felt free to go his own poetic way, appending his verses to copies of the engravings in *Typus Mundi* and the *Pia Desideria*. Arwaker, when he set himself the task of translating Hugo more faithfully, clearly had problems with the Latin. He pruned the mythological allusions, reduced the epithets and the periphrases. Like Quarles, he avoided specifically Catholic doctrinal points, and he severely pruned the citations from the Church Fathers at the end of each emblem. But these are no

76

concessions to a younger readership. His verses are still long-winded. The text is crudely emotionally charged, as if the scenes between Amor and Anima were being played out in the Castle of Otranto: 'icy Horror chills my freezing Blood' (1, 10); 'The shackl'd Captive . . . shakes with wild Affright' (1, 14). The skeletal figure of Death stalks all and sundry:

> Nor *Sex* nor *Age* the grim Destroyer spares,
> Unmov'd alike by *Innocence* and *Tears*.[25]

However ludicrously grotesque we might find this, it is the stuff of nightmares for any self-respecting sensitive innocent. Nevertheless, it must be said that there is a calculated, crude effectiveness in all of this, which depends on the fact that spiritual doubts and fears are graphically registered, carnally embodied, in terms of the expense of bodily fluids: tears and blood.

Extreme, over-theatrical, and lugubriously melancholic postures are struck:

> I wish not time for *Laughter*; . . .
> . . . .
> All I desire, is time for *Grief* and *Tears*. (1, 13)

In reading these lines it is important to bear in mind the melodramatic quality and the emotional excesses of much of the writing for the tragic stage at Arwaker's time, and the emblem writer would not seem to be out of line with the adult tastes of his age when he strikes these notes.

Arwaker had promised to exclude Hugo's reliance on pagan mythology from his verses. But this was not to make the book more accessible to an underage readership. For all his sympathy for the truths embodied in Hugo's book, he was much too Protestant to bring himself to partake in Hugo's post-Tridentine rhetorical belief that pagan theology and Christianity were compatible. Nevertheless, he could not exclude the mythological references entirely. And when they do appear, they carry on the element of Gothic horror that pervades the emotional temperature of the volume. 'Sad *Philomel* unlocks her mournful Throat' (1, 14). Time appears as the devourer of children:

> This Truth the *Ancients* weightily Exprest,
> Who made the *Father* on his Off-spring feast. (1, 13)

If this weighty presence were not enough, expressed as an undeniable Truth, endorsed by the almost overbearing authority of the '*Ancients*', the babes-in-the-wood nightmare scenario of the Minotaur's maze is invoked as a mere shadow of the terrors that await the lost soul:

> Not the fictitious Labyrinth of old
> Did in more dubious Paths its Guests infold; (2, 2)

Again, the spiritual message is graphically incarnated: the sad, mournful infolding and devouring of the human frame.

If Arwaker's rhetoric invokes bodily fluids, Mme de Guyon's translation of Hugo is airier. She consistently invokes breathings, pantings, sighs and whispers – the whole Aeolist repertory of religious enthusiasm. In her French adaptation she pruned Hugo even further than Arwaker dared. It is compressed, intensely emotional and highly moving. The text becomes an introspective dramatic monologue or extended soliloquy. She did not simply excise Hugo's Baroque excrescences, she relocated the emotional centre. But not towards a putative childish reader. Where Hugo's first emblem is based on a contrast between the darkness of spiritual night as opposed to the illumination conferred by the face of Christ, the true Phoebus, Mme de Guyon finds enlightenment in a self-lacerating spiritual darkness: consciousness of sin and a sense of unworthiness leads to conversion. This emphasis on spiritual paradoxes, light in darkness, love amidst self-hatred is typical of the passionate Quietistic piety that informs the collection. 'I hate this ungrateful heart; I love my Chastisement'.[26]

Hugo frequently refers to Love as a snare and a deception, which needs to be tamed by rational means. Mme de Guyon emphasizes, even glories in, the corrupted state of the human will. For her, the way of human amendment is through pain, desire and love, the very emotions that Hugo eyes with enormous suspicion. In fact, Mme de Guyon comes to long for pain, because her pain might attract the attention of the Heavenly Lover. The Soul is so corrupt, that nothing except its sufferings can commend it to the 'Adoreable Master'. Longing for union with the Creator leads to extreme emotions: 'yea, hell, even hell, might I be but near to thee, should be to me a blessed inheritance, its Torments should be sweet unto me. Heaven with all its joys without thee would be my torments'. Such a faith renders even the terrors of death and the last judgment into a game of hide-and-seek (illus. 77).

The Amor–Anima formula continued in use. Hugo and Vænius were translated into almost every European vernacular language. Editions of the original or the vernacular adaptations remained continually in print for 200 years – often well into the nineteenth century. Further, others saw the potential of the emblematic formula and adopted and adapted it. Faith, Hope and Charity, for example, appear as angelic children in Gulielmus Hesius's *Emblemata sacra de Fide, Spe, Charitate* (Antwerp, 1636). Hesius had the good fortune to employ the brilliant woodcut designer Christoffel Jegher to fashion his cherubs for the *picturae*. They delightedly play all sorts of musical instruments and games throughout the volume. A good example of the effectiveness of these is the emblem 'Spes viuida semper amanti est' (Lively Hope is always in love). The woodcut, set into the text without a frame – at a date when the woodcut had been all but totally superseded by copper engraving – shows Spes throwing up her hands in delight

77

as a sky-rocket flies heavenwards. Jegher's Spes is 'in love' because, of course, she appears in the iconographic, cherubic panoply of Cupid. But what Jegher's brilliance brings to the cut is to make her in no uncertain terms *vivida*: lively, animated, full of life, vigorous, yes, we can even say, if we mean 'true to the life of the emotion', she is indeed 'true to *life*': *vivida* would have been the term any contemporary art critic would have used to describe her. Hesius's verse does the rest: we all aim for the skies, Heaven is our goal, our blessed destination. The underpinning scriptural verse is from I Corinthians 13: 'Charitas omnia sperat' (Charity . . . hopeth all things).[27]

Some kind of miniaturizing process was obviously required when figures were operating in the theatre of the Heart.[28] Figures shrunk to childish dimensions appear in the *Cor Iesu* series of emblems, where their size enables them to crawl into the confined and obscure corners. This produces some interesting effects: the visual sphere is miniaturized, but its intense focus paradoxically and grotesquely magnifies the problems visualized. A further mutation of this form occurs in the cardiomorphic emblem, in which the heart functions as a kind of visual synecdoche for the human soul – the physical part standing for the whole.

In 'The Circus Animals' Desertion', W. B. Yeats would later see the 'foul rag and bone shop of the heart' as the standing place from which 'all ladders start'. Christopher Harvey anticipated this in his 'Ladder of the Heart', the stanzaic form of which mirrored the ladder. Yet the religious sensibility of the age insisted on tidying, mopping, cleansing, sweeping out the trash and reforming the heart into a clean habitation.

SIX

Fame's Double Trumpet

Pompes, Pagents, Motions, Maskes, Scutchions, Emblems, Impreases,
strange trickes and deuises...[1]

the triumph itself requires jollity[2]

Videsne...?
Video et gaudeo![3]

Not without the utmost pleasure should Emblems be seen, read,
meditated upon, understood, discussed, sung and heard.[4]

Emblematics, given the date of their conception and subsequent development, could never be a totally self-pleasing exercise. The genre emerges from a distinct perception of the poet's social role and function. As a public utterance the emblem was bound to observe certain responsibilities towards an essentially public, epideictic rhetoric: a duty to administer praise or blame. In this its appropriate iconographic attribute is Fame's trumpet (illus. 78).

In considering the emblem from a chronological perspective, it is important to remember that many books of this kind referred to a single, special occasion, and involved a specific gratulatory design. Zincgref in 1619 styled this species of emblem the 'emblema singulare'.[5] The term is more apt than may be realized at first unblushed view. It, of course, implies a 'one off', an emblem for a special event, but, in the context, the term should be translated as 'an emblem (or an emblematic programme) dedicated to a single (and, by implication, exceptional) individual'. Often these emblems had in their sights only a single, ideal reader, or, however public the occasion, one ideal spectator: the patron or dedicatee. Many emblematic manuscripts were precisely of this kind, magnifying the deeds and accomplishments of an individual in a private act of fealty between the author and his noble lord. In the English tradition, Thomas Palmer, Geffrey Whitney and Henry Peacham all produced manuscript works of this kind. When published, those emblem books commemorating a particular occasion were intended to serve as a permanent record of what would have been otherwise lost, even though these may have been a rather muted, black-and-white reflection of a very colourful show. The publication's hidden (or not so hidden) agenda may have been to bring together a specific religious or political community in the interests of a common cause. On the other hand, the same strategy could be satirically directed to arouse popular fear and loathing towards a common perceived enemy, harnessing an archetypal folk memory of particular resentments and animosities in order to vilify and anathematize. This latter tendency will, of course, be more prominent at times of national anxiety and crisis.

78

These factors also go some way towards explaining the necessarily ephemeral nature of the genre. Zincgref's adjective 'singulare' also points to the visual and verbal opulence of works of this kind: they are, indeed, 'extraordinary' works designed for 'extraordinary' individuals for a 'unique', 'special' occasion. Yet the emblem's dedicated commitment to festivity and to particular satire has caused difficulties, even embarrassment, for some commentators.

Henry Green rather regretfully conceded that 'emblem books . . . were generally the trifles for a day',[6] but missed the point that certain species of *emblemata* were required to be just that: trifles. Moreover, they were occasional, festive outpourings: 'for a day' rather than for all time. It is essential to recognize that a sense of ephemerality and occasion was the very essence of many emblematic productions, just as it was for the emblematic sister art, the court masque. Ruscelli early on grasped the essential connection between the figures in emblem books and those 'in plays, and in jousts, and in masquerades'.[7] Colonna's proto-emblematic *Hypnerotomachia* (illus. 79) contains all sorts of triumphal 'Pompes' and 'Pageants' that anticipate later developments in the emblem genre. To underestimate the strength of this tradition of public celebration, and to fail to appreciate the importance of the festive, the ceremonial, the comic, the playful, the jocose and the satiric is to misunderstand the aims and

79

purposes of particular emblem books, and, indeed, the genre as a whole. These were public, festive ejaculations in the Renaissance *silva* tradition: collections including epigrams of praise, encomia, odes, epithalamia, genathliacon, consolations, valedictions. The culture of the Renaissance and Baroque would seem to have anticipated by several hundred years the solemn follies of the 1960s counter-culture, which desired to 'institute a sense of festivity into public life whereby people could . . . wear fancy dress' if not exactly 'all the time', as the Underground might have wished, at least with a gratifying frequency.[8] At such celebrations, everyday dress would be discarded in favour of masks and allegorical costumes, in order to impersonate gods, nymphs and satyrs. As noted above, the Roman festivals described by Apuleius and Dionysius of Hallicarnassus are precursors of, and to some extent sources of, the emblem. This common image stock brought together the emblem books and the rhetoric of public celebration.[9]

Emblems and Devices for Festivities and Funerals

Mario Praz's bibliography that concludes his *Studies in Seventeenth-century Imagery* seems to betray a similar embarrassment to Green's. It is strangely and inconsistently bifurcated. It is divided into two parts: 'A Bibliography of Emblem Books' and 'Emblems and Devices for Festivities, Funerals, Degrees, etc'.[10] The second division of the bibliography comprises some 30-odd pages that include various *Acta*, triumphal entries, *Glückseligkeiten*, *Iubel-Gemälde*, *Solenes Fiestas*, *Festivos cultos*, *Gratulationes*, *Epithalamia Symbolica*, *Genii Nuptiales*, *Esequie*, *Funebre Pompae*, tournaments, triumphal arches. These publications celebrate anniversaries, coronations, weddings, births, royal visits, academic ceremonies. They extol past or present achievements of royal households, holy saints, or princes of the Church, living or dead. The number of such publications, Praz notes, is vast. Nor does he pretend to cover them exhaustively. The implication behind this is that these works are somehow different, even, perhaps, qualitatively inferior, to those in the primary bibliography of 'Emblem Books'. But the truth of the matter is that the division between the two parts of the bibliography is figuratively paper thin. Many of the emblematic works that appear in the 'Bibliography of Emblem Books' might just as legitimately have found a place among the 'Emblems and Devices for Festivities', for there is no discernible difference between them. Their inclusion in the second section would have enlarged the catalogue of occasional festive emblems and brought the two bibliographies more into balance.

For example, in the first part of the bibliography Praz includes various *Essequie*, by Alessandro Adimari (Florence, 1614), Giovanni Altoviti (Florence, 1612), Aurelio Biondi (Florence, 1590), Andrea Cavalcanti (Florence, 1634), Carlo Roberto Dati (Florence, 1644) and Renato Malsucio (Padua, 1664). Ottavio Caputi (Naples, 1599) and Baldo Catani (Rome, 1591) give us two works entitled *La Pompa funerale*, while Marcello Marciano describes *Pompe funebre* (Naples, 1666). Carolus Bovio provides an 'honoraris tumuli et funebris pompae descriptio' (Rome, 1671), Felice Benedetti, *L'Imprese ... rappresentate nel tumulo ...* (Aquila, 1599), Joseph Cajetan Khuen, *Apparatus Funebris Litterarius ...* (Munich, 1727).

On a happier note, we have various emblematic celebration of weddings and births: Engelbert Bischoff's *Epithalamium* (Vienna, 1699) was followed after a decent interval by a *Genathliacon* (Vienna, 1701). Filippo Maria Bonino supplies a *Racconto historico del felicissimo maritaggio* (Vienna, 1677), and Johan Ebermaier a SYZYGIA *Connubialis* (Stuttgart, 1653).

Ecclesiastical dignitaries are remembered or fêted in Ottavio Boldoni's *Theatrum* (Milan, 1635), Carolus Bovio's *Heroica virtutum ... Clementis XI* (Rome, 1702), which did double duty as a celebration of the author's own 90th birthday. In addition, there are Benedetto Buommatei's *Descrizion delle Feste* (Florence, 1632), and Principio Fabricii, *Delle allusione, imprese, et emblemi ... sopra la vita di Gregorio XIII* (Rome, 1588).

The visits and triumphal entries of temporal lords are commemorated by Willem vander Beke, *Triumphalis Introitus* (Antwerp, 1636), Joannes Bocchius *'Pompae triumphales', 'Descriptio Pompae et Gratulationis'* and *'Descriptio Triumphi et Spectaculorum'* (Antwerp, 1602), Cornelius Graphaeus, *Spectaculorum ... Mirificus Apparatus* (Antwerp, 1550), Jan Baptista Houwaert, *Sommaire beschrijvinghe van de triumphantelijcke Incompst ...* (Antwerp, 1579), Peter Antonio Bendinelli, *Il Nobilissimo ... torneo* (Piacenza, 1574). Academic festivities are found in Paris Gille, *Juvavi ter felix Urna* (Salzburg, 1668), and in his *Corona Gratulatoria seu Gratulationes diversae* (Salzburg, 1681) and in Caspar Mandl, *Emblemata philosophica* (Dillingen, 1692).

These are only a selection of works that might equally properly have found a place in the second part of Praz's bibliography. But I can perceive absolutely no difference in kind between the works mentioned in the preceding paragraphs as 'Emblem Books', and the works relegated to the 'festive' second division of his bibliography. It would be tedious to labour the point by heaping up even more examples of this kind. However, I note that I have not even begun to mention in this connection the many works that were devoted to the cultivation of the royal image of Louis XIV by Le Jay, Menestrier, Le Moyne, La Rue, Le Vasseur, Le Vavasour, and others. The point by now has, I think, been sufficiently made.

Festive eruptions characterize the genre as a whole. They can hardly be described as late, decadent developments in the history of the genre. Festivity was present from the very beginning, as can

be seen, for example, in the explosion of triumphal pageantry in
Colonna's emblematic dream vision (illus. 80). Alciato's manuscript was composed, after all, 'in festivis horis' (during the holiday
period). The very first vernacular French emblem book, Guillaume
de la Perrière's *Le Theatre des bons engins* had its origin in a royal
visit to Toulouse in 1535. On this occasion, La Perrière presented
Marguerite de Navarre with 50 manuscript emblems, regretting
only that he did not have time to complete the 100 he had

80

intended. These were duly prepared for publication in 1536, without accompanying woodcuts. The finished work, complete with its
emblematic *picturae*, had to wait until 1539 to see the light of day.
With a fine sense of self-mockery, the author alludes to his slowness in perfecting the work in his final emblem, which shows Diligence 'en grand magnificence' seated in her triumphal car drawn
by ants. This emblem immediately precedes a concluding epistle to
'ladicte tresillustre princesse', which thoroughly confesses the
author's devotion to the royal personage, while acknowledging his
slow-paced negligence in following through with the swiftness
such an enterprise deserved.[11] The shaping impetus of the book
from beginning to end, from its initial occasion to the last pages of
its eventual publication, was obviously festive, gratulatory, and
occasional. Janus, the god of the beginning of the Year, presided
over ancient triumphs, and, as Vincenzo Cartari tells us, gave his

name to the triumphal arch.[12] It was actually called a Janus. It is generically appropriate, therefore, that the god stands at the beginning of La Perrière's theatre of emblems (illus. 81). The book was itself, after all, a beginning of sorts.

Sambucus, who was among other things a court poet, included several individual festive emblems within his *Emblemata*, which appears to be specifically constructed along the lines of the *silva* tradition outlined above. He includes a betrothal poem, 'On the

81

betrothal of John Ambius, an Englishman, and Alba Rollea, the daughter of Dr Arnold of Ghent'. He celebrates their union with a musical offering, an image of their harmonious relationship. The author summons gods and goddesses to bless the couple, and strews roses, myrtles and laurels before them. Mirth later turns to sadness as he erects a funeral monument in verse to the memory of Lotichius; and he engraves an epitaph for a young man cut off in his prime at the early age of twenty.[13]

Festive notes are struck on the very title-pages of other emblematic works. Heinrich Khunrath's *Amphitheatrum sapientiae aeternae* (Hamburg, 1595) announces its emblematic, joyous wisdom with a three-fold 'Hallelu-IAH!', an elaborate 'Phy' thrust into the face of the very face of the Devil himself: 'Phy diabolo!' Emblematic jubilees would be celebrated in festive recognition of the Holy

Trinity.[14] The Virgin would be celebrated in pious works of Marian devotion. Fantastic and even more elaborate constructions would be erected: an emblematic altar and a 'Ballet emblématique' graced a royal entry into Lyon in 1658.[15] One suspects, given the nature of the work and the place, that Claude-François Menestrier would have had a hand in this production.

The ephemeral nature of such festivities meant that in some cases there are no surviving detailed records to commemorate the event. Material of this festive kind would have bulked even larger in our consciousness of the form had these existed. It was far from uncommon for royal visitors or ecclesiastical dignitaries to be greeted by, or presented with, emblematic displays on their arrival or departure. When Elizabeth I made her visits to Oxford and Cambridge, the students hung emblems and devices from college windows. Unfortunately, no detailed record appears to have been made of the images and verses.

Some emblem books were mere paper exercises, but many others commemorated real monuments and real events. This was in some sense street theatre on a large scale – public celebration, involving stage machinery, allegorical spectacles, and perform-ances in costume and song. These public festivals were essentially 'civilizing' in their functions, promoting by means of public performance the civic virtues: Concord, Justice, Fortitude, Temperance. This was a programme erected on biblical principles, fulfilling Solomon's vision of Wisdom uttering her words 'in the streets, in the top of the high places, in the chief concourse, and in the opening of the gates'.[16] The books commemorating these civic celebrations would describe them in a fashion 'true to life, just as it was', in the words of Cornelius Graphaeus's title-page to his *Miri-ficus Apparatus* (Antwerp, 1550).[17] But their printed utterance must have been a black-and-white shadow of the colourful and magnif-icent entertainment for the eye and the mind. The printed text was no more than a set of ephemeral programme notes for those who were there. Or, when produced retrospectively, they explained what must have been a sequence of visual puzzles, arising from an erudite, recondite imagery, which could not yield up all its mean-ing to a single glance. Of this kind is the anonymous *Narrazione dell' Apparato fatto da P.P. di S. Domenico, nello loro chiesa in Cremona* (Cremona, 1734), which describes the church decorations at the canonization of Pope Pius v. These included sixteen emblems designed by Giuseppe Natali affixed to the pillars of the aisle. Similarly, the sumptuous folio *Racconto delle sontuose esequie fatte alla Serenissima Isabella, reina di Spagna* (Milan, 1645) records in engravings by Paolo Bianchi the 32 emblems that decorated her catafalque.

In other instances, however, the books themselves were the festive celebration. Their sumptuously ambitious designs reflect this. Martin Gosky produced a mammoth 585-page folio celebration of Duke August of Wolfenbüttel.[18] Mara Wade has recently drawn attention to elephantine motifs in the *Triumphus Nuptialis Danicus* (Copenhagen, 1648), that records the festivities surrounding the celebration of the wedding of Prince-Elect Christian of Denmark in 1634.[19] Ottavio Boldoni produced his *Theatrum Temporaneum Aeternitati* (Milan, 1636) to celebrate the life, works and distinguished genealogy of Cardinal Monti, who had been elevated to that rank the previous year. The engraver, Paolo Bianchi, allowed his imagination and artistic fantasy full reign in his grotesque, playful ornamentation of the frames around 44 emblems. We come close in some of this to illustrated hagiographies. But where the saints' lives tend to have plates that function simply as narrative illustrations of events in the holy person's earthly career, emblems celebrate – under the veil of symbols and allegories – the inner qualities, ideals, aspirations and moral principles that governed such lives.

The Jesuits were just the men for 'some delightful ostentation, or show, or pageant, or antic, or firework'. They might even, consciously or unconsciously, show themselves capable of producing 'eruptions or breaking out of mirth'. Indeed, they could themselves become the subjects of the mirth, as we can see from Praz's amusing account of the quarrel between the young Jesuit, Menestrier and the priest Claude Le Laboureur, which rendered both men ridiculous.[20] The quoted phrases at the beginning of the current paragraph are, of course, from Shakespeare's *Love's Labours Lost*, v. i, 103–6, and they show how schoolmasters and teachers might become advisers to a royal household on matters relating to festive entertainments. Truly, the Jesuits were indeed the masters of lavish emblematic celebration, bringing all their arts of post-Tridentine eloquence and iconographic sophistication to bear on their praise of notable political or ecclesiastical dignitaries and saintly heroes. As Praz has noted, De Backer-Sommervogel lists many device books. These occupy fifteen closely printed columns.[21] This gives some general idea of the vast scope and scale of the Jesuits' activities. There were emblematic ballets, madrigals, heraldic displays, ceremonies and rejoicings designed and performed under their auspices. Carolus Bovio's *Rhetoricae Suburbanum* (Rome, 1676), for instance, runs through a whole range of elegant gratulatory forms: odes, emblems, and theatrical productions. The book celebrates the heroes and the heroics of the Faith in displays of engraved devices. There are also naked emblems with precisely described pictures, which are not only expounded and explained, but joyously hymned and sung.[22] The attributes of the Virgin are praised. The most extravagant in a book of extravagances is an operatic performance on the subject of Aeneas' journey to the underworld, where the speeches are punctuated by 'symphonia'. One of the most playful of these contrivances is a barking trio sung by Cerberus from the Gates of Hell, a 'Symphonia ad Cerberi latratum', with a part assigned to each of his heads. This barking is, of course, *ad maiorem gloriam Dei*! In return, joy is said to pour down from Heaven itself.

Not least, the Jesuits occasionally made an exhibition of themselves. The *Imago primi saeculi* was a flamboyant celebration in the form of a printed folio of the first centenary of the founding of the Jesuit Order in the Low Countries. The book attracted the criticism of the Jansenists because of its visual and verbal opulence. Its 'lascivious' rhetoric seemed incongruous when applied to an institution founded on a vow of poverty. The copperplate engravings were lavish and many. Those who knew, could estimate the cost. The volume was further loaded in each and every rift with the ore of golden eloquence. The incense of rhetoric is bought at a cheaper rate, but the message was the same. In the eyes of many it was a totally misdirected work – a triumphal arch to commemorate a century of marvellous achievement – but erected *Ad maiorem gloriam Societatis* rather than to the greater glory of God.

The Jesuits in this book appropriated the image-stock and applied it monotonously and insistently to themselves. Amor divinus applies himself as he had done before in profane and sacred emblems to his profession as a cooper. But this time he is working for the Jesuit Order (illus. 82). He hammers out on his anvil the hot iron into a circle, as before, but now the cooper's art symbolizes a pre-Einsteinian space–time theorem, where the straight-line continuum of the achieved century is bent into a projected hieroglyphic circle of an eternity of Jesuit dominion. Surrounding the frame are the engraved fruits of achievement, a harvest festival of grapes, apples and pears. Behind the Divine smithy grows the proud and lofty palm, triumphant over adversity, and the Heaven-aspiring heliotrope. In the distance a ship continues its voyage, its

ÆTERNVM
FORMET IN ORBEM

IHS

Iungenda primo fæcula fæculo
Rex fæculorum fabricat, ANNVLVM
Æternitatis in perennis
Fœdera connubij daturus

82

sails filled with a prosperous gale. Roses and lilies – the flowers of the Virgin – bloom around the blacksmith's door. The engraving's boast is as grandiloquent as it is finely wrought. As the book begins, so it continues. The fire from the smitten flint is St Ignatius, the founder of the Order. Noah's ark is the Society sailing triumphantly through the waves of adversity. However, the image cannot help but imply a smug, exultant superiority over all those unrighteous, wicked heretics who have, by this stage, drowned in the foaming flood that sustains the Order's onward progress. A bear (illus. 83), engaged in its usual emblematic activity of licking its cub into shape, is none other than the rough tongue of the Jesuit preacher, refining his (by implication) infantile and malleable congregation into whatever shape the Society might wish: 'Vos mentes fingite lingua' (Polish your minds with [his] tongue). A labourer in a vineyard, going about his normal, seasonal occupation of dressing his vines, is pressganged into the service of a witty paradox: 'Nil dabit inde minus' (It will give nothing, unless it is made less). But the bucolic innocence of the image leads to a threatening, apocalyptic verbal shuffle, which exposes the Order's ruthless pursuit of sin and heresy: *Societas Iesu*, anagrammatically transposed, becomes 'Vitiosa seces' (Cut off the wicked things).[23] The fate of these emblematic 'cuttings from the vine', we can be

Vos mentes fingite linguâ. ⎰ *Sy de leden,* ⎱ *Ghy de seden.*

almost certain, is to be burnt: now or later. In the volume, we may find that the pagan pantheon has been converted, and now works in full support of the Order. The *Imago* lets all stops out in a triumphant organ-blast of self-praise, invoking an unashamed, post-Tridentine rhetoric: Mercury points, in his time-honoured fashion, to the right path (illus. 84). But here he does not quite as he had done previously. The motto 'Hac monstrat eundum' (He/It shows the way we must go), now appears in a more restricted, overcoded application than Alciato or the previous humanist emblematists would have suspected or allowed: Mercury's directions are none other than those found in Ignatius's book of *Spiri-*

Hac monſtrat eundum. { *Vraeght hier raedt, Eer ghy gaet.*

84

tual Exercises, a more reliable guide, we are infallibly assured, than Ariadne's thread through the labyrinth of this world. We are also led to believe that the Jesuits also hold the keys to Hell itself: Orpheus's lyre, by whose aid he softened the heart of the infernal king to win back the shade of his departed wife, is interpreted as the 'cithara Iesu', which is immediately anagrammatically crucified into 'Eucharistia', administered, almost certainly, according to the Catholic rather than the Protestant rite. Self praise, they say, is no commendation. But this volume served in the eyes of many only to confirm their perception of the Order's massive self-conceit at that date. The publication rather blackened their reputation, rather than enhanced it,[24] as the articles of the faith were trivialized into anagrams and acrostics, and piety became little more than a witty game.

Gratulatory and Political Designs: Two English Examples

The most famous piece of English emblematic gratulation was, of course, William Marshall's emblematic frontispiece for *Eikon Basilike* (illus. 85). This established the executed Charles I as a martyr. The King rejects a golden crown of this world, and accepts the crown laid up for the faithful in Heaven. The palm, weighted down but resisting its oppression, and the storm-beaten rock symbolize

85

the King's steadfastness. The imagery was particularly potent and long-lived. Copies were made by many printers. Single prints survive and copies went on being made even into the eighteenth century both in Britain and on the Continent. Stained glass windows, paintings in churches, embroidery pictures, one in the Victoria & Albert Museum, all repeated Marshall's image or its copies to the point where the symbolism was imprinted on the national consciousness. The particular ends and purposes of the emblematically encoded print are hard to miss.

In some cases, the particular gratulatory design of an emblem book has been overlooked, even though it is proclaimed from every corner of the volume. Needless to say, failure to recognize the book's occasional and festive nature has contributed to a misunderstanding of its author's intentions. Whitney's *Choice of Emblems*, mistakenly credited for many years as the 'first' English emblem book, is famously a case in point. Rosemary Freeman influentially saw Whitney as little more than a translator and anthologizer almost entirely lacking in originality.[25] His printed book, however, actually formed part of a series of magnificent civic pageants and triumphal entries to welcome Robert Dudley, Earl of Leicester, and his train into the major cities of the United

Provinces in 1585. Whitney was, to all intents and purposes, nothing less than a propagandist for the English interventionist policy in the Low Countries.[26] Subsequent embarrassment at the failure of the military campaign, and the passage of time, has conspired at first to muffle, and then to obscure, the precise nature of Whitney's intentions. But the subject of Whitney's *Choice* was stated plainly at the outset: to blazon forth the 'Dudlaei *illustria facta*' ('the magnificent deeds of Dudley'), and as such it was 'required' as part of a concerted effort to publicize Leicester's campaign against the Pope and the Spanish forces.[27] The book was meant to project his public image, and to create a climate of opinion, both in England and United Provinces, that would render the English 'invasion' acceptable. Since the occasional and explicitly political nature of the work has often been overlooked, it may be worth examining in detail its strategies of appropriation and particular gratulation.

Whitney placed his book under the aegis of the Roman god Janus. His image stands not at the beginning, but at the structural centre. Looking backwards and forwards, the god advertises Whitney's strategy of relating ancient examples of Roman military heroism, courage, and valour to present-day heroes. Janus controls 'time past, and time to comme', 'the newe, and eeke the oulde'.[28]

Ambiguity was evidently considered appropriate to the double-faced god. In Whitney's *Choice* puns may be negotiated between the verbal and the visual. Often such puns are used to praise particular individuals. The dedication to Edward Dyer of the fable *De morte, et amore* ('Of Death and Love') is based on the mortal implications of the dedicatee's name, while the emblem on the dyer's art, *In colores* ('On colours'), adapted from Alciato's original emblem, is transposed into a hymn of praise to the English 'Dyer most of fame'. Elsewhere, puns may be more obscurely heraldic. Alciato's helmet, which has become a hive for bees in *Ex bello pax* (From war comes peace), is appropriated to 'Hugh Cholmeley': the Cholmondeley crest was a squire's helmet.[29] Janus's responsibility for such practices is driven home in the manuscript motto *Ianus quid* ('What Janus is').[30] This contains a punning reference to Jan van der Does, father and son, Whitney's Dutch hosts, active promoters of the Anglo-Dutch alliance, and Whitney's literary patrons. Both men were known by the Latinized form of their name, Janus Dousa. It must have occurred to Whitney that the double identity of this Dutch Janus agreed almost exactly with the conventional representations of the double-visaged god, one of whose faces was shown as that of a man of mature years, the other as much younger.[31] The Dousas must have seemed like real-life embodiments of this traditional iconography: the father expressing the mature face, the son the more youthful, both sharing the name Janus. The joke has a serious side, in that it also may serve to compliment the pair on their common wisdom and prudence. Here we have an example of a kind of semiotic overcoding, in which a general moral symbol is applied specifically to an individual. Here it is used for the purposes of praise. Later in this chapter we will see that overcoding can work no less effectively for the purposes of satire.

Specific emblematic gratulation can be seen in Whitney's volume. His praise of English justice is most fully explored in 'Sine iustitia, confusio' (Without justice there is disorder), which is based, in part, on an emblem with the same motto in Barthélemy Aneau's *Picta poesis*.[32] Aneau's *pictura*, a cut his printer had earlier designed for a projected edition of Marot's translation of Ovid's *Metamorphoses*, illustrates the war between the elements before they were disposed into order by 'God – or kindlier nature'.[33] Aneau turns his Ovidian source and *pictura* into an emblem on Justice, by comparing the primordial confusion of the elements to the strife-riven state of things when Justice is absent.[34] Whitney made use of the *Picta poesis* woodcut design and had it copied at the Plantin press. He considerably expanded Aneau's eight-line epigram. He describes the confusion of the elements at greater length than Aneau had done, with the Ovidian original directly in view. This was a debt he did not wish to hide. Ovid's lines are cited in Whitney's side note to his epigram. Whitney then gives ten lines to a description of the prosperity that ensued after disorder was quelled, when the 'goodly worlde' was created. The original of this passage is not in Aneau, but in Ovid.[35] Similarly, Whitney follows Ovid rather than Aneau, by describing the subsequent history of the created world, the four ages of gold, silver, brass and iron.[36] The Age of Iron receives Whitney's most extensive treatment. He sets out the various mischiefs and crimes that occur in this last and worst phase, when prosperity and plenty decline and abuses abound. Whitney at this point makes Aneau's connection between primordial Chaos and the degenerate world where Justice is lacking:

Nowe, into the worlde, an other *Chaos* came.

Thus far Whitney has closely followed Ovid's scheme. He now abandons Aneau and Ovid. In Ovid's account, Justice at last flees from a world that has become steeped in blood.[37] For Whitney, however, this is the moment when Justice arrives:

> But *God*, that of the former heape: the heauen and earthe did frame,
> And all things plac'd therein, his glorye to declare:
> Sente *Ivstice* downe vnto the earthe: such loue to man hee bare.

Where Ovid's God was almost synonymous with nature,[38] Whitney's is hardly distinguishable from the Christian, or the Psalmist's God: his handiwork declares his glory; He loves mankind sufficiently to send His emissary to earth for man's salvation; and He regards the reformation of men as a challenge as great as that He faced when He created the world out of darkness.[39] But Whitney's departure from the Ovidian model cannot be attributed simply to a preference for Christianity over the cashiered pantheon of the Graeco-Roman world. Whitney abandons Ovid in favour of Virgil, and in so doing transmutes Aneau's sober admonition on the necessity of justice into patriotic congratulation on the righteousness of Elizabethan imperial ambitions. Where Ovid saw the decline from the Golden to the Iron Age as a presage of the near-universal destruction of humanity,[40] Virgil, following the esoteric tradition of the Sibylline prophecies, viewed the Age of Iron as the end of an era, whose completion ushered in universal reform, and the return of a new Golden Age:

> Now is come the last age of the song of Cumae; the great line of the centuries begins anew. Now the Virgin returns, the reign of Saturn returns; now a new generation descends from heaven on high. Only do thou, pure Lucina, smile on the birth of the child, under whom the iron brood shall first cease and a golden race spring up throughout the world.[41]

What Virgil meant is irrelevant. The meaning was beyond doubt for every patriotic Englishman: 'iam redit et Virgo' referred not only to Virgil's Goddess of Justice, Astraea, but to the coming of the Royal Virgin, Elizabeth, whose coronation fulfilled the Virgilian prophecy by bringing about a new Golden Age of plenty, prosperity, justice and peace. William Camden, the English antiquary, records that the words 'Jam redit et virgo' were applied to Elizabeth 'in the beginning of her . . . Reign'.[42] Whitney does not quote the famous Virgilian tag, but his allusion to Virgil's prophetic vision is so plain, and the identification of Elizabeth and Astraea so well known, that, by the time Whitney finishes embroidering upon Aneau's original, the identity of the Latin epigram's abstract 'Regina . . . Ivstitia' has been rendered unmistakable. Such concealment of particular intimations behind the public statement of commonplaces is of the essence of emblematic composition. Yet Whitney's withholding of explicit identification is not opaque. The land where Justice flourishes, this 'paradice, of blisse', is revealed as 'happie England', whose institutions of Justice are founded on Reformation principles, a recognition of the 'dewties' to both 'God, and Prince'.[43]

Whitney does not confine his gratulation to his sovereign. Virgil's prophecy also embraced 'the golden race' that was to spring up under the tutelage of the returned Virgin ('toto surget gens aurea mundo'). Accordingly, Whitney's final couplet, introduced for the first time in the printed text of the emblem, plainly declares his nationalistic pride:

> Then happie England most, where *Ivstice* is embrac'd:
> And eeke so many famous men, within her chaire are plac'd.

These final words recall an earlier emblem (*Choice*, page 38) dedicated to Sidney, in which 'iustice cheare' is similarly allotted to famous men:

> men of iudgement graue,
> Of learning, witte, and eeke of conscience cleare,
> In highe estate, are fitte theire seates to haue,
> And to be stall'd, in sacred iustice cheare.

Accordingly, we may infer that Whitney's praise of famous men in the final lines of *Sine iustitia, confusio* embraces not only the two judges, Wyndham and Flowerdewe, to whom it is explicitly dedicated, but other 'men of iudgement', whose gifts have made England 'happie', and who exemplify the virtues of the 'gens aurea' that banish Iron Age barbarism and set their mark on the new Golden Age of Justice under Elizabeth. Nor can Virgil's prophecy that the golden race should spread itself over the entire world ('toto surget gens aurea mundo') be considered an understatement given Whitney's later celebration of Sir Francis Drake's circumnavigation of the globe.[44]

Explicit praise of Sir Philip Sidney similarly refers back to the apocalyptic prophecy from Virgil's *Eclogue*, which prays for Lucina's blessing on the birth of the child that will bring peace ('nascenti puero . . . casta fave Lucina'). At *Choice*, page 196, line 10 (see illus. 78), the child is explicitly identified as Sidney in a marginal note. Elsewhere, further explicit praise is worked into the

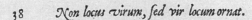

38   *Non locus virum, fed vir locum ornat.*

To the Honorable Sir P H I L L I P S I D N E Y Knight, *Gouernour*
of the Garrifon and towne of Vlifing.

T H E trampinge fteede, that champes the burnifh'd bitte,
Is mannag'd braue, with ryders for the nones :
But, when the foole vppon his backe doth fette,
He throwes him downe, and ofte doth brufe his bones :
    His corage feirce, dothe craue a better guide,
    And eke fuch horfe, the foole fhoulde not beftride.

By which is ment, that men of iudgement graue,
Of learning, witte, and eeke of confcience cleare,
In highe eftate, are fitte theire feates to haue,
And to be ftall'd, in facred iuftice cheare :
    Wherein they rule, vnto theire endleffe fame,
    But fooles are foil'd, and throwne out of the fame.

Claud. 4. Honor.
Tu ciuem, patrémque
geras, tu confule cun-
ctu,
Nec tibi, nec tua te mo-
neant, fed publica
vota.

Horat. 1. Ser. 6.

————*magnum hoc ego duco,*
Quòd placuit tibi, qui turpi fecernis honeftum.

Medio-

86

volume. Whitney may have known Sidney's *Defence of Poesie* in
manuscript. The dedication to Sidney of the woodcut device of the
horseman from Alciato's Emblem 35 (illus. 86) may have been
chosen as a conspicuous allusion to the opening paragraphs of
Sidney's poetic treatise.[45] But the mounted equestrian figure also
has moral and philosophical import. Platonic control over the
horse of the passions yields to larger themes of government and
the conquest of Evil.

Emblematic Theatres and Cavalcades

As noted earlier, many emblematic works of public celebration were placed under the tutelage of the god Janus. His famous 'doubleness' may account for the binary oppositions that govern some emblematic celebrations. The programmes for the annual public celebrations of Corpus Christi organized by the Jesuit College at Brussels were based on paired contrary concepts placed in complementary opposition. Annually the students 'set up a formal public exhibition to give some proof of what they have learned, by hanging up emblems and similar literary ornaments in the street (on the square) on the day that the reverend Sacrament was carried around in a festive procession'.[46] 'Pairings' may be set at some distance apart, or may be more closely advertised by juxta-position. In 1660 the topics were *Mors et Vita* (Death and Life). A book devoted to the one is followed by another book concerning its contrary. In 1665 the topics chosen were *Tristitia–Laetitia* (Sadness–Joy). Here one emblem on *tristitia* is followed by another on *laetitia*. They are not separated into different books. The juxta-posed exercises for 1657 were *Temperantia* and *Intemperantia*.

These Brussels celebrations must have been magnificent theatrical spectacles. Not only were there displays of the painted emblems, but processions and cavalcades. It was not for nothing, therefore, that many books of emblems were conceived as 'Theatres', because they were connected with public perform-ances. Not only the festive works that began this chapter, but other books of emblems go under the title of *Theatrum* or its various vernacular equivalents. Van der Noot, Boissard, La Perrière and others produced works of this kind, and they might profitably be considered in the light of a wider culture of theatrical festivity. This is not the drama of Shakespeare, Racine or Goethe, even though their theatre was contemporary with many of the emblems I discuss in this book, and even though these dramatists may use or make allusion to particular emblems or emblematic forms. These emblematic theatres are more akin to the play of *Everyman*. Allegorical personifications take part in the drama – Death, Faith – just as the emblem theatres introduce their person-ifications of Fortuna, Occasio, Fama, Mors, Fides, Spes. A whole set of representative human characters from history play out in a single emblematic scene the drama of their life or death – Ajax, Agamemnon, Hercules, Brutus, Penelope, Helen. Readers, just like the character Everyman, are confronted with various role models and choices. These *Theatres* could be Theatres of Honour in that one's choices of action could be ennobled by implicit comparison with past precedents of the great and good. Or they could become Satiric Theatres enlarging and magnifying individual follies. The latter was more congenial to the temper of the age, and, indeed, was encouraged by a religious view of the world that tended to view the temporal against the broader backdrop of eternity. This was Thomas Browne's perspective, 'the world to mee is but a . . . mockshow, and wee all therein but Pantalones and Antickes'.[47] In either case, these 'mockshows' – whether honorific or satiric – mirror back to the reader images of the choices that are to be made or have been made, and what the reader is, or what he or she might become.

The Globe of emblematic performance is sometimes shrunk to the miniature form of the medal or *jeton*. The medallic praise of Louis XIV organized and orchestrated by Le Jay in *Le Triomphe de la Religion* and in Claude-François Menestrier's *Histoire du roy Louis-le-Grand par les medailles* (Paris, 1689) is of this kind. The royal image was a hostage to fortune in such productions. An edition of Menestrier's *Histoire* was published at Amsterdam in 1693 'augmentée de cinq planches', which satirized the King. A medal was struck showing Joshua stopping the sun with the motto *Ecquis Cursum Inflectet* (Who will deflect its course?). This plainly applied to Louis xiv, the Sun King. This thin iconographic divide between praise and blame indicates that we should now turn our attentions to Fame's posterior trumpet.

Political and Ecclesiastical Satire

It soon becomes apparent that, if emblematic strategies could be used for praise, they could also be used for blame. There was an element of satiric reprehension of vice in the works of Alciato, La Perrière and other early emblematists. Here the satire tended to be general, directed against the Sin rather than an individual sinner, for there was a perceived generic convention that prohibited the outright naming of individuals. But, as time went on, satire became more and more particular, or more transparent. Yet, ever since Alciato first styled his book of manuscript emblems a *libellus*, he opened up the form's potential for 'lampoon' and 'pasquinade' – for these were subsidiary meanings of the Latin word. This element of satiric coarseness would always remain a generic possibility. Indeed, as we have seen in the case of the *Imago primi saeculi*, the dividing line between conscious and unconscious praise and blame could sometimes be precariously thin.

The Dutch, more than any other nation, and from the earliest period of their republic, were masters of the satiric medal and lampoon. They galled both the French and the British. They rendered the English 'cheap and ridiculous by their lying Pictures and libelling pamphlets',[48] when they depicted a lion, the national heraldic emblem, with its tail cut off, along with three reversed crowns. This was a national insult, which Henry Stubbes cited as part of the *casus belli* against the Dutch. To anyone except the offended party, this must have seemed an unreasonable over-reaction. Peter de la Court's disingenuous, though utterly rational, response must have been altogether infuriating: 'God preserve us from such Christian Princes, as for a Picture or a medal make no scruple to stir up commotions in Christendom and to cause the effusion of so much innocent blood'.[49] But sensitivities about questions of honour, and the injury that laughter could inflict, were greater then than now.

Satiric medals go back to the first years of the emblem, even to the proto-emblematic period of the history of the form. These became a potent weapon in political and ecclesiastical satire, and formed the basis of much engraved work. '[T]urn't upside down' urges the sportive Flesh in Quarles's *Emblemes*, III, xiv, and this is exactly how Reformation satiric medals worked. A variant on the Janus-headed medal was the *phisionomie à double visage*: the profile of a Pope, when turned upside-down, would appear as the Devil. The motto, *Ecclesia perversa tenet faciem Diaboli* (A church gone wrong presents the face of the Devil), verbalized the satiric point. Elsewhere, the image of a cardinal when inverted would appear as a jester (illus. 87).[50]

Obverse and reverse emblematic pairings were also fruitfully exploited for satiric purposes. Martin Luther's *Passional Christi und Antichristi* with cuts by Hans Cranach juxtaposed the Life of Christ with the luxury of the Pope: Christ washes the disciples' feet, the Pope magnanimously allows princes to kiss his toe. This technique gained a certain satiric currency and was imitated by Simon Rosarius in his emblem book *Antithesis Christi et Antichristi, videlicet Papae*.[51] The antitheses were exposed on left and right hand sides of an opening in the book: Christ on the left, 'Antichrist' (i.e., the Pope) on the right. On the opening at pages 74–75, for example, Moses receives the Ten Commandments from God on one side; on the other, the Pope takes his orders from the

Devil. The work includes a ribald spoof of a saint's life: *La Vie de Papesse Ieanne* (The Life of Pope Joan). Later, Puget de la Serre's *Le Breviere des Courtisans* and *L'Entretien des bons Esprits* in a less virulently sectarian vein will contrast the religious and the worldly life.

The advice to 'turn't upside down' is echoed by the 'Overturn! Overturn!' of the Diggers and Levellers of the English Civil War. Emblematic satire often emerges during periods of national crisis and was used to fuel popular fears and phobias. At such times we find eruptions of 'Emblematical' or 'Hieroglyphical' prints, where the word 'emblem' is used for any picture with moral or, more

87

usually, political significance. We also have 'Hieroglyphical letters' – which was the contemporary term for what we would term a 'puzzle print'. There is also the 'Hieroglyphic Portrait' that seeks to anatomize symbolically a political figure's moral qualities *in bona* or *in mala parte*. Emblematic frontispieces of political tracts are expounded in the 'Meaning of the Emblem' or the 'Mind of the Frontispiece'. Wenceslaus Hollar's plate 'The World is Ruled & Governed by Opinion' is explicated in verses by the emblematist Henry Peacham. Opinion perches in a tree. On her arm is a chameleon, because in established emblematic lore it 'can assume all Cullors saving white', i.e., the hypocrite cannot imitate honesty. On her head is the republican cap of freedom, the *pileus*, cunningly transmuted into a Tower of Babel. It falls over her eyes. Her chameleon descends directly from Alciato's little beast that featured in his emblem 'In Adulatores' (On flatterers), who in turn descended from Pliny via Erasmus's *Parabolae*. In Peacham's 'Square Caps turned into Round Heads' (1642), Opinion retains her chameleon, as she turns Fortune's wheel: 'her Camelian feedeth upon aire'.

The bestiary can satirically cage and emblematically label perceived public enemies. One of the orators at the Altdorf Academy took the motif of the antipathy between swinish grossness and the pleasant odour of the rose bush to show that, even as an offence is committed, so punishment swiftly follows.[52] The orator begins with St Paul's comparison of the 'acceptable' right-thinking and right-acting Christian community to 'an odour of sweet smell' (Philippians 4. 18). He quickly moves on to identify the particular pigs that threaten his own garden: Jews, Mohammedans, Papists, Socinians and Anabaptists. He then takes comfort in God's past judgments on Sennacherib, Antiochus and Herod in biblical history. A similar fate, he feels, must now await latter-day heretics – the Romish asses and mules, the grunting monkish swine, the Purgatorial ravens, the sepulchral night-owls, the hissing monastic snakes and vipers.[53] Part of what fuelled this outpouring of abuse in 1595 were the anxieties occasioned by the recent successes of the Islamic forces against Rudolf II.

Thomas Stirry served up for the appetites of England at the outbreak of Civil War *A Rot Among the Bishops, Or, a Terrible Tempest in the Sea of Canterbury, Set forth in lively Emblems to please the judicious Reader*. It is 'An Aegyptian Dish drest after the English Fashion with a Tribute for Mr. Quarles of never dying memory, set forth in four silent Parables'. The four emblems are expounded in verse: First, the ship, 'High Commission', is under sail to Hell Mouth. The sea, on which it sails, is identified as 'The Church and Commonwealth of England'. The ship is next struck by the lightning of Justice. The last two are more narrative: Laud goes to the Tower; Laud looks from the Tower to the Gallows. In 1641 there is a print, Charon's ferry boat, in which Laud sails to Hell in company with a monk, a cardinal, a pope and a bishop. Later in the century the hysteria of the Popish Plot gave birth to *The Protestants Vade Mecum or Popery display'd in its proper Colours in thirty Emblems* (London, 1680).

The language of such emblematic satire is not unduly recondite, and has much in common with satiric broadsides and *Flügelblätter*. Cerberus, the three-headed guard dog of the classical Hades, was adopted for various satiric applications: *The Kingdomes Monster uncloaked from Heaven* (1643) shows three clusters of heads emerging from three elongated necks that are poised to devour the Church, the Parliament, the Kingdom and the City. Conveniently, the predatory jaws are precisely labelled 'Papist Conspiritors', 'Bloudy Irish', 'Malignant Plotters'.

The whore mounted upon her seven-headed beast from the Revelation of St John was, of course, an enduring Protestant metonym for Rome situated on her seven hills. Cranach's woodcuts to Luther's *New Testament* (1522) depict the Pope as Antichrist, the Scarlet Whore wears the Papal tiara, fallen Babylon is Rome. She figured among Alciato's emblematic *dramatis personae* (illus. 129) as 'Ficta Religio' (False Religion). But any current popular *bête noire* at different times could find him- or herself portrayed in such a form. Laud, Cromwell (particularly in anti-English Dutch prints), and Napoleon all were seen mounted on such a steed. On a memorial medal struck in Saxony following Charles I's execution in 1649, *Heu Quaenam Haec Insania Vulgi!* (Alas what a madness is this of the rabble!), shows the many-headed republican monster poised above the royal corpse. Whole raree shows of monsters are unleashed. It is a *Wunderkammer* of the popular imagination – monstrous fish, strange births, hermaphrodites – that gives form and substance to nameless fears and phobias.

Other monsters can be built up of worthless objects: the *Gorgoneum caput* that adorns Stephen Batman's *The Doome* depicts a pope's head constructed of disparaging objects. Arcimbaldo produced a head of Calvin for Maximilian II assembled out of chickens and fish.[54] The fashion for such things was started by Tobias Stimmer, beginning a whole race of 'Hieroglyphic Portraits', which continues into a *Pilorie-Phrénologie*.

In many cases these political emblems 'need[ed] no learned Exposition' in the words of the anti-monarchist, anti-Scottish Commonwealth emblematic print *Old Sayings and Predictions verified and fulfilled* (1651). They were designed to appeal to a popular audience, and such things attracted the scorn of those who considered themselves of superior taste and judgement.

The Catholic iconography of St Michael weighing the souls of the departed is cunningly appropriated for Protestant purposes in the woodcut colophon of John Foxe's *Book of Martyrs*: 'A liuely picture descrybing the weight and substaunce of God's most blessed word, agaynst the doctrines and vanities of mens traditions' (illus. 88). The Bible placed in the balance easily outweighs the scale containing the papistical paraphenalia. A demon strains every nerve to drag down the lightweight pan. A more learned allusion to Ovid's *Metamorphoses* portrays a modern Diana exposing the sexual failings of her lapsed follower, Callisto, enacted respectively in the form of England's Virgin Queen, Elizabeth I, and a pregnant pope, hatching his deformed iniquities.

Eirwen E. C. Nicholson has argued that much writing on eigh-
teenth- and nineteenth-century graphic satire has shown a reluc-
tance to take account of the emblematic roots of the form.[55] James
Gillray is a case in point. He was a satiric genius, but his success
depended on his early training in the drawing schools. Here he
would have copied emblems, iconologies and images of the gods
and goddesses from various manuals. He soon tired of this, but his

88

training familiarized him with the conventional encoding of types
and allegorical figures. These furnished him with a ground plan
for an interpretation of many aspects of the contemporary political scene, for it became obvious to him that real-life politicians,
consciously or unconsciously, often re-enacted the roles previously
set down in the emblem books. Gillray brought to his craft an
uncommon ability to translate to the engraved copper plate a
manneristic swirling energy, and an unabashed, Rubensesque
delight in the expansive rolls and folds of naked human flesh. It
perhaps comes as little surprise, that, at the end of Gillray's life (he

died in 1815), when he was totally insane, he actually thought he *was* Rubens. Some examples of his reliance on emblems in interpreting the history of his times are as follows.

The fable of Daedalus and Icarus, as we have seen, had been used by various emblematists as a means to sundry ends. Alciato, for instance, in Emblem 104, had applied it to the fraudulent claims of astrologers. Gillray brilliantly transposed the myth to a current, topical fraud (illus. 89). *The Fall of Icarus*, published 28 April 1807, shows an awareness of the various precedent emblematic models, the iconography and the long-standing association with fraud. On quitting office, Earl Temple, Joint Paymaster of the Forces, it was reported, had taken with him a large quantity of stationery. We see vast quantities of the stuff being loaded onto a cart outside his official residence in Whitehall at the bottom-right of the engraving. In his local application of the Ovidian story, Gillray furnishes wings for his 'Icarus' out of quills and sealing wax. Unfortunately, as Temple departs the scene, temporarily borne aloft on his purloined wings, the sun, in the shape of the beatifically beaming visage of George III, exposes the theft: the wax melts, and the quills fail to sustain him in his flight. In the inevitable consequent fall, a painful recompense awaits the exposed, ample buttocks of the fraudulent minister: 'a spike out of the public hedge'. This detail is Gillray's own sadistic, delighted departure from his Ovidian source. But this unusual addition to the traditional iconography gives a new focus – one is tempted to say 'point' – to the scene. The gross, physical actuality of the instrument of punishment, the unerring geometry of its construction, thrusts itself on our attention. Gillray, with manneristic brilliance, arrests his victim in mid-fall. But punishment has not yet been inflicted. Rather, it is deliciously and anxiously suspended. Nevertheless, this part of the plate ineluctably implies the same physical laws that govern the spectator. The eye calculates the body's trajectory and estimates the most likely point of impact. The sheer physical bulk of the descending victim minimizes any chance of reprieve. The penetratingly sharp contours of the pain to come are mentally explored, revolved in the mind, indeed, almost savoured, in the instant before they are to be anticlimactically enacted. How much more subtly satisfying than a rendition of the next frame of the implied narrative, had it had been allowed to run on for a few more short moments! But this is no decision based on a tasteful squeamishness. Gillray's corrosive craft has, on reflection, sadisti-

89

cally managed to prolong Temple's torment. The engraving has no
past, no future, only a present. Temple is suspended within the
frame of the plate in anguished anticipation, a torture akin to that
of Hell in that it has no end.

Temple's 'Daedalus', the Marquis of Buckingham, at the top left
of the engraving has his rear massively exposed, but it escapes the
painful end that awaits Temple's. Buckingham's more reliable
wings support him in his flight to higher things: they are labelled

'Tellership of the Exchequer'. The indifferent self-interest of his onward, unimpeded flight procures some little sympathy for the fatally descending Temple.

The engraving and the satire work because the Ovidian myth is translated detail by detail to a current, specific, political event. Gillray engages in a busy dialogue, which negotiates between his contemporary application and the traditional iconography of the Ovidian narrative: he retains some features, alters others, and translates the old tale to modern undress. This process, in which an artist applies a more specific, restricted interpretation of a myth or an emblem, a twentieth-century semiotician would call 'overcoding'. An early modern rhetorician would see it as a species of metonymy, the basis of one of Whitney's emblematic procedures:

> The couetous man, this fable reprehendes,
> For *chaunge his name*, and *Tantalvs* hee is.[56]

But Gillray did not need the name of a rhetorical figure or a theory of signs to do what he did. He simply pushed Whitney's exercise in metonymy one step further: he names not only the sin, but the sinner. Or if the name is withheld, it is covered by a 'poetic' veil so tissue thin it is transparent. In this engraving 'Icarus' *is* Earl Temple; or, perhaps we should say, Earl Temple *is* Icarus: the translation in these local, satiric equivalences depends for its effect on an instantaneous, explosive fusion: the mythic archetype is that immediately contemporary, ephemeral subject at that time and in these circumstances. The one, within the frame of that engraved plate and for that political moment, is the other, and no other. Where allegory is committed to an expansive continuance of its tropes and dark conceits over a longer narrative span, emblematic satire is responsible only for the immediate effect of a single plate. It is not committed to any further application of the archetype to that individual or to any other similar circumstance. If it wishes to elaborate or repeat a lucky hit, it can and will; but it may be more appropriate to surprise its quarry using different veiled motifs.

Specific overcoding strategies are similarly used in Gillray's *Gloria Mundi* (illus. 90). It, too, pushes an iconographic type to the point where not only sins, but names are named. A man stands on the globe of the World, as Fortuna had frequently done in previous emblems. He has a fox's legs and tail, a possible Ripaesque moral biography of a sly and deceitful individual, but here also a direct allusion to the man's name: Fox. Gillray would probably insist that the traditional iconography was no less appropriate as an index of the man's moral character. Fortune's wheel is still that, but it is more specifically a roulette wheel, a biographical allusion to Charles James Fox's addiction to gambling. His moral and literal bankruptcy is recorded by the fact that his pockets are empty. The hapless, scowling politician is demonized by a quotation and adaptation of lines from Milton's *Paradise Lost*, a source also alluded to in the alternative title to the plate, 'The

GLORIA MUNDI.
or ___ The Devil addressing the Sun.

Devil addressing the Sun'. This 'Sun' is subjected to particular overcoding strategies too: it takes on itself the sublime features of Lord Shelburne, who remained beatifically in power. Fox, of course, was out of office, out of cash, and out of luck. Gillray interestingly appropriates an English classic, as previous emblematists had used Horace, Ovid or Virgil.

The classical underworld comes to Gillray's aid in his demonization of the 'Ministry of the Talents', or the 'Broad-Bottoms', as

they styled themselves (illus. 91). Published on 16 July 1807, Gillray
has taken as his basic framework the representation of Charon's
barge on its journey to Hell. The iconographic model can be seen
in an engraved frontispiece of the *Mythologia Latina* of 1681 (illus.
92). But various detailed inscriptions and allusions worked into
Gillray's plate specifically identify each hapless mariner on his last
voyage in the listing, over-freighted craft. The Prince of Wales's
coat of arms, for instance, three feathers with the motto *Ich Dien*,
is found on the mast of the barge. The brilliance of Gillray's design
is that it manages to cross the po-facedness of the iconography of
a mythographic school-book with the ribald, satiric tradition of
the *Narrenschiff* – for the Ministry of the Talents was on a self-
destructive mission that revealed, for all its talent, its innate foolishness. Various satiric tropes are invoked: the undulating,
trembling nakedness of the talented 'bottoms', broad or otherwise,
is amply exposed to the satirist's cane or purge. Scatological
punishment is fulsomely and joyously administered, as the characters are liberally befouled and bespattered by low-flying birds,
Purgatorial ravens of another feather, who unstintingly and unerr-
ingly empty the contents of their bowels on the hapless mariners.

A suppressed plate, 'Patience on a Monument' (illus. 93), once
more appropriates a tag from an English classic, this time, Shakespeare.[57] It joyfully and wholeheartedly embraces an emblematic
scatological tradition. Here we have fairly close-to-the-surface

MYTHOGRAPHI LATINI.

Amstelodami, apud Viduam Joannis à Someren. 1681.

92

"PATIENCE on a MONUMENT."

93

94

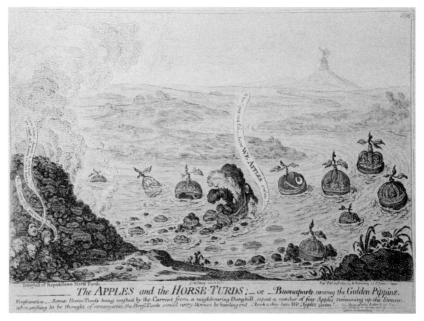

The APPLES and the HORSE-TURDS; — or —Buonaparte among the Golden Pippins.
Explanation.—Some Horse-Turds being washed by the Current from a neighbouring Dunghill, espied a number of fine Apples swimming up the Stream, when wishing to be thought of consequence, the Horse-Turds would every Moment be bawling out, "Lack-a-day how We Apples swim!"

95

quotations from a number of emblematic models: Alciato's so-called 'obscene' emblem, 'Adversus naturam peccantes' (illus. 94) and Harrington's *Metamorphosis of Ajax*. The triangular form of the funeral monument is copied from the format used in Baroque displays of the attributes of the Virgin in Catholic works of devotion. Gillray's woman, of course, is no virgin, and an object of satiric ridicule rather than devotion. But Gillray's satire is like a vortex, and he is powerless to resist the undertow of a subsidiary anti-Catholic gibe. Gillray pursued his quarry (whatever and whoever) uninhibited by any sense of shame.

In *The Apples and the Horse-Turds; or, Buonaparte among the Golden Pippins* (illus. 95), Gillray vents his xenophobic hatred of the French in uninhibited scatological vein. He styles France a 'Dunghill of Republican Horseturds'. These are individually itemized as the articles of the Republican Faith and its heroes: 'Egalité', 'Falshood', 'Atheism', 'Regicide', 'Licentiousness', 'Voltaire', 'Rousseau', 'Godwin', 'Paine's Rights of Man', etc. The satire rests on sound emblematic precedent: the motto from Harrington's *Metamorphosis of Ajax* – 'These apples swim!' The crowns of Europe, the 'Pippins', float by in a ditch, as Napoleon, no true 'Pippin' but a 'Horseturd' of substantial proportions, tries to emulate them. In the distance, atop a neo-Classical tempietto, stands Fame, blowing her trumpet over this running sewer.

These examples show an adaptation of emblematic models and themes for the purposes of eighteenth- and early nineteenth-century political satire. It is a commonplace of early modern emblem theory to say that emblems handle general moral principles, not specific individual vices. These general moral principles are shadowed under types, allegories and fables. What we have in Gillray is a natural evolution of the form, in which the allegorical figure is applied to a specific individual. He moves emblematic insinuation and indirectness firmly in the direction of personal, libellous innuendo. But he was far from the first to do this. His emblematic satire is rooted in the very beginnings of the genre.

SEVEN

Licentious Poets and the Feast of Saturn

Io Saturnalia!

Turpe est difficiles habere nugas
Et stultus labor est ineptiarum.[1]

Chapter Six dealt with collections of *emblemata* as they relate to particular occasions and to particular individuals. Saints' days, weddings, funerals, births, jubilees and royal visits might occur at any time of the year, and provided excuses to paint the town as well as the calendar red. Johann Michael Dilherr went so far as to propose a sub-genre of emblems, *Festag-Emblemata*,[2] but this has not become generally accepted. There were, however, some exercises in the genre: Henricus Engelgrave dealt with the feast days and deeds of the Saints during the whole year,[3] and these also provided Casimirus Fuesslin with emblematic sermons on the festivals of the Church.[4] Other collections of emblems can be tied to specific annual festivals: Christmas, New Year, Shrove Tuesday, May Day, etc. This culture of festivity – whether it arose from a humanistic appropriation of ancient rites and ceremonies, or from a genuinely popular insurgences of seasonal merriment – dictates major features of the genre.

Johann Bissel celebrated the delights of summer in *Deliciae Æstatis* (Munich, 1644). In *The Returne of Pasquill*, Thomas Nashe proposed, or threatened, a 'May-game of Martinisme', which was to have included requisite emblematic decoration.[5] If this project ever progressed beyond its announcement, it never attained public utterance. But the idea in such matters often exceeds the performance, or runs foul of the censor. It is enough that Nashe saw the connection between emblematic forms, holiday merriment and festive satire. Three centuries later, but in the same vein, Stevenson sent a copy of his *Moral Emblems* as an April Fools' Day gift to Dr Alexander Japp.[6] In writing of them to his friends and relations, he repeatedly emphasized their sheer playfulness: 'Are they not fun?'; 'I enclose a good joke'; 'I hoped they might amuse you'; 'Here's a copy of *Moral Emblems* enclosed. If these combined do not cheer you, the devil's in it.' 'I doat on them'![7]

Giovanni Bernardino Giuliani's *Descrittione dell'Apparato* (Naples, 1631) commemorates the popular festivities surrounding one celebration of the feast day of St John – 24 June, Midsummer's Eve. This was marked by bonfires, torchlight processions and, in some cultures, certain masonic rituals. In Britain, it was the anniversary of the founding of the Order of the Garter. Ercole Cimilotti's *Il superbo torneo* (Pavia, 1587) celebrates Carnival – the *festa larvorum*, many of whose customs and practices derived from the Roman Saturnalia. But it was Christmas that was to become the pre-eminent emblematic festival. Not so much for its Christian message, but as a revival or survival of the traditions of license and misrule of the feast-days of Saturn,

> Lo! tipsy midwinter demands new jests[8]

In that season, and with that demand in mind, the emblem was born, and in that environment emblems were nurtured and continued to flourish (illus. 96). The festival demanded that social divisions between masters and servants were temporarily abated, and even the gods joined in the revelry on equal terms with mortals. Lucian's comic dialogue, *Saturnalia*, which was translated by Alciato's friend, Erasmus, and edited by the emblematist Joannes Sambucus in a bilingual Greek–Latin edition of the *Opera*,[9] describes how, during these intercalary days, the ancient scythe-bearing god briefly reassumes and recreates his ancient regime, the Golden World, where plenty abounded and all men were free. For a brief period at the year's end, he revels with mortals, drinking and getting drunk, appearing naked, shouting, clapping his hands, telling jokes, playing games and dicing. The *Sigillaria*, the feast of images, took up the final days of the ancient Saturnalia. How apt that its prolongation into the early modern period should also present us with a feast of emblematic images!

The first emblems were composed 'His Saturnalibus' (in this holiday season), Alciato told Calvo in that now famous letter.[10] The time and the occasion shape the content and the style of the poems. Alciato would have known from reading his Martial that this was the time in which it was permitted to disport oneself in toil-free verse.[11] The poems are 'toil-free' ('non laborioso'), since all serious business was suspended during this period. We might, therefore, see a further witty justice in Alciato's description of his collection of manuscript emblems as a 'libellus'. The word could

refer to a lawyer's brief, but during this holiday this lawyer's brief
was the composition of *emblemata*, festive poems designed to
please by the grace of their wit and erudition. Alciato by means of
a pun negotiates his way between the world of work and the world
of poetic play. The emblem is meant to be amusing, recreative,

96

even satiric: *libellus*, as I mentioned in a previous chapter, also
carried with it the sense of 'lampoon', 'pasquinade' – an element of
satiric coarseness that remained a generic possibility for the form –
and as such it was appropriate for a period of holiday freedom and
license. *Liber* also meant 'free'. Here we are granted, in the form of
the 'libellus', a little, if much appreciated, freedom. In Emblem 151,

Alciato reminds us that the Romans loved liberty so much that they would literally kill for it.

Some of Alciato's emblems explicitly allude to this festive period. His dedicatory epigram announces that these newly-created emblems were fit to adorn hats ('petasis'). There is certainly an allusion here to the contemporary fashion of adorning one's clothing with emblems and devices, and there is, as well, a metaphoric allusion to the 'covered' nature of emblematic utterance. More specifically, though, Alciato alludes to the headgear of the god of eloquence, Mercury, whose winged hat and caduceus, Giovio records, formed part of Alciato's own personal device.[12] Mignault, however, in his commentary on the dedicatory epigram to Peutinger more plausibly identifies this particular hat as the *pileus*, the cap of freedom worn by ancient Romans – masters and servants alike – during the Saturnalia: 'the *pileus* is the symbol of freedom', notes Mignault in relation to Alciato's Emblem 151, 'Respublica liberata',[13] which hoists aloft the cap of liberty. In the tipsy days of Saturn, according to Martial, 'decent ... pilea sumpta', it is fitting to wear the cap of liberty. At this time, he says, all Rome was 'pilleata', given over to licence and revelry.[14] To show how readily the ancient Saturnalia was assimilated to the early modern Christmas revels, we need look no further than the Puritan Philip Stubbes, who refers to the revellers' custom of 'wear[ing] their badges and their cognizances in their hats or caps openly', while Ben Jonson describes in his Christmas Masque a character, New-Yeares-Gift, with 'his Hat full of Broaches'.[15]

These early modern badges would seem to be directly descended from those of the antique Saturnalia, which explicitly forbade the circulation of money. To offer the coin of the realm was considered an act of madness. Instead, medals cast in lead or copper became the legal tender during this time of misrule. To ridicule the very idea of money, the basest metals were used, stamped with grotesque figures and odd devices – a sow, a chimerical bird, an emperor in his chariot with a monkey behind him; an old woman's head, Acca Laurentia, traditionally, the old nurse of Romulus, or an old whore of the same name who bequeathed the profits earned from the labours of her loins to the Roman people. All things were done in mockery. The base coinage was stamped *S.C.*: not the *senatus consulto*, but *Saturnalium consulto*. The reverse showed four *tali*, or bones, which they used as dice, with the motto *Qui ludit, arram det, quod satis sit* (Let them who play give the pledge). This pledge was called in Latin, a *symbolus*.

Alciato presents a boar's head (illus. 97) as a New Year's gift in Emblem 45, 'In dies meliora' (Things gradually getting better). Pork was the centrepiece of the traditional Saturnalian feast. Having set the darkness of the winter solstice behind, the emblem promises a steady progression towards a brighter future.[16] At Emblem 123 the god Faunus is honoured, whose festival was celebrated in December, as every reader of Horace would know:

All the flock gambols o'er the grassy field whene'er December's Nones come round for thee; in festal garb the country folk make holiday amid the meads, along with resting steers.[17]

97

His was a rural festival. The rustics party, and they, like the beasts of burden, enjoy some time off during this holiday.

In this spirit, many other emblem books and emblematic manuscripts were specifically designed as New Year's gifts: Hadrianus Junius's dedicatory epistle to his *Emblemata* (Antwerp, 1565) speaks of the ancients' custom of sending New Year's gifts (*strenae*) to celebrate the beginning of the year. He says that he is imitating this practice in dedicating his book to Cobelius.[18] The dedication is significantly dated 'sub Idus Ianuarias'. Sambucus's treatise *De Emblemate* is similarly dated ('Kalen. Ianuarijs'). Robert Whitehall's *Hexastichon Hieron* (Oxford, 1677) was a New Year's gift, as was Thomas Palmer's manuscript 'The Sprite of Herbes and Trees', now in the British Library (Add. MS 18040), its dedication dated

January 1598/99. Palmer's intended dedicatee, William Cecil, Lord Burleigh, did not live to receive it. In the event the manuscript served as a funeral tribute to the deceased lord, and a new object for its dedication was found in Burleigh's son, Robert Cecil. His Emblem 22 takes its motto from Luke 1. 52, 'Deposuit potentes de sede' ('He hath put down the mighty from their seats'), the text that had authorized the Saturnalian cult of the Boy Bishop, still practised in Palmer's living memory in England during the reign (1553–8) of Queen Mary. But, in the suddenly enforced change from festivity to mourning, the motto could be seen, if more sombrely, as equally appropriate. Palmer's first manuscript book of emblems, 'Two hundred poosees', dedicated to Robert Dudley, Earl of Leicester, most probably was also a New Year's gift. It is determinedly festive and gratulatory in tone. In the seventeenth and eighteenth centuries the emblematic New Year's gift took on a specifically spiritual character.[19] Yet William Blake's 'songs of happy cheer' are designed 'to welcome in the Year', but this is March rather than January, for the 'new year' is 'Spring'. Yet even here there is a kinship with the Saturnalia, for Blake's spring corresponds with the freedom anciently celebrated on the Ides of March when the republican *pileus* was held aloft.[20]

Thomas Palmer explicitly associated his first collection of emblems with this Saturnalian tradition by referring to them explicitly as 'poosees'. These are, of course, emblems,[21] but the rhetorician Puttenham later defined 'posie' as a particular kind of epigram, the classical *apophoreta*, a form that was identified with the celebration of the Saturnalia in classical times.[22] A host would usually give to his guests small gifts, which they could take away with them, and these were therefore called *apophoreta*, from the Greek verb meaning 'to carry away'.[23] Augustus, and other Roman Emperors, according to Suetonius, kept up the custom in particularly lavish fashion,[24] but for others the gift may have been no more than a small motto inscribed on a sweetmeat or piece of paper. Martial devoted the last two books of his *Epigrams* to this genre, the *Xenia* (New Year's gifts) and the *Apophoreta*. Puttenham accommodated Roman Saturnalia to English New Year, *apophoreta* becoming English *posies* 'sent vsually for new yeares giftes or to be printed or to be put vpon their banketting dishes of suger plate, or of march paines, and such other dainty meates as by the curtesie and custome euery gest might carry from a common feast home with him to his owne house'.[25] New Year's gifts formed an important part of Elizabethan court ceremonial.

Among the gifts of gold and silver usually dispensed at this festival, poetical tributes were also to be found. John Lyly's verses for
the Entertainment at Harefield correspond exactly to Martial's
apophoreta.[26] This tradition was already established in Martial's
day, and presumably formed a precedent for Renaissance authors.
'You may send a poem instead of a gift', the Roman epigrammist
advised; 'poems are not to be despised in the month of December'.[27] Lucian, in setting out the laws for the Saturnalia, allows the
poor scholar to send a rich man any pleasant, convivial old book,
or a work of his own devising.[28] In this vein, the learned Vorberg
offered his annotations to Antonio Beccadelli's *Hermaphroditus* –
a collection of epigrams on the erotic fantasies and depravities of
both sexes, which were enlarged and padded out with a collection
of the more explicitly salacious passages from Virgil, Ovid and
Martial. Vorberg styled his volume of notes *apophoreta*, a second
course of delectable scholarly sweetmeats.[29] At the emblematic
board Alciato serves in his Emblem 36, the sweets of learning are
offered: these 'bellaria dulcia' hold the place of honour among the
courses at the Muses' banquet.

Foolish Labour

If modern readers ignore the festive provenance of many of these
collections, and approach *Emblemata* as serious moral utterances, they can be totally disconcerted, even puzzled. Moral seriousness there may be, but it is often mixed with the nugatory, the
festive and the comic; implicit gratulation with fables and puns;
the learned and erudite with satiric coarseness; pious instruction
with worldly wisdom. It is difficult to know how to take these
texts: are they meant as jokes? as academic exercises? In many
cases it is almost impossible for us to look at them as pieces of
serious moral advice. Nor is it only modern readers who respond
to this oddly mixed form with a sense of puzzlement. Alciato's
early commentators also struggled to define the register in which
they operated. The lines from Martial that form one of the
epigraphs to this chapter,

> *Turpe est difficiles habere nugas*
> *Et stultus labor est ineptiarum.*

> It is degrading to undertake difficult trifles,
> and foolish is the labour spent on silliness.

found their way into Wolfgang Hunger's preface to Wechel's Latin–German edition of Alciato.[30] These 'difficiles nugas' (difficult trifles) might align the emblem with various word–image collocations, lapidary inscriptions, pattern poems, 'Province[s] in Acrostick Land', where not only are 'wings display['d] and Altars rais['d]',[31] but labyrinths and ceremonial cups are presented in artful verse and shaped prose. Although Alciato did not, several emblem writers (Willett, Quarles, Harvey, Bouquet, Harsdörffer, Liceti, among others) deployed stanzas in the form of axes, lozenges, wings, hour-glasses, and ladders – visual analogues to poetic onomatopoeia. Even the learned Valeriano did not disdain an exercise in pear-shaped verse in punning recognition of his nickname, *Pierius*, given to him because he was dedicated to the Muses (the Pierides) and because of his prodigious learning: *pirus* is the Latin name for the pear tree. This may itself stand as a fitting emblem for the whole enterprise. When it embarked on this course, the whole emblem tradition went peculiarly pear-shaped, and lent itself prey to easy ridicule.

But Hunger's allusion to Martial's epigram would seem to be more specific, and go to the heart of the preoccupations of much emblematic writing. Hunger deploys the quotation as a species of rhetorical *occupatio*, in which the author offers an excuse for not prolonging his argument, while at the same time outlining the areas of the subject, which he prefers not to elaborate. The German scholar implies that Alciato's newly invented *Emblemata* are similar in kind to those species of composition that Martial originally derided as unworthy elsewhere in this epigram: 'carmine ... supino' (topsy-turvy verses), 'Sotaden cinnaedum' (sodomite Sotadics), 'versus echoici', or 'mollem debilitate' (voluptuous and broken) galliambics. To pin down this innuendo with any certainty we would have to be sure that Hunger could be confident that at least some of his readers would be able to contextualise the lines he quotes. But it is likely that he could, and they did. Later in this chapter we will examine how appropriate some of these kinds of composition are to emblems, which, as products of holiday mirth and levity might also be seen as the trophies of 'supine' study.[32]

However, we can be certain from the fact that Hunger quoted these two lines from Martial, that he considered *Emblemata* to be elegant trifles: books full of *ineptiae* – jokes, absurdities, puerilities – in which the author is deliberately 'playing the fool'. The verb *ineptio* means precisely that. Nor was his perception an isolated one. Other emblematists were pleased to join in the game. Wither, for one, openly acknowledges the strategy: 'I am ... contented to seeme *Foolish* (yea, and perhaps, more foolish than I am)'.[33] La Perrière produced a whole book of emblems that he advertised as a 'Foolosophy' – *La Morosophie* (Lyon, 1553). In the next century Jan de Leenheer put together an emblematic *Theatrum stultorum* (Brussels, 1669). These are only a few examples of the perceived generic connection between licensed folly and *emblemata*.

Under the banner of such license a book can cross the boundaries of decorum and indulge itself in the indecorous, the tasteless, the pedantic and the silly. The normal distinctions between serious and unserious, sacred and profane, foolish and wise melt and dissolve. The fact that this may be done with stylish elegance or satiric sharpness bolstered by an uncommon erudition merely adds to the fun.

Emblematic Wine

In Alciato's Emblem 25 (illus. 98) Bacchus, the god of wine, disports himself in his full, rubicund nakedness, playing a toy drum (a sign, we are told, of joy and hilarity) and waving a rattle (the instrument played by the Egyptian priests to accompany the lascivious rites of Isis), while wearing a set of horns on his head. These, Alciato tells us, are the attributes of a raving fool ('dementeis'). The wine flows sweetly ('dulcè fluit'). But, in Horatian fashion, the *dulce* is mixed with the *utile*, and vice versa. Isis, for all her lascivious rites, presided over the mysteries of hieroglyphic wisdom,[34] while Bacchus' nakedness befits a book of emblems, for, in his drunken state, hidden truths are revealed, as the mythographer Phornutus recté cornutus pointed out and Mignault's commentary confirms.[35] *In vino veritas*, or, as Alciato says elsewhere: Wisdom is increased by wine.[36] Emblem 205 celebrates the Ivy Bush, the plant of Bacchus and the poets he inspires. Elsewhere other emblematists elaborate the point: Bacchus, his brows crowned with ivy, sits astride the wine vat, or mounts the poetic horse of inspiration, Pegasus. Wine has always been the prop and stay of the poet, giving, according to Henry Peacham, 'quick Invention' to the 'spright', mirth to the heart and delight to the senses.

Others endorse Alciato's commitment to Bacchic pleasures. Mathias Holtzwart similarly connects wine with the revelation of secrets and mysteries, the *arcana*: 'a heart swollen with wine cannot keep secrets, and a full mouth usually tells the truth'.[37] Wine is, after all, the traditional sacred drink of the Mysteries. The 'animus

PRVDENTIÆ.   31

In ſtatuam Bacchi.

DIALOGISMVS.

Bacche pater:quis te mortali lumine nouit?
Et docta effinxit quis tua membra manu?
Praxiteles,qui me rapientem Gnoſida uidit.
Atque illo pinxit tempore qualis eram.
Cur iuuenis,tenera& etiam lanugine vernat
Barba,queas Pylium cùm ſuperare ſenem?

98

turgens' (the swollen heart), the 'os plenum' (the full mouth) are all appropriate organs of the 'oratio referta' (the stuffed, or crammed speech) that Mignault identified as characteristic of the emblem. In all of this, one reveller is propped up by another: Holztwart leans heavily on Horace, the source of so many emblematic mottoes and sentiments.[38]

Sambucus, too, expresses a plain, unashamed preference for honest conviviality, and freedom of expression, irrigated by the festive juice: 'I want cups [of wine], and free words, games and jokes, too'.[39] This is an invitation to life-enhancing liveliness and merriment, rather than to dissolute drunkenness. The emblematic moralizer of Aristotle, Del Bene, in his celebratory statuary of the sense of taste, does not disdain to place a carousing Ceres and Bacchus at the very summit (illus. 99). There were plenty of warnings, of course, against taking things too far. But goodness ought to be pleasurable, nor should honest pleasure be considered bad.

The emblematic culture of festivity moderates between the profane and the sacred, for the emblematists were heirs of both a Classical and a Christian tradition. Thus Augustin Chesneau turns to the festive etiquette of the dinner table to illustrate the joys of the Eucharist.[40] Emblematic wine is often drawn from a well-stocked cellar. These drinkers seriously repeat the Rabelaisian jest 'J'ai la parolle de Dieu en bouche' (I have the word of God in my mouth).[41] Alonso de Ledesma, in his Spanish translation of Vænius's *Amoris Divini Emblemata*, invites all and sundry to the 'taberna', where one can partake freely of the 'wine of divine love'.[42] From his well-stocked wine cellar, Abraham à Sancta Clara furnishes many a refreshing allegorical draught for a thirsty soul.[43] The preacher's supplier was the Holy Scriptures. A good, early vintage came from Christ's first miracle at Cana in Galilee, and an even more productive one was bought from the Song of Solomon, where the Bridegroom regales the Spouse with 'flagons', saying, 'yea, drink abundantly, O beloved'.[44] This biblical wine was, of course, an allegorical type of Christ's Passion: Christ himself entered the Eucharistic wine-press (illus. 100). In Harvey's emblem 'Mustum cordis' (The New-Wine of the Heart), the underpinning Scriptural text is Psalm 104: 15: 'Wine that maketh glad the heart of man'. The Psalmist points typologically to the New Testament fulfilment of this prophetic utterance: Christ is the true vine, and the wine-press is the Crucifixion. 'Draw ... and spare not', enjoins Harvey in his epigram, 'Here's wine enough for all'. Hugo, Vænius, Van Haeften and all their vernacular translators and imitators,

P·DEL·GVSTO·

A.   Ceres & Bacchus epulantes in faſtigio portæ guſtatus.
B.   Auctumnus offerens poma ſiue auctumnitatem.
C.   Pomona Dea etiam ipſa cum munere ſuo.

100

including Quarles, Arwaker and Harvey, have visited this fountain-head. 'The fragrant odour of wine, O how much more ... celestial and delicious it is than oil'.[45] Rabelais's adjectives, 'céleste et déli-cieux', show how sacred and profane merriment can coincide and live delightedly together. Further, the inspiration of much emblematic writing derives as much from bibulous conviviality as from fusty book-learning that smells of the lamp.

The genial potential for the emblematic reconciliation of appar-ently irreconcilable opposites, the sacred and the profane, pleasure and virtue, is shown in Achille Bocchi's emblem 'Cum virtute alma consentit vera voluptas' (True pleasure is consistent with genial virtue), a celebration of Saturnalian excess: a tipsy Silenus, whose tottering steps are supported by young satyrs (illus. 101). Above him sits an armed Minerva, who embraces a naked Venus attended

XXIIII   LIB. I.

CVM VIRTVTE ALMA CONSENTIT
VERA VOLVPTAS.

Symb. X.

101

by her son. Virtuous Wisdom and Carnal Pleasure are caught in
the act of joyful reconciliation. To celebrate their agreement, the
goddesses are in the act of crowning the aged tippler with a laurel
wreath in recognition of a lifetime's pursuit of the pleasures of
virtue, and the virtues of pleasure. Aneau's inclusion of Alciato's 'In
statuam Bacchi' under the heading 'Prudentia' in his edition of the
Emblemata (see illus. 98) gives rise to the same pleasing conclusion: that wisdom ought to be pleasurable, and that seasonable

revelry is essential to the good life. Around the frame of Alciato's Bacchic emblem in Rouillé's edition, naked boys disport themselves in evident, uninhibited delight. Similarly, in Battista Pittoni's engraving for Lodovico Dolce's *Imprese nobile di diuerse prencipi* (Venice, 1578) the long snake-like necks of enigmatic sphinxes, their breasts exposed and wings displayed, support the *impresa* of the 'Proveditore Canale', as satyrs look on at the theatrically framed exposé of his virtuous device in sportive wonderment, bearing bunches of grapes as nymphs languorously and sensuously recline. In the same book serene caryatids and satyrs embracing satyresses support the arms of Conasalva Perez. Nobility is bolstered by these primitive, festive, joyous energies.

Emblematic Festive Games

To gamble for nuts at the Saturnalia was the order of the day.[46] The stakes were nuts because 'Nuts seem a small stake, one not ruinous'.[47] Alciato's prefatory epigram alludes to the practice. This dedication to Peutinger that began the first and all subsequent editions of the *Emblemata* confirms their Saturnalian provenance. Here Alciato likens emblems to children's games, to games of chance, dice and cards, fit recreations for a holiday season. Emblems vie with the nut, the die, the playing card – in Alciato's day, the tarot deck – and ancient medals as pastimes to beguile or to improve the shining hours at the year's end. Later, in Emblem 130, 'Semper praesto esse infortunia' (Misfortune is always close to us), Alciato shows three young women playing dice. The emblem 'Impossibile' (An impossible thing), which illustrates the proverb *Aethiopem dealbare* (To whiten the Ethiop), alludes to one of the silly games played during the Saturnalia: participants, faces blackened with soot, were pushed into a tub of cold water. Part of the ritual merriment of the Fête des Fous in early modern Europe also involved smutted faces.[48]

We can appreciate the wit of a young orator's feigned surprise when his rector called on him to undertake an emblematic oration: 'What are you telling me to do ...? To throw dice? To gamble? To play cards? To indulge in alcohol? To get drunk? Are you casting before me the instruments of dissipation?'[49] But emblematic discourse turns out, after all, to be consistent with the Academy as a 'palace of modesty'.

Wither's surprising addition of a 'lottery' at the end of his book (illus. 102) – possibly in imitation of the Jesuit Jan David's even

103

more surprising inclusion of the same feature in his *Veridicus christianus* – takes part in this time-honoured feature of Saturnalian celebration. *Accipe sortes* (Accept these lots), Martial proposed, as his contribution to the feast days of the scythe-bearing god.[50] Whitney also commemorated the lottery presided over by Elizabeth I, and John Lyly included a lottery as part of the princely Entertainment at Harefield.[51] Wither appropriately talks of the 'libertie of his Muse' and embraces the utility of festive 'levitie', 'a childish delight in trifling objects' – 'Rattles, and Hobbyhorses'.[52] But, in Wither's hands, we see that the activities of Augustus's court and princely entertainments had 'levitated' down the social scale. Such things have now become entirely suitable to

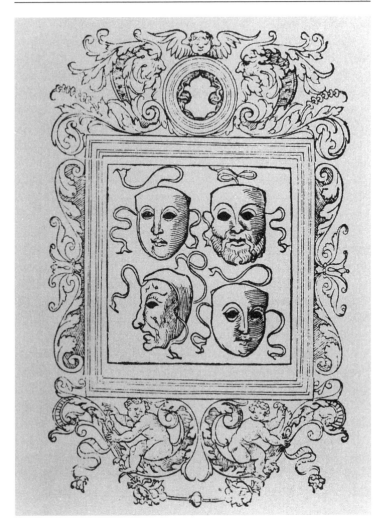

104

emblematic modes of bourgeois instruction, in so far as they are
meant to teach the way to a good life by means of jocose playfulness. Moral instruction, after all, ought not to be without pleasure.

A rustic, carnivalesque burgomasque finds its way into Vænius's
Q. Horatii Flacci Emblemata to show the continuity between the
ancient Roman and modern Flemish festivity (illus. 103), though
the background scenes sound a sombre warning, that the price of
pleasure must be paid. La Perrière's Emblem 6 (illus. 104) derives
from these ancient disguisings and refers to their use 'en banquet
ou en feste'. Today, he wryly observes, everyone uses them on a
daily basis – hypocrisy is so rampant. But such things were allowed
during Saturnalian holidays. Since all things assumed a quite other

appearance than in the days of normal business, masks and disguisings were part of the festivity, and form part of the associated emblematic stock in trade, for emblems and *imprese* were meant to depict the human figure clad in some exotic or unusual costume or disguise, in masquerade or allegorical dress, presenting them in the shape of gods, nymphs, or satyrs, as if in a comedy, in tournaments or a masque.[53] Alexander Barclay, in his translation of 1570 of the *Narrenschiff*, attributes such goings-on to 'The frowarde festis of the Idoll Saturnus'.[54]

Saturnalian Games and Jokes

La Perrière's Emblem 6 (illus. 104) also exposes an offence against the festive code, also seen in the everyday abuse of language: the hypocrite hides 'soubz contrefaict langage' (under counterfeit terms). Such 'counterfeit terms' were part of the Saturnalian revelry – and therefore ought to be strictly confined to that period. Verbal games – riddles concealing common objects under 'misleading names of ambiguous meaning' – were among the games at Augustus's banquets.[55] In emblems, puns and double meanings tease out the significance of fables, or hide the familiar under a cloak of obscurity. In 'Two hundred poosees' Thomas Palmer exuberantly celebrates his patron, drawing on the ancient forms of festive merriment, proclaiming honours the Earl has won, and, under the protection of a kind of licensed folly, recommends by means of jokes, riddles, gnomic sentences and popular rhymes, virtues and skills of statecraft that his patron has or may yet acquire. Father Poirters in his *Het Masker van de Wereldt afgetrocken* introduces 'handfuls of clever puns' ('handvollekens aerdighe punt-redenen').[56] Such puns were keys to unlock the meaning embedded in an image. For Palmer, the ornithological kites in 'The Picture' of Emblem 181 become kites of a different feather in the epigram: rapacious knaves who prey on the undiscerning were so termed in Elizabethan slang; 'foules' (birds) in Emblem 159 become nothing more than 'foule tongde ... knaves'. Elsewhere, puns are more playful: in Emblem 44, the pine 'repin[es]'; the fable of two pots is a warning to all, lest everything 'goes to pot'. Many of Alciato's emblems have a superficially 'correct' and unexceptionable construction. Looked at another way, they can often assume a more licentiously ribald meaning. The prudent, sober man who shuns wine in favour of water in Emblem 201 is rendered ridiculously effeminate when viewed in a

festive light: he is endowed not with balls, but a clitoris. Alciato's
male personification of Gluttony is furnished not with a penis, but
a vulva ('tumida aluo'), what Spenser would call the 'Gulfe of
Greediness'. Emblem 11, 'In Silentium', or 'Silentium', is another
case in point. It enjoins under the sign of Harpocrates the sensible
advice that silence may sometimes be more prudent than speech.
But the phrase 'premat labias' contains a *double entendre*: in
Martial's epigrams, silence is seen as the activity associated not
with the sage, but with the *fellator* or *fellatrix*.[57]

Some of the favoured methods of rhetorical disposition in
emblem books may be determined by the festive origins of the
form. It was usual to arrange the Saturnalian *apophoreta* in pairs.[58]
Alciato experimented with this method in his 1546 edition, when
he followed his emblem 'Maledicentia' (Saurrility), with its
'Contra', on the soothing eloquence of a good leader. Both
emblems were printed on a single leaf to emphasize the topsy-
turvy qualities of the arrangement, where the top half of the page
contradicts the bottom. When the emblems were rearranged the
juxtaposition was lost, and the two emblems found themselves
widely separated, the second acquiring a new motto: 'Principis
clementia' (A ruler's forbearance).

Nevertheless, Alciato's imitators quickly grasped the principle.
Even whole books could be organized according to patterns of
contraries: Antonius à Burgundia's *Mundus Lapis Lydius* (Antwerp,
1639) presents the false appearance of the values of this world at the
top of a page, and confronts them with the truth of the matter in
the bottom line of the page. One emblem (illus. 105) presents us
with Riches, which are, from Truth's perspective, nothing more
than 'A Necessary Evil'. Each emblem is constructed on the same
format. In his *Linguae Vitia et Remedia* (Antwerp, 1631) he corrects
the vices of the tongue by confronting them with their corresponding remedies; the first two sections of Chesneau's *Orpheus
Eucharisticus* deal first with *humana sacra* and then with *humana
profana*. In the academic forum it was common for one scholar to
take one side of an argument, while another would argue the
contrary case. Thus in the Altdorf academy, for example, one prize-
winning orator would take the subject 'HAC ITVR AD ASTRA' (this is
the way to Heaven), while his fellow would argue 'HAC ITVR AD
ORCVM' (this is the way to damnation).[59] Juxtapositions of this kind
figure among Palmer's favourite organizational devices in 'Two
hundred poosees'. Emblem 59 deals with Riches, Emblem 60 with
Poverty:[60] both, we see, have their inconveniences. Emblem 57

represents Pallas, and Emblem 58, Hercules: each represents Virtue, the one feminine, the other masculine, the first founded on wisdom, the other on strength. Both are deemed necessary. The pairing of Emblems 11 and 12 is another example. The same *pictura*, an hourglass, is repeated for both, but the meanings drawn from it are exactly opposite: in 11 the hourglass stands for time, mortality and death, while in 12 it symbolizes resurrection and new life. The numbering of the emblems felicitously alludes to a calendrical symbolism: at Emblem 12 the hourglass is turned over and 'ginns a newe to runne'. A new year begins after twelve months. But the significant process here is that the same image is looked at from different perspectives. The pairing functions almost like the obverse and reverse of a medal. Eventually, however, Palmer moves beyond binary opposition to an inclusive view that encompasses life *and* death.

Palmer advertises this 'topsy turvy' approach to his symbols early in the volume. It is no surprise that this is followed by other 'World-upside-down' motifs: the ass plays the harp, the fool teaches the wise man, the cobbler preaches a sermon (Emblem 94). In Emblem 142 the woman wears the breeches, the Lady marries the servant. Alciato's Emblem on Gluttony (see illus. 117) presents before our eyes a pregnant man, whose stomach is not a stomach but a swelling womb ('tumida alvus'). There was a whole repertory of characteristic inversions in this vein, which had a wide popular currency. The title-page (illus. 106) of John Taylor's *Mad Fashions, O[d]d Fashions, All out of Fashions, or, The Emblems of these Distracted Times* (London, 1642), written at the time of the outbreak of the Civil War, collects a mini-anthology of some of these. A man wears boots and spurs on his hands, gloves on his feet. Trousers cover his torso, his doublet his legs. The Church and a candlestick hang upside down. A horse drives, while a man pulls a cart. A mouse chases a cat; the hare pursues the hound. These are part of the pan-European popular iconography of the *verkehrte Welt*, *le monde renversé*, and the *mundus alter* that could figure in political satire, in inn signs or in sermons. The underlying joke, of course, was that this 'other world' was actually the same as the one we inhabit, if we could only see it from the right perspective.

The perverse, subversive command to 'turn't upside down' became a specifically emblematic strategy, as when the Flesh – the girl with kaleidoscope eyes – in Quarles's *Emblemes* III, xiv, excitedly invites experimentation into the potentialities of an altered visual perspective. Vænius adopts a topsy-turvy approach when he defines love as an 'Inversvs crocodilvs' (an upside-down [or an inside-out, depending on your point of view] crocodile):[61] while a crocodile might shed a few proverbial tears for its victim, Cupid kills lovers with a smile on his lips. Emblems frequently depend on such inversions and perversities. Vænius's verbal games advertise this strategy when, on page 32, he turns the same words and phrases upside-down and inside-out:

MADFASHION s, 30

OD FASHIONS,

All out of Fafhions,

OR,

The Emblems of thefe Diftracted times.

By *Iohn Taylor*.

LONDON,
Printed by *Iohn Hammond,* for *Thomas Banks,* 1642.

106

Amour par tout, Par Amour tout.
tout par Amour, par tout Amour.

This is the merry humour of Shakespeare's Puck:

those things do best please me
That befall prepost'rously.

Yet the preposterous can assume erudite proportions, as when Curio and the author of the *Mikrokosmos* follow Plato in defining humanity as an inverted tree: 'Homo arbor inversa'.[62] Johann Mannich depicts a preposterous fool, who ignores the evidence before his eyes, by twisting his head backwards (see below illus. 142). Such strategies can be determinedly comic, as in the third of Glarus's satiric moral plays, which treats the backward journeys of this world.[63] Blake's 'contrary states' of Innocence and Experience, and his *Marriage of Heaven and Hell* stem from this tradition, inverting the conventional wisdom of 'all Bibles and sacred codes', making 'devils' the energetic exponents of 'Eternal Delight' while 'Angels' are pallid creatures wholly subservient to a stiflingly restrictive, conventional morality. It is not impossible that in some copies of Blake's *Songs*, Experience preceded Innocence.[64]

In Pignoria's epistle to the reader for Tozzi's 1618 edition of Alciato, the ignorant engravers and illustrators were castigated in no uncertain terms. But his criticisms may indicate that they, consciously or unconsciously, may have entered into the spirit of Alciato's Saturnalian grotesquerie. Pignoria describes their work as 'praepostera' – outrageous. Further, these artists revel ('debacchatur') as if drunk or raving mad, giving free license and reign to their own imaginations in utter contempt of standards of scholarly exactitude and correctness. In Pignoria's view, they have clearly gone too far. But it may be argued that they may have instinctively got it more right than wrong, responding in kind to the popular, festive, holiday humour of the project.[65]

Inverse, perverse and reverse emblematic views of the world are, in Martial's phrase, *carmine supino* (poems 'on their backs'). They take a topsy-turvy approach. 'Sotaden cinnaedum' ('sodomite Sotadics'), on the other hand, go the another way about and present an 'arsy versy', 'bottom-up' view of life. De Brune's *Emblemata, of Zinnewerck* (Amsterdam, 1624) reworks the *vanitas* motif by depicting a child with a filled nappy in Emblem 17. The child's bottom, ready for wiping, is thrust directly in the viewer's face, presented centre-stage in the *pictura*. Alciato's 'Ignaui' (Emblem 84) robustly compares the worthless busybody to a seductive, arse-wriggling catamite.[66] Van der Noot inveighs against 'Sodometrie' and the 'Sodomish chastitie' of the Roman priesthood.[67] In the hierarchy of the genres, it is well to remember that the epigram was not so much the 'foot' but the 'bottom' – 'the bottom of all poetry' according to Dryden. Thus, Wither in Emblem 11 of his Book 4 sings of the World's 'arseward Iourney'. Alciato looks at the preposterous through a frankly erotic glass: the 'Venus *praepostera*' or 'Venus *aversa*' of inverted sexuality: the effeminate man, the masculinized woman, the pederast, the deviant, the cinnaede. If the festive emblem is supposed to deal with *turpia* (base things),

Alciato turns to the *turpissima* (the basest things of all). He would have known Cicero's opinion, that there is nothing worse than an effeminate man.[68] Although Alciato's Emblem 4 presents an extremely high-minded allegory of the rape of Ganymede, at the back end of the *Emblemata omnia* (at page 497) we see it for what it is: 'paederastia'. The gallant's tender posterior is exposed to the predatory whore in Alciato's Emblem 74. Cats chooses to point to the world's monkey-business: the higher one climbs, the more one reveals one's shameful parts (illus. 107):

> *La scimia quanto più in alto sale*
> *Tanto più scuopere le sue vergogne.*[69]

'Le sue vergogne', the 'shameful parts', are also exposed in human form in Flitner's *Nebulo nebulonum* (The knave of knaves).[70] But *nebulones* can also mean 'slaves': it is therefore entirely appropriate that they step into the Saturnalian spotlight. This festive humour was not confined to, or designed only for, an exclusive, learned or aristocratic elite. The logic of the Saturnalian provenance of emblematic writing points to democratization, a social levelling. During this period Roman slaves were allowed to cheek their social superiors, and any laws against such libellous insubordination were suspended. Such indulgence did not always translate easily to the early modern period. Roger North scathingly identified the 'low' appeal of emblems, when he referred to their 'notable Eloquence for the Eye', which was directed at 'the Rabble and drunken Sottish Clubs'. The verse was 'in Ballad Doggerel', with a 'witty Picture affixed'. These were precursors of the catches and glees of the late eighteenth century and Victorian Song & Supper Clubs. When North used the term 'witty', he was being sarcastic. In his view these were nothing more than 'Libels, Lampoons, Satyrs, Pictures and Sing-Songs'.[71] Jan van der Veen had earlier used a combination of 'emblems, songs and sonnets' to put on public display 'the old and iniquitous use of life' in its portrayal of the follies of Adam's offspring.[72]

The Puritan kill-joy, Stubbes, in his *Anatomie of Abuses*, sneered at the distinctly vulgar, down-market 'papers, wherein is painted some bablery or other of imagery work'. These were 'my Lord of Misrule's badges', a designedly irregular eruption into the popular festive insurgences at Christmas, Carnival or May Day, in which Morris men attempted to filch coins from the purses of their 'betters'. '[W]hoever will not be buxom to them and give them money for these their devilish cognizances, they are mocked and flouted at', fumed Stubbes.[73] These 'cognizances', devilish or otherwise, are emblems. Wither also offers surprising evidence – given the large, expensive format of his book – for the essentially popular audience for his emblems in 1635. Wither, without the scorn that attaches to Stubbes's or North's comments, states in his prefatory comments that his book is 'sutable to meane capacities', 'common Readers', and 'Vulgar Capacities'. He admits that his book has 'some faultes', but 'they are such, as *Common-Readers* will never perceive'. Cornelis Plemp observed the same shift in the audience for emblems in the Low Countries around the beginning of the seventeenth century, when he remarked, 'Even the common people have developed a taste for emblems'.[74] Nor should we be distracted by the fact that Wither dedicated each of his books that make up his *Collection of Emblemes* to members of the Royal Household: this was an appeal to an essentially popular piety, loyalty to the King, the reigning monarch, which still could be strongly invoked, even though we know that within the decade this would fall apart, and these traditional allegiances could no longer be widely sustained. Charles's court was far less erudite in its tastes than was the case under Charles's father, James I. But the popular appeal of Wither's book can be demonstrated by the fact that it continued to circulate, not in its folio format, but in the cheap, possibly pirated, copies of

108

Wither's verses, that went under the title *Delights for the Ingenious, in above Fifty Select and Choice Emblems, Divine and Moral, Ancient and Modern* and under the alternative title *Choice Emblems Divine and Moral.* These reproduce crude copies of De Passe's elegant plates, William Marshall's frontispiece, and the lottery. The man responsible was the publisher Nathaniel Crouch, who regularly used the pseudonym Richard Burton. These went through a number of editions: a 'sixth edition' was printed for Edmund Parker in 1732. It must have continued to sell, for there were subsequent editions in 1781, 1784 and 1812.

In emblematics there is a 'democritization' in another sense: there is, as we have seen, a social levelling. But, more specifically, 'democritization' can refer to the view of the world taken by the laughing philosopher Democritus. Rabelais, as a contemporary of the founding father of emblematics, with an eye on his Aristotle, could confidently affirm: 'rire est le propre de l'homme' (To laugh is natural to the human race).[75] One could either view the world through the eyes of the laughing philosopher, or through those of his weeping companion, Heraclitus.[76] Alciato rehearsed these options in his emblem on human life, 'In vitam humanam' (illus. 108). This is the ultimate Janus-inspired perspective. We see it in Erasmus, and it was a guiding principle of the Counter-Reformation. But in this emblem Alciato edges towards the Democritan view: '[vita] magis ludicra facta fuit' (Life has become more of a joke). It is therefore doubly appropriate that Alciato devotes a proportion of the *Emblemata* to the Saturnalian activity of telling old jokes. He repeated the jests of others, and others repeated his. Emblem 155, 'De Morte et Amore' (On Death and Love), attempts to explain by means of a fable why old men should fall in love and young men die. This paradoxical state of affairs came about because of a mix-up over two sets of luggage at an inn. Cupid and Death each went off with the wrong arrows: Cupid with the bony ones, and Death with Cupid's golden shafts. This is a 'figmentum lepidum et festivum' (a witty, humorous story) according to Mignault. Whitney styles this 'jocosum' – a funny story. In Du Bellay's hands, this becomes one of life's little jokes ('ludibria vitae'), and, as such, thoroughly in tune with Saturnalian perversities, for this involves an inversion of Nature's laws:

You, too, Nature, learn to invert your laws! [77]

Another of Alciato's jokes is the one about an ass carrying a shrine on its back. The animal mistakenly thinks it is the object of worship, when people kneel in reverence as it passes along the street. There is probably in this emblem an allusion to more than the *asinus portans mysteria*, the foolish person of limited capacities who overreaches himself. It may also allude to the Carnivalesque *Festum asinorum*, where an effigy of an ass is borne through the streets of the city.[78] Traditions of Carnival are accommodated to the Saturnalia, another piece of evidence that bespeaks their common origin.

Yet jokes allow the emblematic writer to reproduce things that were formerly seen as manifest offences against Classical good taste and common sense. Horace denounces the image of a beautiful woman with the tail of a black and ugly fish ('turpiter atrum / desinat in piscem mulier formosa superne') as ludicrously mirth-provoking.[79] But just such a fishy-tailed female appears in Alciato's emblem 'Sirenes': 'mulier, quae in piscem desinit atrum' (illus. 109). Other emblems depend for their effect on a raree show of such ludicrous monsters, sports and tricks of nature, where head and tail, bottom and top are disgustingly mismatched: Chiron the Centaur, the Chimaera, the Giants, the Harpies, the Minotaur, Pan, Scylla and the Sphinx. This category of imagery is specifically associated not only with the ludicrous, but with depraved, low, shameful ('turpe') and unworthy things.[80]

The perspective of *Vanitas* often comically exposes the pretensions that mask the reality of things. Antonia à Burgunda shows the ludicrous fragility of the high-flying upper classes in the image of a kite (illus. 110). They are at the mercy of the wind ('ludibrium venti'), and as such are comically exposed. Another 'ludibrium ventorum' appears in a satiric political print of 1605, which

109

compares the embarrassment of the Spanish Armada in 1588, whose threat was lightly tossed aside by the gales of Heaven, to the exposure of Guy Fawkes' plot to blow up Parliament. In these comical emblematic stage plays (also 'ludibria'), Heaven has the best seat in the house, and God has plainly enjoyed the performance. 'Video et rideo' (I see and I laugh) is His pleased critical comment (illus. 111). Rosicrucians and Alchemists also sometimes referred to their emblematic works as *ludibria* (jokes). How can we possibly be sure what these things are or mean? Maier advertises a *Iocus serius* – the fact that the merest trifling fables, silly stories, drawings and images should point to the fundamental secrets of the universe, a profound philosophical wisdom must have provoked at least a smile, given the vast disproportion between vehicle and tenor. From our perspective the joke is often at their expense: so much labour, so much windy verbiage, so many smoky circumlocutions to cover such empty, and finally unproductive, conclusions, their speculations, like so many of their experiments,

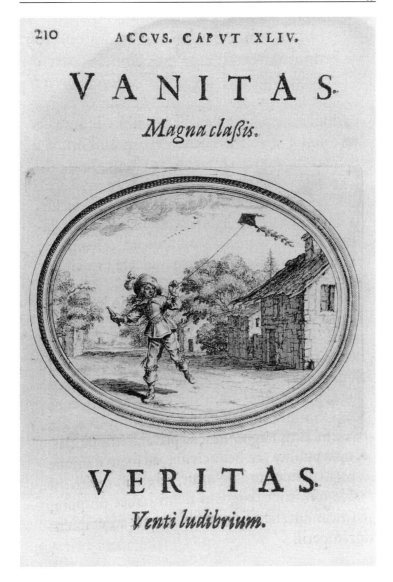

disappearing in a puff of smoke. These *ludibria* (frivolities) can at times be quite impenetrable to a modern taste. But the past is, we must remember, another country, and there they speak a different language – a language we understand imperfectly. Especially when it comes to humour. What they described as a joke, *jocus, ludibrium, facetiae, figmentum festivum*, a modern reader may not necessarily find particularly funny. Often the early modern joke can be simply too grim and lugubrious for our present eyes and ears. Fajardo Saavedra's final emblem in his *Idea de un Principe*

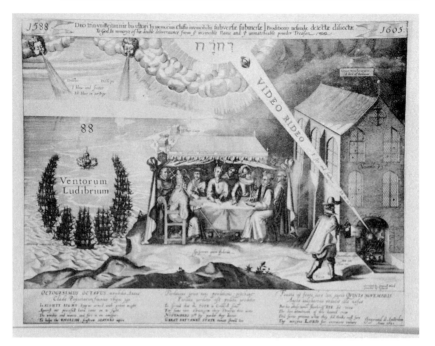

111

politico Christiano gives a whole suite of LUDIBRIA MORTIS (illus.
112) that we might freely translate as 'Death's Alchemy'. The
emblem subjects his protagonist, the Christian prince, to a final
indignity, or, more properly, a whole series of indignities. This last,
absurd scene in his emblematic progress shows a discarded crown,
a sceptre and a broken column lying at the foot of a cracked
sarcophagus. On it rests a skull covered by a spider's web. After his
exit from the world's stage, the prince is far from forgotten. Time
and its agents – the worm, the spider and all the ineluctable
processes of decay – work their last, subtle, strange and secret
attendances on him. Death is the ultimate democrat, the final
social leveller. At the emblematic Saturnalian feast he was a
frequent, if not a compulsory guest.[81]

Father Poirters collected a whole string of jokes and used them
as an aid in recognizing the vanity of the world. In this he makes
subtle distinctions between the laughter of lovers, the worldly, and
the pious.[82] Alonso Ledesma, the Spanish translator of Vænius's
Amoris Divini Emblemata, prided himself on teaching moral and
religious truths under the cloak of 'burlas y juegos'.[83] This kind of
witty piety, sometimes known as scripture jests or 'concetti predi-
cabili', can prove something of a shock to modern sensibilities. Two
centuries after the fashion for this sort of thing reached its peak,

388   I M P R E S A.
li effetti,che le caufe.Coprìua a'fuoi Ambafciatori li fuoi difcegni,quàdo vo
che ingànati perfuadeſſero meglio il còtrario. Seppe gouernare per metà cc
Regina,& vbbidire à ſuo Genero . Impofe tributi per la neceffità,non per l'
ritia,ò per il luſto , Quello che tolſe alle Chieſe,obbligato dalla neceffità, i
tuì quàdo ſi vidde ſenza quella.Rifpettò la giuridittioneEcclefiaftica,e còſ
la Reale. Nò tène Còrte ferma,girando come il Sole per li circoli de fuoiRe
Trattò la pace con la tèpetanza,& con l'integrità,& la guerra con la forza,&
l'aftutia. Non affettò queſta,nè ricusò quella.Ciò che occupò il piede man
il braccio,e l'ingegno,reſtàdo più poderoſo cò le ſpoglie.Tāto operauano l
negotiationi come le ſue armi. Quel che puote vincere cò l'arte non rimeſ
la ſpada.Ponea in queſta l'oftentatione della ſua grandezza,& la pompan
roce delli ſquadroni . Nelle guerre dètro del ſuoRegno ſi trouò ſempre pr
te, Operaua il medeſimo che ordinaua .Si confederaua per reſtare arbitro
ſoggetto . Nè vittorioſo s'infuperbì, nè ſi diſperò vinto. Stabilì le paci ſot
ſcudo . Viſſe per tutti,& morì per sè,reſtando ſempre nella memoria degl
mini,per eſſempio delli Prencipi, & eterno nel deſiderio de ſuoi Regni ,

LAVS DEO.

LVDIBRIA MORTIS

Efle mortal defpojo , ò Caminante ;   Donde antes la Sobervia, dando leyes
Trifte horror de laMuerte,en quiē laAraña   A la Paz, i à la Guerra,prefidia ,
Hilos anuda, i la Inocencia engaña ,   Se prenden oi los viles animales .
Que à romper lo futil , no fuè bastante .   Que os arrogàis ò Principes ò Reyes ?
Coronandofe viò,fe viò triunfante   Si en los vltrajes de la Muerte fri
Con los trofeos de vna , i otra bazaña ,   Conmunes ſois con los demàs Mortal
Fabor ſu riſa, fue te rror ſu ſaña ,
Atento el urbe à ſu Real ſemblante,

112

Charles Lamb wrote to Robert Southey, disapproving of Quarles:
'Religion appears to Quarles no longer valuable than it furnishes
matter for quibbles and riddles; he turns God's grace into wantonness'.[84] Yet Arwaker's exercises in the form are sometimes given his
own epigrammatic point by a felicitous use of the couplet:

> Thus, when too freely Noah had us'd the Vine,
> He who escap'd the Flood, lay drown'd in Wine.[85]

This is Arwaker's very own acknowledged, *original*, italicized contribution to pious desires. He leaps free from his Jesuitical source only to sink under his own metrical weight and measure. Pope would have doubtless adduced such 'wit' as further evidence that Dullness does indeed love a joke.

Some humour can only be seen *sub specie aeternitatis*, as in Arwaker, II, i:

> How do we weary Heav'n with diff'rent Prayers!
> The medly, sure, ridiculous appears.

Arwaker inherits a Classical world-view that placed the human race at centre stage in a comedy for the gods. The Judaeo-Christian Supreme Being apparently had a season ticket for re-runs of this classical farce.[86] Arwaker, as some species of *entrepreneur*, a ticket tout for this divine comedy, encourages us to participate in the ineffable, divine amusement. The very term *ludicra* that Alciato used in relation to Democritus' vision of the world in his emblem 'In vitam humanam' (illus. 108), refers specifically to stage plays and to theatrical spectacles. Many books of emblems are advertised as theatres: the *'Theatrum ...'* or *'theatre'* or other vernacular equivalents.

Priapic License

But the jokes appropriate to Saturnalian holiday mirth came from a theatre more like Martial's – a theatre that was given over to 'the festive games and license of the common people'. This allowed for an 'uninhibited freedom of expression'.[87] Wither appealed, as we have seen, to the 'Vulgar Capacities' of 'Common Readers', while North noted the appeal of the emblem to the 'Rabble' and the 'Drunken Sottish Clubs'. Martial's choice of matter and manner, although he is talking of his epigrams, and the festival he refers to specifically here is the *Florales*, may be considered as a model for later Renaissance humanist developments in the field of emblematics, as a species of *carmina iocosa*. Festive emblematics, particularly those associated with the Saturnalia, may be aligned with the traditions of old comedy with its 'Bacchic songs ... full of drunkenness and phallic license'.[88] It is no secret that humanist writers of the sixteenth century had a robust taste for the scurrilous and the scatological. Theodore de Bèze in his own day was perhaps more famous for the obscene poems of his youth than as the leader of Calvin's Protestant flock in Geneva; Celio Calcagnini, the admired translator of Plutarch's *De Iside et Osiride*, one of the most difficult of Greek texts, was also responsible for the salacious epigram 'De cunnis' and the learned trifle 'De pulicis' (On fleas). Antonio Beccadelli's *Hermaphroditus* was anathematized, burnt in the public square in Bologna, Milan and Ferrara, even though it sprang from the learned pen of the founder of the Accademia Pontaniana; Justus Lipsius, the champion of neo-Stoicism, was known to take pleasure in the verbal lubricities of Petronius; Valeriano, however disingenuously, in Book XVIII of the *Hieroglyphica* opined that a reading of wittily suggestive verses on the hermaphrodite might lead to higher knowledge. Sambucus identifies epigrammatic sharpness with the salacious: 'salsa, quod salacia'.[89] This is generically obligatory, and was proclaimed as such: 'This is the rule assigned to jocular poems, to be unable to please, unless they are prurient.'[90]

Martial's epigram that forms the epigraph to this chapter invokes the name of Sotades, by reputation one of the most scurrilously obscene poets of antiquity. In citing this epigram Wolfgang Hunger seems to suggest that emblems, in his view, are in this Sotadic tradition. Acccordingly, Alciato's comic theatre is marked by lascivious, lewd or obscene jests. He intended his emblems to be entertaining and enjoyable. One of his emblems, 'Maledicentia', commemorates the archetypal scurrility of Archilochus. In his pursuit of the coarse and the obscene, he causes his commentators to blush on more than one occasion.[91] However, in spite of some embarrassment, Mignault comments approvingly on his use of a shocking, obscene diction.[92] The comedy here resides in the use of bawdy words. Alciato's legless embodiment of sly deceit in Emblem 5, a man's head and torso joined to a serpentine tail, is disgustingly sharpened by the author's bold recourse to 'low' diction: the nether limbs are 'farted' out; the torso is 'burped' up. Mignault applauds the willingness to apply gross words to gross deeds. In Emblem 84 Alciato literally dives to the bottom of the linguistic register, coming up with the abusive verb *cevere* to describe a degenerate busybody fussing over other people's business: he wiggles his backside enticingly, as though he were the willing, passive partner in a sodomite coupling.[93] The very origins of the word *obscene* are necessarily plumbed in relation to Alciato's Emblem 79, 'Lasciuia'.[94] Alciato set a standard in such matters, which others followed.

But we now come to the nub of much of the vehement disapproval voiced against the Rabble's immoderate delight in the 'notable Eloquence for the Eye' by North and others. When

Stubbes referred to the Morris men's 'devilish cognizances' as 'painted ... bablery', he obviously did not only mean to dismiss them as mere nonsense. He may, of course, have implied that they are a species of confused 'Babel-ry' in scorn of emblematic polyglottism, or worse, that they were tainted by some species of 'devilish' necromancy, which was literally 'characterised' by nonsensical, barbarous obscurities: mangled verbiage, a tortuous, incomprehensible script, or utter nonsense and silliness.[95] But the devil he really fears in all these 'cognizances' is their priapic obscenity: the fool's 'bauble', the 'foolish thing' in Feste's seasonably ribald song from Shakespeare's *Twelfth Night*.[96] In translating the pet names for the infant's 'chose' in Rabelais's *Gargantua*, Chapter 11, Urquhart overgoes his original. One of the names he produces that explains Stubbes's disproportionate disgust at mere 'nonsense' is 'bableret'.[97] This, in Stubbes's demonology, would have been no less a sign of unmistakable demonic Sabbath-breaking lewdness, showing the Morris men to be indubitable masters of lust, practitioners of the most shameful kinds of depravity.[98] Yet, emblems with blatantly priapic obsessions are found in the canonical works of Alciato himself. His spoof heraldry of the god of love in 'In statuam Amoris' (illus. 113) is blatantly and physically engrossed:

> *signum*
> *Illius est nigro punica glans clypeo*
> (His heraldic device is an empurpled *glans* on a black ground)

It is impossible to distinguish this small object picked out on the shield in many of the illustrations to the *Emblemata*. Chaste and more modest eyes and ears distinguished the 'glans' as a pomegranate![99] The contemporary technical heraldic term for the device on such a shield as Cupid bears is the 'prick', because it was hammered out on the metal with some sharp object. And with punning justice, this is exactly the device that the god of Love bears: a prick. Edmund Spenser, for one, would have recognized 'this pricke of highest praise' (*Faerie Queene*, 11, xii, 1, 3) for what it is. If there was any doubt about the emblazoned object, Mignault's commentary can allow no escape from the obvious: 'it is the top part of a man's penis, which in Latin is called the *mentula*.'[100] This is anatomically clear to any common understanding. There can be no doubt that the 'glans' in question is the male organ – empurpled, engorged and glistening. Further, the 'glans' is obviously meant to 'stand out' against the black background of his shield. But

113

that detail, too, contains various other bawdy innuendoes, emblematic 'secrets'. These are blush-worthy, and contemporary commentators are in difficulties over explicating them in plain terms: 'modesty forbids me from saying anything openly about this'.[101] Sufficient to say, these involve sexual 'covering': the word for shield, 'clypeus', is derived from 'celo' (to cover, conceal by covering). The 'black shield' thus alludes to the 'deed of darkness' and to its sweet and viscous joys.[102]

Other examples of a delight in priapic license and obscenity are to be found elsewhere in Alciato's emblems. The god Pan in Emblem 98, openly displays his venereal parts: 'Veneris signaque aperta gerit', in keeping with the sexually 'open', unrestrained spirit of Carnival. Emblem 153 focuses on the 'virilia' (testicles), where one cannot but savour the witty justice of Alciato's precise choice of the epithet 'propendulus' in the first line of his epigram: the semantics of the adjective chart the movement of the epigram as the attention swings from the 'sagging' belly, to the 'dangling' male appurtenances. Venus's amulet in Emblem 77 knowingly alludes to the magic talisman that hangs not from the neck but from the male loins. The first word of the emblem's epigram closes the gap between any honest construction of the meaning of the motto and its suspect bawdy innuendo by directing the reader's attention immediately to the appropriate part of the anatomy: 'INGVINA' (the groin, the privy member). Emblem 123 celebrates the god Faunus as a benefactor of the human race. He had bestowed on humanity an inestimable gift – none other than the war trumpet – and was consequently deified! But many early illustrations of the emblem prefer to depict him in his more familiar Horatian role, as 'Nympharum fugientum amator' (the lover of the fleeing nymphs).[103] We therefore see him in loud pursuit, raising his 'horrido corno', as Marquale's choice Italian translation so aptly puts it (illus. 114).[104] One need only point to Lewis and Short's primary entry in their *Latin Dictionary* for *horridus* to savour the full, phallic implications of the sixteenth-century Italian epithet: 'standing on end, sticking up, rough, shaggy, bristly', and, finally and decisively, 'prickly'.[105] The very word *satyr* derives from the Greek, *sathé*, the male organ. Alciato's Latin phrase 'inflat cornua' (who blows my horn) contains an equally, if different, phallic *double entendre*. When Pignoria advised on the redesigned plates for Tozzi's 1618 and 1621 editions of the *Emblemata* he directed readers' attention away from the erotic pastimes of the god. The *pictura* presents a straight-forwardly militaristic Captain Faunus: there is not a nymph in sight. Pignoria and Tozzi therefore reduce the chance that the tumescent implications of Faunus's *inflat*[ed] *cornua* would come into view. But Colonna, in the area of furtive eroticism (illus. 115), as in so much else, has already laid the groundwork that will be built on in the sixteenth-century emblem.

   No discussion of emblematic priapic obsessions can avoid the heraldic device of the Colleoni. Like Alciato's shield of Cupid this lascivious heraldry emblazons the *virilia* – the testicles. The image was entirely, if blatantly, appropriate – a punning visual allusion to the name of the noble bearers. Unfortunately, it did not seem appropriate to everyone. Mario Praz describes at some length a learned dispute over these 'sales monuments de ... lubricité'.[106] Claude Le Laboureur's *Discours sur l'origine des armes* failed to recognize them for what they were. Menestrier criticized the book severely, and one of the features he seized on to discredit the volume was the little matter of the unidentified or misidentified testicles. The two men fell into prolonged dispute, and in the ensuing combat of verbal tennis, whose weapons included *termes de bordel*, these balls were batted back and forth over the net. Menestrier was not afraid to lower the tone by imputing more than scholarly impropriety to the aged priest. The artist who had drawn the item was, apparently, a young woman, Claudine Brunant.

In vn subito terrore.

Mentre intento a suonar l'horrido corno
  Fuggir ratto le genti il fauno vede:
Non virtù, ch'in mio cor faccia soggiorno
  Dice ha riuolto a questi in fuga il piede,
Ma la viltà, che con vergogna e scorno
  Fa che'l miglior al manco degno cede.
Così misera al mouer de le frondi
  Fugge la lepre, e doue puo s'asconde.

ΠΑΝΤΩΝ ΤΟΚΑΔΙ

115

Who, Menestrier wondered, had served as the male model for the objects she illustrated? The participants in the quarrel had rapidly moved beyond the stage where either of them could see the joke. It was the onlookers who saw and enjoyed the game.

Anti-Catholic polemic, too, revolved around the *virilia*. In one emblem in his *Quinquaginta emblemata* Cornelis Plemp depicts what looks like a toilet – but this is, in fact, the papal *cathedra pertusa*: not so much a holy throne, but a throne-with-a-hole; not a privy, but a crudely simple machine designed for the inspection of the privy member. The papal candidate was obliged to sit on this noble edifice, whereupon the action of gravity would render his male credentials accessible to tactile inspection by the youngest choirboy. This invention of ingenious piety was developed to

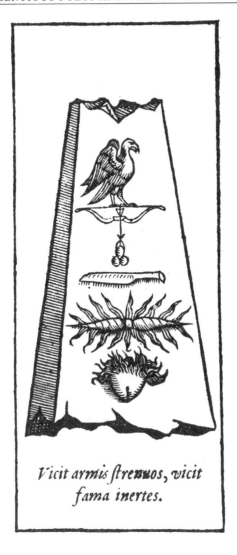

*Vicit armis ſtrenuos, vicit
fama inertes.*

116

ensure that there would be no repetition of the embarrassing
aftermath of the election of Pope Joan.[107] Religious folly is also
priapically displayed in Flitner's invocation of the 'cauda Diaboli'
(the Devil's penis), on which the man who despairs of God's salvation is said to ride (see illus. 138).

We should not be altogether surprised to find that the 'secret
parts' adorn the emblematic mysteries. The origins of the hieroglyphs lay in Isis' search for the dismembered phallus of Osiris.[108]
Valeriano's exhaustive catalogue of animals, agricultural implements and discrete body parts includes, inevitably, the *pudenda*
(see illus. 116).[109] Nor is our emblematic Saturnalia devoted exclu-

sively to the priapic. The genitalia of both sexes are celebrated –
not unsurprisingly, since contemporary medical treatises held that
a woman had all the sexual attributes of a man, except that they
were internalized and concealed.[110] The 'arvum genitale' (the fruitful field) of Alciato's Emblem 77 is as feminine as it is masculine,
but the impudent female 'pubes' (private parts) of the monstrous
Scylla are uncompromisingly feminine: they form the emphatic
opening of Emblem 68: 'PVBE tenus mulier' (Down to the private
parts a woman).[111] Here, Alciato anticipates Shakespeare's 'waist of
shame' of Sonnet 129 – Scylla is none other than Shame ('Impu-
dentia'). Not content to stay his investigation at that point, Alciato's emblem explores her deformed 'infra', her underneath. These
nether parts form the classically dreaded monstrous cavern,
Virgil's 'spelunca' of *Aeneid*, III, 424, that both contains and is her
body. Other sexualized caves and caverns are found in Ausonius's
Crispa, whom Thuilius cites to explicate Alciato's Emblem 79:
'Lascivia' (Lust): 'she masturbates, fellates, lets herself be done in
either hole'.[112] Finally, the *clitoris* itself is necessarily discussed in
the annotations to Alciato's emblem on the willow.[113]

Scatological humour

Priapic displays do not exhaust the vulgarities of the emblem
theatre. Alciato's 'Gula', for instance, turns to another engorged
member, the tumescent belly, showing the effects of appetite on
the human form (illus. 117). But the gross turpitude depicted in the
emblem is not so much directed towards the grotesquely physical
deformities that result from over-indulgence. Alciato describes
here a moral turpitude: the figure in the emblem actually *wants* to
look this way! Alciato directs his attack on the state of mind that
produces this physical obscenity. 'How ingenious is gluttony!'
exclaimed Thuilius,[114] who goes on to produce a menu of all that
once swam, walked, flew, hopped or crawled that finds its way onto
the dinner plate. Indeed, he rivals the Tempter himself in Milton's
Paradise Regained:

> meats of noble sort
> And savour, beasts of chase, or fowl of game
> In pastry built, or from the spit, or boiled,
> Grisamber-steamed; all fish from sea or shore,
> Freshet, or purling brook, of shell or fin,
> And exquisite name . . .[115]

58   GVLÆ.

GVLÆ.

Curculione gruis tumida vir pingitur aluo,
   Qui Laron, aut manibus gestat Onocrotalum..
Talis forma fuit Dionysi, & talis Apici,
   Et gula quos celebres deliciosa facit.

117

The ingenuity of the human palate extends not only to the methods of hunting, trapping or slaughtering the prey, but to the means
of preparing it. To Thuilius this becomes a huge joke, because in
the end it all is dissolved into the chamber-pot, the *matella* or the
scaphium – a huge, expensive cacastrophe.

Nor is Thuilius alone in revelling in this mirth-provoking

EMBLEMA XXXVIII.

Belidas fingunt pertufa in dolia vates
Mox effundendas fundere femper aquas.
Nomine mutato,narratur fabula de te,
Ebrie,quæ meias qui fine fine bibis.
Quin etiam hoc in te quadrat turba ebria,quòd fint
Corpora quæ fuerant,dolia fatta tibi.

118

excremental emblematic vision. In the previous chapter we observed Gillray's scatological enthusiasms and we have already noted De Brune's exercise in the genre, when he produced his emblematic child with a filled nappy under the motto 'Dit liif wat ist, als stanck en mist?' (What is life, but stink and shit?). The picture of a defecating man, introduced in the 1546 Venice edition of the *Emblematum libellus* (see illus. 94), also graces Alciato's Emblem 80 in the Tozzi 1621 edition.[116] Gillray inverts the sex of Alciato's sitter in his 'Patience on a Monument' (see illus. 93). Sir John Harrington adorned his newly-invented water-closet with an emblem. Jakob Cats goes further to show an emblem of a fool engaged in a furious fight. His chosen weapons are missiles formed of his very own excrement. Woefully bewrayed in his own ordure, he clutches one of the few certainties of life: in such a battle, no matter whether one wins or loses, one is bound to come away dirty.[117] Thuilius freely acknowledged the example and the mastery of Théodore de Bèze, whose emblem on the urinating drunkard he cites as a *locus classicus* (illus. 118). Improving on his source, De Bèze applies to this character the fable of the grand-daughters of Belus, the Egyptian king. In Hell, these murderesses were sentenced to fill throughout eternity a perforated barrel: as fast as they brought water, as quickly would it drain away. So the drunkard condemns himself to just such an interminable ('sine fine') hell-on-earth. The infernal tun is his body; as fast as he drinks, he pisses it away.[118] A 'bitter' end, one might opine, if the jest were not so tired.

Ultimately, one may refer these jests to an aspect of Baroque spirituality, which encouraged the believer to regard the things of this world as no more than trash and trifles, dirt and excrement: a view tersely summed up in the two sardonic echoing synonyms that form the motto of Cramer's Emblem 32: 'LIMUS FIMUS'.[119]

Sexual humour

We have it on St Augustine's authority, 'In vino luxuria est' (In wine there is lust). The remark was so frequently anthologized in collections of *apothegmata*, and from thence acquired with comparatively little effort, that it became an inspiration to many. Peacham, for one, warns against 'Blaspheming, whoredome, oathes, and deadlie hate' that follow excess of 'daintie fare, / And drunken healthes'. But emblem books provide *luxuria* with and without the wine. Even the pious Benedictine Van Haeften, in his *Schola Cordis*, and, consequently, his translator, Christopher Harvey, in *The School of the Heart*, catalogue 'Base lust and luxury', 'sensual delight', 'riotous excess', 'effeminate desires', 'spumy pleas-ures'.[120] All this raises our interest, even though the 'pleasures' and 'delights' are vague, general and unspecified. But Van Haeften and Harvey only allow us the merest glimpse of these excesses in order to reprove them in manifest self-loathing disgust. Fortunately, elsewhere, the emblematic corpus manages to put more delightful flesh on these bare lenten bones.

Love is, according to Alciato, a 'Iucundus labor' (delightful labour).[121] With the phrase, he frankly acknowledges that he has made love, and enjoyed it! He also insinuates that his *emblemata* are similarly delightful. Little wonder, then, that standard reference works of the period, such as Mirabellius's *Dictionarium*, cite Alciato's emblems as authoritative statements on topics such as *fornicatio, amor venereus, adulterium, scortatio* (see illus. 119) and *libido*. And the index to Alciato's *Reliqua opera* indicates that he had a healthy, professional interest in the legal ramifications of human sexuality, marriage, adultery and illegitimacy. His solution, in his annotations on Tacitus (*Annales*, XI, 26), to the sexual conundrum of the Roman matron who was said to have her birthplace in both Naples and Cos,

138　　*Andreæ Alciati*

In amatores meretricum.

EMBLEMA LXXV.

V ILLOSÆ *indutus piscator tegmina capræ,*
  Addidit vt capiti cornua bina suo;
Fallit amatorem stans summo in littore sargum,
In laqueos simi quem gregis ardor agit.
Capra refert scortum : similis fit sargus amanti,
  Qui miser obscœno captus amore perit.

EXPLICAT. CLAVD. MIN.

P R I M A huius comparationis pars sumpta est ab
  Aeliano, lib. De animalib. 1. cap. 23. Vt sargus piscis
facilè à piscatore capitur, si caprinam pellem induerit
(genus enim hoc piscis instinctu quodam naturæ, amore
caprarum detinetur) ita deperit amasius visa quadam
formosula, vel potius laruata capra, cuius laqueis irre-
titus,

was admired as much for its justice, as for its wit, and ingenuity: she denied in the privacy of the bedroom (and hence *Nola*) the sexual favours she willingly agreed to in the public forum of her dinner parties (hence *Coa*).[122] Alciato supplies a humane correction to the abusive term *Cuckoo* – Shakespeare's (and James Joyce's) 'word of fear', and source of so many tiresomely repeated jokes in Renaissance comedies – usually applied to the wronged husband in the relationship. The term, opines Alciato, should more fitly be attached to the adulterer, who has polluted the matrimonial nest.[123]

120

Many early modern emblem books are little more than a voyeuristic peep-show, revealing sexual practices and proclivities, aligning them even more firmly with the excesses of the ancient *Florales*. Unfortunately, no contemporary Jesuit encyclopaedist applied his indefatigable industry to this topic. However, we can go so far as to say that the the whole gamut of licentious conjugations, licit and illicit, *nequitiae* of all colours and shapes are catered for: voyeurism (illus. 120), prostitution (male and female), incest, homosexual rape, sodomy, paedophilia (*amor puerilis*), carnal lusts, adultery and bestiality. Alciato's Emblem 141, 'In desciscentes' (On degenerates, or, perhaps, more properly, On deviants) exposes the shameful end ('fine turpi') of self-abuse, as the milky riches are squandered and spilt ('proprias . . . profundit opes'). Additions to Valeriano's *Hieroglyphica* show the gods' pursuit of mortal beauty under feigned shapes (illus. 121). Aneau's *Picta poesis*, in particular, deals with a range of strange sexual practices, which we might

121

122

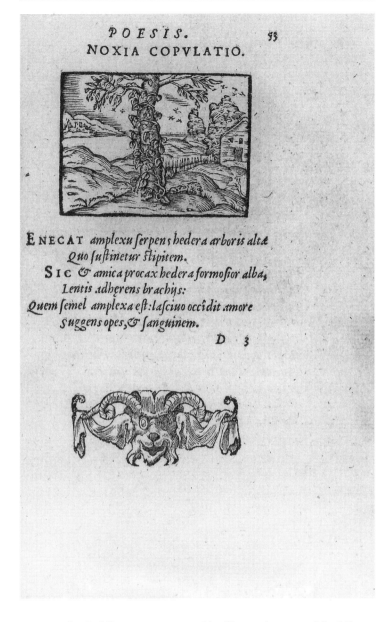

POESIS.   53
NOXIA COPVLATIÕ.

E NECAT *amplexu ferpens hedera arboris altæ*
Quo fuſtinetur ſtipitem.
S I C *& amica procax hedera formofior alba,*
Lentis adhærens brachijs:
Quem femel amplexa eſt:laſciuo occidit amore
Suggens opes,& fanguinem.

D   3

123

trace to the Ovidian provenance of its illustrative materials. Misce-
genation and bestiality are seen in the riotous wantonness of
Pasiphae. Sexual ambivalence or impotence is presented in Aneau's
and in various other representations of the fountain of Hermaphroditus (illus. 122). Aneau's 'Noxia copulatio' (illus. 123) more than
hints at *fellatio*, as the 'amica procax' (wanton slut) sucks her lover
dry ('Suggens opes, et sanguinem'). The Latin *sanguis* refers not

only to his financial lifeblood and his physical well-being, but also to his other bodily fluids – blood, and here, most probably, semen. If the *amica* sucks, she also fornicates. A satyr embraces a raging inferno in Aneau's *Picta Poesis*, to show the painful consequences of meddling with women:

> There is the sulphurous pit – burning, scalding,
> Stench, consumption; fie, fie, fie![124]

One might say he gets what he deserves – Aneau's goat-legged god himself is burnt by his own lusts. Aneau's underpinning biblical text is 1 Corinthians 7. 1: 'It is good for a man not to touch a woman.' But the instrument of punishment is the fire he so eagerly sought: the fire and the woman are emblematically one – this is the 'hell', this the 'darkness', this the burning pit, this the 'beneath' of lascivious women dedicated to the fiend and here tormenting the very fiend himself: the harlotry of Laïs and Flora; the vindictive Medea; the deceitful Scylla; Circe's degrading, bestial appetites; Biblis's and Canace's unnatural, incestuous lusts for their own brothers, Mirrha's for her father, Semiramis's for her son, and Phaedra's burning desire for Hippolitus. Venus presides over the uncontrolled female *libido*. Her various and numerous adulteries – with Anchises, with Apollo, with Mercury, with Mars, with Adonis – are exposed to the mockery of gods and men (illus 124). This catalogue is almost certainly incomplete, for who can number her lapses and indiscretions? Nor should one exhaust oneself in such sums and computations. It is enough that these emblems, almost without exception, carried with them warnings by older and wiser men (priests, doctors, teachers, lawyers) to younger men. 'Hoc itaque dico fratres', says St Paul (I Corinthians 7. 29), and our emblematists follow: this *Gesellschaft* admits an exclusively male membership. If not totally against love, they could go so far as to recommend certain prudential maxims to avoid its worst consequences, and to embrace the best that might be had under the circumstances. Safe sex could only be recommended in terms of a thoroughly tamed, restricted, domestic Venus, an *amor coniugalis*.

The Lessons of Pleasure

But the method of instruction used here is to define 'safe' boundaries. Typically, the favoured themes of the emblematic corpus are Temperance, Abstinence, Prudence under the mottoes *nequid nimis*, nothing too much, not too high, not too fast, not too slow, observe the norm, *aurea mediocritas* (the Golden Mean). But the trick with this form of instruction is to know what is 'enough'. What is '*too* high'? What is the norm? Frequently these sensible ideals are recommended by warnings presented by those who have gone too far or risen too high, and suffered the painful consequences: Phaeton, Icarus, Thyestes' or Polyphemus' banquet. Recommendations to virtue thus take the form of explorations into excesses and transgressions, by flirting with the boundaries that separate Virtue and Vice. These boundaries are tested, explored and defined by transgressions into the illicit, the abnormal. These excursions are allowed, even actively encouraged, by festival license. Indeed, they cannot be resisted, as Vænius pronounced in his Love Emblems: 'True Love does not know how to keep to any measure'.[125] This Blake well understood, when he delivered as one of his Proverbs of Hell: 'The Road of Excess leads to the Palace of Wisdom'.

Alciato's so-called 'obscene' emblem on those that sin against nature sums up the notion of transgression, though we must probably doubt whether it can be any more obscene than the rest of his output. Martial says 'Turpe est ...' in the epigram that forms the epigraph to this chapter; 'Turpe ... est' begins Alciato's emblem. Perhaps Hunger's citation of the Martial epigram suggested this opening, for Alciato's emblem appeared in print for the first time three years after Hunger's preface. Alciato then goes on to explore obscenity in words (i.e., as it is talked about) and obscenity in deeds (i.e., as it is actually carried out). Is one, in fact, worse than the other? Why should we be afraid to speak, what we are not afraid to do? 'We have taught Ladies to blushe, onelie by hearing that named, which they nothing feare to doe', Montaigne was later to state according to Florio's translation. Alciato then goes on to point to all sorts of deeds that go under the name of unchaste acts. These run the gamut of perversities: homosexuality, lesbianism and other voluptuous species of delectable unchaste (*i.e.*, etymologically *incestuous* = unchaste) turpitude, which find specific utterance elsewhere in the *Emblemata*.[126] These are headed by the scatological image of defecation. 'I am not ashamed to find pearls even in a dungheap' ('me non pudebit . . . stercore margaritas legere'), Thuilius opined. 'Under a dirty cloak, wisdom is sometimes hid', the proverb states. As Alciato began, others carried on. If the emblem consists, according to its early theorists, of 'body' and 'soul', in this species of emblem the body speaks loudly, insis-

BART. DELBEN.   19

P. DEL'TATTO

A.   Porta contactus siue tangendi, operta hederis, quibus nomen ip-
sum ab herendo & tangendo. In hyperthyro autem Mars &
Venus irretiti à Vulcano.

125

tently and purposefully. Characters burp, fart, vomit, spew, shit, piss and spit their way through numerous emblem books. Flitner's knave is given to minute inspection of his own ordure, literally raising a stink as he passes it through a sieve (illus. 125).[127] The upturned pisspot becomes a weapon in Xantippe's hands, as she pours its contents over Socrates' defenceless head in Palmer and Vænius (illus. 126).[128] De Bèze produces an emblem 'On a man spitting at Heaven', which begins 'Do you see how this man who spits at the sky from his filthy lips', and ends by showing him vomiting all over himself.[129]

The taste of the early modern period for such material was in many ways more robust than ours. But these ejaculations can be seen as a healthy, comic inversion of a tragic catharsis – a purging through comic orifices: the mouth, the urinary tract, the genitals,

126

the anus. The eyes might be thought the sluices for tragic emotions
– unless, of course, they give vent to tears of laughter. Alciato saw
his emblems as recreative and entertaining: a relief and respite
from graver labours. He also hoped that these elegant trifles might
amuse. In so doing he did not stint to indulge his genius, and the
taste of the humanists was frequently for the ribald and the scatological. But emblematic forms can be seen to be predicated on a
current medical and physiological theory that underpinned,
among other things, the vogue for the bastard form of tragicom-
edy: 'comedy shakes off that gloomy and foggy humor [melan-
choly], generated in us by too much mental concentration'. The
comic recreations afforded by emblems may similarly be seen to
'take away the parts which by passing their natural bounds corrupt
the symmetry of life and cause disease ... moderating and reducing

them to that proper consistency which can contribute to a virtuous habit'.[130] No less a moralist than Milton would agree: 'the spirit of man cannot demean itself lively in the body without some recreating intermission of labour and serious things'.[131] This reminder of being 'lively in the body' is a necessary corrective to the weariness of the workaday world. To remind each reader of the particular

Elck heeft de zijn.

Dit is de mijn.

127

bodily imperatives under which each labours is the role of none other than the festive Fool. 'Elck heest de zijn' cries the Fool at the end of Roemer Visscher's *Sinnepoppen* (illus. 127).[132] To each his own particular bauble. Everyone is afflicted with his own peculiar species of folly. If hierarchical differences are eroded by Saturnalian revelry, they are resolved and harmonized at the basic level of a common recognition of individual human frailty, and the common bond of foolishness that joins us all. On this base foundation the whole fantastic edifice of emblematic ornament is erected.

Similarly, Shakespeare's Feste at the conclusion of *Twelfth Night* flaunts his 'foolish thing' on the cusp between the festivities of the Saturnalia and the experienced 'hey ho' world of the 'wind and the rain'. He brings together licensed satiric wantonness with the consciousness that the holiday must end, and the world resume its normal, harsh appearance. 'POST IUBILA, FLETVS' (After jubilation, tears) was one of the sobering emblematic lessons taught to the scholars at the Academia Altorfina.[133] As the sage Socrates remarks in Thomas Palmer's emblem, dripping beneath what, only an instant before, were the contents of Xantippe's chamber-pot: 'I knew that after thunder clappes, / was like we shulde have rayne.'[134]

EIGHT

Last Things

'I can't remember things before they happen.'
'It's a poor sort of memory that only works backwards,' the Queen remarked.
'What sort of things do you remember best?' Alice ventured to ask.
'Oh, things that happened the week after next,' the Queen replied in a
careless tone.[1]

Doomsday not come yet? I'll draw it nearer by a perspective [2]

does thy Prospective please
Th'abused fancie with no shapes but these? [3]

Is this the promised end?
Or image of that horror? [4]

Respice finem!

The form and structure of many emblem books are dictated by a
chiliastic horror, and their attitudes are shaped by an acute *post
mortem* consciousness. The world was transitory; its joys an
evanescent, deluding dream, mere trivia when weighed against the
considerations of eternity and the fate of one's eternal soul. Daily
devotional practice on both sides of the sectarian divide
demanded that people 'in al places, at al times so lead their lives, as
if each day were the last they should ever see, and have so wary an
eye over their conscience in all thoughts and works, as if they were
instantly to dye'.[5] In this spirit, Jakob Cats offers us his *Dootkiste
voor de levendige* (A coffin for the living).[6] Cramer's emblem, 'POST
MORTEM VEL DECVS VEL DEDECVS' (After death [there is] either
honour or shame) cites Syrach 7. 40: 'In all your works remember
your latest end'.[7] This attitude of mind exerted an influence over
the way one lived, and, inevitably, the way one regarded the world
and the images it contained. If the emblem book is related to the
Ars memorativa, it is related to it in a way that can only recall the
Janus-like 'both ways' memory system of the White Queen's looking-glass world as detailed in the first epigraph to this chapter. But
the emblematic 'prospective glass' is extended throughout the
panorama of world history. With that end in view, Jan David
provided not one, but twelve mirrors for those that hereafter

hoped to see God.[8] From the certain knowledge of impending death and the Last Judgment that is to follow, some things must be 'remembered' before they have happened.

There is a local conceitful justice in Whitney's positioning of the emblem 'Interdum requiescendum' (We must sometimes rest) at the point where his own emblematic sequence breaks off at the end of the first part of his book, while 'Tempus omnia terminat' (Time brings all things to an end) concludes the work.[9] The structure is designed to spur the reader to poignant, even chilling, final moral reflection. Since emblems refer to all aspects of life and death, it is perhaps not unsurprising that Time and Eternity should figure among their repertory of subjects. Yet as long as emblem books were conceived of as rag-bag anthologies of iconographical motifs by modern students of the subject, it could never be possible to see their overarching organizing principles. Janus's instruction, 'to beare in minde ... time to comme', which begins the second part of Whitney's *Choice of Emblemes* directs us to the book's final examples. Here we find that 'time to comme' offers trial, 'tormentes straunge, and persecutions dire'; the quickening passage of time; the consciousness that 'God ... all thy waies doth see'; the imminence of death; and the certain knowledge that 'all must ende'.[10] Such eschatological reflection exerts constant pressure on the individual towards well-doing and virtuous achievement, for therein lie man's hope of salvation, and of immortality, through faith and fame.[11] 'Honour, fame, renowme, and good reporte, doe triumphe ouer deathe, and make men liue for euer', Whitney had earlier assured the Earl of Leicester.[12] The promise of 'euerlasting honour, which is alwaies permanent', which Whitney offered Leicester in the opening 'Epistle Dedicatorie', he extends more generally in the final emblems of the *Choice*.

Of course, it is hard to underestimate the millenarian expectation, which imbued Whitney's *Choice*. Leicester's campaign in the Low Countries was seen as nothing less than a latter-day crusade against the Pope, Spanish political oppression and religious persecution by the Inquisition. The heroism of Leicester, Sidney, Essex and others was displayed in a great symbolic and idealized posture as a conflict between Virtue and Vice, Right and Injustice, Truth and Iniquity. Here and elsewhere, in Van Dorsten's and Strong's words, the English intervention in the Netherlands was to herald 'the day when the Empire of the false Antichrist of Rome and his adherents [should] crumble away and the reign of God and his Saints [should] be ushered in'.[13]

Whitney's emblematic strategies are far from atypical. Many emblematic works of the period drew eschatological inspiration from the Apocalypse, and from the four last things: death, Judgment, Heaven and Hell. These subjects derived from approved schemes of Catholic meditation as much from a Calvinistic anxiety concerning predestination, a self-examination on the state of one's soul in eternity, whether it was to be saved, or damned. The Huguenot Jan Baptista van der Noot, a refugee from religious persecution in the Low Countries, and smarting under his feelings of loss and injustice, comforted himself in his exile by looking forward to the imminent settling of scores in his *Theatre for Voluptuous Worldlings* (1569), a heady cocktail of antiquarianism, vitriolic anti-Catholicism, militant Protestantism, the visionary and the apocalyptic. Since there was daily evidence before one's very eyes that the world was in a state of decay, and that all that was left were the mere ruins of all that was good and virtuous, the time must be ripe for the Second Coming. His four concluding emblems are based directly on the Revelation of St John: the blaspheming beast, the 'Woman sitting on a beast' dispensing the 'wine of hoordome', the 'faithfull man' on his white horse and 'the holy Citie of the Lorde' (illus. 128). Even the humanist Alciato had earlier included, in his 1546 edition of hitherto unpublished emblems, the image of the Whore of Babylon (illus. 129) out of the Revelation of St John as a depiction of False Religion. Although he appears to have had a different image in mind – a woman seated on a royal throne plying her drunken followers with wine from a large cup (illus. 130) – his illustrators soon accommodated the emblem to the more familiar biblical iconography to show the harlot mounted on a seven-headed dragon. The four horsemen of the Apocalypse gallop into Reusner's 29th Emblem: only the foolish in heart would ignore their warning, that the mighty were about to be put down from their seats, and that the meek would be exalted. Part of the satiric pressure exerted on and by Simon Rosarius's *Antithesis Christi et Antichristi* lies in the fact that the appearance of Antichrist is prophecied in the latter days of the world, a sign that the Second Coming is at hand.[14] Georgette de Montenay's *Emblemes chrestiennes* (Lyon, 1571) – one of Whitney's sources, and arguably the first specifically Christian emblem book – takes as a guiding point of reference the imminence of the Second Coming and the certainty of the Last Judgment. The parable of the wise and foolish virgins encourages her readers to take immediate action now to prevent any future embarrassment in the last days. Her penultimate

128

129

emblem depicts an angel summoning the dead to the general resurrection – the righteous to the joys of Heaven, the unjust to an eternity of damnation. Quarles thrusts before our unwilling gaze the
fearful future prospect of 'how the queazy-stomach'd graves / Vomit
their dead', and goes on to show the resurrected bodies of the
damned writhing amid the scalding purple waves of Hell.[15] 'Dira
canuntur' (Ill omens are prophesied) was the motto taken out of
Ovid by the scholars of the Jesuit College in Brussels when they
began their set task of producing emblems of Eternity.[16] In spite of
many warnings to the effect that divine matters should not concern
us (*Quae supra nos nihil ad nos*), emblem writers constantly exhibit
a nagging, but damnable curiosity:

> ... would fain
> Pry in God's cabinet, and gain
> Intelligence from heav'n of things to come,
> Anticipate the day of doom.[17]

The Jesuit Claude-François Menestrier termed this type of emblem 'emblèmes sacrez' (sacred emblems).[18] These were literally *hieroglyphs*, sacred writings, concerning the mysteries of the faith imparted through dark types and allegories by the the Old Testament prophets – Moses' verdant but burning bush, the brazen serpent, the loves of the Bridegroom and the Bride in the Song of Solomon – and, not least, by the visions of the Revelation of St John. In Menestrier's view, emblems based on this mysterious theology were by far the most ingenious, and, perhaps inevitably, assumed first place in his catalogue of emblematic kinds. Yet the hermeticist Michael Maier may indicate that there is more to Menestrier's sense of priorities here than an obligatory professional preference. During his strange and secret peregrinations across Europe from Prague to London, Maier declared in his *Arcana arcanissima* (Oppenheim, 1614) that the Egyptian hieroglyphs were invented during a period when the world was undergoing enormous religious and political change. Those entrusted with occult wisdom thought it prudent to write these secrets down in a language few could understand. Maier obviously saw himself and his world in just such a situation. Other emblematists were similarly committed to a hieroglyphic wisdom, but saw themselves heir to a tradition that did not derive from ancient Egypt, but from the Judaeo-Christian holy books. Taking the Old and New Testaments as their model, many emblematists cast themselves in the role of the purveyors of parables and the 'dark sayings' of old. Alciato styled himself as a 'vates', a poet and also a prophet. These volumes were books of secrets akin to the prophet's fiery flying roll or St John's book with seven seals. Near the beginning of Thomas Palmer's first emblem book is 'the booke with claspes seven'.[19] Drechsel would later compare his works with those ultimate heavenly books, which should only be opened at the Last Judgment: the Book of Life. The Soul, in Hugo and Arwaker, quakes before the Book

> in which are writ
> All the black Crimes I rashly did committ.[20]

Jesuit writers exploited the appeal of popular catchpenny titles – the popular forms of almanac, horoscope, or fortune-teller's manual – as a way of overcoming initial resistance to purchasing the book, and then as a way of insinuating their doctrine. Perhaps, one might see this as way of reclaiming symbolic territory that had been usurped by the occultists and hermeticists. Alciato's Emblem 130, 'Semper praesto esse infortunia' (Misfortune is always close to us), alludes to the habit of divination by dice. Cartomancy and bibliomancy were also used, and we can legitimately assume that this habit of the breaking up of texts was perceived as essentially emblematic in kind. Jan David's *Veridicus christianus* contains a lottery, and this is where Wither may have got the idea. Drechsel's *Christians Zodiake* unashamedly played on natural human anxieties, targeting those who might on other questions have appealed to an astrologer, just as Hugo had addressed the soul blind to the future.[21] Arwaker takes his cue from Hugo, when he asks (I, xv, 1): 'What *lowring Star* rul'd my unhappy Birth?' But Drechsel and Hugo are concerned not with superstition, but with more serious questions regarding the fate of the eternal soul within a future, predestined, eschatological framework. The Calvinists' God at least allowed people to sin before they were damned, but the pietists opened up the dreadful doubt that even a person who had led an exemplary moral life might not, at the end of the day, find his or her name in the Book of Life. At the beginning of the final chapter of the *Christians Zodiake*, Drechsel asks: 'Seeing then (as it is most certaine) we have no certainty, ought it not to be most gratefull to us, to gather some probable signe of this our election?' The text moves from uncertainty to a certainty, which holds little comfort, to a probability, which may bring some. But this hope is anything but certain. As Drechsel verbally shuffles his fortune-teller's deck, he points to the absolute inevitability of death and the certainty of the Last Judgment. Such certainties the popular astrologer cannot match, because Drechsel is dealing with eternity, the astrologer with the merely temporal. Weighed in that balance, the astrologer's concerns are lightweight, trivial. The scrutiny and determination of these 'signs' and auguries of the Christian zodiac – *signum vitae, signum praedestinationis* – now become vitally important, essential. In spite of his tone of reasonable assurance, Drechsel extorts our attention. One cannot but attend, for not to do so is a foolish, unreasonable neglect of one's eternal health and safety.

Another work that uses the planets and zodiacal signs (see illus. 131) in some of the fifteen emblems depicting the progress of human life from conception to death is Quarles's *Hieroglyphikes of the life of Man* (London, 1638). This book also makes use of a catch-

penny title. But this is no humanistic encyclopaedia of erudite
symbolism derived from Horapollo, as it pretends on its title-page.
In fact, it takes but one symbol from Horapollo and orchestrates it
with a grimly determined, mathematical logic. The title also further
misleads, for the subject of the book is not so much 'life' as death.
Quarles evokes an irresistible arithmetic: the traditional Seven Ages

Jam ruit in Venerem 362

131

of Man marked off in seven decades, each with their planetary
guardian, to make up the biblical allotted span of threescore years
and ten. Each emblem is constructed around the image of a burning taper. It is lit in a conspiratorial dialogue between Time and
Death (illus. 132) and ends when the flame is finally snuffed out.
The candle gradually diminishes, each stage of its dwindling
progress corresponding to a decade of human life from x to LXX. It
brings to mind the anxieties of Lewis Carroll's shrinking Alice:

It might end . . . in my going out altogether, like a candle. I wonder what I should be like then?' And she tried to fancy what the flame of a candle looks like after the candle is blown out, for she could not remember ever having seen such a thing.

Alice may not remember, but Carroll may well have been thinking of Quarles. But even Quarles draws back from showing such an ethereal substance as 'the flame of a candle ... after the candle is blown out'.[22]

'Tempus erit'

342

132

The *Bilderbibel* tradition initiated by Martin Luther, with cuts by Hans Cranach, was committed to the whole panorama of world history from the creation to the Second Coming. Although it did not begin its life as an emblem book – the plates merely illustrated the Biblical narrative and the impulse behind its first invention was nothing more than to stimulate Protestants to read their Bibles. But the emblematic potential of the form was quickly recognized as a way of purveying the sacred emblematics of world history. There is no way that the first creators of a genre can dictate the way it will later develop. Nor can we, with the benefit of hindsight, narrowly confine subsequent developments to the limited vision of its first practitioners. This is as true of the *Bilderbibel* as any other generic form. The word–image collocation was irresistibly emblematic: mottoes were supplied from classical authors, and the epigrammatic verses drew appropriate moral applications. Robert Whitehall's *Hexastichon hieron* took the illustrations of Nicolas Visscher's *Bybel printen* and pressed them into emblematic service in an exercise that married the book production processes of the printing press with the still current manuscript tradition.[23] Such a reapplication of the illustrative material was emblematic in its orginal Ciceronian sense. Earlier, Benito Arias Montano adapted biblical materials for his emblematic *Humanae Salutis Monumenta* (Antwerp, 1571), but he had the full resources of the Plantin Press, no strangers to the art of emblematic publishing, fully behind him. Engraved illustrations of the Bible, for the most part by Jan and Jeronimus Wierix and Abraham de Bruyn after P. van der Borcht, were each followed by a poem and 'Annotationes in Odas'. This was an emblematic complement to the masterly *Biblia regia*, financed by Philip II, and which would make the Plantin Press financially secure. Johann Lauterbach's *Enchiridion veteris et novi testamenti* (Frankfurt am Main, 1573) follows the same biblical course to produce a Protestant version of the same message. The types and allegories of the books of Moses, which Menestrier claimed had furnished the divine Plato with his most mysterious allegories, equally provided Guillaume Borluyt with his *Historiarum Memorabilium ex Exodo* (1558) and Augustus Callias with his *Emblemata sacra e libris Mosis excerpta* (Heidelberg, 1591). This preoccupation with the works of Moses is punningly apposite to the emblem: it is 'Mosaic' work.[24] Yet the emphasis in many of these emblematic books given over to a survey of world history falls inevitably on the concluding emblems, where the whole plot reaches its spectacular conclusion, where old things are swept away to be replaced with a new heaven and a new earth. The triumphant final emphasis of Whitehall's book, as it had been for Van der Noot over a century earlier, exults more in *omega* than it had done in his *alpha*: 'Gods glory exceeds the *Sun*'. His last act of universal history, the production of the New Jerusalem, magnificently overgoes the first issue of his handiwork, Light. This is an ultimate emblematic topsy-turvy evaluation: the last shall be first!

Many emblematic works are predicated on the premise of just such a universal eschatological promise, where a new order is ushered in. Giordano Bruno posited this in his hermetic and heterodox *Spaccio della bestia trionfante*, where the heavens are purged of a zodiac that commemorated the amatory indiscretions of the gods, and new moral imperatives are put in their place. Yet the same strategy appears in the more orthodox Jeremias Drechsel's enormously popular *Zodiacus Christianus*, translated into English as *The Christians Zodiake, or, Twelue Signes of Predestination unto Life euerlasting* (London, 1647). Drechsel systematically replaces the twelve pagan zodiacal signs with twelve *signa* 'collected at spare houres out of the sacred Scriptures and holy Fathers; which for the helpe of memorie beare each one their Device or Impres in the front of them'.[25] In the preface to the dedicatory epistle to the third edition, Drechsel advises his reader to substitute this corrected and emended Zodiac for the previous one.[26] Father Engelgrave followed this tactic in his *Coelum Empyreum* (Cologne, 1668), when he replaced the fictive monsters of the pagan heavens with the apostles, saints, martyrs, professors of the Faith and the holy Virgin. He also went on to propose a 'Coelum novum' in his *Caeleste Pantheon*.[27]

That anxieties over the last things – death, Judgment, Hell and Heaven – caused a radical review and purgation of the image stock is evidenced in Luzvic's *The Devout Hart*: 'Wipe al away', he demands:

> And make the foure last things appeare:
> That no Chimeraes of the brayne,
> Or Phantasies I may retayne.[28]

The 'images and fading shadowes of worldly things', the 'idols' and fantasies of wickedness, are driven out and replaced with the images of the four last things. These form the chief preoccupations of many emblem books. With these, the rest of the chapter is concerned.

Death

Readers of emblem books cannot escape Death. In Gerlach's *Allegories and Emblems* the Grim Reaper surveys his necropolis, the tombs and funeral monuments (illus. 133). Drechsel 's *Æternitatis Prodromus Mortis Nuntius*[29] makes the point that whether one is sound in body and mind, sick or dying, one cannot avoid the consideration of one's mortality. The catalogue of works given over to the iconography of death is enormous, when we take into account the innumerable occasional texts devoted to the commemoration of the funerals and obsequies that we touched on

133

at the beginning of chapter Six. Alciato led the way, including six emblems on the subject that were duly collected under the heading 'Mors', and these do not include the numerous depictions of murders, suicides, tombs and mourning in the rest of the volume. But these do not touch the individual directly. Erasmus deflected the hostile criticism aroused by his device of the Roman deity Terminus (god of boundaries and death) with the motto 'Cedo nulli' (I yield to none), by claiming that it referred, not to his arrogance and intransigency, but served as a reminder of his own mortality. This, one cannot help suspect, was something of a witty subterfuge. But as part of the meditative tradition, the first 'holsome and profitable Picture' that is to be placed before the penitent is a deathbed scene: his own. The eyes are sunk into the head; the visage pale; children, gathered at his bedside, weep. Beside the bed lies the coffin. By means of such contemplation, one was encouraged to anticipate one's death. One was called on to be dead to the world, though technically still in it. The verbal details of this deathbed scene are taken from Hawkins, though the idea was Luzvic's. But they might have come from any number of emblems of this kind. Gailkircher early in his *Quadriga Æternitatis* (the chariot of Eternity) shows just such a scene, with the addition of a priest in attendance, who is in the act of administering the Last Rites to the dying man.[30] The motto, however, is taken not from some religious writer, but from Seneca: 'Mors nos sequitur, vita fugit' (Death follows us, life flees).

Nor should we be surprised at this use of the virtuous pagan philosopher in a book of Christian devotion. Death was an inescapable topic in religious writings as much as in humanistic studies. There was a contemporary vogue for Neo-Stoicism, promoted by and particularly associated with the professor Justus Lipsius. It became a fashionable pose – the wise should not expect too much, or be moved by the various vagaries of Fortune. It imbues parts of Drechsel 's *Christians Zodiake*:

> what is our life, which wee are so fearefull to be deprived of, but a scene of mockeries, a sea of miseries, where, in what ship soever we embarke our selves, . . . there is no avoyding of the swelling waves, of being often dashed against the opposite rocks, and oftener grounded on perillous flats and sholes. Happy is he who hath passed this dangerous sea, happy he who is safely landed in the haven, and hath no more reason to complaine, who chances to dye before he is well struck in years, than one for comming too soon to his journies end. Why then should we feare death which is but the end of our labors, the beginning of our recompence? It is the judgement of God upon all flesh, which none in former ages could ever avoyd, nor ever will in any ensuing times, all must follow. . . . Death is the end of all, to many a remedy, and every good mans wish, as being to godly men, no other than a deliverance from all paine and griefe, and

the utmost bound beyond which no harm of theirs can advance apace. What madnesse then were it in us, to oppose our selves to such an universal decree of Almighty Gods, to refuse to pay a tribute, that is duely exacted of every one, and pretend to an exemption that is granted to none?[31]

I quote at length, because the passage manages to string together so many of the common topics of the genre that succeeded also in working themselves into consolatory oratory. The melancholy, world-weary cadences that exert a gentle, if insistent, pressure towards acceptance of one's Fate are typical of the tradition, and need to be sampled in a longer passage to give an idea of the intended affect. If there are echoes of Donne, of Hamlet's 'To be or not to be', or of Spenser's Despair, it may well be that the translator had read Shakespeare's play and *The Faerie Queene*. However, it is just as probable that he was drawing on the same common stock of fashionable Neo-Stoic commonplaces.

Vænius's *Q. Horatii Flacci Emblemata* (Antwerp, 1607) did much to further this attitude of mind. Frequently reprinted, it was translated into French by Marin Le Roy, sieur de Gomberville, as *La Doctrine des moeurs* (Paris, 1646). Thomas Manington Gibbs's English translation, *The Doctrine of Morality* (London, 1721), derives from the French and further spread its popularity. A second edition, *Moral Virtue Delineated*, appeared in 1726. James Ford produced another translation under the title *Ut Pictura Poesis* as late as 1875. One scene (illus. 134) shows Death as the unwelcome guest at both prince's palace and beggar's hovel, and the facing page collects various statements to this effect from classical authors. There is no word here of Christian consolation, but rather an emphasis on the common bond that unites all humanity, pagan or Christian, rich or poor. 'Death is the end of all' – everyone and everything – in Drechsel's phrase quoted above. The iconography of the plate, for all its classicizing detail, draws its considerable strength from the popular tradition of the *Totentanz* or Dance of Death.[32] Here a vigorous skeleton bearing a huge scythe and clad in a tattered shroud is beating down the palace door. Although not emblem books themselves, *Totentanz* motifs were easily accommodated to the emblem. Jost Amman, at the end of his *Enchiridion artis pingendi, fingendi et sculpendi,* shows Death about to cut down two lovers with his scythe, as Cupid hovers over them. Marc Gerard's etching in Jan Moerman's *Apologi creaturarum* depicts Death summoning a youth with a hawk on his fist to the church-

134

yard. Nicolaus Reusner's *Aureolorum emblematum liber* has Tobias Stimmer's print of Death leading away a woman who has been stung by a serpent. Arwaker's insertion of various mementos of the tradition is perhaps a more sustained example:

> Nor *Sex* nor *Age* the grim Destroyer spares,
> Unmov'd alike by *Innocence* and *Tears*.
> . . . .
> Here sprightly Youth, there hory bending Age
> Sweet Boys, and blooming Virgins
> . . . .
> Each *Sex*, each *Age*, *Profession*, and *Degree*.[33]

Yet these hyperactive skeletons in emblematic works do not always derive simply from the *Totentanz*. One of Theodore Galle's strange, emblematic plates to Jan David's *Veridicus Christianus* depicts a skeleton climbing a ladder towards one of two open upper windows of a shed (illus. 135).[34] But we observe, too, that the barn resembles a human head: its thatched roof, the hair; its upper windows, the eyes; its open door, the nose and mouth. In case we miss the point, a large human ear grows on the side of the shed. The scaling skeleton, on closer inspection, derives not from the Dance of Death but is a visual transliteration, or a starkly literal illustration, of Jan David's text: 'Mors intrat per fenestras oculorum' (Death enters through the windows of the eyes). Behind this dictum lies a lattice of classical, patristic and biblical antecedents, which validate and underwrite the grotesque visual

HORATIANA.   199

136

image. Quintilian: 'Vitiis nostris in animum per oculos via est'
(Our vices enter our soul through our eyes); St Augustine: 'Oculi
fenestrae sunt mentis' (The eyes are the windows of the soul); and
the prophet Jeremiah: 'Ascendit mors per fenestras nostras'
(Death is come up into our windows). David annotates his
sources in a hanging side-note: 'Quintil. *Declam.* 1 ... August. *in*
Psal. 41 ... *Ierem* 9. [21]'. We are meant to recognize the verbal
provenance of his imagery.

A similar verbal network validates Vænius's 'Commvnis ad
letvm via' (The universal road to death – illus. 136). This resorts to
a more straightforwardly classical iconography in its representation of the Neo-Stoic tenet that death is a 'tribute, that is duely

exacted of every one'. Here the virtuous man pays his toll to Charon, the infernal ferryman of classical myth. It shows, too, how all conditions of life from the earliest times have been brought to that place and that condition: behind him on the shore stands a crowd of men, women and children. The use of classical myth has the effect of universalizing the allegory. The facing verso page contains the passages from Horace, Ovid and Seneca, which in turn provided mottoes for innumerable emblems: 'Tendimus huc omnes' (We all travel by that road), 'Metam properamus ad unam' (We all make haste for the one finishing-post), 'Omnia sub leges suas' (Everything is under [Death's] laws), 'Ad inferos una via est' (There is but one path to the infernal regions). These sentiments were so far in agreement with Christian teachings that they could be adopted with little strain. 'All of us tend unto one onely goale' does not strain the resources of Drechsel's English translator when he has the full weight of Golden Age Latinity behind him. The fact, too, that the poets of intiquity confirmed that there was an afterlife, wherein rewards and punishments would be exacted, meant that the fables of the classically damned could all be pressed into emblematic service: Ixion bound to his wheel for eternity, Prometheus chained to a mountain-side suffering the pains of repeated evisceration, Sisyphus condemned to eternal hard, futile and repetitive labour, and Tantalus (see illus. 137), immersed up to his neck in the infernal lake and suffering perpetual hunger and thirst.

The scholars at the Jesuit Academy in Brussels were encouraged to reflect on all circumstances and manners by which different people in different stations in life might come to their end. The prospect of holy martyrdom for the faith was not the least of the possibilities considered. But equally, death might come violently in battle, in bed, by natural causes, on the scaffold, from hunger, from the plague, from ambition, from wrath, inflicted by the ungrateful, often by members of one's own family. Death might come to kings from political plots, children might be cut off before their time, or one's neighbours might be the cause of one's death. It is paradoxically unexpected, though its inevitabity is universally acknowledged. It begins as soon as we are born. The pupils' delighted choice of associated symbolism is ingeniously if lugubriously repetitive: the death's head, the dwindling taper, the hourglass and other timepieces of strange and intricate design, the setting sun, the funereal cypress, the black robes of mourning.[35] In spite of its gloomy topic, the collection is not at all pessimistic. It begins with

137

the paradox that Christ's death is the gateway to eternal life: 'Mors Christi nostra vita': a rhetorical chiasmus that itself makes the sign of the Cross. There is even some grim satisfaction that the hand of divine Providence might be seen or inferred in some premature deaths. The collection concludes with the pious hope that after death comes the Resurrection.[36] The exercise, by familiarizing death, makes it acceptable. Grasping his Christian consolation with both hands, Hieronymus Ammon does not resist the chance to play at a kind of joyous poetic alchemy, turning 'funus' (death) into 'foenus' (profit) and 'horror' into 'honor'.[37]

In the last chapter of the *Christians Zodiake*, Drechsel reports the vision of 'a certaine holy *Anchoret*' of 'soules falling as thick into hell as flocks of snow, or drops of raine, insomuch as the damned ... imagined the world to be at an end, as thinking it impossible, considering their number who descended into hell, that any more persons should be left alive'. This impression is reinforced by other collections of emblems. Otto Aicher's mammoth *Theatrum funebre* (Salzburg, 1674) collects into four scenes, a 1,200-page catalogue of the heraldry and formal ostentation that adorns the tombs of the famous dead: trophies, *imprese*, hatchments, inscriptions. Each part deals with a different order of humanity: ecclesiastical dignitaries; kings, emperors, and the aristocratic nobility; the learned, musicians, medical doctors, painters, sculptors, poets and politicians; the list concludes with those cut off before their time: children, young men and women. Finally, Aicher provides a catalogue of epitaphs: for the noble, for the young, for women, for animals; for those undone by the gout. The whole is rounded off by a series of enigmatical epitaphs. Who would have thought that death had undone so many? It is a monument to the vanity of worldly honours and distinctions, which are reduced to a huge quintessence of dust.

The dangers of creating such an overwhelming impression of mortal futility is to promote a despair that leads to the ultimate sin, the despair of salvation, for which there is no remedy. As St Ambrose pronounced, 'Desperatio certa mors est' (Despair is certain death). Flitner concludes his book with an emblem depicting the ultimate act of worldly folly, the man who sits on the Devil's tail (illus. 138). There is an obscene innuendo that the illustrator chose not to follow, but he provides one literal, visual translation of a proverb applied to those who believe that the door of salvation is closed to them. This is a death before death: once entered into that labyrinthine snare there is no way back. The goat-horned, goat-footed demon that stalks the emblem is a creature from the Breughelesque twilight of the Flemish imagination. Since Flitner's book can be seen as a mock encomium of the upside-down world of Folly, it is no surprise that this concluding emblem reverses the concluding topos of so many emblem books: the sight of the New Jerusalem.

This emblematic contemplation of the overwhelming universe of Death seems to have resulted in an opposite effect: an anticipation and a longing: a desire, in St Paul's words, 'to be dissolved, and to be with Christ'. It forms the motto to emblems by Hugo, Quarles, Arwaker and Drechsel.[38] The enamoured Quietistic soul runs with desire from this world into the next: 'break ... ye thread of my life ... ravish [it] from me by ye Darts of strong [and] powerfull Love', pants Mme de Guyon.[39]

The emblematic preoccupation with death persists well on in the tradition. Stevenson's personal circumstances may well explain why he found the form congenial when he undertook his *Moral Emblems*. Stevenson had made a revealing use of the word 'emblem' in a letter written just after his marriage and before his first visit to Davos in the Swiss Alps in desperate search of a cure for his tuberculosis. When he wrote this letter, he could not have suspected his later involvement in the writing and printing of the *Moral Emblems*.

ODA XXXIII.   161

Caudæ hic Diaboli insidet.

Si paululum infortunio
Incessitur, mox perditus
Desperat, & turpissimas
Ore euomit blasphemias,
Deumq; multis questibus
Iniuriarum postulat,
Quod immerentem talibus

                                        L   Se

it was not my bliss that I was interested in when I was married; it was a sort of marriage *in extremis*; ... I was a mere complication of cough and bones, much fitter for an emblem of mortality than a bridegroom.

'Emblem' here is a synonym for 'personification', and Stevenson presents his desperate state of health in a macabre, self-mocking representation of himself as a *memento mori*. The term 'emblem of mortality' also picks up a dominant organizing motif in numerous emblem books and their related genre, the Dance of Death. Berne and Basle, staging-posts on the way to Davos, both boasted famous representations of the *Totentanz*, as did Roslyn Chapel, much closer to home, just south of Edinburgh. Even closer to the parental home was the *imago mortis* in Greyfriars Churchyard, which Stevenson would have passed on his way to the University, or to his meetings with the prostitutes who plied their trade in its vicinity.

Stevenson's consciousness of his own precarious mortality seems to have drawn him to this particular emblematic form. His grim description of his wedding reminds one of an emblem in Meisner's *Sciographia cosmica*, which depicts a man and woman chained together in the bonds of matrimony, which Death brutally breaks by taking a bone and striking the chain that binds them. The ironic motto is 'Conjugii vinculum firmissimum est' (The bond of marriage is very strong) – but not, it is implied, so strong that death cannot break it.[40]

It is impossible to say whether Stevenson knew this cut, or others like it, but there can be no doubt about the insistence on death throughout the Davos poems. The 'Martial Elegy' invokes grim Death, who 'smote each leaden hero low'. In the *Moral Emblems* Death lies in wait for the Beau, who 'from the poor averts his head', and the poem threatens him with an eternity of regret; a murderer is haunted by thoughts of a 'mangled body' (illus. 139); all hands are lost when an emblematic ship sinks at the beginning of the second book of *Moral Emblems*; sudden death strikes an Abbot, one of the traditional victims in the *Totentanz*, as he walks in a wood (illus. 140); an explorer lies dead on the frozen peaks. Pirate Ben remembers the 'untended dead' beneath the Tropic sun. Death is administered by both the Pirate's cutlass and the Apothecary's drug in the *Moral Tales*. In Alciato's Emblem 130, 'Semper praesto esse infortunia' (Misfortune is always close to us), a young woman is killed when she is struck by a falling roof-tile while play-

139

140

ing dice. That is a minor accident compared to the 'Builder's Doom'. Death lurks everywhere:

> Death in the falling window-blind
> Death in the pipe, death in the faucet,
> Death in the deadly water-closet!
> A day is set for all to die:
> *Caveat emptor*; what care I?

One of the traditional ploys of the late-eighteenth-century emblem book was to try to frighten young readers into virtue, by pretending that death, destruction and ruin would instantly over-take those who were foolish enough to stray from the paths of conventional morality. John Huddlestone Wynne, for example, depicts a boy falling from a tree as he tries to rob a nest (illus. 141):

141

> When lo! the faithless branch in pieces broke,
> His limbs are shatter'd with the dreadful stroke.
> > MORAL
> So, when we seek some dear-priz'd joy to gain,
> And buy *our* Pleasure with *another's* Pain;
> Our slipp'ry steps to evil are betray'd,
> We fall unpitied in the snare we made.[41]

And the danger of temptation is illustrated by:

> The silly fish, while playing in the brook,
> Hath gorg'd and swallow'd the destructive hook;
> In vain he flounces on the quiv'ring hair,
> Drawn panting forth to breathe the upper air;
> Caught by his folly in the glitt'ring bait,
> He meets his ruin, and submits to fate.
>   MORAL
> Avoid base bribes; the tempting lure display'd,
> If once you seize, you perish self-betray'd.
> Be slow to take when strangers haste to give,
> Lest of your ruin you the price receive.

Self-denial is recommended because the paths of pleasure lead but to the grave:

> With hasty steps, at the first dawn of day,
> The cheerful traveller pursues his way;
> But tir'd at noon, he seeks a shady grove
> Of lusty trees, whose branches meet above:
> Conceal'd beneath the Grass the Serpent lies,
> The swain draws near, and by his venom dies.
>   MORAL
> Thus he, who leaving Virtue's sacred ways,
> Securely thro' the paths of Pleasure strays:
> Wounded by Vice, his Peace and Honour lost,
> Buys late experience at too dear a cost.

While Death stalks Stevenson's emblems no less relentlessly, it is not always with any distinct or discernible moral purpose. Death for Stevenson is much more adventitious and casual. On it hangs no comfortably useful moral. Indeed, in the 'Builder's Doom', Death takes on a grotesque, truly frightening, all-consuming form. In the poem's apocalyptic catastrophe, the builder-cum-architect's skeletal structure, like some insatiable monster with a life of its own, turns on its creator and finally devours all:

> A helluo of lath and plaster!
> This structure on the Deacon's crown
> Came from above redoubling down,
> And Hell, the empire of Astarté,
> Gaped and engulphed that dinner party.

And thus, they who did eat were not so much eaten, as swallowed whole.

The emblem was to Stevenson more than just a form made up of word and image, with which he could occupy himself while working towards a cure. It represented for him an acute consciousness of the imminence of death, judgment and eternity that seems to have shaped much of his thinking at this time. Death was never far from his conscious or subconscious mind. Preoccupied with the very real possibility of his own imminent demise, surrounded by those for whom the medical profession prognosticated, at best, an abbreviated future, frequently struck by the oddly unforeseen, but permanent absences of fellow patients, it is not surprising that he was acutely aware of mortality. The emblematic form gave him a way to deal with it.[42]

Judgment

There are comparatively few emblematic works entirely devoted to the Last Judgment. Erasmus Francisci, *Die Letzte Rechenschafft jeglicher und aller Menschen* (Nuremberg, 1681), which was followed by a revised and enlarged edition in 1684, is probably an exception. The reason for this is no doubt the controversial status of the topic. Even various shades of Protestant opinion could not agree on when this act was to take place. Some thought it was to be at the general resurrection of the dead, others that it happened immediately after the soul left the body. Some would even doubt whether it would happen at all. During the Thirty-Years War emblematists from both religious traditions tended to avoid the controversies that divided Protestants from Catholics, concentrating instead on areas of doctrinal agreement. It is, perhaps, no coincidence that the most fruitful periods of emblematic activity in England occurred during times when Protestant and Catholic opinion was converging. The first appearance of Quarles's *Emblemes* coincided with the High Anglican reforms of Archbishop Laud; the first edition of Arwaker's translation of Herman Hugo appeared during the, albeit brief, reign of the Catholic James II. But, notwithstanding how far we should weigh these events, when Drechsel speaks of the Last Judgment in the *Christians Zodiake*, he bases his account on biblical authority, which would be acceptable to both sides:

> each one of us is to render account unto God Almighty onely of himself; each one to undergoe his owne burthen; each one according to his works that he hath done shall receive reward. [Romans 21.12; Galatians 6.5; 1 Corinthians 3.8.] And this is that

which made our Saviour break forth into those dolefull words, *Multi sunt vocati, pauci verò electi*, Many are called, but few are chosen [Matthew 20. 16].[43]

The attention-grabbing potential of a biblical drama was a chance few religious emblematists could resist. Johann Mannich offers a cataclysmic scene of the latter days, the shaking of the Heaven and the earth, and God as a consuming fire. The scene is not, however, devoid of humour. Against this spectacle a foppishly dressed fool sets his face (illus. 142). His whole anatomy is contorted to avoid the circumstances that would confront him, if he were only the right way about. 'Quid tune venire recusas?' (What will you plead in your defence?), the emblem asks. The verb 'recusas' invokes the judicial process, while the construction 'Quid tune' implies that there is no plausible response that this preposterous individual can offer. He is embarrassed by having no reply, and is rendered an object of mirth. He who laughs last, laughs longest, one might say.

Hugo, and then Arwaker in more abbreviated form, adopted Augustine's words for his epigraph to Book I, Emblem 14, to concentrate the mind of each of his readers on the dilemma that is to face all, and which must give each of them pause for reflection in the here and now. The question is idle when posed in general terms, of absolute importance when focused on the individual. What will be said to my soul, when it comes to judgment?

> *What more lamentable and more dreadful can be thought of, than that terrible Sentence,* Go? *What more delightful, than that pleasing Invitation,* Come? *They are two Words, of which nothing can be heard more* affrighting *than the* One, *nothing more* rejoycing *than the* Other.

Although written a millennium before the first emblem book, their citation of Augustine at this point, with their focus on the individual, is at the core of emblematic forms of expression. We ought also to recognize the emblematic structuring of the string of juxtaposed binary opposites: 'Go . . . Come'; 'One . . . Other'; 'affrighting . . . rejoycing'; 'dreadful . . . delightful'. The emblem verses fill out the circumstances of trial and sentence in melodramatic terms, which orchestrate the exquisite dilemma of the forward and backward motion of these contrary states:

> The *Soul's Immortal*, tho' the *Body Dies.*
> Which, soon as from its Pris'n of Clay enlarg'd,

142

At Heav'ns Tribunal's *sentenc'd* or *discharg'd*.
Before an awful Pow'r, *just* and *severe*,
Round whose bright Head consuming Flames appear;
The shackl'd Captive, dazl'd at his Sight,
Dejected stands, and shakes with wild Affright.
While, with strict Scrutiny, the Judge surveys
Its Heart, and *close Impieties* displays.
The Wretch *convicted*, does its Guilt *confess*,
Nor hopes for *Mercy*, for *Concealment* less;
While *He*, th' *Accuser*, *Judge*, and *Witness* too,
Damns it to an *Eternity of Woe*;
Where, since no hope of an *Appeal* appears,
'Twou'd fain dissolve and drown it self in Tears.
What Terrors then seize the forsaken Soul,
That finds no *Patron* for a *Cause* so foul?
Then it implores some *Mountain* to prevent,
By a kind Crush, its *Shame* and *Punishment*.
O wretched *Soul*, just *Judge*, hard *Sentence* too!
What harden'd Wretch dares Sin, that thinks on *You*?

The final line of this quotation encapsulates the moral to be drawn
now from the circumstances of the Last Judgment. The second

143

table that Hawkins commands to be painted in the penitent's heart is of Christ: 'sitting in the clouds, with the mouth armed, with a two edged sword, and with an eternal separation of the sheep from goats'. In 'Omnes sistentur tribunali Christi' (illus. 143), Oræus depicts the division of humanity at the Last Assizes. It is as though it is taking place on a huge stage set. The purpose of this piece of majestic theatre is to prevent the sinner rushing 'into the precipices of vnbridled appetites'. Similarly, Gailkircher's corresponding emblem in the *Quadriga Æternitatis* agrees: 'When the appetite invites you to sin, think of the Last Judgment'.[44] Drechsel is equally confident that 'many ... have, as it were by some sudden clap been awaked out of the dead trance of their licentious lives' by contemplating this future judgment.[45]

Hugo, Arwaker and Quarles depict the heavenly tribunal (illus. 144), before which the quaking wretch is summoned. Justice, holding her scales aloft, dominates the scene, as does the image of the Ten Commandments prominently displayed on the wall above the head of the Master. On the table are the dreaded spiritual account books that are about to be opened. 'How can *sinners* that strict place abide?' is the question that concludes the emblem. This is

144

directed out to the reader, as much as towards the participants in the unfolding drama.

Hell

Hell is the dreadful sentence that hangs over the eschatological judicial process. 'IBVNT MALEDICTI IN SVPPLICIVM ÆTERNVM' (Depart ye cursed to eternal punishment), announces Gailkircher's motto above his emblem of Hell.[46]

Yet images of the underworld appeared in emblem books long

before the religious emblem book made its appearance. As we noticed above, the tortures of Tantalus, the punishment of Prometheus, Ixion's wheel, the rock of Sisyphus, the fateful tun of the Belides are all part of the emblematic repertory. *Aeneid*, vi, 575ff. made it easy for anyone who wanted a catalogue of the classically damned. The ethical message is summed up in a single line: 'Learn to be just, and do not despise the gods'.[47] This is unexceptionable advice, from whatever tradition. Exemplary torments could be particularized to various moral failings with some witty justice, according to the formula 'Ubi culpa, ibi poena' (Where the fault is, there the punishment shall be).[48]

Virgil produced a ready moral guidebook to the infernal regions, which was seized on by the hard-pressed emblem writer. His 'facilis descensus Averni' (The descent to hell is easy)[49] provided a motto for many emblems. A connection could be made to the Pythagorean glyph, the twentieth letter of the Greek alphabet, Υ. The letter splits from a common downstroke into diverging branches, one thin the other thicker: a physical embodiment of two paths, one of good, the other of evil.[50] The Virgilian motto permitted an easy accommodation to the Christian road map, where the broad, and primrose path led to destruction, the 'strait gate' to Heaven. Drechsel harmonizes the two traditions, where the first half of the sentence is based on the Gospels, the second on Virgil:

> The way of life is narrow, that of perdition, broad, rosie and pleasant; there we must climbe up a craggy clift, here we slide easily downe into a dale.

Drechsel found the comparison congenial, for he was to use it on more than one occasion:

> the gate is broad, and the way spacious which leads to perdition, and many there are who enter by it; whereas the gate is straight, and the way narrow which conducts to life, and there are few who finde it (Matthew 7. 13.) . . . . *Inforce your selves to enter by the narrow gate, For I say unto you, there are many who are desirous to enter in, and yet cannot* (Luke 13. 24).

The iconography was variously appropriated. William Marshall drew on this and the *Tabula Cebetis* to produce the folio frontispiece to Wither's *Emblemes* and, among others, the emblematist Gilles Corrozet produced an emblematically moralized Table of Cebes, which broke the whole scene down into separate emblematic tableaux.[51] 'The Broad Way' (illus. 145) shows a procession along the biblical highway that leads to destruction. It almost parodies the triumphs of Colonna's *Hypnerotomachia* discussed in a previous chapter. Here Time and the Devil strut vigorously at the head of the parade, while Death on the side lines strikes up the tune. And behind them in a meandering crocodile follows the vast rout of humanity.

145

Even though some of the discomforts of the classical Hades were identical to those suffered by the Christian damned, the dangers of this syncretistic line for the religious emblematist was to equate the reality of the Christian Hell with a pagan fable. Ripa attempted to get round the problem by introducing some medieval iconography from Dante's *Inferno* into the *Iconologia*,[52] but this did not prove a generally popular solution for the emblem books of the period. The more usual course was Drechsel's. When he codified his nine infernal torments, he made sure to ground them on firm biblical authority.

  1. Darkness
  2. Weeping, wailing, horrible roaring (or rumbling in the bowels: his word 'rugitus' can bear both senses) and gnashing of teeth
  3. Hunger, and incredible thirst
  4. Incredible stench
  5. Fire

6. The worm that does not die
7. Abominable lodgings and execrable company
8. Total despair
9. Eternity: i.e., these things would last forever[53]

Each sense is exquisitely catered for and suffers its particular torture: the first will torment the eyes; the second, the ears; the third, the taste; the fourth, the smell; and the fifth and sixth the touch. Drechsel's *Infernus Damnatorum Carcer et Rogus Aeternitatis Pars IIa* (Munich, 1631) set the scenes before one's eyes in nine full-page engravings.

Other emblem books were to include some or all of Drechsel's catalogue, as they rehearsed their vision of eternal torment. Some took only one of Drechsel's categories, but embellished it with further nastiness. Sucquet's first emblem allows us to peer through Hell gate. Hawkins opens up 'this lamentable abysse of infinit euils' to show 'the vnhappy soules cheyned together', the howling, the despairing cries, the darkness, the gnashing of teeth, the horrible blasphemies, oaths, bans and cursings. He describes the damned as 'they cruelly teare one another'. Hieronymus Ammon seizes on Isaiah's undying worm as the quintessential torment of Hell in 'Meditatio xv' of his *Imitatio Crameriana*: 'qui cavet, ille sapit' (He who is on one's guard [against this] is wise). The Brussels scholars in their manuscript on Eternity pick out various infernal pains: there is no way out; the fire lasts forever, as does the torture.[54] Arwaker provides his own gloating addition to Hugo, when he smugly observes:

> Thus guilty Souls in Hell are scourg'd for Sin;
> Their never-ending Pains thus still begin.

Quarles's *Emblemes*, iii, 14, in a dialogue between the Flesh and the Spirit, has the Spirit bring before the Flesh's squeamish gaze the awaiting infernal tortures:

> I see a brimstone sea of boiling fire,
> And fiends, with knotted whips of flaming wire,
> Tott'ring poor souls, that gnash their teeth in vain,
> And gnaw their flame-tormented tongues for pain.
> Look, sister.

The Flesh's reply is understandable:

> Can thy distemper'd fancy take delight
> In view of tortures? these are shows t'affright:

Her disgust echoes the thoughts of a number of contemporary theologians who were frankly sickened by the 'abhominable fantasy' of Hell, and could not conceive of a merciful God, who would disproportionately punish a sinner.[55] Any temporal ruler would be considered a tyrant for doing as much. How could we admire the Ruler of the Universe who would indulge in sadistic behaviour that we would abhor in another human being? It must, too, have struck some as a sick joke that the damned should have the benefit of a resurrected body so that they could suffer tortures in it for eternity. Unlike the mortal body, the new one would not wear out.

But Quarles's Spirit is unswayed by the Flesh's protestations, and drives his point home:

> Foresight of future torments is the way
> To baulk those ills which present joys bewray.

This insistence on the necessity of the doctrine of Hell shows the conservative morality of the emblematic culture, the adherence to traditional forms of popular piety, and a traditional image stock.

Other emblematists wondered how one could possibly restrain immoral individuals from doing just as they pleased in this life, if one removed the threat of eternal retribution. Gailkircher saw the threat of Hell as a 'FRAENVM PECCATORVM'.[56] Arwaker similarly claimed that the atheists called God's existence into doubt only because they might more easily continue their wicked way of life unchecked and unhindered (I. ii). The restraining influence of the doctrine of divine retribution for sins committed in this life was, to him, clearly necessary.

The first book of Joannes Mantelius, *Speculum Peccatorvm* (Antwerp, 1637), takes a different approach. Sin is not punished in the afterlife, but here and now. One might be tempted to associate this with a seemingly modern, existentialist stance, until we remember that we are on familiar emblematic ground. The book is essentially satiric and moral. The *Christians Zodiake* also turns from the fifth torment of Hell, fire, to consider the rampant presence of sin in the here and now:

> *Hell hath dilated its soule* (saies Isaiah) *and opened its mouth boundlesse wide;* and that because *impiety like a fire imbraces* (all.) *It shall consume the thorne and bryar, the very thicket of the grove shall be burnt, and the pride of the smoak shall roule along;*

for thorns and bryers shall overgrow the universall earth. [Isaiah 5.
14; 9. 18; 7. 24.] And where shall you not find whole wildernesses
of briars of libidinousnesse and luxury? what place is free from
the pricking thornes of cares, and solicitude, not so much of
purchasing heaven, as wealth?

The emblem book scores many palpable hits in castigating vice,
and exhorting the sinner to amendment. Once the sinner is
damned, all that remains to the emblematist is a smug satisfaction.

Heaven

It ought to be confessed that the resources of emblematic forms
are stretched when it comes to Heaven. In that place there ought to
be no need of shadows and types. The dark glass of allegory is
there redundant. It is not surprising, therefore, that some emblematic treatments of the topic strike uncertain notes, and the miniature form of most emblematic *picturae* can scarce accommodate
the Baroque splendours of contemporary paintings of the subject.
The eye-dazzling Celestial City built of gold and precious stones is
ill-suited to be rendered in a black and white woodblock. The
heavenly reward is in the shape of golden diadems and immortal
laurels. Yet, for all the described opulence, these all seem out of
place as grossly and gaudily materialistic, however much they are
meant to be understood as anagogical symbols. The priest Henry
Hawkins looked forward to nameless 'chaste delights' in the certain
biblical knowledge that in Heaven there will be no giving or taking
in Marriage.[57] Yet, this strikes one as bloodlessly ethereal, given
that one is promised a new, resurrected body. Others look forward
to an unremitting round of choirs, and anthems of divine praise.
One must say that the prospect of eternal choir practice palls.

Nevertheless, the vision of Heaven is the scope and end of many
emblem books. Van der Noot and Whitehall both close with St
John's vision of the New Jerusalem. Others will take a more
cautious approach and end their books by 'shadowing' this eternal
glory and beatitude, rejoicing in the witty paradox that these are
'without end'. Others will place Heaven beyond the logical end of
the book: De Zetter's penultimate emblem in his *Kosmographia
iconica Moralis* (Frankfurt am Main, 1614) depicts Time's chariot
accompanied by the Seasons, which is his natural conclusion. After
this he places his emblem of the Triumph of Christ the Redeemer.
Similarly, Kreihing's final eschatological emblem, depicting the

different destination of the Good and the Reprobate, comes as a coda after his two previous emblems had already given a firm sense of ending: 'Sic transit gloria mundi' (So passes the glory of the world) and 'Nil ultra in terra' (Nothing further on earth).[58]

Emblem writers are on surer ground when they adopt the successful generic ploys and strategies that worked well when dealing with other matters. Otto Vænius's Neo-Stoic heaven (illus. 146) imaged in the last emblem of his *Q. Horatii Flacci Emblemata* successfully reconciles a classical iconography with an imputed Christian heaven. Angelic *putti* fly over the large tomb. They hold the attributes of the four moral virtues: the scales of Justice, the pillar of Fortitude, the grain measure of Temperance, the torch of Wisdom. These are not inconsistent with Christian virtues and Justice. The tomb is in the form of a winning-post, and before it are laid symbols of all aspects of human life: toil, study, the insignia of various offices and duties. In death these are all left behind, and what is exalted, after the earthly race has been run and won, are virtuous achievements: 'sola Virtus manet'. Ethical paganism ought not to be inconsistent with Christian faith. Nor should the pagans be seen to outdo Christians in virtue. The drift of the collected, facing classical texts is that this consciousness can put all earthly troubles and achievements within a larger perspective. It is with no sense of impropriety that the Jesuit Johannes Kreihing will take the Horatian motto to Vænius's emblem and apply it to his own final emblem depicting the ultimate destination of the good on one hand, and the damned on the other.

When identifying the fifteen joys of Heaven, Drechsel follows the same tactic as he did when working with the torments of Hell. Each joy is supported by a concensus of Scriptural quotation and footnoted references. Further, he sees Heaven as the obverse of Hell. Thus, where Hell is darkness, Heaven is light; the dreadful din caused by the infernal wailing, teeth-gnashing and stomach-rumbling is contrasted to the music of the celestial Choirs; Hell's thirst is increased by the sight of the flowing fountains of living water in Heaven. Arwaker, following Hugo, adopts the same tactic, bringing the joys of Heaven into sharper focus by contrasting them with the pains of Hell: nectar is served in Heaven, fire and brimstone in Hell; the one has music, the other hideous yells; the celestials inhabit temperate climes, the damned endure extremes of cold and heat; eternal rest is opposed to ceaseless toil:

HORATIANA.

146

Here rich Caelestial Nectar treats the Soul;
There Fire and Brimstone crowns the flaming *Bowl*:
That, fill'd with Musick of th' Angelick Quire,
Shall each blest Soul with Extasies inspire;
While *This* disturb'd, at ev'ry hideous yell,
Shall in the Damn'd raise a new dread of Hell:
That knows no sharp Excess of *Cold* or *Heat*,
In *This* the Wretches always *Freeze* or *Sweat*.
There reign *Eternal Rest*, and *soft Repose*;
Here, *painful Toil* no *end* or *measure* knows.
That, void of Grief, does nought Afflictive see;
This, still Disturb'd, from Troubles never free.
O happy *Life*! O vast unequall'd *Bliss*!

> O *Death* accurs'd! O endless *Miseries!*
> For *that* or *this* must be the doubtful *cast,*
> Nor may we *throw* agen when once 'tis past.
> Be wise then, Man, nor will thy Care be vain,
> To shun the *Mis'ry,* and the *Bliss* obtain;
> Give Heav'n thy *Heart,* if thou its *Crown* wou'dst gain.[59]

Hugo produces a bravura rhetorical flourish in a six-fold repeated 'Illa ... Haec' comparison that mirrors the flipping of an emblematic medallion from obverse to reverse. In so doing he mirrors the stark choice that confronts the reader now, in this life. This is a game of dice at the end of the universe, and the stake is the fate of a human soul.

Quarles (illus. 147) shows Heaven as a prize to be striven for, but his methods are oblique and indirect. Instead of showing the eternal joys, he presents us with the alternative – an earthly game of bowls in which the prizes are tawdry: a 'glorious garland' held by Gill Fortune, a 'crown for fools'. The player draws back in disgust, once the recognition dawns that the stakes are what they are, and concludes:

> I'll cease to game, till fairer ground be given
> Nor wish to winne untill the mark be heaven.[60]

The 'fairer ground' is, of course, celestial.

Thomas Palmer's last emblematic manuscript, 'The Sprite of Herbes and Trees', evaluates his youthful ambitions in the light of his hopes for the next world. He becomes preoccupied with sin and the processes of amendment of life, intent on preparing himself for Heaven and avoiding Hell. Throughout his life this English emblematist took comfort in a macaronic, homonymic pun: the Latin *palma* (a palm tree) identifies the author with the virtuous tree. Palmer took a particular pleasure in the usual contrast between the noble uprightness of the palm and the slimy nastiness of the envious. He wrapped himself in a superior consciousness of his own virtue by association. The palm, that most constant of trees ('arbor ... inter caeteras constantissima'),[61] gives in his Emblem 119 an earnest promise of the heavenly reward that awaits those that persevere in this life:

> Constans in verbis suis.
> Et folium eius non defluet.
> The Palme tree leaves doe never falle:
> but from that first they spring

147

> They groe to their perfection still,
> as Basill notes the thing.
> Whiche constancie in wordes and dedes
> dothe passing muche commende
> For suche shall raigne in blisse, that doe
> persever to the ende.

Palmer's final book of emblems takes comfort in his religious faith
and looks intently to the rewards of the next life. In an almost apocalyptic stance he judges this world by the values of Heaven. Inspired
by the words of St John the Divine, Palmer takes his emblem of the
upright palm branch as a sign of Christian apotheosis:

> Sic virtus vinco. Apoc. 7.

> Godes martyr beares a boughe in hand:
> of that victoriouse tree,

Whiche pressed rysethe vp agayne:
whiche is the palme yow see.
In showe that he subdued in earthe
above the skyes dothe raigne,
Where conquering his conquerors,
true conquest he dothe gayne.

The traditional symbolism of the palm 'whiche pressed rysethe vp agayne' was based on thoroughly Classical sources when Palmer first used it in 1565. There it celebrated the moral virtue of fortitude. In Palmer's last book of emblems it celebrates the Christian virtue of perseverance. And in 'rysethe vp againe' he confidently asserts his faith in the glorious resurrection of the faithful. The palm is now the heavenly reward of those that overcome in this life. Classical symbolism is totally subsumed by the biblical vision of the faithful who surround the throne of God in Heaven:

After this I beheld, and, lo, a great multitude, which no man could number, of all nations and kindreds, and people, and tongues, stood before the throne, and before the Lamb, clothed with white robes and palms in their hands. . . . These are they which came out of great tribulation.

Palmer's sights are, by now, towards the end of his life and poetic career, firmly set on the consolations of religion and of Heaven. This prospect of Heaven is shown in Dilherr's view of eternity from the here and now. His emblematic prospective glass brings the sight of Heaven before his eyes as the *putto* of Charity plays about his feet and he is sustained by the anchor of Hope (illus. 148).

Palmer's translation of emblematic metaphors to anagogical ends shows that the most successful treatments of celestial subjects occur when the emblem does not abandon its traditional methods. Similarly, Arwaker's 'O wretched man' (illus. 149) gives by implication one of the most potent arguments for the joys of Heaven by presenting them as no more than a blessed release from this prison house of the soul.

Conclusion

The high point of artistic representations of the Last Judgment was in the thirteenth and fourteenth centuries. It was portrayed in cathedral sculptures, in wall paintings and in illuminated manu-

F: N. Vilhernns Freudenblick in das ewige Leben.

148

scripts. Johan Huizinga in *The Waning of the Middle Ages* noted
that the *Quattuor hominum novissima* was popularly disseminated
in engravings and by the printing press in the fifteenth century.[62]
The great art of the Counter-Reformation, none the less, did not
contain many Last Judgments. It tended to concentrate on the
doctrinal points of difference between Protestants and Catholics.[63]
The emblem books, however, perpetuated a traditional image
stock that centred on the Last Things. Here both sides of the
sectarian divide could find common cause.

But the doctrine of the Last Judgment as it was taught was thoroughly amenable to emblematic treatment, and accords with many
of the features identified as part of the corpus described earlier in
this book. The Second Coming was supposed to be a joyous,
triumphal occasion (at least for some), and as such it chimes with
emblematic modes of gratulation and celebration. It is a party to
end all parties. It also enacts an ultimate praise of virtue and reprehension of vice. There is even a contemporary satiric edge to all of
this, since the Second Coming was imminently expected. Calvin
had, after all, identified the Antichrist and given his current
address.[64] 'Sacred scripts' and 'mysteries' were now seen as having
an immediate relevance. These were not the ancient hieroglyphs of

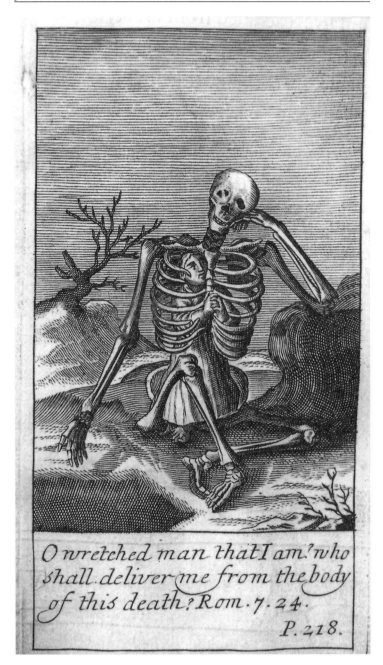

O wretched man that I am! who shall deliver me from the body of this death? Rom. 7. 24.

P. 218.

the Egyptians, but imminent signs and wonders foretold in the Judaeo-Christian sacred texts and prophecies that had an immediate bearing on the individual.

'We would see a sign', said Christ's doubting contemporaries.[65] As we have seen, signs were forthcoming during the Renaissance and Baroque in encyclopaedic quantities, many darkly intimating that the 'end' was indeed nigh. But the calendar has flipped over into a new millenium, and we are still indubitably here. If anything, our signs and wonders have increased, though these are in the service of Mammon. Visual and text messages – billboards, newspaper advertisements, neon signs, television commercials, the internet (all words and images) – derive from, or have their roots in, what were originally emblematic devices. These are part of our everyday world. Much of this postmodern verbal–visual culture derives from what are basically emblematic constructs. The merest flick through any glossy magazine will reveal that while some images are not, others are self-consciously knowing or ingenuous throwbacks to the images found in early modern emblem books. These were probably assimilated by the artists during their training in the drawing schools. This stock of images appeals to an educated, visually literate clientele. But neither artist nor customer would necessarily think of themselves as emblematically aware. Nor do advertising images always consciously allude to an exact archetypal predecessor. The effect of the image does not depend on an awareness of the 'archaeology' of the invoked symbol. Rather, its appeal tugs at something teasingly half-remembered, half-assimilated, a feeling of subliminal *déjà vu*. These images are part of an inarticulate iconic lexicon that is part of our culture. They are at once familiar, yet new, recontextualized in favour of a persuasive strategy to buy, to own, or to align oneself with a product or a company, capitalizing on emblematic icons for profit. Our experience of these emblematic forms has much in common with that of the majority of the early modern readers of emblem books or spectators at emblematic performances. Renaissance devices often pretended to be new, even when patently they were not. Their intention was identical to that of the modern advertiser, mixing delight with profit, and doing so in order to promote 'brand recognition' of an individual or a product. With the advertisement as with the legitimate emblem, this might involve prudent advice, political propaganda, the image of a leader or an organization, or the promotion of doctrine.

Among others, Peter M. Daly has studied the relationship

between emblems and modern advertising.[66] Not only does he
demonstrate the migration of particular symbols from the
emblematists' stock pile of images to modern advertising copy, he
also argues that the rhetorical strategies of the advertisement
closely parallel those of the early modern emblem. Thus the pelican, who freely sacrifices his life-blood so that the young might
live, becomes the logo of the blood-transfusion service.[67] A rainbow will recommend the happiness afforded by a bottle of Grand
Marnier under the caption 'Paradise Found', though the biblical
parallel is surely that of Noah, the father of viticulture, rather than
Adam and Eve, as Daly suggests.[68] The modern advertiser uses
modern 'gods' and heroes – the stars of the screen or the sports
field – in much the same way as the early modern emblem used the
classical pantheon or the paradigmatic figures from the history
books. Their Venus is our Madonna.

Daly's list is not, of course, exhaustive. It was not intended to be.
Nor do his examples show the full repertory of emblematic rhetorical strategies that can be used in these commercial circumstances.
Consider one of Rex Whistler's sequence of advertisements for
Shell (illus. 150). We have encountered this ploy earlier: the double-
faced physiognomy, which is deciphered by the simple expedient
of turning the plate upside-down.[69] Here, Whistler wittily
promoted the revolutionary advantages of the new fuel, Shell, as
opposed to 'any old' petrol. The face is hermaphroditic, male and
female, with the female having the last, satisfied word in the
matter. This is no isolated case. Whistler also used emblematic
reversals of this kind to recommend the virtues of this fuel from
the perspective of 'Age' and 'Youth'.[70] John Reynold's advertisement
demonstrated progressive advances in fuel technology by a Janus-
headed figure under the caption 'That's Shell – that was!' This
undoubtedly conceals a compliment to the discerning motorist
who chooses this fuel above the others. Alciato had, of course,
identified Janus with 'Prudentia'.[71] Johann Mannich's backward-
facing fop shown earlier in this chapter anticipates by several
centuries Charles Mozley's persuasive image showing the absurdity of not embracing the new.[72] His caption, 'Don't be backward', is
rather less intimidating than the seventeenth-century exercise in
the genre. Mythological allusions can also be found. Mozley
recommended the virtues of speed injected by Shell by invoking
the story of Atalanta and Hippomenes (*pace* Michael Maier): the
wooer now scatters the company ensign rather than the mythological golden apples to assist him in his victory.[73] Calman also drew

on an emblematic bestiary when his prudent snail smilingly displays his 'SHELL'. The visual homonym further implies careful progress, that motoring may involve 'heed' more than speed. There are additional implied compliments to the Shell motorist's self-sufficiency, and safe contentment (*Lentè sed attentè; domus sua, domus optima; omnia mea mecum porto*). [74] How far these additional associations are meant to be articulated or consciously formed is, of course, left undetermined. But the reticence of the minimal text is suggestive, and pushes the reader towards further explication.

There is scarcely any need to remind readers that the modern advertiser in the service of the gospel according to Mammon uses the gestures and postures of the pre-eminently female body –

His Worship the Mayor
uses any old petrol,
but –

– but the Lady Mayoress uses SHELL

clothed, or naked, and bearing whatever fashion accessory – no less fulsomely and relentlessly than any Cesare Ripa. Signed designer labels confer status and prestige. In this way the advertiser's logo works its way back into an assembled visual and verbal text, and becomes in its way emblematic of more than itself.

Facsimile Pages of Three Emblem Books

These pages from three emblem books deploy representative strategies by which word and image relate to one another in emblematic texts. The first is from an edition of Alciato; the second derives from the French Court culture of Louis xiv; the last, from a late edition of Quarles, shows an accommodation of Protestant and Catholic traditions of meditation.

1 From Tozzi's Alciato (Padua, 1618)

Alciato's epigrams are followed by Claude Mignault's brief notes and glosses. The woodcuts were produced under the supervision of the antiquarian scholar Lorenzo Pignoria, whose epistolary preface severely criticized the iconographic philistinism of earlier editions. The cuts are the 'first pulls' of those later used in Tozzi's 1621 edition with Thuilius's compendious *variorum* commentary.

Both the 1618 and 1621 editions were designed to appeal to scholarly readers. The 1618 edition reproduces only the sparest of Mignault's *annotationes*. Commentary is endorsed as an intrinsic part of emblematic reading. The reticence of this edition invited participation in the scholarly game of explicating the gnomic text. Manuscript annotation and marginalia in surviving emblem books from the period attest to the fact that readers took up the challenge.

For all Pignoria's strictures against previous editions, that of 1618 is editorially conservative. The layout of epigram and notes is that found in editions of standard classical authors, and indicates that Alciato's *Emblemata* had assumed the status of a 'modern' classic. In their shorter or longer form, Mignault's commentaries (or those that went under his name) had appeared in editions of Alciato since the 1570s. Like most editions of the *Emblemata* that appeared after their author's death, that of 1618 arranges the emblems under the commonplace, topical headings introduced by Aneau in Rouillé's editions of the late 1540s and 1550s.

The six emblems reproduced here lie under the heading 'Prudentia' (Good Sense), and each presents a piece of sensible advice, gnomically encoded in a succinct visual allegory. These are, or are in the style of, Pythagorean *symbola*, wise utterances of ancient sages, articles of faith passed from master to pupil. Each, in Alciato's hands, reflects on the art of composing *emblemata*.

The motto of the first emblem reproduced here – 'Be moderate and remember to be careful what you believe. These are the sinews of the mind' – is a quotation from the Greek comic dramatist Epicharmus. Some previous editions provided a Latin paraphrase: 'Sobriè vivendum: et non temerè credendum' (We must live in a temperate manner; and we must not tender our belief rashly). Pignoria disdains those with 'small Latin and less Greek': the motto appears in its original Greek with no Latin crutches. Tozzi and Pignoria had in view a classically literate reader.

In the woodcut a disembodied hand floats like a huge cloud over a diminutive landscape. In its palm nestles a single, staring eye. This anatomical dislocation is in the style of 'hieroglyphic' illustration that we have met with in editions of Horapollo. But the iconography is not 'Egyptian', it was introduced by 'Pierre Vase' in the Rouillé editions of Alciato in the late 1540s. In spite of its threatening, almost apocalyptic form, this *manus oculata* is a transcription into visual form of a Roman proverb, to which Erasmus's *Adages* give continued currency. Its source is in the comic dramatist Plautus, who utters the practical, mercenary sentiment 'oculatae nostrae sunt manus, credunt quod vident' (Our hands have eyes: they believe what they see). *Seeing is believing*, we might say, and in so saying we endorse an essential emblematic truism.

Where Vase provided the dominating visual feature of the emblem, Pignoria directed that from the landscape overshadowed by the gigantic hand should spring outsize flowers that do not appear in the earlier woodcut: these blooms exaggerate the size of the humble penny-royal (*pulegium*). Here Pignoria provides a visual embodiment of the other part of Epicharmus's proverbial wisdom: 'Sobriè vivendum'. The allusion is to Heraclitus, not here in his opposition to the laughing philosopher Democritus, but as the author of dense and cryptic aphorisms, as the prophet of the Delphic god who 'neither says nor conceals, but gives a sign'. The herb and the verse allude to a story in Plutarch's *De Garrulitate* (On talkativeness), in which Heraclitus allegorically showed his fellow citizens the virtues of a moderate diet by taking cold water and barley-meal and mixing them with a sprig of penny-royal. The emblematist takes a similar route in rendering his advice by means of visual signs and succinct, pithy sentences.

The motto of the following emblem is a Greek quotation from Pythagoras, who advised his followers when they returned to their houses to say 'Where did I trespass? What did I achieve? And what duties did I leave unfulfilled?' The source is in Diogenes Laertius, *Lives of the Eminent Philosophers*. The emblem translates this piece of oracular wisdom into a visual sign: a flight of cranes, who hold in their feet a stone to prevent them from being blown off course.

The two-faced god, Janus, looking simultaneously to the past and to the future, appears in the next emblem, to recommend Prudence. Silence is recommended in the following emblem, a symbol adopted by the mythical king Cecrops, the founder of religious cults and a virtuous promoter of civilization. The paradoxical art of tempering haste with mature deliberation is next enjoined by the arrow and slug-like remora. The final emblem reproduced here shows a short way to handle slippery customers: an eel can be held by a rough fig-leaf.

In all cases sound advice is delivered through a facetious playfulness: the words of comic dramatists Epicharmus, Plautus, or even Pythagoras, who, despite his sober lifestyle, was thought by some to be a trickster and juggler, using artful verbal riddles and devices. Even the emblem on Janus makes reference to 'sannas' (mocking jests).

34   *Andreæ Alciati*

Νῆφε, καὶ μέμνησ' ἀπιςεῖν· ἄρθρα ταῦτα τῶν φρενῶν.

E M B L E M A   X V I.

NE *credas, ne (Epicharmus ait) non sobrius esto :*
    Hi nerui humanæ membraq̄, mentis erunt.
Ecce oculata manus, credens id,quod videt : ecce
    Pulegium antiquæ sobrietatis olus :
Quo turbam ostenso sedauerit Heraclitus ,
    Mulserit & tumida seditione grauem.

EXPLICAT. CLAVD. MIN.

DVctvm id è dicto Epicharmi,quo duo præcep-
    ta in primis ad vitâ necessaria tradebat; vnû de am
plexanda fobrietate,alterû de vitanda credulitate. Sobri
tas,seu têperantia est vitę custos,mater valetudinis,sapi
tię comes, pacis amica : cui symbolum meritò tribuitu
pulegium,exiguum olus, & paratu facile.Credulitas i
                                                    dicium

Emblemata.   35

dicium impedit , mentémque à sua sede & statu dimo-
uet. Eam qui admittit, sæpe sibi alijsque certum exitium
arcessit: quod exemplis innumerabilibus ostendi potest .
Symbolum est oculata manus , quo ostenditur non esse
credendum alicui , nisi optimè perspecta & cognita hominum fide.

Ne credas.] temerè, vel adeò facilè.

ne non sobrius esto.] esto sobrius.

nerui membraq́;] ἄρθρα , νεῦρα, τὰ μέρη. quod dicitur per translationem.

Ecce.] demonstrandi nota rectè cum oculata manu ,
quæ credit id, quod videt . Huc pertinet præclarus sermo Dionis Chrysostomi περὶ ἀπιστίας: & illud Theo-
criti .

μὴ πίστευε τάχιστα, πρὶν ἀτρεκέως πέρας ὄψη.

pulegium.] herba quædam minima , de qua Plin. 20.
cap. 14.

antiqua sobrietatis olus.] qua veteres, homines frugi ,
& rerum parabilium appetentes vtebantur.

Quo ostenso.] pulegio.

turbam graui tumidam seditione.] populum tumul-
tuantem, iamque ad seditionem se comparantem.

Heraclitus.] vt est apud Plutarch. De garrulitate.

C 2   Πῄ

36   *Andreæ Alciati*

Πῆ παρέβην; τίδ᾽ ἔρεξα; τί μοι δέον ἐκ ἐτελέσθη;

EMBLEMA XVII.

ITALICÆ *Samius sectæ celeberrimus auctor*
   Ipse suum clausit carmine dogma breui :
Quò prætergressus ? quid agis ? quid omittis agendum ?
   Hanc rationem vrgens reddere quemque sibi .
Quod didicisse Gruum volitantium ex agmine fertur,
   Arreptum gestant quæ pedibus lapidem :
Ne cessent, neu transuersas mala flamina raptent .
   Quâ ratione, hominum vita regenda fuit.

EXPLICAT. CLAVD. MIN.

LAERTIVS & Suidas scribunt Pythagoram præ-
cepisse, suos auditores domum repetentes, hunc ver
ficulum pronuntiare.
    Πῆ παρέβην; τί δ᾽ ἔρεξα; τί μοι δέον ἐκ ἐτελέσθης
                                                      Nam

Emblemata. 37

Nam omnis humanæ vitę lapſus in tribus potiſſimum
cernitur,aut cum tranſgredimur , id eſt , ſecus facimus
quàm oportet , quod eſt plus quàm decet: aut quod o-
miſſum oportuit, neq; ſatis conſideratè fecimus: aut o-
mittimus,quod erat faciendum. Id volatu gruum didicit
Pythagoras,quæ dum volant in ſublime,lapillum geſtāt
æqualem viribus,& iuſto libratum pondere : vt ne nihil
tollant,ne nimium efferant ſeſe, neve aduerſis ventis ab-
ripiantur.

Italicæ Samius.] Pythagoras, auctor Philoſophorum,
Italicorum. Cic. Laert. D. Auguſt. de ciuit. Dei.

Samius.] oriundus ex inſula Samo.

Ipſe ſuum clauſit.] ſapientiæ ſuę vim omnem,aut cer
tè pręcipuam vno hoc carmine comprehendit.

Quò prætergreſſus?] quò tranſgreſſus? aut vltra quàm
decuit,feciſti?quod eſt, N I M I S.

quid agis?] vel quid agebas?ſic .n. Gręce, τί δ' ἔρεξας;
qui lapſus eſt in eo,quod P A R V M.

quid omittis agendum?] quid non deceus à te factum
eſt?quo d eſt in omiſſo bono.

Hanc rationem vrgens.] Volebat quiſque ſibi apud ſe
rationem hanc redderet. Idem penè de Seſtio Seneca lib.
3. De ira. 3 6. c.

Quod didiciſſe gruum.] Grues nempe in volatu id do-
cuerunt Pythagoram. Et huc fortè pertinet verbum
Gruere,ſiue Congruere,à Gruibus ductum,quod ſigni-
ficat conuenire. Grues enim ſe non ſegregant , ſiue cum
volant,ſiue cum paſcuntur,ait Feſtus.

mala flamina.] venti oppoſiti & impetuoſi.

38   *Andreę Alciati*

            Prudentes .

       EMBLEMA XVIII.

*I*AN E *bifrons, qui iam tranſacta futuraḡ, calles,*
   Quiḡ, retro ſannas , ſicut & ante, vides :
Te tot cur oculis, cur fingunt vultibus ? an quòd
   Circumſpectum hominem forma fuiſſe docet ?

       EXPLICAT. CLAVD. MIN.

*I*A N V M bifrontem finxit antiquitas , quòd ferinum
 & ſylueſtrem cultum mutarit in ciuilem : vel quòd pa-
ter Grece & Latinæ gentis fuerit : aut quòd Solem, ſeu
Ianum, celeſtis aulæ ianitorem crederent . Quod tamen
permulti referunt ad ſapientiam prudentiamq́; optimi
principis Iani, qui preterita noſſet, & futuris multò ante
proſpiceret.
    tranſacta futuraḡ, calles.] res preteritas & futuras
eque perſpectas habes.

                                              Quiḡ

Emblemata .   39

Quíq́, retrò fannas.] irrifiones. Perfius :
———*poftica occurrite fanna.*   Idem:
O *Iane, à tergo quem nulla ciconia pinfit .*
    Te tot cur oculis.] Inuenio & Ianum non modò bicipi-
tem, fed tripicitem & quadricipitem effictum olim.

Prudens magis quàm loquax .

EMBLEMA XIX.

N OCTVA *Cecropijs infignia præstat Athenis,*
      Inter aues fani noctua confilij .
Armifera meritò obfequijs facrata Minerua ,
    Garrula quo cornix cefferat antè loco .

EXPLICAT. CLAVD. MIN.

N OCTVA Mineruę facra , infigne Athenienfium
      fuit, vel propter oculos cęfios , quibus qui prędití
                              C 4   funt,

40 *Andreæ Alciati*

fant,prꜹſtantioris & acutioris ingenij feruntur eſſe, vel propter lucubrandi & contemplandi munus, quòd animi vis dicatur nocturni potiſſimùm temporis ſilentiò vegetari. Sed & tertia cauſſa redditur, quòd noctuarum nuſquam multitudo maior eſſet quàm Athenis aut ob nummum,in quo eſſet impreſſa imago noctuæ. Ea itaque Athenis,id eſt, emporio diſciplinarum toto orbe notiſſimo,& vrbe optimis inſtituta legibus,ſymbolum fuit, vt ſignificaretur prudens maturumꝗue cõſilium, & recta ciuitatis inſtitutio, in qua inepta hominum loquacitas nullo haberetur in numero.

Cecropijs Athenis.] à Cecrope rege ita dictis.Hinc Cecropidæ Athenienſes.

Inter aues ſani.] quæ pro ſymbolo conſilij habeatur.

Armiferæ Minerua] Ouid.Faſt.6.

Creditur armiferꝗ ſignum cæleſte Minerua.

Garrula quo cornix.] Teſtis Ouid. 2. Metamorph. & perſpicuè Aelianus de animalib. 3.c.9.

Emblemata. 41

Maturandum.

EMBLEMA XX.

M AIVRARE *iubent properè , & cunctarier omnes*
  Ne nimium preceps, neu mora longa nimis .
Hoc tibi declaret connexum echeneide telum :
  Hac tarda est, volitant spicula missa manu .

EXPLICAT, CLAVD. MIN.

I N rebus arduis , & quibus neglectis aliquid periculi
  esse potest, cauendum est à nimia celeritate , nimiave
mora . Videndum enim maximè, vt maturè non modò
rem, quam sumus aggressuri, suscipiamus, sed & susce-
ptam maturè persequamur : ne in capiendo consilio im-
prudentia vel error committatur, aut in mora pericu-
lum. Id ostenditur symbolis duobus inter se iunctis. Te-
lo, & Remora: quod expressit Cæsar Augustus, cum di-
ceret,

42 *Andreæ Alciati*

ceret, σπεῦδε βραδέως, quo monebat, vt ad rem agen-
dam simul adhiberetur & industriæ celeritas,& tarditas
diligentiæ:ex quibus contrarijs simul iunctis fit ea quæ
dicitur maturitas. Sueton & Gellius.

Maturare properè.] accelerare,seu properare opportu-
nè prouideque

cunctarier.] tardare.

omnes.] sapientes,auctores optimi.

Ne nimium præceps.] ne sis nimium festinus & subitus
ad aliquid aggrediendum.

connexum echeneide telum.] Remoræ adiunctum te-
lum.de Remora,in sequentibus.

1 La Rue, Idyllia

The incense of flattery that imbued the Court of the Sun King, Louis
xiv, flavours these emblems by the Jesuit Charles de la Rue. The
verses are not succinct, but they are dominated in terms of layout by
Louis Cossin's fine steel engravings. These accupy a full page, while
the facing epigram is printed in a rather small font. The emblems
commemorate notable events of Louis's reign: here the public
baptism of his son and heir. They also extol the nobility of the royal
personage. The symbolism in each case is based on the iconography
of the Sun King.

Coelestis facit vnda parum

L. Cossinus fecit.

63

LVDOVICO
FRANCIÆ
DELPHINO
POST
PUBLICA BAPTISMI
SOLEMNIA.

SYMBOLVM
Parelius.

LEMMA.

Cæleſtis facit unda parem.

E Gregias refero Patris cum nomine dotes :
    Quantus & eſt, proli gaudet ineſſe Pater.
Totus & hunc, & me totus quoque ſuſpicit orbis :
    Totus & hunc orbis, me quoque totus amat.
Hæ tamen egregiç tanto cum nomine dotes,
    Hic mihi ab çtherea fulgurat ignis aqua.
Cæteraque ut vincam radiis melioribus aſtra,
    CAELESTIS PATRI ME FACIT UNDA PAREM.
        F ij

65

CCCCCCCCCCCCCCCCCCCCCCC CC

AD

GALLICAM

NOBILITATEM

REGIS EXEMPLO

BELLI PERICULA

LACESSENTEM.

SYMBOLUM

Aquilæ in folem defixæ.

LEMMA.

Crefcunt vires animique videndo.

QUOD & procellas inter, & afpera
Depræliantum murmura fulminum,
Dum cuncta terrarum tremifcunt,
   Impavida volitamus ala;

Quod æmularum protinus alitum
Se turba noftris viribus imparem
Non erubefcenda fatetur
   Sponte fuga, domitifque late

F iij

66   EMBLEM.   HEROICA

Decedit auris : non patrium genus,
Non celsa summis e nemorum jugis
    Origo , non acres dederunt
       Indomitę stimuli juventę.

Ipse , ipse tantos addidit impetus,
Quem terra curru gaudet in igneo
    Fulgere sublimem , & remotis
       Pallida nox veneratur umbris.

Hinc ille totis artubus emicat
Fervetque venis ęthereus vigor.
    Phœbęa tanti est irretortis
       Lumina luminibus tueri.

III *Quarles*

The final emblems reproduced here are taken from an eighteenth-century edition of Quarles. The images have been copied countless times from the preceding editions, and this copy is typical of many of those still to be found of this popular emblem book. It does not seem to have been out of print since it was first published in the 1630s. Here we see the childlike Anima leaving her bed at night to seek her beloved by candle-light. The motif of the bed is meant to evoke an erotic context and alludes to the clash between sacred and profane love. The soul's search for the *deus absconditus* is conducted passionately. But, of course, she must leave the bed because this lover will not be found in an environment of lascivious ease. The verses begin wittily, relating the lover's quest with that of the pagan philosopher Diogenes, who, at noon, searched the market-place by torchlight, looking for an honest man.

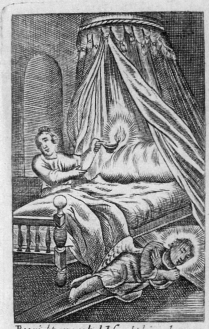

224   *Emblems.*   Book 4.

X.

By night on my bed I sought him whom my
soule loveth: I sought him but I found him not.
Cant: 3:1.   224.

X.

CANTICLES 3. 1.

In my bed by night I fought him that my
foul loveth ; I fought him, but I found
him not.

THe learned *Cynick* having loft the way
     To honeft men, did in the height of day,
By taper-light divide his fteps about
The peopled ftreets to find this dainty out ;
But fail'd : the *Cynick* fearch'd not where he ought ;
The thing he fought for, was not where he fought.
The wife-men's task feem'd harder to be done,
The wife-men did by ftar-light feek the fun,
And found : the wife-men fearch'd it where they ought ;
The thing they hop'd to find was where they fought.
One feeks his wifhes where he fhould ; but then
Perchance he feeks not as he fhould, nor when.
Another fearches when he fhould ; but there
He fails ; not feeking as he fhould, nor where.
Whofe foul defires the good it wants, and would
Obtain, muft feek where, as, and when he fhould.
How often have my wild affections led
My wafted foul to this my widow'd bed,
To feek my lover, whom my foul defires ?
(I fpeak not, *Cupid*, of thy wanton fires :
Thy fires are all but dying fparks to mine ;
My flames are full of heav'n, and all divine)
How often have I fought this bed by night,
To find that greater by this leffer light ?

                                        How

How oft have my unwitnefs'd groans lamented
Thy deareft abfence! ah! how often vented
The bitter tempefts of defpairing breath,
And toft my foul upon the waves of death!
How often has my melting heart made choice
Of filent tears (tears louder than a voice)
To plead my grief, and woo thy abfent ear!
And yet thou wilt not come, thou wilt not hear.
O is thy wonted love become fo cold?
Or do mine eyes not feek thee where they fhould?
Why do I feek thee, if thou art not here?
Or find thee not, if thou art ev'ry where?
I fee my errour, 'tis not ftrange I could not
Find out my love: I fought him where I fhould not.
Thou art not found in downy beds of eafe;
Alas! thy mufick ftrikes on harder keys:
Nor art thou found by that falfe feeble light
Of nature's candle; our *Egyptian* night
Is more than common darknefs; nor can we
Expect a morning but what breaks from thee.
Well may my empty bed bewail thy lofs,
When thou art lodg'd upon thy fhameful crofs:
If thou refufe to fhare a bed with me,
We'll never part, I'll fhare a crofs with thee.

ANSELM.

Book 4. *Emblems.* 227

ANSELM. in Protolog. 1.

Lord, if thou art not present, where shall I seek thee absent? if every where, why do I not see thee present? thou dwellest in light inaccessible; and where is that inaccessible light? or how shall I have access to light inaccessible? I beseech thee, Lord, teach me to seek thee, and shew thy self to the seeker; because I can neither seek thee, unless thou teach me; nor find thee, unless thou shew thy self to me: let me seek the e in desiring thee, and desire thee in seeking thee: let me find thee in loving thee, and love thee in finding thee.

EPIG. 10.

Where should thou seek for rest, but in thy bed?
But now thy rest is gone, thy rest is fled:
'Tis vain to seek him there: my soul, be wise;
Go ask thy sins, they'll tell thee where he lies.

References

Preface

1 Peter M. Daly and Mary Silcox, *The English Emblem: Bibliography of Secondary Literature* (Munich, 1990), p. xv. He later notes (p. xvi) that this estimate 'must be revised' upwards.

Introduction

1 'non mihi si linguae centum sint oraque centum, / ferrea vox, omnis *emblematum* comprendere formas, / omnia symbolorum percurrere nomina possim'. Based on Virgil, *Aeneid*, VI, 625–7.
2 'al l'impossibile nessuno e tenuto' (G. Rouillé, *Prontuario de le Medaglie*, Lyon, 1553, sig. a₃ʳ.)
3 *De Anima*, 431 a 17.
4 Earl Leslie Griggs, ed., *Collected Letters of Samuel Taylor Coleridge, Volume 4: 1815–1819* (Oxford, 1959), p. 885.
5 Claude Mignault in his 'Syntagma de symbolis' (*Omnia Andreae Alciati Emblemata* [Antwerp, 1577], pp. 29–43) distinguishes these as: a seal or mark of ownership; a watch-word or war-cry; a contribution of money towards a celebratory dinner; a sign by which communicates a meaning to someone; the coin of the realm; a gnomic, cryptic utterance, such as the *Symbola* of Pythagoras, designed for the ears of the learned. The last is the closest to the emblem.
6 Mignault: 'Emblemata vocantur carmina'. These sorts of poems, he goes on to say, describe works of art, which conceal an erudite meaning.
7 *Oxford English Dictionary* (Oxford, 1969), *s.v.* 'Emblem 2'.
8 Mario Praz's bibliography of emblems and emblem books in his *Studies in Seventeenth-century Imagery*, 2nd edn (Rome, 1964) is still the most complete. The fullest bibliography of Alciato is Henry Green's, published in 1872.
9 Stephen Orgel's reprint series, though useful in their own way, 'The Renaissance and the Gods' and 'The Philosophy of Images', published by Garland, are cases in point.
10 Edmund Gosse, 'Mr R. L. Stevenson as a Poet', *Longman's Magazine*, 10 (1893), pp. 623–31; rptd in *Questions at Issue* (London, 1893), pp. 237–54.
11 See Peter M. Daly, *Emblem Theory: Recent German Contributions to the Characterization of the Emblem Genre* (Nendeln, 1979).
12 Ian Hamilton Finlay and Ron Costley, *Heroic Emblems*, with an introduction and commentaries by Stephen Bann (Calais, VT, 1977). See also, Ian Hamilton Finlay, *Poems to Hear and See* (New York, 1971).
13 See André Breton, 'The Crisis of the Object', in Patrick Waldberg, *Surrealism* (London, 1965), pp. 85–6.
14 Both quotations are from Paul Hoover, ed., *Postmodern American Poetry* (New York, and London, 1994), pp. 659 and 311. The last quotation is from Clayton Eshleman's 'Notes on a Visit to Le Tuc d'Audoubert'.
15 Ben Jonson, *Every Man out of his Humour*, 'After the Second Sounding', ll. 247–70 in *Works*, III, p. 437.

16 'Sed ut in ceteris fere omnibus rebus, quamvis eodem genere comprehensis, magna est diversitas: ita in *Emblematibus* quoque' (G. Rollenhagen, 'Candido et Benevolo Lectori', in *Nucleus emblematum selectissimorum* (Arnhem, 1611), sig. A₃ᵛ.

17 *Oedipus Aegyptiacus*, 3 vols (Rome, 1652–4); *Turris Babel* (Amsterdam, 1619).

18 Genesis 9. 11. This divine *impresa* is cited by Luca Contile, *Ragionamento ... sopra la proprietà dell' imprese* (Padua, 1574), fol. 31ʳ. Contile also cites the Tree of the Knowledge of Good and Evil with the motto 'NE COMEDAS' (Thou shalt not eat thereof), as an even earlier exercise in the art.

19 'Vna eademque alicuius animalis, plantaeue figura, varijs animi sensis explicandis inservire potest' (*Symbolicae philosophiae liber quartus et ultimus*, ed. John Manning, New York, 1991, pp. 22–3).

20 Blake, *The First Book of Urizen*, chap. II, ll. 24–30, in *The Complete Writings of William Blake*, ed. G. Keynes (London, 1966), p. 224.

21 Henry Hawkins, *The Devout Hart* (Rouen, 1638), pp. [58] and [71]. The plates first appeared in Etienne Luzvic's *Le coeur devot* (Paris, 1626).

ONE: Talking with the Dead: The Beginning and Before the Beginning

1 Daniel Russell, *Emblematic Structures in Renaissance French Culture* (Toronto, 1995), chaps 1–5.

2 Peter van der Coelen, 'Emblemata Sacra? Biblical Picture Books and Emblem Literature' in Manning and Van Vaeck, eds, *The Emblem and the Low Countries* (Turnhout, 1999), pp. 261–78, argues that the emblem and the picture Bible had separate beginnings and on that basis they should continue to be treated separately. But this did not prevent authors such as Jan Phillipsz. Schabaelje calling their works *Emblemata Sacra* (1653–4). Robert Whitehall used a suite of Bible illustrations as the basis of his emblem book *Hexastichon hieron*.

3 'His saturnalibus ... libellum composui epigrammaton, cui titulum feci Emblemata' (*Le lettere di Andrea Alciato Giureconsulto*, ed. Gianluigi Barni, Florence, 1953, Letter 24). For careful definitions of the term, see Hessel Miedema, 'The Term Emblema in Alciati', *Journal of the Warburg & Courtauld Institutes*, XXXI (1964), pp. 234–50; Claudie Balavoine, 'Archéologie de l'Emblème littéraire: la Dedicace à Conrad Peutinger des Emblemata d'André Alciat', in M.T. Jones-Davies, ed., *Emblèmes et devises au temps de la Renaissance* (Paris, 1981), pp. 9–21; Denis L. Drysdall, 'Préhistoire de l'emblème: Commentaires et emplois du terme avant Alciat', *Nouvelle Revue du Seizième Siècle*, 6 (1988), pp. 29–44, and Bernhard Scholz, '"Libellum composui epigrammaton cui titulum feci Emblemata": Alciatus's Use of the Expression Emblema Once Again', *Emblematica*, I (1986), pp. 213–26.

4 'Maturare iubent properè, et cunctarier omnes; / Ne nimium præceps, neu mora longa nimis. / Hoc tibi declaret connexum echeneide telum: / Hæc tarda est, volitant spicula missa manu.'

5 *Selecta epigrammata Graeca Latine versa* (Basle, 1529). The *Greek Anthology* as we know it today was not yet discovered. The collection known to Alciato was the shorter version by Maximus Planudes. Altogether about 50 out of Alciato's 212 published emblems can be said to have their source in the *Anthology*. See Praz, p. 26 and J. Hutton, *The Greek Anthology in Italy to the Year 1800* (Ithaca, NY, 1935), p. 204.

6 *Le Theatre des bons engins* (Paris, 1539).

7 The presence of sketches or pictures in Alciato's manuscript is almost an article of faith for some scholars. For a detailed account of these views and an argument against them, see John Manning, 'A Bibliographical Approach to the Illustrations in Sixteenth-century Editions of Alciato's *Emblemata*', in Peter M. Daly, ed., *Andrea Alciato and the Emblem Tradition* (New York, 1989), pp. 127–76.

8 *Reliqua D. Andreae Alciati opera* (Lyon, 1548) and *Opera, ab ipso quidem autore tomis digesta quatuor* (Basle, 1549).

9 For detailed discussion of this point, references, and particular examples, see John

Manning, 'A Bibliographical Approach to the Illustrations' cited above (Reference 7). Jean de Tournes' editions of 1547 and 1556 lack illustrations for 79 emblems; Rouillé's first edition of the *Emblemata* (Lyon, 1548) does not have *picturae* for 72 emblems; Plantin's first edition (Antwerp, 1573) includes 44 non-illustrated emblems.

10 'In librum emblematum Praefatio, ad Chonradum Peutingerum Augustanum', l. 3.

11 On the prevalence of these forms and their influence on Alciato, see Daniel Russell, *Emblematic Structures*, particularly chap. 5.

12 Aldus's text of Horapollo was published in 1505. For an English translation and introduction, see George Boas, *The Hieroglyphics of Horapollo* (New York, 1950). On the hieroglyphic tradition, see L. Volkmann, *Bilderschriften der Renaissance* (Leipzig, 1923). In the context of the present argument, it is important to realize that Aldus's text was not illustrated. The first illustrated edition of Horapollo was not published until 1543 by J. Kerver at Paris.

13 Lyon, 1550.

14 All early commentators (Sambucus, Junius, Mignault) give this derivation: Emblem is 'something set in for the sake of ornament' ('quicquid inseritur ornatus causa'). Whitney refers to 'suche figures, or workes, as are wroughte in plate, or stones in the pauements or on waules, or such like, for the adorning of the place'. 'Everything cultivated when grafted on to what is uncultivated, is called emblema', according to the Renaissance encyclopaedist Caelius Rhodiginus, in connection with the cultivation of olive trees (*Lectionum antiquarum libri xvi*, Basel, 1517, Book 7, cap. 14: 'omnia syluestribus insita dici Emblemata'; cited Miedema, p. 239). The Greek moralist Dio Chrysostom had much earlier used the metaphor of grafting to describe the process whereby 'an idle tale might become a parable of the real and the true' ('The Fifth Discourse: A Libyan Myth', in Dio Chrysostom, trans. J. W. Cahoon, London, 1932, vol. 1 ,p. 237).

15 'ut tesserulae omnes / arte pavimento atque emblemate vermiculato' (Each word highly polished, taking its place like a tile in a mosaic design). See Warmington, *Remains of Old Latin*, vol. iii, p. 20. The lines from Lucilius were frequently cited by Mignault, Thuilius and others in their prefaces to editions of Alciato's *Emblemata*.

16 *Actio in Verrem* (Against Verres), 2.4.22 and 2.4.17: 'scaphia cum emblematis'.

17 See Alciato's prefatory dedicatory epigram to Conrad Peutinger, 'In libellum Emblematum praefatio', l. 4.

18 'singulis enim epigrammatibus aliquid describo, quod ex historia, vel ex rebus naturalibus aliquid elegans significet' (*Le lettere di Andrea Alciato*, Letter 24).

19 See Claude Mignault's commentary reprinted in Tozzi's Padua 1621 edition of Alciato's *Emblemata omnia*, p. lxiii: 'We will acknowledge that the cogency of the emblem depends upon the *symbolum*' ('Fatemur Emblematis quidem vim in simbolum sitam esse'). Mignault had previously defined *symbolum* as, among other things, a species of Pythagorean gnomic allegory. Plutarch had, even in antiquity, conflated the Pythagorean symbolum with the hieroglyph: they are 'not unlike the writings called hieroglyphs' ('De Iside et Osiride', *Moralia*, pp. 354–5).

20 'ratio non sat aperta mihi est' (Emblem 79, l. 2); 'abdita in arcanis' (Emblem 47, l. 3); 'Samij dogmata sancta senis' (Emblem 83, l. 2) and Emblem 187: 'Dicta septem Sapientium'; 'exemplo ut doceas dogmata certa tuo' (Emblem 104, l. 4), 'fabula prisca fuit' (Emblem 84, l. 2), 'dictus ab antiquis vatibus' (Emblem 84, l. 6); 'docta per ora virum volat' (Emblem 138, l. 12), 'fides sit penes historicos' (Emblem 84, l. 4).

21 'Poetrie, ... a more hidden and diuine kinde of Philosophy, enwrapped in blinde Fables and darke stories, wherein the principles of more excellent Arts and morrall precepts of manners, illustrated with diuers examples of other Kingdomes and Countries: ... Cicero testifieth in his *Tusculanes*' (*The Works of Thomas Nashe*, ed. R. B. McKerrow, 5 vols, Oxford, 1966, i, p. 25). See also Edgar Wind, *Pagan Mysteries in the Renaissance* (Harmondsworth, 1967), p. 17: 'Pico claimed that the pagan poets used hieroglyphic imagery: their myths and fables protected the divine secrets from profanation by shrouding them in the garb of trifling tales.'

22 Emblem 122 in the *Emblemata omnia* of 1621 published by Tozzi. Unless there is

a good reason for not doing so, I will usually refer to the numbering in this edition for the sake of convenience.

23 These find their way into Emblems 68, 38, 176, and 71 from Virgil, *Eclogues*, VI. 74: Scylla 'fama secuta est / candida succinctam lantrantibus inguina monstris' (the story is still current that her white waist is girt about with barking monsters); *Aeneid*, VIII. 702–3: 'et scissa gaudens vadit Discordia palla, quam cum sanguineo sequitur Bellona flagello' (and in rent robe Discord strides exultant, while Bellona follows her with bloody scourge); *Aeneid*, IV. 173–97; *Aeneid*, I. 294–5: 'Furor impius' (impious Rage).

24 Barthélemy Aneau, for example, Alciato's French translator and editor, whose novel arrangement of the emblems exerted enormous influence on the appearance of the book after Alciato's death, praised the 'licentieuses eclypses and synalephes' of Alciato's style (*Les Emblemes de Seigneur André Alciat*, Lyon, 1549, p. 11).

25 C. G. Jung, *Mysterium Coniunctionis*, trans. R.F.C. Hill (London, 1963), p. 58 draws attention to a similar paradox, 'The enigma at Bologna', that exercised most of the early emblematists (Maier, Drechsel, Mylius and others). Some took it highly seriously, others saw it as a practical joke.

26 'De Cameleonte vide Plin. natur. histor. libro VIII. Cap. xxx'. Modern editions have the passage at VIII, 51.

27 Trans. H. Rackham (Cambridge, MA, 1983), p. 87.

28 Plutarch, 'Quomodo adulator ab amico internoscatur' (*Moralia*, 53D–E; Erasmus, *Parabolae* in *Collected Works of Erasmus*, vol. 23, ed. Craig R. Thompson (Toronto, 1978), p. 252, ll. 6–8: 'The chameleon, which from time to time changes its colour, imitates every colour except red and white. The toady imitates everything in his patron except what is honourable'.

29 'Antiquae inscriptiones veteraque monumenta patriae' (published in facsimile by Cisalpino in 1973). On the influence of this manuscript on Alciato's idea of the emblem, see Pierre Laurens and Florence Vuillemier, 'De l'archéologie à l'emblème: La genèse du *Liber Alciat*', *Revue de l'Art*, 101 (1993), pp. 86–95.

30 'Quae supra nos, nihil ad nos'. Emblem 103. Alciato's caution about embarking on these areas is not a symptom of the generic limitations of the emblem or the epigram: Tasso similarly confined the author's interests in the field of the epic: 'The poet should not become fascinated with material too subtle, and fitted for the schools of the theologians and the philosophers rather than the palaces of princes and the theaters, and he should not show himself ambitious in the questions of nature and theology' (Tasso as cited in Allan H. Gilbert, *Literary Criticism: Plato to Dryden*, Detroit, 1962, p. 489).

31 *Mikrokosmos* (Antwerp, 1579), sig. A₁ᵛ.

32 Terence, *Heautontimorumenos*.

33 Strabo, XVII, i, 27; Pliny, *Historia naturalis*, XXXVI, lxiv–lxxiv; Plutarch, 'Isis and Osiris', *Moralia*, 354–55; Diodorus, *Bibliotheca*, I, 94; II, 81, III, 4; Tacitus, *Annales*, II, lx, XI, 14; Ammianus Marcellinus, XVII, 4.6–11, 14–23; Clement of Alexandria, *Stromateis*, Book V.

34 Ammianus Marcellinus, 17, 4. 10: 'singulae litterae singulis nominibus serviebant et verbis; non numquam significabant integros sensus'.

35 Ammianus Marcellinus, 17, 4, 10: 'per vulturem naturae vocabulum pandunt, quia mares nullos posse inter has alites inveniri, rationes memorant physicae, perque speciem apis mella conficientis, indicant regem, moderatori cum iucunditate aculeos quoque innasci debere his rerum insignibus ostendentes'. The interpretation is grounded on natural history of the ancient world: on the vulture, see Aelian. 2. 46; on the bee, see Seneca, *De Clementia*, i. 19, 2ff.

36 'Die Hieroglyphenkunde des Humanismus in der Allegorie der Renaissance' in *Jahrbuch der Kunsthistorischen Sammlungen des allerhöchsten Kaiserhauses*, XXXII/1 (1915), p. 146ff.

37 Apuleius, *Metamorphoses*, XI, 8. Vænius's emblem is on p. 115 of his *Amorum emblematum*.

38 For a discussion of this point, see Denis Drysdall, 'The Hieroglyphs at Bologna',

Emblematica, 2 (1987), pp. 225–47 and Claudie Balavoine, 'Le Modèle hiéroglyphique à la Renaissance' in Jean Lafond, ed., *Le Modèle à la Renaissance* (Paris, 1986), pp. 73–85.

39 'Two hundred poosees'. For Palmer and Valeriano, see introduction and notes to *The Emblems of Thomas Palmer*, ed. John Manning (New York, 1988).

40 *Hieroglyphica* (Lyon, 1602), p. 60: 'Porro Sphinges in Ægyptiorum templis hieroglyphice admonent mystica dogmata ... per aegnigmatum modos à profana procul multitudine inviolata custodiri debent'. Valeriano's source is Plutarch, 'De Iside et Osiride', 9 (*Moralia*, 354C). Proclus, *Theologia platonica*, Book I, chap. 4, also held that those who dealt with divine matters should only speak of them symbolically or mythologically, or through similitudes or images.

41 Valeriano, p. 244 (Book 24: *De Ansere*). The authority here is Francesco Colonna's *Hypnerotomachia*.

42 *Dialogo dell' Imprese* (Rome, 1555).

43 Lyon, 1602, pp. 331–2.

44 Exodus 24: 15–18.

45 Percy Bysshe Shelley, 'A Defence of Poetry' in Duncan Wu, ed., *Romanticism: An Anthology*, 2nd edn (Oxford, 1998), pp. 950–51.

46 Nashe, *Works*, III, p. 252.

47 *Hypnerotomachia* (Venice, 1499), pp. 74, 195, 203, 206, 295, 355.

48 *Hypnerotomachia*, pp. 125–6. The motto is 'velocitatem sedendo, tarditatem tempera surgendo'.

49 *Odes*, I, 34, 14–16: 'hinc apicem rapax / Fortuna cum stridore acuto / sustulit, hic posuisse gaudet'. The glossator on this passage notes 'volubilis fortunae rotam, ejusque rapidae conversionis stridorem notat. Et quidem non sine gravi mortalium concussione, perturbatione, querimonia, fiunt illae mutationes, quibus imperia ab his ad illos transferuntur'.

50 (Rome, 1555). I cite the first illustrated edition, by Rouillé (Lyon, 1574). The *impresa* conforms to the pattern we have discerned elsewhere in relation to the emblem and the hieroglyph: the illustrated text appears later.

51 See, for example, Pierre L'Anglois, *Discours des Hieroglyphes* ... (Paris, 1584), p. 5ff.

52 See Scipione Bargagli, *La prima parte dell'imprese* (Venice, 1589), pp. 39–40, which influentially states that 'an *impresa* is the unique representation of some idea conceived within the mind'. By the mid-seventeenth century, the Latin neologism *Phrenoschema*, which reflects this definition, had come to be adopted in place of the overburdened *symbolum*. We also find the coinage *Impresia*. See Athanasias Kircher, *Oedipus Aegyptiacus*, 3 vols (Rome, 1652–4), II, i, p. 3.

53 Giovio, *ed. cit.*, p. 16: 'la bellissima impresa, che portò la S. Hippolita Fioramonda Marchesana di Scaldasole in Pauia, laquale all'età nostra auanzò di gran lunga ogn'altra donna di bellezza, leggiadria, e creanza amorosa; che spesso portaua vna gran veste di raso di color celeste, seminata a farfalle di ricamo d'oro, ma senza motto; volendo dire et auuertire gl'amanti, che non si appressassero molto al suo fuoco, accioche tal hora non interuenisse loro, quel che sempre interuiene alla farfalla, laquale per appressarsi all'ardente fiamma, da se stessa si abbrucia'.

54 Giovio, *ed. cit.*, p. 16.

55 Giovio, *ed. cit.*, p. 20.

56 Giovio, *ed. cit.*, p. 12: 'Prima, giusta proportione d'anima e di corpo; Seconda, ch'ella non sia oscura, di sorte, c'habbia mistero della Sibilla per interprete a volerla intendere; ne tanto chiara, ch'ogni plebeo l'intenda; Terza, che sopra tutto habbia bella vista, laqual si fa riuscire molto allegra, entrandoui stelle, Soli, Lune, fuoco, acqua, arbori verdeggianti, instrumenti mecanici, animali bizzarri, ed vccelli fantastichi. Quarta non ricerca alcuna forma humana. Quinta richiede il motto, che è l'anima del corpo, e vuole essere communemente d'vna lingua diuersa dall'Idioma di colui, che fa l'impresa, perche il sentimento sia alquanto più coperto.'.

57 Girolamo Ruscelli, *Le imprese illustri* (Venice, 1566); Alessandra Farra, *Settenario* (Venice, 1571); Luca Contile, *Ragionamento* ... *sopra la proprietà delle imprese*

(Padua, 1574); Scipione Bargagli, *La prima parte dell'imprese* (Venice, 1589).

58 Lodovico Domenichi, 'Ragionamento nel quale si parla d'Imprese d'Armi, e d'Amore' and Gabriele Simeoni, 'Le imprese heroiche e morali'.

59 'De arte symbolica ad Erastum' in *Symbolographia* (Augsburg, 1702), pp. 2–72. Book 3 is specifically devoted to 'Leges Jovianae generales'.

60 Emblem 143: 'Princeps subditorum incolumitatem procurans' (A prince looking after his subjects' safety). Simeoni would turn his imprese into emblems as *Tetrastichi morali*.

TWO: Towards an Emblematic Rhetoric

1 Francis Quarles, *Emblemes*, 1, 14.

2 Robert Burton, 'Democritus to the Reader', *Anatomy of Melancholy*.

3 Giulio Cesare Capaccio, *Delle Imprese* (Naples, 1592), 1, fol. 52.

4 Gilles Corrozet, *Hecatomgraphie* (Paris, 1540); Guillaume de la Perrière, *Le Theatre des bons engins* (Paris [1539]).

5 'In libellum Emblematum praefatio', l. 6.

6 Cornelis Plemp, 'Dedicatio' in *Quinquagenta emblemata* (Amsterdam, 1616).

7 G. Rollenhagen, 'Candido et benevolo lectori', in *Nucleus emblematum selectissimorum* (Cologne, 1611), sig. A₄ʳ: 'Figuras enim non in lignum, ut illi, sed in æs incisas damus, nec nudas, sed parergis non invenustis exornatas. Versus pauci sunt; sed apti, perspicui, rotundi'.

8 'Andreas Alciatus ... parvo quidem sed docto edito Emblematum libello, magnam laudem consequutus est: quem Sambucus, Hadrianus Iunius et alii sequuti sunt, quamquam dispari passu.'

9 Elmer Adolph Beller, *Caricatures of the 'Winter King' of Bohemia from the Sutherland Collection in the Bodleian Library and from the British Museum* (London, 1928).

10 Nicolaus Reusner, *Emblemata ... partim ethica, et physica: partim ... Historica, et Hieroglyphica ...* (Frankfurt am Main, 1581). The fourth book consists only of lemmatized epigrams.

11 *Emblemata, ante quidem Amatoria, nunc vero in Moralis Doctrinae sesum magis serium translata; Emblemes traduits des jeux d'Amour au Reiglement des Mœurs.*

12 *Le lettere di Andrea Alciato*, Letter 24.

13 Emblem 27: 'Continet et cubitum, duraque frena manu' (She holds in her hand both a cubit rule, and a sharp bridle.)

14 *Saturnalia*, I, 22, 1. The mythographers Vincenzo Cartari (*Le imagini dei Dei de gli antichi*, Lyon, 1581, p. 388) and L. G. Giraldus (*De Deis Gentium*, Lyon, 1565, p. 393) popularized this iconography.

15 Pope, *Dunciad*, I, 119–20. The revised *Dunciad* (I, 139–40) chooses to single out Quarles for the pillory ('And Quarles is sav'd ...').

16 *Institutio Oratoria*, I, iv, 2.

17 See *FQ*, III, Pr. 8; V, vii, 8; I, xii, 40; II, xii, 46; III, ii, 33; II, ix, 3. Note Spenser's references to spectacles, shows, signs and monuments: 'false showes' (I, i, 46); 'coloured showes' (III, Pr. 3); 'pompous showes' (VII, vi, 41); 'the dreadfull spectacle of that sad house of Pryde' (I, v, 53); 'piteous spectacle' (I, ix, 37); 'pitifull spectacle' (II, i, 40); 'spectacle of sad decay' (II, x, 62); 'piteous spectacle' (II, xii, 45); 'sad pourtraict Of death' (II, i, 39); 'hevenly pourtraict' (II, iii, 22); 'the Faery Queenes pourtract' (II, viii, 43); 'pourtraicts of deformitee' (II, xii, 23); 'there stode an Image all alone' (III, xi, 47); 'An Altare, carv'd with cunning ymagery' (I, viii, 36); 'antickes and wyld ymagery' (II, vii, 4); 'curious ymageree' (II, xii, 60); 'painted imagery' (VII, vii, 10); 'the signe of gelosy' (I, iv, 24); 'the signe of shame' (VI, iii, 17); 'suffice it heare by signes to understand' (I, xii, 40); 'a boxe ... Embowd with ... gorgeous ornament' (I, ix, 19); 'sure he weend ... by many tokens plaine' (V, vi, 34); 'the moniments of passed age' (IV, xi, 17); 'speaking markes of passed monuments' (VI, xii, 29); 'detestable sight' (I, i, 26); 'uncouth sight' (I, viii, 31; II, vi 43); 'great Jove these pageants playd' (III, xi, 35); 'devicefull sights' (V, iii, 3); 'devicefull art' (V, x, 1);

'a Porch with rare device' (II, xii, 54); 'a worke of rare device and wondrous wit' (III, i, 34); 'rare device' (v, ix, 27). 'Painted in a table plaine' (I, ix, 49); 'wals Were painted faire with memorable gestes' (II, ix 53); 'Princes bowres adorne[d] with painted imagery' (VII, vii, 10); 'in those Tapets weren fashioned Many faire pourtraicts' (III, xi, 29); on every side With costly arras dight' (I, iv, 6); 'arayd ... With royall arras' (I, viii, 35); 'costly clothes of Arras and of Toure' (III, i, 34); 'embroder'd quilt' (III, i, 61).

18 'Behold the ymage of mortalitie' (II, i, 57); 'Behold, O man' (II, vi, 15); 'Behold ... with mortall eye' (II, vii, 38); 'Behold this heavy sight' (II, viii, 7); 'Behold, who list, both one and other' (II, ix, 1); 'Behold th'ensamples in our sights' (II, xii, 9); 'Behold the man!' (III, iii, 32); 'Come thou ... and see' (II, vii, 20); 'See, whoso fayre thing doest faine to see'; 'See the Virgin Rose'; 'See soone after' (II, xii, 74); 'See the mind of beastly man' (II, xii, 87); 'See how the heavens ... Doe succor send' (III, viii, 29); 'See, how they doe that Squire beat...'; 'See, how they doe the Lady hale and draw!' (VI, viii, 6); 'Looke! how the crowne, which Ariadne wore' (VI, x, 13); 'Lo! there before his face his Ladie is' (I, i, 49); 'Lo! underneath her scorneful feete was layne' (I, iv, 10); 'Loe! this dead corpse' (II, i, 49); 'Lo! where they spyde ... One in a charet' (IV, iii, 38); 'And loe! his hindparts, ... ugly were' (IV, x, 20).

19 Praz, *Studies in Seventeenth-century Imagery*, p. 348, notes the first appearance of these heart emblems in an edition of 1685, but I have not seen this. The first unemblematized edition of *Quinquaginta meditationes sacrae* was published at Jena in 1607 by Christopher Lippold. It proved enormously popular in its unemblematized state and was translated into English by Ralph Winterton (Cambridge, 1627).

20 MS Rawlinson Poetry 146; MS Harleian 6855 art. 13; Royal MS 12 A lxvi.

21 Bartolomeo del Bene, *Civitas Veri sive Morum* (Paris, 1609).

22 *Odes*, III, 2.

23 To John Rickman, 19 January 1803, in Kenneth Curry, ed., *New Letters of Robert Southey*, 2 vols (New York and London, 1965).

24 Cesare Ripa, *Iconologia* (Rome, 1603), 'Proemio': 'Le Imagini fatte per significare vna diuersa cosa da quella, che si vede con l'occhio, non hanno altra più certa, ne pij vniuersale regoli, che l'imitatione delle memorie, che si trouano ne Libri'.

25 Princeton University Library holds ten of these engravings ([Ex]N7710.A35.1874f).

26 '... le feu de devotion se perd et s'esteint par un discours diffus ...'

27 *Emblems*, p. 67.

28 *Emblems*, sig. A₁ʳ.

29 *Emblems*, (*Les emblèmes sacres sur le Tres-Saint et Tres-Adorable Sacrement de l'Eucharistie* [Paris, 1660]) A₂ʳ.

30 Seneca, *De Beneficiis*, I, iii. For a masterly study of the Three Graces and the antiquarian culture of the Renaissance, see Edgar Wind, *Pagan Mysteries of the Renaissance*, revd enlarged edn (Harmondsworth, 1968), esp. chap. 2: 'Seneca's Graces'.

31 *Epistles*, I, 1, 60–1.

THREE: The *Imaginotheca*: Curators and Janitors

1 Christopher Harvey, 'The insatiableness of the Heart', *Schola Cordis* (London, 1664), p.42

2 William Blake, *For the Sexes, The Gates of Paradise*, ll. 47–8, in *The Complete Writings*, ed. Geoffrey Keynes (London and New York, 1957), p.771

3 In English, E. M.'s *Ashrea* (London, 1665); in Latin, Vincentius Hensbergh's *Viridarium Marianum* (Antwerp, 1615), Heinrich Oræus' *Viridarium Hieroglyphico-Morale* (Frankfurt am Main, 1619), Daniel Stolcius' *Viridarium Chymicum* (Frankfurt am Main, 1624) and his *Hortulus hermeticus* (Frankfurt am Main, 1627). The anonymous *Viridarium moralis philosophiæ* (Cologne, 1594) is, strictly speaking, a zoological garden.

4 *Emblemata* (Lyon, 1550), sig. A₂ᵛ: 'ex promptuario instructissimo'. The domestic

meanness of Betty Knott's translation, 'well stocked cupboard', misses the point. Rouillé's rearranged format first appeared in 1548. The privilege, dated 9 August 1548, states that the book groups the emblems under themes and topics to render it more useful to readers.

5 Lyon, 1620, and subsequent editions. The book cites motto and epigram only. The encyclopaedia also draws on Valeriano's *Hieroglyphica*.

6 (Bologna, 1555), the copperplates by Giulio Bonasone. There was a second edition in 1574.

7 *Heures de la Vièrge* (Lyon, 1548).

8 From *Don Juan*, Canto I, stanza 46.

9 It is a matter of debate whether the first religious emblem book was Protestant or Catholic. The honour probably belongs to the Huguenot Georgette de Montenay, who in the 1560s began composing the emblems that made up her *Emblemes, ou Devises Chrestiennes* (Lyon, 1571). The Catholic Benedictus Arias Montanus *Humanae Salutis Monumenta* was published in the same year at Antwerp.

10 *I Discorsi . . . sopra l'Imprese recitati nell'academia d'Urbino* (Bologna, 1575).

11 *C. Julius Caesar, sive historiae imperatorum Caesarumque Romanorum* (Bruges, 1563). By 1645 an annotated edition of his *Opera omnia* appeared in five volumes.

12 Christoph Weigel, *Oculum animumque delectans Emblematum Repositorium . . . Aug- und Gemütbelustigendes Sinn-Bilder-Cabinet . . .* (Nuremberg, 1718); Christian Weidling, *Emblematische Schatz-Kammer* (Leipzig, 1702); Clemens's work was published at Lyon in 1635; Schiebel's *Neu-erbauter Schausaal* (Nuremberg, 1684) contains 300 'künstlich eingerichteter Sinn-Bilder'.

13 *La Devise du Roy justifiée . . . avec un Recueil de cinq cens Devises faites pour S. M. et toute la maison Royale* (Paris, 1679).

14 John Evelyn, *Numismata* (London, 1697), p. 64.

15 Guillaume Rouillé, *Prima (-secunda pars Promptuarii Iconum insigniorum a seculo hominum subjectis eorum vitis per compendium ex probatissimis autoribus desumptis* (Lyon, 1553); 2nd edn (Lyon, 1578); *La premiere (seconde) partie du Promptuaire des Medalles des plus renommees personnes qui ont esté depuis le commencement du monde: avec brieue description de leurs vies et faicts, recueillie des bons auteurs* (Lyon, 1553); 2nd edn (Lyon, 1576–81); *Prima (-seconda) parte del Prontuario de le Medaglie de piu illustri e fulgenti huomini e donne, dal principio del mondo insino al presente tempo, con le lor vite in compendio raccolte* (Lyon, 1553); 2nd edn (Lyon, 1577, 1578); *Primera parte (parte II) del Promptuario de las medallas de todos los mas insignes varones que avido desde el principio del mundo. . .*, trans. J. M. Cordero (Lyon, 1561).

16 Padua, 1618. See his epistle to the reader (sig. b$_2$^{v}–b$_5$^{r}). The collaboration between this printer and the scholar was not new: they had worked on iconographically authoritative editions of the mythographer Natalis Comes and the iconographer Vincenzo Cartari.

17 'Gravissimum esse imperium consuetudinis' (sig. B$_2$^{v}).

18 'nihil quantumvis tritum, et commune, apud maiores illos nostros, mysterio vacabat' (*Symbolarum epistolicarum liber primus* (1628; Padua, 1694), p. 7. The letter is dated 1596.

19 *La Saincteté de Vie, tirée de la considération des Fleurs* (Liège, 1642).

20 *La Vertu enseignée par les Oiseaux* (Liège, 1647).

21 *Symbolorum et Emblematum ex re Herbaria desumtorum centuria una* (Nuremberg, 1590); *Symbolorum et Emblematum ex animalibus quadrupedibus desumtorum centuria altera collecta* (Nuremberg, 1595); *Symbolorum et Emblematum ex volatilibus et insectis desumtorum centuria tertia collecta* (Nuremberg, 1596); *Symbolorum et Emblematum ex . . . aquatilibus et reptilibus desumptorum centuria quarta* (Nuremberg, 1604).

22 (Paris, 1657). A decade later there was a French translation, *Emblemes Sacrez sur le Tres-Saint et Tres-Adorable Sacrement de l'Eucharistie*.

23 *Currus Israel* contains a list of the emblems to be found in the Church of the Holy Cross in Biberbach, where Ginther was *Decanus et Parochus*. The book was many

times reprinted. The Antwerp edition of 1752, however inaccurately, is described as the eighth.

24 Ginther, *Mater Amoris et Doloris* and *Speculum Amoris et Doloris*; [Henry Hawkins], *Parthenia sacra* ([Rouen] 1633); Joannes de Leenheer, *Virgo Maria Mystica sub solis imagine emblematica expressa* (s. l. 1681); Joannes Pauwels, *Elogia beatissimae Virgini-Matri Mariae attributa, decem iconibus . . . adumbrata* (Antwerp, 1775); Maximilianus Sandaeus, *Maria Flos Mysticus* (Mainz, 1629), *Maria Gemma Mystica* (Mainz, 1631), *Maria Luna Mystica* (Cologne, 1634), *Maria Sol Mysticus* (Cologne, 1636), *Astrologia Mariana* (Cologne, 1650), *Maria Mons Mysticus* (Cologne, 1650).

25 Munich, 1635.

26 *Emblemata sacra de Fide, Spe, Charitate* (Antwerp, 1636).

27 *Virtutes Cardinales Ethico Emblemate expressae* (Antwerp, 1645); *Virtutes et vitia bis Septem . . .* (Rome, n.d.).

28 Michel Cuvelier's *Annona spiritualis* (Cologne, 1646) contains three emblems depicting the three stages of meditation: purgative, illuminative and unitive. On these trinitarian structures, see John Manning, 'De tribus potentis animae: A Seventeenth-century Jesuit Manuscript in the Royal Library, Brussels', in *The Jesuits and the Emblem Tradition*, ed. John Manning and Marc van Vaeck (Turnhout, 1999), pp. 323–39.

29 See, for example, *Virtutes Cardinales Ethico Emblemate Expressae* (Antwerp, 1645) and André Félibien, *Les Quatres Elemens* (Paris, 1665) and *Tapisseries du Roy, ou sont representez les Quatre Elemens et les Quatre Saisons* (Paris, 1670).

30 Gerard de Jode, *Septem Planetae Septem Hominibus aetatibus respondentes* (Antwerp, 1581) and *Speculum vitae humanae* (Antwerp, n.d.). Emanuele Tesauro, 'Trattato degli Emblemi: Planetae' in *Il Cannochiale Aristotelico* (Venice, 1682), pp. 412–13. Francis Quarles's *Hieroglyphiques of the Life of Man* (London, 1638) is based on the scheme of the Seven Ages. See the discussion in my chapter Eight.

31 For example, August Casimir Redel, *Annus Symbolicus* (Augsburg, 1695); Ignatius Franciscus Xavier de Wilhelm, *Annus Politicus* (Munich, 1731); J. Drechsel, *Zodiacus christianus* (Munich, 1618) and subsequent editions; Emanuele Tesauro, 'Trattato degli Emblemi: Signa Zodiaci' in *Il Cannochiale Aristotelico*, pp. 412–14; Richard Pigot, *The Life of Man Symbolized by the Twelve Months of the Year* (London, 1866); Jan David, *Duodecim specula* (Antwerp, 1610) and its German translation, *Himmliche Kunstkammer* (Munich, 1626). Robert Farley's *Kalendarium Humanæ Vitæ* (London, 1638), though it suggests a scheme based on twelves, contains 16 plates.

32 *t'Jaar d'xII Maanden, vII Dagen en IV Getyden* (Amsterdam, 1698).

33 J. Drechsel, *Orbis Phaëton* (Munich, 1629) has 23 plates, one for each letter of the alphabet; J. Harrewyn, *De xxv letteren van het ABC* (Amsterdam, 1694) has 25, as does Thomas Boyles Murray, *An Alphabet of Emblems* (London, 1844).

34 Cornelis Gijsbertszon Plemp, *Emblemata quinquaginta* (Amsterdam, 1616); Daniel Cramer, *Emblemata sacra. Decades quinque* (Frankfurt am Main, 1624); Jean Mercier, *Emblemata* (s.l. 1592); Michael Maier, *Atalanta fugiens* (Oppenheim, 1617).

35 Jakob Bornitz, *Emblematum ethico-politicorum* (Heidelberg, 1664) is made up of two parts, divided fifty and fifty, as are the last two books of Juan de Horoczo y Covarrubias, *Emblemas morales* (Segovia, 1589); book one is a theoretical treatise, and contains no emblems. Other 'centuries' of emblems are, for example, Gilles Corrozet, *Hecatomgraphie* (Paris, 1540); Guillaume de La Perrière, *Theatre des bons engins* (Paris, 1539); Georgette de Montenay, *Emblemes, ou Devises Chrestiennes* (Lyon, 1571); Jan Luyken, *Het Menselyk Bedryf* (Amsterdam, 1694); G. A. Hiltebrant, *Neu-Er'ffneter Anmuthiger Bilder-Schatz* (Frankfurt am Main, 1674); J. W. Zincgreff, *Emblematum Ethico-Politicorum Centuria* (Heidelberg, 1619).

36 Filippo Picinelli, *Mondo simbolico* (Milan, 1653), translated into Latin by A. Erath as *Mundus symbolicus* (Cologne, 1681); C.-F. Menestrier, *La Philosophie des images* (Paris, 1682). On this symbolic configuration, see Michael Schilling, *Imagines Mundi: Metaphorische Darstellungen der Welt in der Emblematik* (Bern and Frankfurt, 1979).

37 'Benevole Lector', *Mundus symbolicus* (Cologne, 1681), sig. c_2^r.
38 Torquato Tasso, 'Discourses on the Heroic Poem', in Allan H. Gilbert, *Literary Criticism: Plato to Dryden* (Detroit, 1962), p. 500.
39 *Mundus symbolicus*, Book 21, caps 9–11: 'Horologium arenarium', 'Horologium rotarum', 'Horologium solare'.
40 Paris, 1618.
41 *Mundus symbolicus*, Book 8, cap 2, para. 101.
42 'invisibilia Dei per ea quae facta sunt'. The English version in the text is based on the King James 'Authorized' translation. Interestingly enough, neither Picinelli nor any of the other symbolographers were deterred by St Paul's following condemnation of idolatry in vv. 22ff: 'they ... changed the glory of the uncorruptible God into an image made like corruptible man, and to birds, and fourfooted beasts, and creeping things'.
43 *The Path of Life, And the way that leadeth down to the Chamber of Death ...* (London, 1656).
44 *Pseudoxia Epidemica*, in *The Works of Thomas Browne*, ed. Geoffrey Keynes, 4 vols (London, 1928), ii, 175 and 52.
45 '*L'Intelletto humano in guisa di purissimo specchio*' (Emanuele Tesauro, *Il Cannochiale Aristotelico*, p. 9).
46 See Thomas Palmer, 'Two hundred poosees', Emblem 85: 'Falshode vnto a lokinge glas / men did of olde compare / Where thoughe the faces like appere, / yet fals we knowe thei are. / What on the lefte hande standes in dede, / semes on the righte to be; / And what is on the righte, we thinke / that on the lefte we se.' Palmer's emblem is a close translation of Valeriano, fol. 307[41]: 'De Speculo. Falsum'.
47 Amsterdam, 1695. This is a Latin translation of *La Philosophie des images* (Paris, 1682).
48 'Jugement des autheurs, qui ont écrit des Devises' (pp. 1–126).
49 Amsterdam, 1699.
50 *Emblemata: Handbuch zur Symbolkunst des XVI und XVII Jahrhunderts* (Stuttgart, 1967).
51 For example, and preeminently, Scipione Bargagli, *La prima parte dell'imprese* (Venice, 1589); Luca Contile, *Ragionamento ... sopra la proprietà delle Imprese* (Padua, 1574); Girolamo Ruscelli, *Le imprese illustri* (Venice, 1566).
52 The following is a partial list of such publications and sufficiently indicates the existence of the fashion north of the Alps: Theodore de Bèze, *Icones* (Geneva, 1580); Jean Jacques Boissard, *Icones diversorum hominum fama, et rebus gestis illustrium* (Metz, 1591) and *Bibliotheca siue thesaurus virtutis et gloriæ: in quo continentur illustrium ... virorum effigies et vitæ* (Frankfurt am Main, 1628–32); Hubert Goltz, *Vivæ fere Imperatorum imagines* (Antwerp, 1557); Hendrik Hondius, *Icones* (The Hague, 1680); Marco Mantova Benavides, *Illustrium imagines* (Padua, 1559); Nicolaus von Reusner, *Icones sive imagines impp., regum, principum* (Leipzig, 1597); Johannes Sambucus, *Icones veterum* (1574; Leiden, 1603); Valentin Thilo, *Icones heroum* (Basle, 1589).
53 For this iconographical association of the rooster, see Cesare Ripa, *Iconologia* (Padua, 1611), *s.v.* 'Sanità'.
54 Venice, 1591.
55 'Plures erant modi Philosophiam et Theologiam tradendi apud veteres, et plerumque arcani. Faciem velabant veritati, ac si vetuisset pudor nudam ostendere populo. Hos modos ita notat Proclus [Theol. Plat.lib. 1. c. 4] Qui enim per demonstrationem de rebus divinis tractant, vel symbolice et mythologice, vel per similitudines et rerum imagines loquuntur' (Thomas Burnett, *Archaeologiae philosophica*, London, 1728, p. 124).
56 Chronologically, he progressed from *Prodromus Coptus, sive Aegyptiacus* (Rome, 1636), *Obeliscus Pamphilus* (Rome, 1650), *Obeliscus Aegyptiacus* (Rome, 1650), *Oedipus Aegyptiacus*, 3 vols (Rome 1652–4), *Obelisci Aegyptiaci* (Rome, 1661), *Lingua Aegyptiaca* (Rome, 1664), and, finally and triumphantly, to *Sphinx mystagogus*, 5 vols (Amsterdam, 1676).

57 *L'Art des Emblemes* (Paris, 1684), pp. 86–167: 'Des Emblêmes Moraux, Politiques, Doctrinaux, Chymiques, Heroïques, Satyriques, Passionez'.

58 *Emblemata. . . . Partim Moralia partim etiam Civilia* (Gouda, 1618).

59 Frankfurt am Main, 1581.

60 *L'Huomo . . . con Figure, Simboli, Anatomie, Imprese, Emblemi morali, Mistici, Proverbi, Geroglifici, Prodigi, Simolacri, Statue, Historie, Riti, Osservationi, Costumi, Numismi, Dedicationi, Signature, Significatione di Lettere, Epiteti, Favolosi, Mirabili, Fisonomie, e Sogni . . . .* (Bologna, 1684).

61 Cited *Choice*, pp. 79; 109; 144; 114; sig. **$*_1^6$; sig. $*_3^7$; 16; 113; 188; 169; 60; 202; 215; sig. $*_1^8$; 123; 144; 197; sig. $*_3^9$; 13.

62 Cited sig. $*_3^r$ and $*_4^r$.

63 *Choice*, pp. 3; 5; 10; 18; 34; 35; 49; 53; 54; 67; 118; 126; 188; 229.

64 *Choice*, pp. 50; 51; 73; 87; 97; 144; 147; 177.

65 *Choice*, pp. 10; 45; 49; 120; 193; 194.

66 Sturmius, I, 8: No. 6.

67 Viz. *similitudo, oppositio, alienatio*, and *allusio*. For analysis of emblems based on these terms, see J. J. Müller, *Introductio in Artem Emblematicam* (Jena, 1706).

68 Emanuele Tesauro, *Il Cannochiale Aristotelico*, pp. 7–8.

69 Cesare Ripa, *Iconologia* (Rome, 1603), 'Proemio': 'Le Imagini fatte per significare vna diuersa cosa da quella, che si vede con l'occhio, non hanno altra pij certa, ne pij vniuersale regoli, che l'imitatione delle memorie, che si trouano ne Libri . . .' (Images made to mean more than meets the eye have no other nor more universal rules than the imitation of the memorials of what is found in books . . .).

70 Luis de la Puente, *Meditations vppon the mysteries* (s. l. 1618), pp. 56–7. The seventeenth-century translation is by Fr. Richard Gibbons.

FOUR: Children and Childish Gazers

1 MS translation of Mme de Guyon. On this manuscript see 'An Unedited and Unpublished English Manuscript Translation of Hermann Hugo's *Pia Desideria*', *Emblematica*, 6 (1993), pp. 147–79, and 'An Unedited and Unpublished English Manuscript Translation of *Les Emblemes d'Othon Vænius*', *Emblematica*, 6 (1992), pp. 325–55.

2 'Quisne Iouem tactum puerili credat amore?' (Alciato, Emblem 4, l. 3).

3 On Jourdain and his book, see John Manning, 'An Unlisted and Unrecorded Sixteenth-century Emblem Book: Charles Jourdain's *Le Blason des Fleurs*', *Emblematica*, 6 (1993), pp. 195–9.

4 *Libellus emblematum* (Paris, 1542), p. 11: 'hic accedit quoque pictura, quae grato quodam oblectamento primam etatem ad amorem sapientiae severioris adliciat' (Here a picture is added, which by its pleasing diversion will lead young people to the love of more serious wisdom). Hunger addressed his preface to two young brothers, Baldasar and Werner Sybelsdorf.

5 *The Emblems of Thomas Palmer: Two Hundred Poosees*, ed. John Manning (New York, 1988), p. 190.

6 Palmer, Emblem 9. This is loosely based on Alciato's Emblem 4, 'In Deo lætandum'.

7 2nd edn (Nuremberg, 1602), sig B_4: 'Tandem putrefacta resurgent'. This is an emblem of the Resurrection.

8 'Amoris semen mirabile'. See Praz, pp. 119 and 122, on this motif in Heinsius and the *Thronus*.

9 On the iconographic influence of this work well into the eighteenth century, see E. H. Gombrich, 'A Classical Rake's Progress', *Journal of the Warburg & Courtauld Institutes*, XV (1952), pp. 254–6. Raimonde van Marle, *Iconographie de l'art profane au moyen-âge et à la renaissance*, 2 vols (The Hague, 1932), II, p. 157 describes the influence of the iconography of the *Tabula*. Hans Holbein based a woodcut border on it that was pressed into service for such diverse publications as an edition of Cebes (Cracow, 1519), Erasmus' *New Testament* (Basle, 1522) and Strabo's *Geography* (Basle, 1523).

10 'Dum pueros iuglans ... fallit'.

11 Its corollary is *relinquere nuces* (to give up childish sports, to get on with the serious business of life).

12 *Epigrams*, 14, 1, 12.

13 Henry Peacham, *Minerva Britanna* (London, 1612), p. 81. George Wither, *A Collection of Emblemes, Ancient and Moderne* (London, 1635), 'To the Reader', sigs A₂ʳ and A₁ᵛ.

14 In *Silenus Alcibiadis* (Middelburg, 1618). The text used here is from the anthology *Zedenkundig vermaan voor jong en oud uit de prentenboeken van Jakob Cats*, ed. G. A. van Es (Culemborg, 1977), pp. 48–53.

15 'To the Reader', sig. A₁ᵛ.

16 'Maar, lieve vrient, en merckje niet, / Dat ghij u selfs hier med'in siet?'

17 'Sic in vita hominum, quasi cum ludas tesseris'.

18 'Periculosæ plenum opus aleæ' (*Odes*, II, 1, 6).

19 Rabelais, *Gargantua*, chap. 24: 'ilz ... revocquoient en usage l'anticque jeu des tales .... En y jouant recoloient les passaiges des auteurs anciens esquelz est faicte mention ou prinse quelque metaphore sus iceluy jeu'. The English translation is Urquhart's. Works that make use of this technique are Nicholas Leonicus Thomæus, *Sannutus, sive de ludo talario* (Lyon, 1532); Jules-César Boulenger, *De ludis privatis, ac domesticis veterum liber unicus* (Lyon, 1627); Joannes Meursius, *Graecia ludibunda, sive de ludis Graecorum* (Leiden 1625); and Daniel Souter, *Palamedes, sive de tabula Lusoria, alea et variis ludis, libri tres* (Leiden, 1622).

20 Plato, *Laws*, I, 644 DE, trans. B. Jowett.

21 *Emblemata moralia nova*, Emblem 7 (p. 25).

22 'nunc hac nunc fluctuat illac' (*Emblemata moralia nova*, p. 53, referring to Ephesians 4. 14).

23 On Alonso de Ledesma, see Praz, *Studies in Seventeenth-century Imagery*, 2nd edn (Rome, 1964), pp. 142 and 139.

24 S. Foster Damon, *A Blake Dictionary: The Ideas and Symbols of William Blake* (Providence, RI, 1965), *s.v.* 'Children'.

25 'Ut sphaerae Fortuna, cubo sic insidet Hermes'. Betty Knott's translation (p. 107) of the line is plainly inadequate, stating as it does, 'Fortune rests ...'. She misses the point of the epigram and its iconography: Fortune *never* rests! Her sphere is a symbol of inconstancy and change.

26 *Symbolicae philosophiae liber quartus et ultimus*, ed. J. Manning (New York, 1991), p. 8: 'figuras vel pueri percipiant expedite satis'.

27 *Oxford English Dictionary*, *s.v.* 'Gay C 3': 'A picture in a book'. First cited use, 1646.

28 'To the Reader', sig. A₂ʳ.

29 Graven-Hage, 1632, p. 29.

30 Richard Taverner, *Proverbes or adagies* (London, 1539), fol. 30.

31 'Angustum virtutum iter'. See Levinus Hulsius, *Epitome Emblematvm Panegyricorvm Academiæ Altorfinaæ* (Nuremberg, 1602), p. 6.

32 'Spinosa, ad astra, mollis ad Stygem, via est'. Royal Library, Brussels, MS4040, fol. 48ʳ. Cf. Virgil, *Aeneid*, VI. 126: 'facilis descensus Averno' (the descent to hell is easy). Hadrianus Junius, *Emblemata* (Antwerp, 1565), Emblem 44 represents the choice of Hercules, which is between the easy path of Vice and the thorny road of Virtue. It is based on a fable by the philosopher Prodicus, recorded by Xenophon.

33 G. Rollenhagen, *Nucleus Emblematum*, 93: 'Culmen ad Eonidum RECTO contendere CVRSV / Fert animus Pindi saxa per et tribulos.'

34 *The Reason of Church Government*, Introduction to Book 2.

35 Freeman, *English Emblem Books*, p. 6.

36 'a pueris debent virginibusque legi' (*Epigrams*, III. 69. 8).

37 'sunt apinae tricaeque' (*Epigrams*, XIV, 1, 7).

38 *Symbolicae philosophiae liber quartus et ultimus*, ed. J. Manning (New York, 1991), p. 6: 'Plura sunt apud Jouium ineptiarum exempla ...'.

39 The title-page reads: 'Apprime Epheborum aliquot Praenobilium in Usum exculta, qua ad SS. Scripturas alliciantur' (Prepared especially for the use of a few youths

from very noble families, by which means they might be drawn to the Holy Scriptures). On Whitehall, see Gillian Manning, '*Hexastichon Hieron*: A Hitherto Unrecorded English Emblem Book of the Restoration Period', *Emblematica*, 6 (1992), pp. 307–22.

40 'The Place of Laughter in Tudor and Stuart England', *Times Literary Supplement* (21 January 1977), p. 80.

41 Wither, 'To the Reader', sigs. A$_1$–A$_2$^{r}. For Spinoza, see *Tractatus theologico-politicus*, ed. C. H. Bruder (Leipzig, 1846), III, p. 83.

42 *Premierement en Allemand . . . et maintenant en François, pour le bien de la jeunesse, et du simple peuple*. *Emblemes nouveaux* (Frankfurt am Main, 1617).

43 See Wendy Katz. 'Miss Thoughtful's *Instructive and Entertaining Emblems*, an American Emblem Book for Children', in *Emblematic Perceptions: Essays in Honor of William S. Heckscher*, ed. Peter M. Daly and Daniel S. Russell (Baden-Baden, 1997), pp. 111–21.

44 *Memoirs of the Life and Writings of Alexander Pope*, 2 vols (London, 1745), II, p. 192.

45 All quotations from the *Dunciad* are from the Twickenham edition, ed. James Sutherland, 3rd revd edn (London, 1963).

46 L'Estrange, 'Preface', sig. A$_2$^{v}.

47 *Symbolicarum Quaestionum de universo genere quas serio ludebat libri quinque* (1555; Bologna, 1574).

48 Oppenheim, 1616, and Frankfurt, 1617.

49 'Preface', sigs. A$_2$^{v} and A$_3$^{r}.

50 'Quo semel est imbuta recens, servabit odorem, Testa diu' (*Epistles*, I, ii, 69–70).

51 'Everything cultivated when grafted on to what is uncultivated, is called *emblema*', explained the Renaissance encyclopaedist Coelius Rhodiginus in connection with the cultivation of olive trees. (*Lectionum antiquarum libri XVI*, Basel 1517, Book 7, cap. xix: 'omnia syluestribus insita dici Emblemata.' Cited Miedema, p. 239).

52 *Emblemata Anniversaria* (1617), sig. Bbb$_4$^{v}; Taurellus, 3.

53 Valeriano, fol. 85; La Perrière, *Le Theatre des bons engins* (Paris, 1539), Emblem XCVIII; and my illus. 83.

54 As in the Jesuit College at Brussels, 1660 manuscript Mors-Vita 20318: fol. 79v, *Vita Iuuenum Flexilis* (The life of young people is pliable).

55 'Rami correcti rectificantur, trabs minimè.' Jacob Cats, *Spieghel van den Ouden Ende Nieuwen Tijdt* (Graven-Hage, 1632), p. 1.

56 *Emblematum liber* (Frankfurt am Main, 1593), p. 3.

57 'Preface', sig. A$_2$^{v}.

58 Sig. Bbb$_2$^{r}.

59 'Preface', sig. A$_2$^{v}.

60 Daniel Cramer, *Octaginta emblemata moralia nova* (Frankfurt am Main, 1630), p. 5. The scriptural authority is I Timothy 6. 7, but the first line of the epigram paraphrases Job: 'Nudus ingredior, sic egredior quoque nudus'. The emblem's motto is 'NIHIL APPORTO, NIHIL ASPORTO' (I bring nothing with me, I carry nothing away). Schoonhoven, *Emblemata* (Gouda, 1618), Emblem 27, 'Semper pueri', will, on Senecan authority, overgo the popular notion that a man is twice a child, in infancy and again in old age, by claiming that man is *always* a child: 'Verissimè Seneca inquit, Non bis pueri sumus, ut vulgò dicitur, sed semper . . .'.

61 'Preface' sig. A$_3$^{v}.

62 Taverner, fol. 38f.

63 Cramer, pp. 40–41: Emblem 11.

64 *Icones* (Geneva, 1580), Emblem 27: 'Ludicra ridemus fabricantes tecta puellos'.

65 'Æternitas porta vitæ aut mortis' (MS 20.326: fol. 12).

66 MS 20318: fol. 109^v.

67 'caducæ mortalitatis vmbra'; 'nihil . . . vanius aut inanius' (Hadrianus Junius, *Emblemata*, Antwerp, 1565).

68 Frontispiece, *The Hieroglyphikes of the Life of Man*.

69 Page 76: 'De Schoonheydt is verganckelijk'.

70 'Constans in ververa perstat' (MS 20318: fol. 119^v).

71 MS 20.326: fol. 14.

72 'Grave sit, tamen ibit ad astra' (MS 20.326: fol. 52).

73 'Qui stat, videat ne cadat' (MS 20.326: fol. 88).

74 'Tempori blando nulla fides' (MS 20.326: fol. 106^v).

75 Wynne's *Choice Emblems* was also known as *Riley's Emblems*, and was first published in 1772 at London by George Riley. Thereafter it went through numerous editions in England and America during the rest of the eighteenth and the nineteenth centuries.

76 On Stevenson's period at Davos, see William George Lockett, *Robert Louis Stevenson at Davos* (London, 1934); J. C. Furnas, *Voyage to Windward: The Life of Robert Louis Stevenson* (London, 1952), pp. 143–7; 184–9; Jenni Calder, *RLS: A Life Study* (London, 1980), pp. 156–78. For the history of the production of the emblem texts, see the 'Preface' by Lloyd Osbourne in *Moral Emblems by Robert Louis Stevenson* (London, 1921), pp. v–xviii, and James D. Hart, *The Private Press Ventures of Samuel Lloyd Osbourne and R.L.S.* (San Francisco, 1966).

77 *Moral Emblems*, no. 2. The begging pauper and a more generous Elizabethan beau appears under the motto 'Bis dat qui citò dat' (He who gives quickly gives twice), in Whitney's *A Choice of Emblems* (Leyden, 1586), p. 190, and in Gabriele Simeoni, *Le imprese heroiche e morali* (Lyon, 1559).

78 *Moral Emblems*, no. 3. In the tradition of the many emblems commemorating the heroic deeds of classical kings and generals. See also the various *Icones illustrium*, which were devoted to commemorating ancient and contemporary worthies. On this tradition, see Chapter Three above, n.52.

79 *Abies* (the fir or pine) appears as one of the emblematic trees in Alciato, while a disputatious pine argues with a gourd in Palmer's Emblem 44, Whitney, p. 34, and Alciato's Emblem 125; the eagle is a fit companion for heroes in Alciato, Emblem 33, and Palmer, Emblem 62; the elephant is a symbol for piety in Palmer, Emblem 10, and in Valeriano Bolzani, *Hieroglyphica* (Basle, 1556); Valeriano's Book 17 includes the hieroglyphic ibis.

80 The angler appears in Palmer, Emblem 47, and in Barthélemy Aneau, *Picta poesis* (Lyon, 1552), p. 103. The foundering ship can be found in Whitney, p. 11, and in Joannes Sambucus, *Emblemata* (Antwerp, 1564), p. 46.

81 See, for example, *Industria naturam corrigit*, Whitney, p. 93: 'the man on whome dothe Nature froune, / Whereby, he liues dispis'd of euerie wighte, / Industrie yet, maie bringe him to renoume, / And diligence, maie make the crooked righte'. John Huddlestone Wynne advised: 'Be *frugal*, be *industrious*'.

82 For example, Alciato's Emblems 57: 'Furor et rabies', and 63: 'Ira'. Wynne's Emblem 54 warns against 'Passion' (i.e., rage).

83 *Moral Emblems: A Second Collection*, Emblem 5. Pirates appear in earlier emblem books, e.g., Whitney, pp. 144 and 203, but are not commended.

84 Sidney Colvin, ed., *The Letters of Robert Louis Stevenson*, 4 vols (New York, 1899), I, pp. 235–6.

85 Colvin, ed., *Letters*, I, pp. 236–7.

86 Bradford Allen Booth and Ernst Mehew, *The Letters: August 1879–September 1882* (New Haven, CT, 1994) p. 359.

FIVE: Carnal Devotions

1 See Samuel Fletcher, *Emblematical Devices* (London, 1810), discussed by Praz, pp. 132–3, 132n. 1. See also, Praz, p. 54, for examples of Vænius emblems on cabinets and glassware. See also Ria Fabri, 'Amor, amor divinus — anima, virtus: Emblematic Scenes on Seventeenth-century Antwerp Cabinets', in John Manning, Karel Porteman and Marc van Vaeck, eds, *The Emblem Tradition and the Low Countries: Selected Papers of the Leuven International Emblem Conference, 18–23 August 1996* (Turnhout, 1999), pp. 357–68.

2 *The Complete Works in Prose and Verse of Francis Quarles*, ed. Alexander B. Grosart, 3 vols (New York, 1967), I, p. lxxiv.

3 Henry Hawkins, *The Devout Hart* ([Rouen] 1638), p. 217. This is an English translation of Etienne Luzvic's *Le coeur devot* (Paris [1626]).

4 See respectively pp. 188 and 196: 'pour du vin il verse du poison'.

5 See respectively pp. 14, 164, and 66.

6 Page 120: 'Solus Amor morbi non amat artificem' (Only love does not love a cure for his disease).

7 Page 154.

8 'Amans Amanti medicvs' (p. 168); 'Morbvm nosse, cvrationis principivm' (p. 176).

9 Page 114: 'Amor addit inertibus alas' (Love gives wings to the lazy).

10 Page 2: 'Perfectus amor non est nisi ad vnvm'; p. 4: 'e geminis concinnat amantibus unum'; p. 16: 'Amoris finis est, vt dvo vnvm fiant'.

11 Respectively p. 6 and p. 126, and p. 182.

12 Page 86: 'iocos inter vincula miscet Amor'.

13 I, vii, 1 and I, ii, 21, 'Aequalem uxorem quaeere' (Seek a wife that is your equal) and 'Simile gaudet simile' (Like delights in like).

14 Vænius himself used the fable in this way in the *Emblemata horatiana*, p. 18: 'IN MEDIO CONSISTIT VIRTVS'.

15 P. Renouard, *Les marques typographiques parisiennes des xve et xvie siècles* (Paris, 1926–8), pp. 616–18. The *Emblemata Anniversaria* (Nuremberg, 1617), sig. Ll₂ʳ records a use of this device with the same motto by a pupil in 1595.

16 Page 5: 'Optimus est medius, sic ego vera loquor' (The middle course is best; I speak the truth). Or, the last part of the verse might be more properly rendered: I speak plainly – an obvious inversion of the indirect, dark utterances expected from emblems.

17 'Préface', sig. *₃.

18 'Ce que nous faisons aujourd'hui, les Anciens l'ont sçeu faire'.

19 A punning reference to the Latin *cunnus*, French *con*.

20 On this point see my chapter Eight. Jeremias Drechsel was particularly given to this tactic. See his works variously titled *Zodiacus christianus*; *Horologium*; *Trismegistus*.

21 'Perfectus amor non est nisi ad vnvm; 'In unitate perfectio'; 'Amoris finis est, vt dvo vnvm fiant'.

22 Mark 10. 15; Luke 18. 17: '. . . shall in no wise enter therein'.

23 Book 2, Emblem 18: 'Sustineor fragili puerilia membra curuli / Quæque vehunt socias ipsa propello rotas.'

24 Quarles, *Emblemes*, 4, 3. Arwaker, *Pia desideria*, 2, 3 refers to 'this *slight Engine*' and 'my *slow-wheel'd Chariot*'.

25 1, 14. For Arwaker's inclusion of and relation to the *Totentanz* tradition, see my chapter Eight.

26 Mme de Guyon, *L'Ame amante de son Dieu* (Cologne, 1717). The English translation here is from the manuscript in the British Library. For a full transcription and discussion see John Manning, *Emblematica*, 6 (1992), pp. 147–79 and pp. 325–55.

27 Page 334: 'In cælum properemus: illa meta est, / Tot desideriis petita meta; / Curarum scopus, et beata meta est. / Ingens hinc iter est, inane magnum est . . .'.

28 The subject, in spite of the miniaturization of the form, is huge. I have not the space to do it justice here. For further study of this motif, see K. A. Wirth, 'Religiöse Herzenemblematik' in *Das Herz, 2, Im Umkreis der Kunst* (Biberbach a.d. Ris n.d.), pp. 63–105, Sabine Mödersheim, *Domini Doctrina Coronat: Die geistliche Emblematik Daniel Cramers (1568–1637)* (Frankfurt am Main, 1992), pp. 149–99. For the profane tradition of heart emblematics, see Marc van Vaeck, 'The *Openhertighe Herten* in Europe: Remarkable Specimens of Heart Emblematics', *Emblematica*, 8 (1994), pp. 261–91.

six: Fame's Double Trumpet

1 Nashe, *Works*, I, 83.

2 'lusus ipse triumphus amat' (Martial, *Epigrams*, VII, 8, 10).

3 'Do you not see?' / 'I see and rejoice!' (Shakespeare, *Love's Labours Lost*, v, i, 29–30).

4 'Emblemata . . . non absque singulari jucunditate videnda, legenda, meditanda, intelligenda, dijudicanda, canenda et audienda' (Michael Maier, *Atalanta Fugiens*, Oppenheim, 1618, t.p.).

5 Julius Wilhelm Zincgref, *Emblemata ethico-politica* (Frankfurt am Main, 1619), 'Praefatio', sig. xx₃ʳ.

6 *Andrea Alciato and his Books of Emblems*, p. ix.

7 'nelle comedie, e nelle giostre, e nelle mascherate' (Girolomo Ruscelli, *Le imprese illustri*, Venice 1566, pp. 15–16).

8 Jeff Nuttall, *Bomb Culture* (1968; London, 1970), p. 239.

9 *Symbolicae philosophiae liber quartus et ultimus*, pp. 14–15.

10 Praz, pp. 235–543 and pp. 544–76.

11 Guillaume de la Perrière, *Le Theatre des Bons Engins* (Paris, 1539), sig. O₃.

12 *Le Imagine de i dei de gli antichi* (Lyon, 1581), p. 41.

13 Antwerp, 1564, 'In sponsalia Ioannis Ambij Angli, et Albae Roleæ D. Arnoldi Medici Gandauensis filiæ' (pp. 124–5); pp. 194–5; pp. 228–9.

14 See, for example, Johannes van Sambeek, *Het geestelyck jubilee van het Jaar O.H.M.DC.L* ([Amsterdam] 1663).

15 Anon., *L'Autel de Lyon consacré à Louys Auguste . . . Ballet dédié B Sa Majesté en son entrée à Lyon* (Lyon, 1658).

16 Milton, *The Reason of Church Government*, 'Introduction to Part II' as cited in Allan H. Gilbert, *Literary Criticism: Plato to Dryden* (Detroit, 1962), p. 591. Milton typically paraphrases and conflates several verses in this 'quotation' from the Book of Proverbs (8. 2–3; 9. 3).

17 'vere, et ad vivum accurate'.

18 *Arbustum vel Arboretum Augustæum* (Wolfenbüttel, 1650).

19 'Emblems of Peace in a Seventeenth-century Danish Pageant', *Emblematica*, 5 (1992), pp. 321–40.

20 Praz, p. 180ff.

21 Praz, p. 544. His reference is to cols 1882–97 in the volume of *Tables*.

22 'Figura carmine iuuabatur', 'Carmen fabulæ accinebat'.

23 *Imago*, p. 203.

24 See M. Fumaroli, 'Baroque et classicisme. L'*Imago primi saeculi Societatis Jesus* (1640) et ses adversaires', in Alphonse Vermeylen and François Chamoux, eds, *Questionnement du Baroque* (Brussels, 1986). Fumaroli defends the Jesuit authors of the volume.

25 Freeman, p. 56.

26 For a full discussion of the political and cultural links between England and the United Provinces in these years, see J. A. van Dorsten, *Poets, Patrons and Professors: Sir Philip Sidney, Daniel Rogers and the Leiden Humanists* (Leiden and London, 1962) and R. C. Strong and J. A. van Dorsten, *Leicester's Triumph* (Leiden and London, 1964). The present discussion is an abbreviated version of my article 'Whitney's *Choice of Emblems*: A Reassessment', *Renaissance Studies*, 4 (1990), pp. 155–200.

27 *Choice*, sig. ***₁ʳ: 'auspiciis *Leycestri*, *Emblemata* lucem / Aspiciunt' ('at Leicester's command the *Emblems* see the light of day'); *Choice*, sig. ***₁ᵛ: '*Leycestrivs* heros / Vindicat auspiciis edita scripta suis' ('The hero, Leicester, commands by his authority that the writings be published').

28 *Choice*, p. 108.

29 On Dyer, see *Choice*, p. 135. On the Cholmondeley crest, see *Choice*, p. 138 and Henry Green, ed., *A Choice of Emblemes by Geffrey Whitney* (1866; New York, 1967), p. 363, who notes the heraldic pun. Green's contemporary Marquess of Cholmondeley was the leading dedicatee of Green's reprint of 1866.

30 The manuscript is in the Houghton Library (shelfmark, MS.Typ 14), and was unknown to Freeman. For a discussion of the differences between the manuscript and the printed text, see Mason Tung, 'Whitney's *A Choice of Emblemes* Revisited: A Comparative Study of the Manuscript and the Printed Versions', *Studies in*

Bibliography, xxix (1976), pp. 32–101. The Janus emblem is on fol. 52ᵛ.

31 Vincenzo Cartari, *Le Imagine de i dei de gli antichi* (Lyon, 1581), p. 36: 'Mostrano anchora le due faccie di Giano il tempo, che tuttauia viene: e perciò l'vna é giouine, e quello che già è passato, onde l'altra è di maggiore età, e barbuta.' Both faces are bearded in the woodcut on *Choice*, p. 108: the one on the left of mature years, the one on the right elderly. In the ms. one face is turned away from the reader, and is partially concealed.

32 Lyon, 1552, p. 49.

33 *Choice*, pp. 122–3. Ovid, *Metamorphoses* I, 21: 'deus et melior ... natura'. The translation cited, unless otherwise stated, is that of Frank Justus Miller (London and Cambridge, MA, 1921).

34 'Est Mundanarum talis confusio rerum / Quo Regina latet Tempore Iustitia' (Aneau, ll. 7–8).

35 *Metamorphoses*, I, 26–31; 69–88.

36 *Metamorphoses*, I, 89–150.

37 'virgo caede madentis / ultima caelestum terras Astraea reliquit' (*Metamorphoses*, I, 149–50).

38 'deus et melior ... natura' (*Metamorphoses*, I, 21).

39 For example, Psalm 19, 1; John 3, 16; John 1, 3–4.

40 *Metamorphoses*, I, 177–347.

41 Virgil, *Eclogue* IV, 4–10: 'Ultima Cumaei venit iam carminis aetas; / magnus ab integro saeclorum nascitur ordo. / iam redit et Virgo, redeunt Saturnia regna; / tu modo nascenti puero, quo ferrea primum / desinet ac toto surget gens aurea mundo, / casta fave Lucina.' The translation cited in the text is by H. Rushton Fairclough in *Virgil: Eclogues, Georgics, Aeneid I–VI*, new and revd edn (Cambridge, MA, and London, 1935).

42 William Camden, *Remains Concerning Britain* (London, 1870), p. 381. Modern scholars owe a great debt to Frances Yates, whose article 'Queen Elizabeth I as Astraea', *Journal of the Warburg Institute*, x (1947), rptd in *Astraea: The Imperial Theme in the Sixteenth Century* (Harmondsworth, 1977), did much to alert us to this aspect of Elizabethan imperialism. Both Yates and Howard Erskine-Hill, *The Augustan Idea in English Literature* (London, 1983), pp. 72–3, associate the identification of Elizabeth with Astraea as a predominantly post-Armada phenomenon, and with an England secure in its own borders. As the quotation from Camden shows it was associated with Elizabeth from the beginning of her reign, and Whitney here invokes it to favour an expansionist, imperialistic foreign policy. These ambitions, we now know, as Whitney did not, were probably more Leicester's than Elizabeth's.

43 Yates explores the religious implications of the Astraea myth in *Astraea*, pp. 38–51.

44 *Choice*, p. 203. For the connection between the Astraea myth and England's maritime expansion, particularly in connection with John Dee's *General and rare memorials pertayning to the Perfecte Arte of Navigation*, see Yates, *Astraea*, pp. 48–9 and 55, which mentions Harrington's praise of Drake's achievement as a sign of England's imperial ambitions.

45 The Norwich ms. was headed 'A treatise of Horsman Shipp': see Mary R. Mahl in the *Times Literary Supplement* (21 December 1967), col. 1245.

46 Royal Library, Brussels MS 4040: 'Moris est in hoc Societatis Jesu Collegio, ut studiosa juventus, quotannis semel praecipuè solemniter doctrinæ suæ specimen publicè præbeat, affixis in plateâ emblematis similibusque ornamentis literariis, eo die, quo per eam celebri pompâ venerabile Sacramentum miraculosum circumfertur.' Translation in Porteman, *Emblematic Exhibitions*, p. 32.

47 *Religio Medici*, I, p. 41.

48 Henry Stubbes, *A Further Justification of the War with the United Provinces* (London, 1673), 3f.

49 *The True Interests and Political Maxims of the Republic of Holland* (London, 1746).

50 For these and other examples, see F. P. Barnard, *Satirical and Controversial Medals of the Reformation* (Oxford, 1927).

51 The full title reads: *Antithesis Christi et Antichristi, videlicet Papae, id est Exemplorum, factorum, vitae et doctrinae utriusque, ex aduerso collata comparatio, versibus et figuris venustissimis illustrata*, revised and enlarged edition (s. l. 1578).

52 *Emblemata anniversaria academiæ altorfinæ* (Nuremberg, 1597), sig. Ii$_3$^{r}: 'POENA COMES SCELERIS'. The lengthy oration continues to sig. Kk$_3$. The same theme appears earlier at sig. E$_1$^{r}, which depicts a Basilisk, whose glance was held to be fatal, staring into a mirror, with the motto: 'IMPROBITAS SVI IPSIVS POENA'.

53 'asini et muli Romanenses', 'sues … monachi', 'Purgatoriani corvi', 'noctuae sepulchrales', 'serpentum et anguium … moniales et Beguttae'.

54 For this tradition, see Doumergue, *Iconographie calvinienne* (Lausanne, 1909). Batman's book is a translation of *Prodigiorum ao ostentorum chronion* by Konrad Lykosthenes.

55 'English Political Prints ca 1640–ca 1830: The Potential for Emblematic Research and the Failures of Print Scholarship', in *Deviceful Settings: The English Renaissance Emblem and its Contexts*, ed. Michael Bath and Daniel S. Russell (New York, 1999), pp. 139–65.

56 *Choice*, p. 74: my emphasis.

57 *Twelfth Night*, II, iv, 114–15: 'She sat like patience on a monument, / Smiling at grief.'

SEVEN: Licentious Poets and the Feast of Saturn

1 Martial, *Epigrams*, II, 86. 'It is degrading to deal with difficult trifles and fooleries are the work of a fool.'

2 *Drei-Ständige Sonn- und Festag-Emblemata* (Nuremberg [1674]). Dilherr also termed his emblem collections a 'Festagsarbeit'.

3 'Festa et Gesta Sanctorum totius anni'. The title of the work is *Cæleste Pantheon. sive cælum novum*. The third edition (Cologne, 1658) adds more materials on saints' days and the festivities of the Church.

4 'conciones in festa occurentia per annum'. *Theatrum Gloriae Sanctorum* (Salzburg, 1696).

5 Nashe, *Works*, I, p. 83.

6 To Alexander Japp, 1 April 1882 (Colvin, ed., *Letters*, II, p. 237).

7 From various letters to Alexander Ireland, March 1882 (Colvin, ed., *Letters*, I. p. 235); to Alexander Japp, March 1882 (Colvin, ed., *Letters*, II, pp. 236–7); to his cousin Bob, quoted from Jenni Calder, *RLS: A Life Study* (London, 1980), p. 158.

8 'postulat ecce novos ebria bruma sales' (Martial, *Epigrams*, XIII, 1, 4).

9 (Basle, 1619), vol. II, pp. 923–82.

10 *Le lettere di Andrea Alciato Giureconsulto*, ed. L. Barni (Florence, 1953), p. 46: Letter 24 to Francesoco Calvo, Milan, 9 December 1522.

11 'versu ludere non laborioso / permittis' (Martial, *Epigrams*, XI, 6, 3–4). Martial's joke in XIV, 10, 'donat vacuas poeta chartas', plays on the same point. The poet's gift can be 'blank sheets of paper' or 'papers containing poems produced during a time of leisure'.

12 Giovio, *Dialogo*, p. 155. See also Alciato, Emblem 119: 'Virtuti, Fortuna comes' and Mignault's note. This device was carved on Alciato's tomb in Pavia.

13 'pileus, signum libertatis'. Later in the sixteenth century the symbol would be appropriated for political purposes: a Dutch medal of 1575 celebrates the Hat of Liberty, 'Libertas aurea cuius habenas ratio' (Golden Liberty whose reins are reason). A cat appears as the ensign of 'Fredome' in Claude Paradin, *Heroica symbola* (Antwerp, 1562), p. 38^v and in Thomas Palmer's 'Two hundred poosees', Emblem 88.

14 Martial, *Epigrams*, XIV, 1 and XI, 6.

15 Stubbes, *Anatomie of Abuses* refers to 'my Lord of Misrule's badges': 'certain papers, wherein is painted some bablery or other of imagery work' – 'whoever will not be buxom to them and give them money for these their devilish cognizances, they are mocked and flouted at'. 'Others,' he writes, wear their badges and their cognizances in their hats or caps openly' (cited in C. L. Barber, *Shakespeare's Festive Comedy*,

1959, p. 28). Ben Jonson, 'Christmas his Masque', in *Works*, VII, p. 439. Christmas himself is attired in 'a high-crowned Hat with a Broach' (VII, p. 437).

16 As Martial, *Epigrams*, XIV, 71 says: 'Iste tibi faciet bona Saturnalia porcus' (This pig will make you a good Saturnalia). For the boar as a symbol of winter, see Alciato's emblem 77, 'Amuletum veneris' and Mignault's notes.

17 'ludit herboso pecus omne campo, / cum tibi nonae redeunt Decembres; / festus in pratis vacat otioso / cum bove pagus' (*Odes*, III, 18, 9–12). The translation quoted is that of C. E. Bennett. For further discussion of Alciato's emblem, see below.

18 Sig. A₂ʳ. On *strenae*, see L. Pignoria, *Symbolarum Epistolicarum Liber* (Padua, 1694), Letter 47, pp. 113–16.

19 The first version of the Jesuit Adrianus Poirters' *Den Spieghel van Philagie* appeared as *Het daeghelycks nieuwe iaer spieghelken van Philagie* (Antwerp, 1673). On this tradition see H. Storme, 'Spiritual New Year's Gifts: Symbolic Presents and Moral Teaching in Seventeenth- and Eighteenth-century Sermons for New Year's Day', *Emblematica*, 8 (1994), pp. 303–20.

20 Blake, *Songs of Innocence*, 'Introduction', l. 10 and 'Spring', l. 9. Alciato's Emblem 151, 'Respublica liberata', depicts a coin with the inscription 'EID. MAR.': i.e., the Ides of March, the anniversary of the assassination of Julius Caesar.

21 *Oxford English Dictionary*, *s.v.* 'posy' I 1 b: 'An emblem or emblematical device'.

22 George Puttenham, *The Art of English Poesie* (London: George Field, 1589), p. 47: Lib. 1. Chap. XXX: 'Of short Epigrames called Posies'.

23 See Martial, *Epigrams with an English translation by Walter C. A. Ker*, 2 vols (London, 1950). Ker notes (vol. II, p. 440): '*Apophoreta* are presents given "to be carried away by guests"'.

24 *The Lives of the Caesars*, II, lxxv; VIII, xix; IV, iv.

25 Puttenham, p. 47.

26 Lyly, *Works*, I, pp. 499–504.

27 'licet hospitibus pro munere disticha mittas' (13, 3, 5); 'non aspernanda Decembri / carmina' (5, 30, 5–6); 'Non est munera quod putes pusilla, / cum donat vacuas poeta chartas' (14, 10).

28 Lucian, *Saturnalia*.

29 *Antonii Panormitae Hermaphoroditus; primus in Germania edidit et Aphoreta adjecit Frider. Carolus Forbergius* (Coburg, 1824).

30 Andreas Alciatus, *Emblematum libellus . . . per Wolphgangum Hungerum . . . rhythmis Germanicis uersus* (Paris, 1542), p. 3.

31 The quotation is from Dryden, *MacFlecknoe*, ll. 206–7. Yet for all the ridicule, the fashion can procure some meaningful local typographical finesses. In Arwaker's revised translation of Hugo we have: 'the *Stars*, whose Light / Chears with kind infl'ence our admiring sight; / Tho' glorious all in our dim Eyes they shine, / Are only small *Opacous Orbs* in thine.' Here, the capitalized O's of those '*Opacous Orbs*', mimic pictorially those 'dim Eyes': 'O . . . O' – poor, blind orbs, which blankly stare back at the reader from the page, mockingly mirroring our 'dim' gaze. Such Socinian mirrors anticipate the horror of Cocteau's parable in our century: 'Les miroirs sont les portes de l'enfer.' The wording in the later version is more firmly and more accusingly honed: where the first edition thoughtlessly describes these '*Orbs*' as 'vast', Arwaker upon mature reflection, realized that the conceit must surely dictate that they must be, more justly, 'small'.

32 Cf. Milton: 'Haec ego mente olim laeva, studioque supino / Nequitiae posui vana trophaea meae' (*The Poems of Milton*, ed. John Carey and Alastair Fowler, Harlow and London, 1968, p. 231). On the emblem and the joke, see Karel Porteman, 'The Emblem as *Genus Jocosum*', *Emblematica*, 8 (1994), pp. 243–60.

33 George Wither, *A Collection of Emblemes, Ancient and Moderne* (London, 1635), 'To the Reader', sig. A₁ᵛ.

34 For Isis as the guardian of the mysteries, see Plutarch, *Moralia*, 351E–F and Apuleius, *Metamorphoses*, Book XI. Plutarch, however, is at pains to emphasize the chaste life of the priests of Isis.

35 'Nuda fiebant Bacchi simulacra, inquit Phornutus, vt naturam vini ostenderent,

quod arcana detegat.' The classical authority for this is Horace, *Epistle* 5, 16: 'quid non ebrietas designat? operta recludit'.

36 Emblem 23: 'Vino prudentiam augeri'.

37 *Emblematum tyrocinia* (Strassburg, 1581), p. 50: 'animus uino turgens arcana tenere / Nescit, et os plenum uera referre solet.'

38 *Odes*, ii, 21, 14–16: 'sapientium / curas et arcanum iocoso / consilium retegis Lyaeo' (Thou, [Wine], unlockest the thoughts of the wise and their secret purpose by merry Bacchus' spell).

39 *Emblemata* (Antwerp, 1564), p. 80: 'calices volo, verbaque libera, / Ludos atque iocos'.

40 Augustin Chesneau, *Orpheus Eucharisticus* (Paris, 1657), Emblem 45: 'I'empesche ceux qui sont à table / D'y rien faire de reprochable.'

41 *Gargantua*, chap. 5. ed. cit., p. 27. Specifically, the allusion is to one of Christ's last words from the Cross: '*Sitio*' (I thirst).

42 'Del vino de Amor divino', cited Praz, p. 137. Note the play on words: 'Del vino … de … divino'.

43 Abraham à Sancta Clara, *Wohl angefhllter Wein-Keller, in welchem manche dürstige Seel sich mit einem geistlichen Geseng-Gott erquicken kan …* (Wurzburg, 1710).

44 John 2. 1–11; Song of Solomon 2. 5 and 5. 1. Hence Rabelais' topers may well say, 'Je boy *tanquam sponsus*' (*Gargantua*, p. 25).

45 Rabelais, *Gargantua*, 'Prologue de l'Auteur', ed. cit., p. 9: '*L'odeur du vin, ô combien … plus celeste et delicieux que d'huile*'. The translation is Urquhart's.

46 'Saturnalicias perdere … nuces' (Martial, *Epigrams*, v, 30, 8).

47 'alea parva nuces et non damnosa videtur' (Martial, *Epigrams*, xiv, 18, 1).

48 On this feature of Saturnalia/Carnival, see 'Von Faßnachtnarren' in *Das Narrenschiff*: 'Sie wollen lieber ihr Antlitz schwärzen / Und sich berußen wie ein Kohl' (p. 432); some 'Defyle theyr faces: so that playne trouth to tell / They ar more fowle, than the blacke Deuyll of hell' (trans. Barclay, ii, p. 269).

49 'Quo me autem vocas …? ad Aleam? Tesseras? Chartas lusorias? ad pocula? ad crapulam? et luxuriae obiicis instrumenta?' (*Emblemata Anniversaria*, Nuremberg, 1617), sig. Ttt₃ᵛ: 'HAC ITVR AD ORCVM'.

50 *Epigrams*, xiv, 1, 5. See also Suetonius, 2, 75: 'Solebat et inequalissimarum rerum sortes … in convivio venditare.'

51 Whitney, *A Choice of Emblemes*, p. 61. R. Warwick Bond, ed., *The Complete Works of John Lyly*, 2 vols (Oxford, 1902), i, pp. 499–504. These lots are modelled on Martial's *apophoreta*.

52 Wither, 'To the Reader', sigs A₁–A₂ʳ.

53 Fraunce, *Symbolicae philosophiae liber quartus et ultimus*, pp. 14–15; G. Ruscelli, *Le imprese illustri* (Venice 1566), pp. 15–16: 'si come nelle comedie, e nelle giostre, e nelle mascherate'.

54 Alexander Barclay, trans, *The Ship of Fools*, 2 vols (Edinburgh, 1874), ii, p. 270.

55 Suetonius, 2, 75: 'alia … titulis obscuris et ambiguis'.

56 On this feature, see Johan Verberckmoes, 'Comic Traditions in Adrianus Poirters' *Het Masker van de Wereldt afgetrocken*', in John Manning and Marc van Vaeck, eds, *The Jesuits and the Emblem Tradition: Selected Papers of the Leuven International Emblem Conference, 18–23 August 1996* (Turnhout, 1999), p. 342.

57 For example, Martial, ix, 5: 'Non tanti fellat Galla. Quid ergo? Tacet.' He threatens Gargilius with irrumation at iii, 96 with the thinly veiled 'tacebis'. Cf. 'comprimere linguam' (Plautus, *Amphitruo*, i, i, 192).

58 See the note by Ker, *Martial*, ii, 440–1: 'Martial's couplets describe [*apophoreta*], and were clearly intended to go in pairs, one couplet describing something that would be given by a rich man, and the next something similar that would be given by a poor man.'

59 *Emblemata Anniversaria* (Nuremberg, 1617), sigs Ttt₂ʳ and Ttt₃ᵛ.

60 Cf. Martial, xiv, 1, 5: 'divitis alternas et pauperis accipe sortes'.

61 *Amorum emblematum*, p. 216: 'Est Amor inuersæ sed conditionis, amantes / Nimirum ridens ille perire facit.'

62 *Mikrokosmos*, Emblem 35. Valeriano, *Hieroglyphica*, p. 634: 'Plato dixit hominem arbori similem esse, verum in hoc ab illa differre, quod illa radices in terra fixas habet, homo autem in caelo.'

63 *Confusio Disposita* .... *Sive quatuor Lusus Satyrico Morales* .... *III Inversum huius mundi Cursum* (Strasburg [1725]).

64 See Peter Ackroyd, *Blake* (London, 1995), p. 141. David V. Erdman, *The Illuminated Blake* (1974; New York, 1992), however, does not include such an arrangement in the census of copies he has examined. Ackroyd does record the fact that poems from *Innocence* and from *Experience* were etched on the reverse of the same copperplate. The two contrary states were thus physically bound together in obverse–reverse relationship.

65 'Laurentius Pignorius Lectori' in A. Alciato, *Emblemata* (Padua, 1618), sig. B_2^v–b_5^r.

66 See below, Reference 93.

67 J. van der Noot, *A Theatre wherein be represented as wel the miseries and calamities that follow the voluptuous Worldlings, As also the greate ioyes and plesures which the faithfull do enioy* (London, 1569), pp. 45^v and 27^r. The translation of the 'Briefe Declaration of the Authour vpon his visions', from which these quotations are taken, is by Theodore Roest.

68 *Tusculan Disputations*, Book 3, xvii, 36: 'Nihil est turpius, aut nequius effœminato viro'. The sentiment had a commonplace currency in the period being cited in, for example, by F. Le Tort, *Gnomologia seu Repertorium Sententiarum* (Paris, 1581), *s.v.* 'homo'.

69 Cats, *Spieghel*, Part 3, Emblem 2.

70 Frankfurt am Main, 1620.

71 *Examen*, 1740, pp 100–101 cited from M. Dorothy George, *English Political Caricature to 1792* (Oxford, 1959), p. 58.

72 Jan van der Veen, *Zinne-beelden, oft Adams Appel* (Amsterdam, 1642). On Van der Veen, see E. K. Grootes's essay in John Manning, Karel Porteman and Marc van Vaeck, eds, *The Emblem Tradition and the Low Countries: Selected Papers of the Leuven International Emblem Conference, 18–23 August 1996* (Turnhout, 1999), pp. 243–59. The translation of the dedication is taken from p. 243 of this essay.

73 See Reference 14 above.

74 Wither, 'To the Reader', sigs. A$_1^v$ and A$_2^r$. See also, Cornelis Plemp, 'Dedicatio' in *Quinquagenta emblemata* (Amsterdam, 1616). On Plemp, see Karel Porteman, 'Emblem Theory and Cultural Specificity' in *Aspects of Renaissance and Baroque Symbol Theory*, ed. Peter M. Daly and John Manning (New York, 1999), pp. 7–8.

75 *Gargantua*, 'Aux lecteurs', l. 10 (trans. Urquhart). Cf. Aristotle, *De partibus animalium*, III, 10.

76 For some recent discussions of this ancient topos, see, for example, Marc van Vaeck, *Adriaen Van de Vennes Tafelreel van de belacchende Werelt*, 3 vols (Ghent, 1994) and B. Bertrand, *Dire et rire à l'âge classique* (Aix-en-Provence, 1995).

77 'Tu quoque disce tuas, Natura, inuertere leges'. Cited by Abraham Fraunce, *Insignium, armorum, emblematum ... explicatio* (London, 1588), sig. N$_2$.

78 *Narrenschiff*, p. 433: 'Den Esel wüste Rotten tragen, / Mit ihm die ganze Stadt durchjagen.'

79 'spectatum admissi risum teneatis, amici?' (Horace, *De arte poetica*, l. 5).

80 Cf. Horace: 'nec pes nec caput uni / reddatur formae' (*De arte poetica*, ll. 8–9). For these figures in Alciato, see pp. 71, 623, 81, 33, 179, 71, 302, 336, 796 of the Padua 1621 edition. Fraunce (p. 22) associates these monstrous forms with the 'depravatum, humile, turpe, indignum'.

81 For the emblematic currency of the idea, see Claude Paradin, *Devises heroiques* (Lyon, 1557), p. 255: '*Quand plusieurs des antiques Egipciens venoient à banqueter de compagnie, la coutume estoit que pendant le repas, l'un d'entre eus portant une image ou simulacre de Mort, s'en venoit le montrer à chacun de tous les assistans: en leur disant l'un apres l'autre, Voy tu? Regardes bien que c'est que cela, faiz tant bonne chere que tu voudras, car ainsi se faut deuenir.*'

82 See Johan Verberckmoes, 'Comic Traditions in Adrianus Poirters' *Het Masker van*

de Wereldt afgetrocken', in Manning and Van Vaeck, eds, *The Jesuits and the Emblem Tradition* (Turnhout, 1999), pp. 341–52.

83 Praz, p. 138ff.

84 8 November 1798.

85 Arwaker (1702): I, ix.

86 Ronsard: 'Le monde est un théâtre, et les hommes acteurs /. . . / Les cieux et les destins en sont les spectateurs.' Cited in E. R. Curtius, *European Literature and the Latin Middle Ages*, trans. Willard R. Trask (New York and Evanston, IL, 1963), p. 140.

87 'non intret Cato theatrum meum aut, si intraverit, spectet'; 'festosque lusus et licentiam volgi'; 'lascivam verborum veritatem' (*Epigrams*, Book 1: Introductory epistle).

88 Giambattista Guarini, 'The Compendium of Tragicomic Poetry', in Allan H. Gilbert, ed., *Literary Criticism: Plato to Dryden* (Detroit, 1962), p. 514.

89 Sambucus, *ed. cit.*, p. 21.

90 'lex haec carminibus data est iocosis, / ne possint, nisi pruriant, iuvare' (Martial, *Epigrams* 1, 35, 10–11).

91 'de quo hic aliquid aperte dicere me pudor vetat' (On 'In statuam Amoris').

92 On Emblem 5, Mignault draws attention to Alciato's use of 'obscoena verba': 'Anguem pedit homo: Obscoena verba. Rem enim turpem turpia verba decent.' See also Thuilius's notes to the 1621 Tozzi edition: 'obscoenum verbum' (p. 856a); 'obscoenum' (p. 335a); 'rem turpem' (p. 35b), etc.

93 Padua, 1621, p. 367a: 'cevere proprie est clunes movere, obscoenum verbum'. Cf. Martial III, 95, 13: 'pedicaris, sed pulchre, Naevole, ceves.'

94 Tozzi (Padua, 1621), p. 349a ('opici mures'), p. 335a ('osci').

95 J. Macarius, *Abraxas*, p. 43, cites St Jerome, *In vita Hilarionis*: 'Tormenta quaedam verborum'; Apuleius, *Metamorphoses*, lib. 11: 'Litterae ignorabiles, apices tortuosi'; and Rabbi Moses Maimonides, *De Idolatria*: 'verbis . . . nulli genti vsitatis, et nihil significationibus; stultitiaque . . .'.

96 v, i, 387, cited from *The Complete Works*, ed. S. Wells and G. Taylor (Oxford, 1986).

97 *Master Francis Rabelais: Five Books of the Lives, Heroic Deeds and Sayings of Gargantua and his son Pantagruel*, trans. Thomas Urquhart of Cromarty and Peter Antony Motteux, 2 vols (London, 1904), I, p. 41. See also Eric Partridge, *Shakespeare's Bawdy*, revd and enlarged edn (London, 1968), *s.v.* 'bauble'. Partridge cites *Romeo and Juliet*, II, iii, 93–5: 'love is like a great natural, that runs lolling up and down to hide his bauble in a hole'. M.E. *babel* applies to Stubbes's 'bablery'. O.F. '*baubel*', toy, plaything is also relevant.

98 *Abraxas*, p. 41: 'Neque adeo eorum Amuleta tam studiosè conquisiuissem, . . . licet valdè pudenda, non erubuisset tamen effari D. Epiphanius, et ex eo Baronius, quibus ostenderet illum fuisse magistratum luxuriæ, turpissimorumque complexuum.'

99 So translated in contemporary vernacular versions: 'Einn Granat' (Hunger); 'Vn Melegran' (Marquale); 'vna granada' (Daza); 'La grenade' (Lefèvre). See Peter M. Daly, ed., *Index Emblematicus: Andreas Alciatus, vol 2: Emblems in Translation* (Toronto 1985), *s.v.* 'Emblem 114'. Betty I. Knott's translation (p. 123) opaquely opts for 'Punic fruit', which she glosses as 'pomegranate' (p. [124]).

100 'estque virilis penis prior pars, quæ Latinis est mentula.' Further, Mignault notes: 'vir doctus quispiam ait, hic glande significari partem obscenum genitalium' (a certain learned man says, that by this *glans* is meant the *genitalia*'). Thuilius adopts this annotation in his edition.

101 'de quo hic aliquid aperte dicere me pudor vetat'.

102 On the etymological play on words between the 'shield' of Love and on the deed of darkness, see Thuilius's note (p. 481) on *clypeum* and *cluere* (to do the will of another, to gratify, to pleasure). On the bitter-sweet joys of Love, see Alciato's Emblem 112 ('Dulcia quandoque amara fieri'), and Emblem 207 ('Malus medica') and accompanying commentary. Cf. Shakespeare's 'saucy sweetness' in *Measure for Measure*, II, iv, 45.

103 *Odes*, 3, 18, 1.

104 A. Alciato, *Diuerse imprese, tratte da gli Emblemi* (Lyon, 1549), p. 86.

105 *A Latin Dictionary* (Oxford, 1969).

106 Praz, pp. 180–85.

107 Cornelis Gijsbertson Plemp, *Emblemata quinquaginta* (Amsterdam, 1616).

108 Plutarch, *De Iside et Osiride* (*Moralia* 358).

109 *Hieroglyphica*, Book xxxiv. But also elsewhere, myrtles signify the female *pudenda*, the myth of Proserpine, a hieroglyph of procreation, etc.

110 A standard piece of Renaissance physiology retailed in the vernacular in Helkiah Crooke, *Microcosmographia: A Description of the Body of Man* (London, 1615).

111 Borrowing from, but slightly altering, Virgil's emphasis: 'virgo / pube tenus' (*Aeneid*, iii, 426–7). The capitalization of the first word of the epigram follows the Tozzi edition of 1621.

112 'deglubit, fellat, molitur per utramque cavernam' (Ausonius, Epigram 71), cited Thuilius (Padua 1621), p. 349.

113 'Salix' (Padua, 1621), p. 856.

114 'Quam ingeniosa est gula' (Padua 1621), p. [3]92.

115 2, 341–6 in *The Poems of Milton*, ed. John Carey and Alastair Fowler (Harlow and London, 1968).

116 Page 353: 'homo nudus ventrem in pateram auream exoneret'. The image first appeared in the Venice 1546 collection of emblems published by the heirs of Aldus. On its publication history, see William S. Heckscher, 'Pearls from a Dungheap: Andrea Alciati's "Offensive" Emblem, Adversus naturam peccantes', in Egon Verheyen, ed., *Art and Literature: Studies in Relationship* (Baden-Baden, 1985), pp. 481–501 and John Manning, 'The Dungheap Revisited: Some Further Reflections on Alciato's Emblem lxxx and the Nature of its Obscenity', in Peter M. Daly and Daniel S. Russell, eds, *Emblematic Perceptions* (Baden-Baden, 1997), pp. 123–34. In the same volume of *Emblematic Perceptions* (pp. 7–32), Michael Bath explores 'Dirty Devices'.

117 'Hoc scio pro certo quod si cum stercore certo, vinco seu vincor semper ego maculor', Cats Part 3, Emblem 18: 'Stultorum est cum stercore pugnare' (It is folly to use excrement as a weapon when fighting).

118 'quæ meias qui sine fine bibis'. De Bèze, *Icones*, Emblem 38.

119 Daniel Cramer, *Societas Iesu et Roseæ Crucis Vera* (Frankfurt am Main, 1616), Emblem 32. Both words of the motto mean essentially the same thing: 'shit, excrement, dung'.

120 'Ablatio cordis'.

121 See the penultimate line of 'In statuam Amoris'.

122 This was the notorious Clodia, according to Alciato. The riddle was propounded in Quintilian, 8, 6. There are other bawdy jokes on this theme. The inhabitants of Naples (the Nolans) were reputedly much given to *fellatio* – cf., Ausonius, Epigram 71: 'Nolanis capitalis luxus'.

123 Emblem 60: 'Cuculi'. The term should not be applied to the wronged husband, but to those that betray other people's marriages. See Thuilius's note (p. 277).

124 Shakespeare, *King Lear*, iv, vi, 129–31.

125 'Verus Amor nullum nouit habere modum' (*Amorum emblematum*, p. 30).

126 (Padua, 1621): 'rem turpem' (p. 35b); 'voluptates turpes' (p. 494a) ; sexual turpitude (p. 349b): 'foeminas absque masculi coitu'; Thuilius notes that to dream of indulging in 'abominable intercourse' (incest) is a symbol of irrumation (Plutarch, *In vita Caesaris*).

127 'Hic merdam cribrando mouet'. J. Flitner, *Nebulo Nebulonum* (Frankfurt am Main, 1620), p. 72. This parodies Valeriano's *Perfectæ vir sapientiæ*. cf. Palmer, *Two hundred poosees*, 175.

128 'Victrix malorum patientia'. From Otto van Veen, *Q. Horatii Flacci Emblemata* (Antwerp, 1607), p. 153. Palmer, p. 123.

129 'Cernis vt hic coelum foedo qui conspuit ore, / non coelum, immo suos conspuit ipse sinus? / Et tu coelorum domini contemptor, in illum / non quot verba iacis, tot tibi probra vomis?'

130 Guarini, 'The Compendium of Tragicomic Poetry', in Gilbert, ed., *Literary Criticism: Plato to Dryden*, pp. 514 and 516.

131 Milton, *Reason of Church Government*, Book 2 'Introduction' in Gilbert, ed., *Literary Criticism: Plato to Dryden*, p. 591.

132 Amsterdam, 1614.

133 *Emblemata Anniversaria* (1617), sig. Ttt₄ᵛ.

134 Palmer, p. 123.

EIGHT: Last Things

1 Lewis Carroll, 'Through the Looking-Glass and What Alice Found There', in *The Annotated Alice*, ed. Martin Gardner (Harmondsworth, 1965), p. 248.

2 John Webster, *The Duchess of Malfi*, IV, ii, 73–4.

3 Quarles, *Emblemes*, III, xiv, 14–15.

4 Shakespeare, *King Lear*, V, iii.

5 J. Drexel, *The Christians Zodiake* (London, 1643), final chapter: 'in omni cogitatu et facto sic suam observat conscientiam, quasi hodie moriturus' (*Opera*, Munich 1628, p. 145).

6 First edition in *Alle de Wercken* (Amsterdam, 1655). I owe this reference to Karel Porteman, 'Cats's Concept of the Emblem and the Role of Occasional Meditation', *Emblematica*, 6 (1992), pp. 70–71. On Cats and Death, see F. W. Wentzlaff-Eggebert, *Der triumphierende und der besiegte Tod in der Wort- und Bildkunst der Barock* (Berlin, 1975), pp. 31–69.

7 *Octaginta emblemata moralia nova* (Frankfurt am Main, 1630), p. 37: 'In omnibus operibus tuis memorare novissima tua'.

8 *Duodecim specula Deum aliquando videre desideranti concinnata* (Antwerp, 1610).

9 Geffrey Whitney, *A Choice of Emblems* (Leiden, 1586), pp. 103 and 230.

10 *Choice*, pp. 108, l. 18; 224, l. 2; 227; 229, l. 4; 229; 230, l. 6.

11 *Choice*, pp. 224; 225; 232; 296–7.

12 *Choice*, sig. **₂ᵛ.

13 *Leicester's Triumph* (Leiden and London, 1964), pp. 2–3.

14 (s.l. 1578), p. 80: 'Description de l'Image de l'antichrist selon l'Escriture saincte'.

15 *Emblemes*, III, xiv, ll. 23–5.

16 fol. 2ᵛ Royal Library, Brussels, MS 20.326: 1682 Aeternitas–Tempus.

17 Christopher Harvey, *The School of the Heart*: 'The Insatiableness of the Heart', st. 7.

18 *L'Art des Emblemes* (Paris, 1684), pp. 61–4.

19 Thomas Palmer, 'Two hundred poosees', Emblem 6. The reference is to Revelation 5. 1–2.

20 *Zodiacus Christianus*, 'Lectori' in *Hieremiae Drexelii Opera* (Munich 1628), p. 84. Arwaker, *Pia Desideria*, I, x. The heavenly books are mentioned in Revelation 20.[12] and Luke 10.[20]: 'which bookes are for the present shut up, not to bee opened, till the last Generall day; when those, who shall not be found recorded in the book of Life, shall be cast into the dreadfull lake of Fire: whereas those, whose names are registred in Heaven, shall participate of a joy, which neither knowes a Measure nor an End' (*The Christians Zodiake*, London, 1643, 'To the Reader').

21 'mens caeca futuri' (*Pia desideria*, I, xiv).

22 Lewis Carroll, 'Alice's Adventures in Wonderland' in *The Annotated Alice*, ed. Martin Gardner (Harmondsworth, 1965), p. 32.

23 On Whitehall, see Gillian Manning, '*Hexastichon Hieron*: A Hitherto Unrecorded English Emblem Book of the Restoration Period', *Emblematica*, 6 (1992), pp. 307–22. The Visschers, father and son, were responsible for a run of illustrated Bibles for much of the seventeenth century. Matthäus Merian of Basle was responsible for the original designs from about 1627. These were revised and augmented by those of Pieter Hendricksz. Schut.

24 For emblem and mosaic, see Chapter 1 above, References 2 and 3. See Henry Hawkins, *The Devout Hart*, p. 144: 'Mosaical work with certain litle stones linked and cimented togeather'. Marvell makes use of the pun in 'Upon Appleton House',

l. 582: 'What Rome, Greece, Palestine ere said in this light mosaic read'.

25 'The Author to the Reader'.

26 'abiecto priore illo Zodiaco, hunc non tantum correctiorem, sed et altero tanto auctiorem substitue' ('Lectori' [To the Reader] in *Hieremiae Drexelii Opera*, Munich 1628, p. 84).

27 *Coelum Empyreum* (Cologne, 1668), t.p.: 'non vanis et fictis Constellationum monstris belluatum sed divum domus Domini Jesu Christi, eiusque illibatæ Virginis Matris Mariæ, Sanctorum Apostolorum, Martyrum, Confessorum, Virginum'. See also his *Cæleste Pantheon* (Cologne, 1658).

28 Henry Hawkins, *The Devout Hart* ([Rouen] 1638), p. 135.

29 Munich, 1628, but numerous reprintings and translations. The anonymous English version, *Considerations of Drexelius upon Death* appeared in 1699 and William Croydon's *The Forerunner of Eternity* in 1642.

30 Munich, 1619, sig. A$_7$^{v}. The plates are by Raphael Sadeler. For the theme of death in emblems, see Gisèle Matthieu-Castellani, *Emblèmes de la Mort* (Paris, 1988).

31 J. Drechsel, *The Christians Zodiake* (London, 1643), 'The second Signe of Predestination, a readinesse to die.'

32 On the Dance, see F. Douce, *The Dance of Death* (London, 1896).

33 Edmund Arwaker, *Pia desideria* (London, 1702), I, xiv.

34 David, *Veridicus Christianus*, p. 210.

35 Royal Library, Brussels: Mors-Vita MS20318 (1660): fol. 9^v: Mors – a Bello –; fol. 11^v: Mors – a Fame –; fol. 13^v: Mors – a Peste –; fol. 15^v: Mors – ab Ambitu; fol. 17^v: Mors – ab Ira –; fol. 19^v: Mors – Sæpe ab Ingratis –; fol. 21^v: Mors – Sæpe a Propinquis –; fol. 23^v: Regi, Sæpe a præsidio; fol. 25^v: Mors – Liberorum, Sæpe a desertus Parentibus; fol. 27^v: Mors Contagiosa sæpe a Vicino; fol. 29^v: Mors a Divinâ Iustitiâ sæpius Intentata – aliquando Infertur. –; fol. 31^v Mors uariis modis opprimit homines; fol. 33^v: Mors omnibus æqualis; fol. 35^v Mors – Ineviabilis; fol. 37^v Mors – Sæpe Inexpectata; fol. 39^v: Mors – Nostra cum vitâ incipit –; fol. 41^v: Mors sæpe in Lecto; fol. 43^v: Mors – Reges etiam sternit –; fol. 45^v: Mors in bello sæpe immatura; fol. 47^v: Mors – Senio Vicina –; fol. 49^v: Mors Damnum infert lacrymis irreparabile; fol. 51^v Mors – Alterius conjugis superstit est oneri –; fol. 53^v: Mors – Filiorum parentibus lacrymabilis? –; fol. 55^v Mors – Furum sæpe in patibulo.

36 Fol. 3^v and fol. 61^v.

37 *Imitatio Crameriana* (Nuremberg, 1647), Emblem 24. The scriptural basis is Philippians 1. 21.

38 Phil. 1. 23. Hugo and Arwaker, 3, 9; Quarles, *Emblemes*, 5, 9; Drechsel, *Christians Zodiake*, 2.

39 *L'Ame amante de son dieu*, Emblem 44. For the translation, see John Manning, *Emblematica*, 6 (1992), p. 347.

40 Nuremberg, 1638–42, C. 9.

41 John Huddlestone Wynne's *Choice Emblems*, also known as *Riley's Emblems*, was first published in 1772. It went through numerous editions in England and America.

42 On Stevenson's period in Davos, see William George Lockett, *Robert Louis Stevenson at Davos* (London, 1934); J. C. Furness, *Voyage to Windward: The Life of Robert Louis Stevenson* (London, 1952), pp. 173–7 and 184–9.

43 *The Christians Zodiake, or, Twelue Signes of Predestination unto Life euerlasting* (London, 1647): 'The Author to the Reader'.

44 Sig. B$_2$^{v}: 'Qvando te invitat appetitus ad peccandum, cogita extremum Iudicium.'

45 *The Christians Zodiake*: 'The Author to the Reader'.

46 sig. C$_1$^{v}.

47 VI. 620: 'discite iustitiam moniti et non temnere divos'.

48 This is Drechsel's formula in *Nicetas* II, cap. 11. Its first edition was published at Munich in 1624. Emblematic plates were provided in Cologne 1631 edition. The edition cited here is from Drexel's *Opera* (Munich, 1628).

49 *Æneid*, VI, 126. Modern texts read 'Averno', but the form cited here is the more usual in sixteenth- and seventeenth-century emblem books. Hadrianus Junius,

Emblemata (Antwerp, 1565), Emblem 44 represents a classical version: the choice of Hercules, based on a fable by the philosopher Prodicus, recorded by Xenophon.

50 On this symbolism, see Franz Cumont, *Recherches sur le symbolisme funéraire des Romains* (1942; Paris, 1966), pp. 425–6. Cf. the equal and opposite motto that was frequently used, 'ANGVSTVM VIRTVTIS ITER' (The path of virtue is difficult).

51 *Le Tableau de Cebes de Thebes* (Paris, 1543). The volume includes Corrozet's 'Emblemes', which are not the same as his *Hecatomgraphie*. The full title advertizes the iconographical route map: 'quelle voye l'homme doit elire, pour paruenir a vertue, et parfaicte science'.

52 Ripa, *Iconologia*, *s.v.* 'Fraude'. I append the translation of the British Library Add. MS 23195: '*Deceit. Dante* paints her in his Hell after this manner, that she hath the face of an honest person, and the rest of the body is like a snake, with many spotts of divers collours, her taile being curled like a scorpion, which she hath gotten out of the river *Cocitus*, or the hell, or puddle of foul water, being thus painted she is called *Gerion*, by her faire face is vnderstood, that the deceiver, most commonly with a fair face, hony words, decent clothing, stately gaith, and other faire shews, deceive men, being alwayes bigg with deceit, knavery and other sorts of Rogueries, being covered with deadly and venomous spotts.'

53 Drechsel, *Nicetas* II, cap. 11 *Opera* (Munich, 1628), pp. 333–46: 1. 'Tenebrae' is based on Job 10. 21–2, Matthew 25. 30 and 41, and Matthew 8. 12; 2. 'Fletus, et stridor dentium, ululatus, et rugitus horribilis' on Luke 13. 28; 3. 'Fames, et sitis incredibilis' on Luke 16. 24; 4. 'Foetor intolerabilis' on Psalm 11. 6 and Rev. 21. 8; 5. 'Ignis' on Matt. 25. 42, 13. 30 and 49; 6. 'Vermis non morietur' on Isaiah 66. 24 and Matt. 9. 44; 7. 'Locus et societas detestabilis' on Luke 17. 26.

54 1682 Æternitas-Tempus Royal Library, Brussels, MS 20.326: fo 28ᵛ: 'EX ÆTERNITATE NVLLVS EGRESSVS'; fol. 29ʳ: 'ad ignis, / Eternum est: reditum ferrea porta negat'; fol. 18ᵛ: 'flamma perennis'; fol. 48ᵛ: 'ÆTERNITAS futura supplicium'.

55 On this topic, see the magisterial study by D. P. Walker, *The Decline of Hell: Seventeenth-century Discussions of Eternal Torment* (London, 1964).

56 Gailkircher, *Quadriga Eternitatis*, sig. C₈ᵛ.

57 Hawkins, *The Devout Hart*, p. 144. For the absence of marriage in the resurrected state, see Mark 12. 25. Yet one of the pupils of the Brussels Jesuit College had no difficulty in wittily imaging the reunion of the soul with the resurrected body as a second marriage. 1682 Royal Library, Brussels Aeternitas-Tempus MS 20.326: fol. 24ᵛ: ÆTERNITATIS DIES ANIMAS PER MORTEM SEPARATAS CUM CORPORIBUS ITERUM CONIUNGET.

58 J. Kreihing, *Emblemata Ethicopolitica* (Antwerp, 1661), Emblems 158–60.

59 Arwaker, *Pia Desideria*, I, 14.

60 Quarles, *Emblemes*, I, 10.

61 Stockhamer's commentary on Alciato's Emblem 24 (i.e., Emblem 36 in the majority of editions of the *Emblemata omnia* after 1573).

62 (New York, 1924), p. 147.

63 Emile Mâle, *Religious Art from the Twelfth to the Eighteenth Century* (New York, 1949), p. 159.

64 *Institutes of Christian Religion* IV, 7, 25.

65 Matthew 12. 38.

66 'Modern Advertising and the Renaissance Emblem: Modes of Verbal and Visual Persuasion', in Karl Josef Höltgen, Peter M. Daly and Wolfgang Lottes, eds, *Word and Visual Imagination: Studies in the Interaction of English Literature and the Visual Arts* (Erlangen, 1988), pp. 349–62. Daly cites predecessors in the discussion of advertising and emblem: Pierre J. Vinken, 'The Modern Advertisement as an Emblem', *Gazette*, 5 (1959), pp. 234–43 and Stefan Bodo Würffel, 'Emblematik und Werbung', *Sprache im technischen Zeitalter*, 21 (1981), pp. 158–78.

67 Gabriel Rollenhagen, *Nucleus emblematum, Centuria secunda*, p. 20; George Wither, *A Collection of Emblemes*, p. 154; J. Camerarius, *Symbolorum et emblematum*, III. Daly discusses the symbolism of the pelican further in *Emblem Theory: Recent German Contributions to the Characterization of the Emblem Genre*

(Nendeln/Liechtenstein, 1979), pp. 38–9.

68 Daly, 'Modern Advertising and the Renaissance Emblem', p. 360.

69 Rex Whistler, 'His Worship the Mayor', April 1932. Pen and ink on paper, 11 x 7 inches, from *Humour from Shell: Shell Advertising Art 1928–1963: An Exhibition of Cartoons and Illustrations from the Shell U.K. Advertising Archive* (Newtown, 1991), p. 20.

70 'The Wisdom of Age', April 1932. *Humour from Shell*, p. 18.

71 1930. *Humour from Shell*, p. 31. Alciato's 'Prudentia' is Emblem 18 in the *Emblemata omnia*.

72 *Circa* 1950s. *Humour from Shell*, p. 33.

73 'Golden Apples', *c*. 1950s. *Humour from Shell*, p. 29.

74 'Snail with Shell', 1962. *Humour from Shell*, p. 10. Wither, *A Collection of Emblemes*, p. 19, commends the snail for its '*Perseverence*' and '*Continuance*': 'some *Affaires* require / More *Heed* then *Haste*'.

Select Bibliography

Adams, Alison, Stephen Rawles and Alison Saunders, *A Bibliography of French Emblem Books of the Sixteenth and Seventeenth Centuries* (Geneva, 1999)

Berge, Domien ten, *De hooggeleerde en zoetvloeiende dicter, Jacob Cats* (Gravenhage, 1979), pp. [226]–262

Black, Hester M., and David Weston, *A Short Title Catalogue of the Emblem Books and Related Works in the Stirling Maxwell Collection of Glasgow University Library 1499–1917* (Aldershot, 1988)

Campa, Pedro F., *Emblemata Hispanica: An Annotated Bibliography of Spanish Emblem Literature to the Year 1700* (Durham, 1990)

Daly, Peter M., and G. Richard Dimler, eds, *Corpus Librorum Emblematum. The Jesuit Series, vol. 1: A–D* (Montreal, 1997)

Green, Henry, *Andrea Alciati and His Books of Emblems: A Biographical and Bibliographical Study* (London, 1872)

Harris, Carolyn, and Ingrid Luckstead, *Emblem Books at the Humanities Research Center: A Checklist, with Selected Emblematic Broadsides* (Austin, TX, 1979)

Heckscher, William S., Agnes B. Sherman and Stephen Ferguson, *Emblem Books in the Princeton University Library: A Short-Title Catalogue* (Princeton, NJ, 1984)

Horden, J., *Francis Quarles (1592–1644): A Bibliography of his Works to the Year 1800* (Oxford, 1953)

Landwehr, John, *Dutch Emblem Books: A Bibliography* (Utrecht, 1962)

— *Emblem Books in the Low Countries 1554–1949: A Bibliography* (Utrecht, 1970)

— *French, Italian, Spanish and Portuguese Books of Devices and Emblems 1534–1827: A Bibliography* (Utrecht, 1976)

— *German Emblem Books, 1531–1888: A Bibliography* (Utrecht and Leiden, 1972)

McGeary, Thomas, and N. Frederick Nash, *Emblem Books at the University of Illinois: A Bibliographic Catalogue* (Boston, MA, 1993)

Platt, Dobroslawa, *Emblematy w osslinskich zbiorach druków i rekopisów XVI–XVIII w.: katalog wystawy* (Wroclaw, 1995)

Praz, Mario, *Studies in Seventeenth-Century Imagery*, 2nd edn (Rome, 1964)

Visser, A. S. Q., P. G. Hoftijzer, and Bart Westerweel, eds, *Emblem Books in Leiden: A Catalogue of the Collections of Leiden University Library, the 'Mattschappij der Nederlandse Letterkunde' and Bibliotheca Thysi* (Leiden, 1999)

Warnke, Carsten-Peter, 'Emblembücher in der Herzog August Bibliothek. Ein Bestandsverzeichnis', *Wolfenbütteler Barock-Nachrichten*, 9 (1982), pp. 346–70

A List of Major Emblem Books

Alciatus, Andreas, *Emblematum liber* (Augsburg, 1531). Woodcuts by Jörg Breu

— *Emblematum libellus* (Paris, 1534–42). Woodcuts by Mercure Jollat

— *Emblematum libellus* (Venice, 1546)

— *Emblemata* (Lyon, 1550). Woodcuts by 'Pierre Vase'

— *Emblemata . . . cum imaginibus plerisque restitutis ad mentem auctoris*, ed. L. Pignoria (Padua, 1618)

— *Emblemata cum commentariis amplissimis*, ed. J. Thuilius (Padua, 1621)

Cats, Jakob, *Proteus ofte Minne-beelden Verandert in Sinne-beelden* (Rotterdam, 1627)

— *Silenus Alcibiades, sive Proteus* (Middelburg, 1618)

— *Maechden-plicht* (Middelburg, 1618)

Corrozet, G., *Hecatomgraphie* (Paris, 1540)

Coustau, P., *Pegma, cum narrationibus philosophicis* (Lyon, 1555)

Drexel, Jeremias, *Heliotropium, seu, Conformatio humanae voluntatis cum divina; libris quinque explicata coram sermo utriusque* (Cologne [rectè Antwerp], 1630). 6 engravings by Philip Sadeler

Heinsius, Daniel, *Quaeris quid sit Amor: quid amare, cupidinis et quid Castra sequi? Chartam hanc inspice, doctus eris* ([Amsterdam], 1601). Engravings ascribed to J. de Gheyn

Hugo, Herman, *Pia desideria* (Antwerp, 1624). Engravings by Boëtius à Bolswert

Junius, H., *Emblemata* (Antwerp, 1565). Woodcuts by G. van Kampen and A. Nicolai

La Perrière, G. de, *Le Theatre des bons engins, auquel sont contenuz cent Emblemes moraulx* (Paris, 1539)

Menestrier, C.-F., *La Philosophie des images* (Paris, 1682)

Montenay, Georgette de, *Emblemes, ou Devises Chrestiennes* (Lyon, 1571)

Paradin, Claude, *Devises Heroiques* (Lyon, 1551)

Peacham, Henry, *Minerva Britanna* (London, 1612)

Picinelli, Filippo, *Mondo simbolico* (Milan, 1653)

Quarles, Francis, *Emblemes* (London, 1635)

— *Hieroglyphikes of the Life of Man* (London, 1638)

Reusner, Nicolaus. *Emblemata . . . partim ethica, et physica, partim vero Historica, et Hieroglyphica . . . cum Symbolis* (Frankfurt am Main, 1581)

Ripa, Cesare, *Iconologia* (Rome, 1603)

— *Nova Iconologia* (Padua, 1618)

— *Iconologia . . . Notabilmente accresciuta*, 5 vols (Perugia, 1766)

Rollenhagen, Gabriel, *Nucleus emblematum selectissimorum* (Cologne, Arnhem, 1611–1613). Engravings by C. de Passe

Rollos, Peter, *Le Centre de l'amour* (Paris, 1680). Engravings by P. Rollos

Saavedra Fajardo, Diego de, *Idea de un Principe politico Christiano* (Munich, 1640). Engraved title-page by Joannes Sadeler

Sambucus, J., *Emblemata* (Antwerp, 1564). Woodcuts by A. Nicolai, C. Muller and G. van Kampen

Sucquet, Antoine, *Via Vitae Aeternae Iconibus illustrata* (Antwerp, 1620). Engravings by Boëtius à Bolswert

Tesauro, Emmanuele. *Il Cannocchiale Aristotelico* (Venice, 1655)

Vænius, Otto, *Amoris Divini Emblemata* (Antwerp, 1615)

— *Amorum emblemata* (Antwerp, 1608)

— *Q. Horatii Flacci Emblemata* (Antwerp, 1607)

Valeriano Bolzani, Giovanni Pierio, *Hieroglyphica* (Basle, 1556)

Visscher, Roemer, *Sinnepoppen* (Amsterdam, 1614)

Whitney, Geffrey, *A Choice of Emblemes* (Leiden, 1586)

Wither, George, *A Collection of Emblemes, Ancient and Moderne* (London, 1635)

Zincgreff, Julius Wilhelm, *Emblematum Ethico-politicorum centuria* ([Oppenheim], 1619)

Modern Emblems, Modern Editions and Translations

Alciatus, A., *Antiquae Inscriptiones veteraq. monumenta patriae* (Cisalpino, 1973)

— *Emblemata Lyons 1550*, translated and annotated by Betty L. Knott, with an introduction by John Manning (Aldershot, 1996)

— *The Latin Emblems and Emblems in Translation*, ed. Peter M. Daly, Virginia W. Callahan, and Simon Cutler, 2 vols (Toronto, 1985)

Boas, George, trans., *The Hieroglyphics of Horapollo* (New York, 1950)

Bourgogne, Antoine de, *Linguae vita et remedia*, with an introduction by Toon van Houdt (Turnhout, 1999)

Buchanan, Hugh, and Peter Davidson, *The Eloquence of Shadows: A Book of Emblems: Emblemata Nova* (Thirdpart, Crail, 1994)

Camerarius, Joachim, *Symbola et emblemata* (Nürnberg 1590 bis 1604), facsimile edn
   with intro. by Wolfgang Harms and Ulla-Britta Kuechen, 2 vols (Graz, 1986–8)
Drijfhout, A. E. (i.e. G. J. Hoogewerff), and M. C. Escher, *XXIV Emblemata, dat zijn
   Zinnebeelden* (Bussum, 1932)
Finlay, Ian Hamilton and Ron Costley, *Heroic Emblems* (Calais, VT, 1977). Introduction
   and commentary by Stephen Bann
Fraunce, Abraham, *Symbolicae Philosophiae liber quartus et ultimus*, ed. with
   introduction and notes by John Manning with an English translation by Estelle
   Haan (New York, 1991)
Klossowski de Rola, Stanislas, *The Golden Game: Alchemical Engravings of the
   Seventeenth Century* (London, 1988)
Leader, Alison B., *Reinventing the Emblem. Contemporary Artists Recreate a Renaissance
   Idea* (New Haven, CT, 1995)
Palmer, Thomas, *The Emblems of Thomas Palmer: Sloane MS 3794*, ed. with an
   introduction and notes by John Manning (New York, 1988)
Peacham, Henry, *Henry Peacham's Manuscript Emblem Books*, ed. Alan R. Young
   (Toronto, 1998)
Rollenhagen, G., *Sinn-Bilder. Ein Tugendspiegel*, ed. C.-P. Warnke (Dortmund, 1983)

Iconography

Bardon, Françoise, *Le portrait mythologique à la cour de France sous Henri IV et Louis XIII*
   (Paris, 1974)
Gombrich, E. H., *Symbolic Images: Studies in the Art of the Renaissance* (London, 1972)
Panofsky, Erwin, *Studies in Iconology: Humanistic Themes in the Art of the Renaissance*
   (New York and Evanston, IL, 1962)
Seznec, Jean, *The Survival of the Pagan Gods*, trans. Barbara F. Sessions (1953; New York,
   1961)
Tervarent, Guy de, *Attributs et symboles dans l'art profane, 1450–1600*, 2 vols (Geneva,
   1958–64)
Wind, Edgar, *Pagan Mysteries in the Renaissance*, 2nd edn (London, 1967)
Wittkower, Rudolf, *Allegory and the Migration of Symbols* (London, 1977)

Emblems in the Material Culture

Böker, Hans J., and Peter M. Daly, eds, *The Emblem and Architecture: Studies in Applied
   Emblematics from the Sixteenth to the Eighteenth Centuries* (Turnhout, 1999)
Grivel, Marianne and Marc Fumaroli, eds, *Devises pour les tapisseries du roy* (Paris, 1988)
Harms, Wolfgang and Hartmut Freytag, *Ausserliterarische Wirkungen barocker
   Emblembücher: Emblematik in Ludwigsburg, Gaarz und Pommersfelden* (Munich,
   1975)
Köhler, Johannes, *Angewandte Emblematik im Fliesensaal von Wrisberholzen bei
   Hildesheim* (Hildesheim, 1988)
Vaeck, Marc van, *Beelden van Omhoog: Hansches 17de-eeuwse plafonddecoraties in
   stucwerk in de kastelen van Horst, Modave en Beaulieu en in het Gentse Brouwershuis*
   (Brussels, 1997)
Young, Alan R., *His Majesty's Royal Ship: A Critical Edition of Thomas Heywood's 'A True
   Description of his Majesties Royall Ship'* (New York, 1990)

Emblems: Authors, History, Theory and Interpretation

Bath, Michael, *Speaking Pictures: English Emblem Books and Renaissance Culture*
   (London and New York, 1994)
— and Daniel S. Russell, eds, *Deviceful Settings: The English Renaissance Emblem and its
   Contexts* (New York, 1999)
Bircher, Martin, and Thomas Bürger, *Alles mit Bedacht. Barockes Fürstenlob auf Herzog
   August (1579–1666) in Wort, Bild und Musik* (Wolfenbüttel, 1979)

Chambers, D. S., and F. Quiviger, eds, *Italian Academies of the Sixteenth Century* (London, 1995)

Chatelain, Jean-Marc, *Livres d'emblemes et devises: une anthologie (1531–1735)* (Paris, 1993)

Choné, Paulette. *Emblèmes et pensée symbolique en Lorraine (1525–1633)*. 'Comme un jardin au coeur de la chrétienté' (Paris, 1991)

Conermann, Klaus, and Günther Hoppe, *Der Fruchtbringenden Gesellschaft geöffneter Erzschein: Das Köthener Gesellschaftsbuch Fürst Ludwigs I von Anhalt-Köthen 1617–1650*, 3 vols (Weinheim, 1985)

Daly, Peter M., ed., *Andrea Alciato and the Emblem Tradition* (New York, 1989)

— *Emblem Theory: Recent German Contributions to the Characterization of the Emblem Genre* (Nendeln/Liechtenstein, 1979)

— ed., *English Emblems and the Continental Tradition* (New York, 1988)

— and John Manning, eds, *Aspects of Renaissance and Baroque Symbol Theory, 1500–1700* (New York, 1999)

Dieckmann, Liselotte, *Hieroglyphics: The History of a Literary Symbol* (St Louis, MO, 1970)

Freeman, Rosemary, *English Emblem Books* (1948; London, 1970)

Harms, W., *Homo viator in bivio. Studien zur Bildlichkeit des Weges* (Munich, 1970)

Heckscher, W. S., and K.-A. Wirth, 'Emblem, Emblembuch' in *Reallexicon zur deutschen Kunstgeschichte* (Stuttgart, 1959), vol. V, cols 85–228

Henkel, Arthur, and Albrecht Schöne, *Emblemata. Handbuch zur Sinnbildkunst des XVI. und XVII. Jahrhunderts* (Stuttgart, 1967)

Höltgen, K. J., *Aspects of the Emblem: Studies in the English Emblem Tradition and the European Context* (Kassell, 1986)

— *Francis Quarles 1592–1644: Meditativer Dichter, Emblematiker, Royalist* (Tübingen, 1978)

Köhler, Johannes, *Der Emblematum liber von Andreas Alciatus (1492–1550): Eine Untersuchung zur Entstehung, Formung antiker Quellen und pädagogischen Wirkung im 16. Jahrhundert* (Hildesheim, 1986)

Leisher, John F., Geoffrey Whitney's *A Choice of Emblemes and its Relation to the Emblematic Vogue in Tudor England* (New York, 1987)

Manning, John, Karel Porteman, and Marc van Vaeck, eds, *The Emblem Tradition and the Low Countries* (Turnhout, 1999)

Massing, Jean Michel, *Erasmian Wit and Proverbial Wisdom: An Illustrated Moral Compendium for François I* (London, 1995)

Porteman, Karel, *Emblematic Exhibitions (affixiones) at the Brussels Jesuit College (1630–1685): A Study of the Commemorative Manuscripts* (Turnhout, 1996)

— *Inleiding tot de Nederlandse emblemataliteratuur* (Groningen, 1977)

Russell, Daniel, *Emblematic Structures in Renaissance French Culture* (Toronto 1995)

Russell, Daniel S., *The Emblem and Device in France* (Lexington, KY, 1985)

Saunders, Alison, *The Sixteenth-century French Emblem Book: A Decorative and Useful Genre* (Geneva, 1988)

Schilling, Michael, *Imagines Mundi. Metaphorische Darstellungen der Welt in der Emblematik* (Frankfurt am Main, 1979)

Schöne, Albrecht, *Emblematik und Drama im Zeitalter des Barock* (Munich, 1964)

Volkmann, Ludwig, *Bilderschriften der Renaissance. Hieroglyphik und Emblematik in ihren Beziehungen and Fortwirkungen* (Leipzig, 1923)

Sider, Sandra, *Cebes' Tablet. Facsimiles of the Greek Text, and of Selected Latin, French, English, Spanish, Italian, German, Dutch and Polish Translations* (New York, 1979)

Stopp, Frederick John, *The Emblems of the Altdorf Academy: Medals and Medal Orations, 1577–1626* (London, 1974)

List of Illustrations

Unless otherwise stated, the illustrations are taken from books in the author's possession.

26 Ants and elephants from Francesco Colonna, *Hypnerotomachia Poliphili* (Venice, 1499), sig. p$_6$^{v}.

27 'Quomodo vitam' and 'Quomodo laborem', from Horapollo, *De sacris Ægyptiorum notis* (Paris, 1574). National Library of Scotland.

28 'Fortuna', from Francesco Colonna, *Hypnerotomachia Poliphili* (Venice, 1499), sig. b$_1$^{v}.

29 'Ex mysticis Ægyptiovm literis', from A. Bocchi, *Symbolicarum Quæstionum de universo genere quas serio ludebat libri quinque* (Bologna, 1574), p. 344. Photo: National Library of Scotland, Edinburgh.

30 'Recedant vetera', from Paolo Giovio, *Dialogo dell'Imprese militare et amorose* (Lyon, 1574), p. 40.

31 'Contemnit tvta procellas', from Paolo Giovio, *Dialogo dell'Imprese militare et amorose* (Lyon, 1574), p. 149.

32 Anchor and dolphin', from Gabriello Symeoni, *Le Imprese heroiche et morali* (Lyon, 1574), p. 175.

33 'Matura', from G. Rollenhagen, *Nucleus emblematum selectissimorum* (Cologne, 1611), Emblem 18.

34 'Amor æternum', from Otto Vænius, *Amorum Emblemata* (Antwerp, 1608), p. 43.

35 'The Palace of Intemperance', from Bartolomeo del Bene, *Civitas veri sive morum* (Paris, 1609), p. 82. Photo: Founder's Library, University of Wales, Lampeter.

36 'Culpam poena premit comes', from Otto Vænius, *Q. Horatii Flacci Emblemata* (Antwerp, 1607), p. p. 181.

37 'I am in a straight between two, having a desire to be dissolved and to be with Christ', from Francis Quarles, *Emblemes* (London, 1718), facing p. 224.

38 The impresa of Gabriello Frascati, 'Hinc rapta iuvat', from L. Contile, *Ragionamento sopra la proprieta delle imprese* (Padua, 1574), fol. 62^v. Reproduced by permission of the Librarian, Glasgow University Library.

39 'Inganno', from Cesare Ripa, *Iconologia* (Rome, 1603), p. 229.

40 'Prima tenet primas rervm sapientia caussas', from A. Bocchi, *Symbolicarum Quaestionum de universo genere quas serio ludebat libri quinque* (Bologna, 1574), p. 60. Photo: National Library of Scotland, Edinburgh.

41 Title-page of Gabriello Symeoni, 'Le imprese heroiche et morali', in Paolo Giovio, *Dialogo dell'imprese militare et amorose* (Lyon, 1574), p. [168].

42 Frontispiece by William Marshall to George Wither, *Emblemes* (London, 1635).

43 'Le Gratie', from Andrea Alciato, *Diuerse imprese, tratte da gli Emblemi* (Lyon, 1549), p. 107.

44 'Murus aeneus, sana conscientia' from G. Whitney, *A Choice of Emblemes* (Leiden, 1586), p. 67.

45 'Dicta septem sapientum', from Andrea Alciato, *Emblemata* (Antwerp, 1577), p. 604. Photo: Glasgow University Library.

46 'Melathesia', from J. Sambucus, 'Partes hominis', *Emblemata* (Antwerp, 1565), p. 118.

47 'Festina lente', from C. Paradin, *Symbola heroica*, trans. Gubernator (Antwerp, 1562). Photo: National Library of Scotland, Edinburgh.

48 Title-page of J. Drexel, *Opera* (Munich, 1628).

49 Title-page of J. Camerarius, *Symbolorum et Emblematum ex re Herbaria* (Frankfurt, 1654).

50 'Omnibus omnia', from *Af-beeldinghe van d'eerste eeuwe der Societeyt Iesu* (Antwerp, 1640).

51 Detail from the engraved title-page of J. Drexel, *Opera omnia*, 2 vols (Antwerp, 1643).

52 'Copiosè', a detail from the engraved title-page of J. Drexel, *Opera omnia*, 2 vols (Antwerp, 1643).

53 'Moraliter', a detail from the engraved title-page of J. Drexel, *Opera omnia*, 2 vols (Antwerp, 1643).

54 Title-page from A. Kircher, *Romani colegii Societatis Jesu Musæum celeberrimum* (Amsterdam, 1678). Photo: Founder's Library, University of Wales, Lampeter.

55 'Svvm cviqve tribve', from Gabriel Rollenhagen, *Nucleus emblematum*

88 Colophon to John Foxe, *Actes and monuments* (London, 1576).

89 James Gillray, *The Fall of Icarus*, 1807, engraving.

90 James Gillray, *Gloria Mundi, or The Devil addressing the Sun*, engraving.

91 James Gillray, *Charon's Boat, or, the Ghosts of all the Talents*, 1807, engraving.

92 Frontispiece. to Thomas Munckerus, ed., *Mythographi latini* (Amsterdam, 1681).

93 James Gillray, *Patience on a Monument*, 1791, engraving.

94 'Aduersus naturam peccantes', from Andrea Alciato, *Emblematum libellus* (Venice, 1546), fol. 26^v.

95 James Gillray, *The Apples and the Horse-Turds; or, Buonaparte among the Golden Pippins*, 1800, engraving.

96 'Prosit Neu Jahr', from Martin Gerlach, *Allegories and Emblems* (Vienna, 1882).

97 'In dies meliora', from Andrea Alciato, *Emblematum libellus* (Venice, 1546), fol. 33^v.

98 'In statuam Bacchi', from Andrea Alciato, *Emblemata*, ed. B. Aneau (Lyon, 1551). Photo: National Library of Scotland, Edinburgh.

99 'Ceres and Bacchus', from Bartolomeo del Bene, *Civitas veri sive morum* (Paris, 1609), p. 18. Photo: Founder's Library, University of Wales, Lampeter.

100 'Mustum cordis', from [Christopher Harvey], *The School of the Heart* (Bristol, 1808), Emblem 47.

101 'Cvm virtvte alma consentit vera voluptas', from A. Bocchi, *Symbolicarum Quæstionum de universo genere quas serio ludebat libri quinque* (Bologna, 1574), p. xxiiii. Photo: National Library of Scotland, Edinburgh.

102 'The Lottery', from George Wither, *Emblemes* (London, 1635), sig. Oo$_4$^{r}.

103 'Sperne voluptates', from Otto Vænius, *Q. Horatii Flacci Emblemata* (Antwerp, 1607), p. 39.

104 'Masks', from Guillaume de la Perriere, *Le theatre des bons engins* (Paris, 1539), Emblem 6.

105 'Divitiae / Malum necessarium', from Antonius à Burgundia, *Mundus Lapis Lydius* (Antwerp 1639).

106 Title-page from John Taylor, *Mad Fashions* (London, 1642).

107 'La scimia quanto piu in alto sale', from Jacob Cats, *Spieghel van den Ouden Ende Nieuwen Tijdt* (Graven-Hage, 1632), Part 3, p. 5.

108 Democritus and Heraclitus, from Andrea Alciato, *Emblemata* (Padua, 1618), p. 271, 'In vitam humanam'.

109 'Sirenes', from Alciato, *Emblematum libellus* (Venice, 1546), fo. 4^v.

110 'Magna classis / Ludiburium venti', from Antonius à Burgundia, *Mundus Lapis Lydius* (Antwerp, 1639).

111 'Video et rideo', Samuel Ward, '1588. To God in memorye of his double deliverance from ye invincible Navie and ye unmatchable powder Treason. 1605' (Amsterdam, 1621).

112 'Ludibria mortis', colophon to Fajardo Saavedra, *L'Idea di un prencipe politico Christiano* (Venice, 1664).

113 'In statuam amoris', from Andrea Alciato, *Emblemata omnia* (Lyon, 1616), p. 395.

114 'In vn subito terrore', from Andrea Alciato, *Diuerse imprese, tratte da gli Emblemi* (Lyon, 1549), p. 86. Photo: National Library of Scotland, Edinburgh.

115 A satyr and nymph from Francesco Colonna, *Hypnerotomachia Poliphili* (Venice, 1499), sig. e$_1$^{r}.

116 'De Pudendis', from J. P. Valeriano, *Hieroglyphica* (Lyon, 1602), p. 349.

117 'Gula', from Andrea Alciato, *Emblemata* (Lyon, 1550), p. 98. Photo: National Library of Scotland, Edinburgh.

118 'The drunkard, or the modern Belides', from Theodore de Bèze, *Icones* (Geneva, 1580), Emblem xxxviii.

119 'In amatores meretricum', from Andrea Alciato, *Emblemata* (Padua, 1618), p. 138.

120 'Nimium vidisse nocet', from *Thronus cupidinis*, 3rd edn (Amsterdam, 1620), sig. G$_4$^{r}.

121 'Europa', from 'Hierolyphicorum commentariorum liber prior. Ea continens quæ per varia Deorum et hominum simulachra significantur' in J. P. Valeriano, *Hieroglyphica* (Lyon, 1602), p. 629.

Index